# Yesterday, Today and Tomorrow with Gib McConnell

# Yesterday, Today and Tomorrow with Gib McConnell

iUniverse, Inc.
New York Bloomington Shanghai

# Yesterday, Today and Tomorrow with Gib McConnell

Copyright © 2008 by Gilbert Lee McConnell

All rights reserved. No part of this book may be used or reproduced by any means, graphic, electronic, or mechanical, including photocopying, recording, taping or by any information storage retrieval system without the written permission of the publisher except in the case of brief quotations embodied in critical articles and reviews.

iUniverse books may be ordered through booksellers or by contacting:

iUniverse
1663 Liberty Drive
Bloomington, IN 47403
www.iuniverse.com
1-800-Authors (1-800-288-4677)

Because of the dynamic nature of the Internet, any Web addresses or links contained in this book may have changed since publication and may no longer be valid.

The views expressed in this work are solely those of the author and do not necessarily reflect the views of the publisher, and the publisher hereby disclaims any responsibility for them.

ISBN: 978-0-595-47310-6 (pbk)
ISBN: 978-0-595-71608-1 (cloth)
ISBN: 978-0-595-91588-0 (ebk)

Printed in the United States of America

# Contents

Foreword—1998 . . . . . . . . . . . . . . . . . . . . . . . . . . . . . . . . . . . . . . . vii
CHAPTER 1    Gilbert Lee McConnell . . . . . . . . . . . . . . . . . . . . . 1
CHAPTER 2    The Younger Years . . . . . . . . . . . . . . . . . . . . . . . . 3
CHAPTER 3    High School . . . . . . . . . . . . . . . . . . . . . . . . . . . . . 8
CHAPTER 4    Girls . . . . . . . . . . . . . . . . . . . . . . . . . . . . . . . . . . . 14
CHAPTER 5    Jobs . . . . . . . . . . . . . . . . . . . . . . . . . . . . . . . . . . . 18
CHAPTER 6    The Service . . . . . . . . . . . . . . . . . . . . . . . . . . . . . 22
CHAPTER 7    Back Home . . . . . . . . . . . . . . . . . . . . . . . . . . . . . 34
CHAPTER 8    McConnell Winding Down . . . . . . . . . . . . . . . . . 44
CHAPTER 9    The Biggest Happening In My Life . . . . . . . . . . . . 47
CHAPTER 10   The Catholics Come To Indianola . . . . . . . . . . . . 56
CHAPTER 11   The Kids . . . . . . . . . . . . . . . . . . . . . . . . . . . . . . . 60
CHAPTER 12   Full Time A & W . . . . . . . . . . . . . . . . . . . . . . . . 64
CHAPTER 13   Sports . . . . . . . . . . . . . . . . . . . . . . . . . . . . . . . . . 67
CHAPTER 14   Cub Scouts . . . . . . . . . . . . . . . . . . . . . . . . . . . . . 69
CHAPTER 15   Building Houses . . . . . . . . . . . . . . . . . . . . . . . . . 71
CHAPTER 16   The Biggie Operator Years . . . . . . . . . . . . . . . . . . 73
CHAPTER 17   The Kids' Stats . . . . . . . . . . . . . . . . . . . . . . . . . . 80
CHAPTER 18   The State Association . . . . . . . . . . . . . . . . . . . . . 83

| | | |
|---|---|---|
| Chapter 19 | The Early 70's | 91 |
| Chapter 20 | 1974 | 99 |
| Chapter 21 | Rome | 102 |
| Chapter 22 | The Bicentennial Year | 107 |
| Chapter 23 | Rio de Janeiro | 112 |
| Chapter 24 | The Orient | 118 |
| Chapter 25 | The end of the 70's | 123 |
| Chapter 26 | 1980 | 134 |
| Chapter 27 | Here Comes the Big Mac | 142 |
| Chapter 28 | 1983 | 153 |
| Chapter 29 | President Gib | 160 |
| Chapter 30 | Northern Italia | 168 |
| Chapter 31 | 1986 | 176 |
| Chapter 32 | Down Under in Australia | 183 |
| Chapter 33 | The Last of the 80's | 192 |
| Chapter 34 | 1990 | 206 |
| Chapter 35 | 1991 | 216 |
| Chapter 36 | 1992 | 224 |
| Chapter 37 | 1993 | 237 |
| Chapter 38 | 1994 | 243 |
| Chapter 39 | 1995 | 254 |
| Chapter 40 | 1996–1998 | 261 |
| Chapter 41 | 1999–2002 | 275 |
| Chapter 42 | 2003 to 2005 | 289 |
| Chapter 43 | 50 Years with A & W | 305 |

# *Foreword—1998*

I'm dedicating this book (jumble of words) to my lifetime partner who has managed to keep everything copasetic these 49 years. Without her there would be no family and everything that goes with that. She was also keeper of the purse strings. My capability in that area would be suspect at best. Remember Mother saying on my wedding day—don't know how you got such a nice girl. There's a lot of people had that same query, including me and especially Father Albers.

I acknowledge help from a number of good people in putting this book together. Brother Jack for remembering the early years. All four of our guys and gal for making a lot of the lines real. Dorene (Sugar, Little Flower) for being a great stabilizer. Tim's girls and Rhonda Pooley for transcribing my writing (free handed, just barely) into print.

Memoirs—It's really an honest autobiography with a few white lies. I'm really not a candidate for sainthood and some things just can't be put in print. A life happy and fun and the writing is meant to show all happy.

# 1

## *Gilbert Lee McConnell*

Born in Mahaska Hospital, Oskaloosa September 5, 1922. Mother & Dad—Byron and Mabel McConnell, on a farm 3 miles east of Bussey. Had many nicknames along the way—some censored. Mom started out Gilbert Lee and settled with Gilbert. Dad's favorite was "Rooster" and "Shikepoke." As a freshman in high school our Coach Bill Dunning, a 6' Dutchman, called me "Wart" and went by that through high school. In the service they lined up alphabetically and I went by Mac and most of my buddies were Mac. Don't really remember where and when Gib came along but it's mostly been forever.

Grew up on the farm but always thought more about the business community. Little too lonely on the farm. Those mules didn't carry on much conversation, a little hee haw and sometimes wiggle the ears. Bussey was the center of our life and, of course, it was during the depression and nobody had nothing from nothing and the Republicans stunted my growth. That's not all bad because the upkeep on small guys is a lot less than on big guys. I thought we were rich. We seemed to have everything we needed, ate good, and got a new pair of corduroys every year for school.

As a small boy my heroes were the merchants of Bussey. Grandpa Doughman was the cashier of the State Bank of Bussey. He was the typical pillar of the community. I remember his car—1933 Chevy Statesman with the two spare tires mounted on the front fenders. Really a classy car. The Palm Beach suit, Panama hat and wingtip brown and white shoes. He was a Democrat and probably never voted other than a straight ticket. He would vote for a dog if he was on the ticket, probably had more sense than any Republican they could run. Remember he made sauerkraut in 10 gallon stone jars and swallowed the seeds when he ate watermelon.

Grandma Doughman spent her time playing tricks on the neighbors, anything for a laugh. The one Uncle in the family (on both sides) that possibly had a little money lived in Chicago (real estate and insurance). For many years a happy bachelor and then took on a bride. By our standards a little fixey. Grandpa and Grandma went in to visit them for a few days. The Uncle thought it would be great for the four of them to have dinner and a show at a popular nightclub. Grandma had to visit the ladies room which happened to be at the other side of the large room and across the dance floor. Grandma came back from the ladies room across the dance floor strutting like a peacock with the back of her dress tucked into her bloomers (remember '30's bloomers). The new Aunt was so mortified they had to leave the club.

Chick's Place with Chick and Nellie Thomas was the place to meet and eat. He was the typical, rather large protrusion in the front and about 5'10" and could say the funniest things in the world without cracking a smile. There was a 16' long counter with stools. Wire ice cream store chairs and tables, booths and 5 cent roller piano. A fellow sitting at the counter one day—Chick, is this pie fresh? Oh, my yes, you bet. Give me a piece of apple pie. Just a minute and I'll dust it off for you. In those days business wasn't always too brisk. A traveling salesman usually made his weekly call about noon. (Carl Johnson—Samuel Mahon) and had asked Chick many times to go along, finish his route and he would drop him off on the way back (he deadheaded at Knoxville). This particular day there was one solitary customer at 12:15 and the salesman said—Chick, this would be a good day to ride up the line. Oh my, can't go now. The rush is on. Had a young man in town—a lot of personality and had polio at a younger age and left him with one gimpy arm. He did odd jobs for Chick. Came thru one evening and went behind the counter and picked up a sack of Bull Durham—Chick, got a sack of Bull Durham and owe you one mouse. One of his jobs was trapping mice for a nickel a head.

Another protractor of really dry humor and sober was A.J. Morris of the local meat market. The State Inspector had been by and warned him he shouldn't have that shoulder of beef on the block, it should be under refrigeration at all times. A year went by and the Inspector comes in. On the block was a shoulder of beef and he proceeds to light into A.J., the volume raising as he goes. A.J. says—Heavens no, that's not the same shoulder of beef.

# 2

## *The Younger Years*

Really don't remember much about the younger years. Older brother Jack, 3 ½ years older, can still remember better than me. I was a misfit with farm work and good thing I left. Jack did the farm work with the mules and I did the chores. Across the road lived the Mehana's—Willis and mother Alice. Willis was a little different and not cut out to be a farmer. He was really good at drawing. He drew Jack and took it to the county fair in Oskaloosa. It got a blue ribbon. The next year he drew me and it got a red ribbon. but when he brought it home and gave it to me the ribbon was blue. Didn't want my feelings to be hurt. Mrs. Mehana was always good for a cookie and she made great ones. The first Christmas I remember Willis dressed up as Santa Claus and came over. I was probably 2 and pretty much scared of the whole deal, wasn't about to talk. He asked Jack—Mind your parents? He didn't know what he meant, but said yes anyway.

The Union Liberty Church was the neighborhood meeting place and always a Christmas program with all the youngers involved. The highlight was a sack of candy with an apple or orange. A Rook Club consisted of 8 families in the neighborhood and met in the winter every 2 weeks at the homes. Play so many hands and establish the couple that won it all, then a desert with coffee and usually Kool-Aid. Remember about 4 of the guys smoking cigars. Uncle Ike was the wild bidder and Joe Tucker would fall off his chair laughing at a joke.

Remember from day one we had Shetland ponies—Midget and Jasper, thanks to John Moore and son Ray with their livery stables. The horse and buggy had gone out of style with the coming of automobiles in the 20's, and they outfitted us with single harness, double harness, bobsleds, carts, wagons, actually anything you could imagine for ponies. We were a big deal for the city cousins and seemed like there was always 2 or 3 visiting in the summer. Jack built a log cabin club house with my help. Cut the logs and whole bit. It was at the far end of our 80 acre field along a ditch. Before long it was decided too far from the house. Disassembled the cabin and moved it into the orchard. I always thought Jack could do anything and he basically could. Remember one day Jack was pulling a sled with Jasper through the pasture and ran over a big bull snake. Billy Rex was riding along and had to go to the house and change his pants.

It seems like we always had a club with the cousins at our cabin. Later with the Bussey guys. About high hchool age for Jack the country guys, Union Liberty neighborhood, had a baseball team. It was mostly Bonnetts with Paul Bonnett pitching. I was too young, but Jack played 3$^{rd}$ base. When Paul was pitching we were hard to beat. Don't remember all the teams, but we did beat Bethel Church team every time we played them. I never had much talent but did later play 4 years in High School partly because there wasn't enough players available. Was a freshman and Coach Bill Dunning would put me in to pinch hit. I was so small they couldn't hardly pitch to me. Coach would say—Make like you'll swing at every pitch, but don't you dare swing and I would get a walk.

Cousin Gilmore Doughman had a Register & Tribune paper route in Bussey. A fringe benefit was a day they would bring all the paper carriers to Des Moines and a day at Riverview Park. The carriers could each bring two friends and Gilmore took Jack and me along. We would ride the train to Des Moines and walk from Union Station to the Coliseum on the river. As I remember, it was a circus at the Coliseum and then they would assemble the whole gang on the river bank and take a group picture. That took a double page of the Sunday Register and took us a half day to spot our position in the picture. They would hand each of us a R & T bag to hang over our shoulder. We would march in a parade, then we would get a sack lunch for each and board the 6$^{th}$ Avenue trolley for Riverview Park. The park was ours all day, then trolley back to Union Station and ride home on the train (Doodlebug). As I remember, we got to Bussey about 6:30 and that was the end of the greatest day in our lives at this point.

Being the youngest, I'm sure, had its advantages and disadvantages. Jack was always the leader and I figured he could and would accomplish anything he set out to do. Jack carried most of the work load in my younger years. They favored me being younger longer than they should have. We did have good parents and they actually gave us more than they could afford. Long Johns, wool with full length arms and legs with the back door opening. I had pneumonia at 2 so it was mandatory I wear the L.J.'s from early in the fall to later in the spring. One time in the 6$^{th}$ grade had done something to deserve a paddling. Miss Thomas bent me over in front of the class and started with the walnut paddle. With my L.J's and heavy corduroy pants, she wore herself out and still didn't hurt me. Mr. Cox, the 8$^{th}$ grade teacher, was a different game. Was afraid of his paddle and never crossed him. Jack was an entertainer in class—learning was secondary. I never lived up to his image, but was no Angel. Dad was always on the school board and was President when I graduated from High School to hand me the diploma. It also meant he respected the teachers and any discipline at school was doubled at home.

The farms in the 20's were self sufficient. Cattle, hogs, sheep, chickens and we even had ducks and geese. In the earlier days we had horses for the work and later had mules. Ray Moore had a Jackass to breed the horses which would produce mules. My Dad believed the mules were better for work than the horse and I thought he was right. Jack was pretty much into the farming and I was relegated to the chores. It seems like chickens were all over the place and I also had ducks and geese that I took care of. Don't remember what the ducks were good for other than make a mess, but the geese made for a good Thanksgiving dinner every year. Gilmore had decided he could make a fortune raising and selling chinchilla rabbits. The market went south by the time he got set up. Don't remember what transpired but we ended up with the rabbits and cages at the farm. It went like gangbusters for a while and we branched into different colors. Of course, you know how rabbits multiply—wow. In the end we out grew the rabbit thing and eventually they were all turned loose. For years there were different color rabbits running around the country.

Mother was easy going and liked to play tricks like her Mother. Dad was a little more serious. We were always giving a hard time to Mom, but when Dad gave an order we jumped. There's a million fun stories about Mom. One time in the summer, the neighborhood ladies arranged a surprise Birthday party on Mom. She got wind of it and dressed up real silly and went down the road and hid out about the time they were to come. They were all settled in and waiting for Mom to come in from her visit. Mom came up the road and knocked on the door. They all tried everything to get rid of this funny looking old lady—traveling sales women. Mom finally had to tell them who she was. Grandma Doughman and her next door neighbor, Laura Metz, were always tricking somebody and if they couldn't find anybody else they would trick each other. Monday was wash day and they tried to beat each other with the wash on the line. Grandpa and Chas. Metz tried to intervene, but they both always had the clothes on the line by 4:30 a.m. Grandma and Laura sent the neighbor girl to the hardware store to borrow a left handed monkey wrench.

As I said before, thought we were rich and had nothing, but pretty much everybody was in the same boat. The farmers lived day to day with the cream and egg check. Some of the ladies churned butter and sold, also dressed chickens both fryers and hens that weren't laying. To the grocery store Ma and Pa brought the cream and eggs and with the money received bought the groceries and supplies for the week—usually oatmeal, sugar, flour, coffee and a banana if there was money left. This normally took place on Saturday night.

I first remember the silent picture (of course black and white) shows run by Clarence Baltzley. Admission was 10 cents and popcorn five cents. Our allowance was five cents and later we moved up to a quarter. My big treat was a five cent fudgsicle. As I remember, Jack was free with his money and I was conservative, Mom would say tight. I would say—Jack, take plenty money and I would have very little if any. I kept my money stashed under the dining room table.

Back in the depression, late 20's and early 30's, the city people were out of jobs and had nothing to eat. The normal farmer didn't face that. They always ate good. We butchered a hog in the fall (beef was too expensive—they could sell it). First it was heart and dressing, liver and onions, brain patties and fresh side in the morning. The refrigerator was the outside cold and a smoke house did the ham and bacon usually with Morton's Smoke Salt. Of course we had fresh eggs right out of the nest plus fresh churned butter, milk and cottage cheese. Mother had a big garden, make the normal farmers market look sparse. A big strawberry patch and raspberries plus apples, pears and peaches along with a pretty good grape arbor. Breakfast was a dream come true. We did about three hours of chores before (got up at 3:30 summer and 4:30 winter), so we were usually hungry. There was always meat, eggs and always homemade bread, biscuits, corn bread, and a very special day with cream gravy. There was always hot cereal, usually oatmeal, and cream so thick you had to stir to pour it. Mom was working on the noodles and made great ones with chicken or beef. Thinking back, that food was the greatest thing in my memory.

Jack and I trapped every winter. It was Jack doing and me following. Caught a lot of civet cats and skunks, a little risky with the smell. Our biggest catch was a mink. This brought about 16 dollars. We never had a gun on the place and to this day have never owned a gun and don't believe Jack ever had one either. Uncle Doc (O.R. Wilson) took Dad and the two of us to Minnesota fishing one summer in a new '28 Model A and sometimes would take us to a pond or river. He was a great fisherman, but it never really caught on with us. He kept in the good graces of Grandma McConnell taking her fresh fish.

Jack and I thought we could make some money raising sheep. It went pretty good for a couple years and then they got sick and died. Put us out of the sheep business. The hazard of the barnyard was a gander that would sneak up and bite you. We also had a billy goat that would butt you. Don't know where the goat came from, guess we inherited it. Goats would really eat anything. One day Dad looked out the haymow door and saw the goat on the hood of the Model T touring car eating the cloth top. Dad hit the goat in the head with a scoop shovel and knocked him to the ground. The goat got up, shook his head, and walked away.

# 3

# *High School*

We lived 3 miles from Bussey in the Bussey Consolidated School District, one of the few, at that time, to be consolidated. Most of the farm kids went to a country school (one room school house) and graduated from the 8$^{th}$ grade and then go to the nearest high school. I started in 1927. Birthday was Sept.5 with no kindergarten, was just 5 in the 1$^{st}$ grade. Our driver was a really great guy—Coon Ver Ploegh. As I remember, the 2$^{nd}$ year Coon had a Model T truck with a Ruxel-Axel and a school bus on the truck bed. Was coming home from school and going up the McConnell hill (McConnell hill was a steep winding hill fronting the McConnell home place), Coon missed the gear shifting which meant the truck was in neutral and back down the hill we came. At the curve the truck left the road and hit a tree. The back door was open and Harley Shipman was thrown out onto the truck step and pinned between the truck and the tree. Miraculously it only hurt his arm which was pinned between. It mashed his arm pretty bad and he carried a gimpy arm rest of his life. As the years went by the school buses (cars & trucks) got better and really decent. The school buses as we know them today didn't come into being until after W.W.II.

Bussey was a great place to grow up. In my high school graduating class (1939 of 25), 8 started in the 1$^{st}$ grade with me. Esther Jean Visser got polio in the 1$^{st}$ grade and she was paralyzed from the waist down. Her Mother, Ruth, was a former teacher and she tutored Esther at home, not uncommon today but unheard of in those days. By the 5$^{th}$ grade they had fit Esther with braces and she could partly walk. Nothing about the school was wheelchair accessible and mostly it was easier to carry Esther around than work with the braces. One bigger boy was paid by the system to carry Esther. We all took our turn carrying her. One day I was carrying her down the stairs and slipped at the top. Down the whole flight we rolled and was sure probably killed the poor girl. She hit the bottom laughing and I was relieved. Esther had a great out going personality and really never missed a trick. Whatever and wherever the class ended up, she was with us. Esther graduated from high school, went on to Central College and paid her own way. Got a job in Des Moines and later married and had a daughter. Her husband had polio in one leg and actually they got along pretty good.

I liked school, but more to entertaining than academics. Probably ended up as an average student. Never figured out how to be ornery until the 6$^{th}$ grade and we gave Miss Thomas fits. Same in the 7$^{th}$ grade with Miss Friberg. The 7$^{th}$/8$^{th}$ shared two teachers, Mr. Cox was the 8$^{th}$ grade teacher and I was afraid of him and his walnut paddle. High school was more of the same. Got my first F in geography as a sophomore mostly because I did more class entertaining than class work. Mr. McClymond was our superintendent the first two years of H.S. He wore sponge rubber soled shoes—silent—you could never hear him coming. One day he lifted me out of the desk seat and proceeded to dress me down of course in front of the whole assembly. Another time he caught James Conway and me passing notes—The XXX kind. We ended up in his office and, of course, Dad heard about it. Things were hairy for awhile.

Manual training and typing were two of my favorite subjects. Walnut was the favorite wood and I made about 4 different things in manual training—end table, desk, lathe turned dish and can't remember the other. They were all just barely and fell apart later. Tim gathered up the pieces for the end table and desk and had Bob Eaton (do everything guy that Tim bought the studio from) redo them and they are beautiful now. Have the end table in the front room and, of course, take all the credit. Jack made a beautiful walnut bed that graces his bedroom today. As I said before, Jack could do everything better than me and I'm still trying to catch up. I took typing 2 years mostly because it was easy and I liked it plus LaVon Wilson, the teacher, was really nice. My average typing after 2 years was in the low 20's, so it wasn't something I could make a living at.

There was only 2 sports offered—baseball and basketball. They had dropped football about 5 years before. Remember Chas Hutch kicking a football a mile with a bare foot. Of course I went out for both sports. In basketball Coach Dunning didn't know what to do with me so I was the student manager and team mascot. Coach kinda liked me because I was somehow responsible for introducing him to his current girlfriend and future wife. She was a nurse buddy of Aunt Margaret's. I did all the odd jobs and the biggest was cleaning up the basketballs for game night. There was a total of 2 basketballs for the season and by game night there was about 3 layers of dirt on them. At least got to go to all the games. Was also in the band. Started out with a trumpet and that gave me a headache so traded for a set of drums. Didn't play either very well and after H.S. gave the drums to somebody. Baseball was a little better. I could throw and catch pretty good. That was our main thing at home—Jack and I playing catch. I played right field as a freshman and then shortstop and second. Fount King was playing second in my sophomore year. He, as a southpaw, made a little different combination. Miss Flockhart taught English. Didn't care for English, but was in glory when we did talks in front of class. Our H.S. class was 26–13 boys and 13 girls. It seemed like the girls were all smart and the boys were just barely. Never really figured out why, but I was class president all 4 years of H.S.

As I said before, we had a close knit class. Think my carney business head blossomed in the junior year. It was the custom, maybe still is, to have a fundraiser to pay for the junior-senior prom. We voted to have a carnival. I got hold of a book to order all the prizes, etc. At that time, a nickel had about the worth of a dollar today and these things for the prizes went for an average of 40 cents a gross. All the games were 5 cents which filled up the little gym floor. Food at a nickel was in the home ec room. The assembly room we used for our skits and plays, and the cost was 5 cents. Can't remember any of the skits but the one Fat Watkins and I did—Edgar Bergen and Charlie McCarthy was the big hit at that time and we played to a full house. Of course I was on Fat's knee jabbering and swinging the head and he was trying to get the jokes out. We got a nice ovation and then they were asking for a rerun. Only had one act so we filled the house with nickels again and gave them the same jokes.

When the smoke cleared away, our class had netted more money than any in history. We bussed the seniors up to Des Moines to the Younkers Tea Room for our banquet and then to a movie at the Orpheum and that was a really big deal. The program at the Tea Room included a speech from the Jr. Class President, which was me. Don't remember the program theme, but it was related to the 3 page speech I was to read. It was going to be real boring and I said—It would be much better to do the speech without the paper. Guess they thought since we made the money and got this far maybe the free wheeling speech would be okay. I went into it having read the speech a couple of times and no notes. Needless to say, didn't get too close to the written version. Got a lot of laughs. Don't know whether the laughs were with me or at me. Sure the grade would have been in red.

As I said before the farms were self-sufficient. With the farming and stock we had extra cows and sold milk in town. Probably the reason it came about, Uncle Jack had the grocery store and needed milk to sell. At that time (20's) there were no A&E Dairies, etc, delivering to small country markets. As we look back, starting house to house delivery was a mistake. About ¾ of the customers were coal miners. The coal market wasn't too stable and there would usually be 4 months in the summer that there was no work. That didn't relate to eating, which was year round. The money would run out, so we would end up carrying them until they got back to work. Probably 1/3 would never catch up. I was relegated to the chores and milk business. Dad would drive the Model A pickup with me and Jack Godfrey standing on the running boards delivering milk to each side of the street. We basically gave Godfreys the milk for the son's help.

At 14 I was basically driving the pickup and running the milk route. Deliver the milk before school and again in the evening. Most of the customers were real good on the pay, some you didn't mind trying to help and some that were just plain crooks. I was easy at first but eventually had heard every excuse and all the ways to hide and dodge. I learned, but it still didn't get the pay for the milk. The milk was pretty much my domain and all 3 of us milked and, of course, I was just barely in that department. Dad & Jack could do at least 2 to my 1. A lot of time in the morning I would go to sleep leaning up against the cow and she would stick her foot in the bucket. Dad laid the law down. You can stay out all night, but you'll be in this cow barn at 3:30 in the morning.

I was probably about 10 and delivering the milk. This cute girl was on the porch every night, gingham dress and all slicked up. Right away I had a crush on this girl, went on for a couple of summers. She would come to Bussey and stay with her Grandpa, Bert Huff. I never said a word to her, but I always ran the pint of milk up to the porch. Bert was a retired coal miner getting along on his old age pension and he never missed paying for his milk. This girl, Mary Patton, lived in the Des Moines area. Her dad was a traveling salesman and ran away. Mother was a school teacher and got in a car wreck. Mary pretty much ended up in an orphanage. Her brother, Bart, finished high school in Bussey, staying and working for Uncle Jack.

Mary later got hooked up and married a young fellow from Berwick, Woody Diehl. He was a farmer and they settled on a farm below Des Moines on the river bottom. He was a sharp operator and had quite a spread when the Red Rock Dam took all their holdings. They came to Indianola and bought the General Mills Research Farm, a really nice (1500 acres) and updated spread that General Mills had moved out of. In the 60's Woody & Mary wanted to have their neighbors in for a party and came to us for the food. Dorene and I brought out the food and Mary got me in the front room and the two of us sat down in the middle of the floor to entertain the guests. It was then I found out, way back when, she had a crush on me and I had a crush on her. Neither one of us said a word to each other. Who knows what might have been but we each did well on our own.

When I went to war, Dad gave up milking the cows. You've heard about the roads starting out as dirt. The first I remember the roads had shale. Shale was the leftover rock similar to slate when they took the coal out. The rock was sharp and would cut up tires. The coal was soft with quite a bit of sulfur which would make big clunkers in the stove ashes. The roads were surfaced with whatever was available. Some areas had gravel and sand which was really better. Later on and still today there is crushed lime rock. At that time there were plenty of dirt roads and they would get deep in muck with wet conditions.

Our farm bordered the area close to Buxton, a coal mining camp of 10,000 in the early 1900's. The railroad owned most of the coal camp and when the coal would run out, they would move the town to the next mine. Buxton, at that time, was the largest in the state. The miners went on strike for more money, working conditions, etc. The Railroad took a train down south and picked up a load of Blacks and put them to work in the mines. It was great for the Blacks. Better money than they mostly made in the South, plus the living conditions were better, plus the community accepted them as part of. I first remember the mid-twenties and Buxton was all gone and there was a Buxton reunion every summer. It was held in a field like a park with a baseball diamond. The Blacks had a team, the Buxton Wonders. They were really good and in my estimation best in the world. They had one white guy playing first base. He was actually a friend of the folks. Remember one of the team members telling the story—We had this white guy playing 1st base, Hjalmar Nylander, and he had hands big as a bushel basket.

In 1938 the Chicago Cubs were in the World Series. Mother had two brothers and two sisters in Chicago. One Uncle, Roy, supposedly had a little money and in our young minds—a big operator. He was in insurance and real estate on the near south side. We called and asked him to get tickets and we would come in to the World Series. Sure—I'll get tickets—come on in. He couldn't get tickets then anymore than Mayor Daley could today. Jack, 18, I was 15 and we brought along two of my buddies, James Conway and Keith Redding. Took our car, which was a 1935 Chevy Standard, and Jack was the driver, the only one with a driver's license. We arrived in Chicago and Uncle Roy was real surprised that a couple farm nephews from Iowa could make it to the Big City on their own.

Of course, there were no regular tickets. There was one chance—400 bleacher tickets would go on sale at 10:00 the morning of the games. Uncle Roy loaded us all in the car, the 4 of us plus Aunt Margaret (Mother's sister) and Delight, Uncle Roy's girlfriend. We lined up outside of Wrigley Field at 8:00 the night before. We were about 15th in line so all we had to do was wait it out. It was August but close to Lake Michigan and it blew in a little cool but we were fixed for that. We bought a wooden orange crate for 25 cents and, of course, we could take turns going to the nearby restaurant, etc, for food and drink plus toilet. There was a couple guys close that entertained us all night. They had taken their paychecks, evidently, and bought the tickets plus booze. They really did entertain us all night, but by the time 10:00 in the morning rolled around they were pretty much out of it and I would say they never made it into the game.

Aunt Margaret was really a screwball and Delight knew absolutely nothing about baseball. Of course, it really was an experience for us and probably none of us had been 100 miles from home. Aunt Margaret asked James—Are you the oldest in the family? Yes, of the kids. Of course Delight asked a lot of silly questions. We got inside Wrigley at 10:00. The game would start at 2:00. The ground crew was getting the field ready. Aunt Margaret told Delight that was the opposing team and it was their job to get the field ready. If the fellow with the club hits the ball, he will win a Maytag washing machine. I don't think any of us slept a wink, know I didn't. When the team finally came out to warm up, Dizzy Dean came out to shag flies in center field. We were in the center field bleachers and got to talk with him. He was a great guy and that was one of his things—to make the fans happy.

To fill in the blanks, it was the Cubs & Yankees in the World Series. The Cubs lost 4 straight. That didn't bother us. We got to see the players in action and that was the greatest. Saw Bill Dickey (catcher for the Yanks) hit 3 consecutive Texas Leaguers out over $2^{nd}$. It was Lou Gehrig's ($1^{st}$ base Yanks) last full year. He had to quit the following year and passed away in '41 with what is now called Lou Gehrig's disease. Saw Phil Cavaretta (right field for Cubs) throw a ball into home on a line with one bounce. It was the year Gabby Hartnett (catcher for the Cubs) won the pennant with a home run in the $9^{th}$ inning and final game of the season. Of course, everything was a first and to see this happening in front of us was out of this world. After the game we rode back to the flat on the "L"(elevated train), another day for sightseeing and then back home. Many, many stories to tell and it went on for years—still pops up once in awhile.

# 4

## *Girls*

There was always eyes for girls but mostly would rather do sports and always had work plus an extra job. My first real date was with Vee Myers. When I brought her home she taught me how to kiss goodnight. Just one date, was a little slow for her. Went with Phyllis Stockwell for a few months. Her Dad was railroad section foreman and they moved away. She was really a nice girl. Was a senior in high school and it seemed like there were times and functions that worked better with pairs. I started going with Ila Wallace in our class and from Marysville. She was a good girl, in fact too good for me. We went through graduation and then split.

Girls were like a lot of other things I did, part of living but just barely. Didn't really want a full timer and most of the girls didn't operate that way. I could, most of the time, talk myself into a date, but the average stay was 2 dates. Had 4 buddies I palled around with. We were all country boys and each one of us kinda had access to a car. Fat Watkins and his Dad just got a new maroon Ford V8 sedan (1940). We hung at Oskaloosa (our County Seat) and did quite a lot of cruising. We had a little advantage over the city kids because they normally didn't get the car. It was Fat, Elmer Patrick, Lloyd Krouse and me. James Conway was also a buddy, but they moved to Keystone (west of Cedar Rapids) before our senior year.

At that time in Oskaloosa, the big thing for young people was El Chappo. It was a dance hall above the Canary Cottage restaurant off the northeast corner of the square. Ten cents to get in and play the jukebox for dance music. The jukebox was 5 cents—6 for 25 cents and they served setups for 10 cents. There was always a good crowd of the younger set and good places to get acquainted. About this time Dr. Bos from Oskaloosa had bought the Woodard Building and Ice House in Bussey. Dr. Duffy and Dr. McClure had their offices upstairs. Georgia Jones' sister's husband took over the pool hall and the sister had a little dance thing downstairs. She tried to teach us young people to dance. I've always really enjoyed, but never attained the good status—just barely. The El Chappo was a regular with us, mostly to hang out and get acquainted. We all had short girl flings. Fat started going with Marge Ballou. Her Dad was the bodyman for Lamberson Ford and Marge was one of the best dancers at the El Chappo. It wasn't too long they were steady daters and a wedding was in the works. I was the best man in the church wedding and Fat was lost from our gang. The pool hall wasn't making any money and they decided to close. The 3 of us bought a pool table for $35.00. Fat & Marge had set up housekeeping at the homeplace and we decided to put the pool table in the bigger upstairs room. You can take a Brunswick pool table apart and the 3 slabs of slate weigh, it seems, a ton. In order to get the pool table upstairs we had to take a window apart, frame and all, and put up a block and tackle on the outside. So that means Bob & Marge are going to have company every night. Marge was a good sport and never heard her complain. Think back, wonder if they ever took the pool table out of the house.

Getting a date with some girls was a challenge. There was one girl in Lovilla, the biggest catch of the time, Carmen Dreibelbies. I worked 3 months and finally managed a date. The date was to the Rivola Theatre (Oskaloosa) for a movie. Everything was going good. They turned on the theatre lights and I was the only one left—sound asleep. Carmen had gone to the car and when I got there she read the riot act to me. The ride home was real quiet and, of course, no more dates. Hadn't heard from Carmen all these years and really hadn't thought about her. Just this year after Harold Miek and I helped the Bussey Library, the picture was in the Oskaloosa Herald. She stopped by the A&W and left her name. Of course the guys said they had never heard that story and I was happy to oblige.

In the El Chappo days there was a cute little freckle faced blonde girl I had taken a fancy for. She was friendly, but wasn't about to date me. One time at a farm-type dance she was there and I approached her and ended up chasing her around the house. Her name was Esther Mae Horn. I was pretty fast at that time, but she was faster. Don't know what I would have done had I caught her, but I didn't, so we'll never know. After the war and running the Bussey Café, Esther stopped by with her husband, evidently anxious to see how I had turned out.

Had different girls along the way, but nothing really took. At the time I went in the Service was going with a farm girl that lived over by the Des Moines River. A super nice girl and the cutest thing I ever laid eyes on. Our second date was walking back to the car after taking her to the door. Their big black dog came around the house and caught up with me just as I got to the car. He took the seat out of my herringbone green suit pants, was really proud of that suit but got the pants fixed.

The deal in the Service—everybody had a girl back home and you would display the picture on the footlocker in the barracks. I was proud of my picture (Lois Denburger) and, of course, somebody to think about and write to. Was in the Cadets and getting ready for open post which we didn't get very often. This little buddy of mine was sitting on the bunk—no going open post, mostly homesick. Best thing to do is write your girlfriend a letter, that gets me cheered up. I was down the first night when I rode the troop train through Bussey heading for St. Louis. Of course thought I would never see home again. Ben Veenstra, fellow from home and a little older, helped me through that first night and was never homesick again. Back to the little buddy. He didn't have a picture or a girlfriend. Tell you what I'm going to do. Lois was really too good for me and I was too busy having fun with new girls and groups I would meet in town. I'll write this girl and tell her the circumstances and you can have this picture and girl for the duration. Lois bought the idea and they corresponded through the war. They also came to see me at the Cafe in Bussey. They didn't marry. He went back to Kansas and Lois married a guy from Oskaloosa and evidently has had a good life. See her from time to time.

While at the Sioux City Air Base I got acquainted with a cute little Greek girl, Stella Siganos. Her dad, Harry Siganos, had the Mayfair Tap at the bus stop. Nice fellow and mother was also nice. One night I had planned a special date with Stella and she stood me up. Found out later she had gone out with my bunk mate. In fact she told me he was a good looking Greek and really a great fellow. She had a chance to go out with him and couldn't pass it up. Couldn't really blame her for that.

Later in the Bussey Café days, Swede had started going with Phyllis Cavender in Des Moines. She was actually a cousin of Jimmy Comer. In order to take her out, Swede had to bring somebody for her sister Bobbi. This had been going on for some time and we were getting along fine and having a good time. One night I couldn't make it and sent along a buddy of ours, Fount King. The next date came up. She gave me to understand good guys were hard to find and she had Fount and wasn't about to go out with me. They are still married. Guess it was okay. Fount still speaks to me.

One of my first business ventures in the outside world—decided to have a stand at the celebration in Bussey on July 4$^{th}$. Serve milk (all sizes), chocolate milk, buttermilk, and a concoction I made up with ginger ale and milk. In first place, didn't have anything the public wanted and second, I got smitten with another one of Jim Comer's cousins. Spent more time trying to capture the girl than run the business. After I asked Dr. McClure what I owed for the stand space. Don't think you made any money—nothing. He was right. Did go with the girl a few times and then we quit.

# 5

## *Jobs*

I never had any real talent in anything. Possibly the best thing I did was shake hands and the—Hi, how are you? Really always and still like people and every meeting and greeting. In the younger years, always had 2 or 3 jobs. Finished up high school on Friday and Grandpa Doughman came out on Saturday and wanted me to take a job in the bank that started on Monday. Always thought of Grandpa as one of my heroes. He chewed Red Man and never passed up a drink and never really fought it either. He also smoked cigars and a pipe on occasion. He also made good sauerkraut in 10 gallon stone vessels. He was a regular guy and had more common sense than the average.

Here's my story on the bank job. Grandpa had run the bank for a number of years and the son, Uncle Ed, needed a job so he did a little Business School and went to work. Ed bought stock so he would have a little say—leverage. Grandpa never bought any stock, all he was interested in was running the bank. It was a two man bank and Grandpa, a little older, couldn't really handle his side of the posting machine. In other words, Uncle Ed, as a member of the Bank Board, would get rid of his Dad if he couldn't handle his half of the work. Grandpa came to get me to do his part of the bookkeeping. He would pay me $5 a month and noon lunch. That kind of a deal sounds a little ridiculous and it was, but in 1939 there wasn't too many jobs available. It was either 3C's or nothing and I could still stay at home and handle the milk for my room and board.

I was originally thinking college in the fall or a real job. Actually I stayed over 2 years and posted my side of the ledger, worked the counter, wrote up the foreign checks, swept and mopped the floor, filled the stoker, washed the windows, scooped the snow and caught rats in the basement. Actually handled every job in the Bank but loan money and was a learning experience. I never complained and did the job plus didn't ask for anything. Uncle made sure I didn't get in over 40 hours a week, which was a problem, but evidently slave labor didn't make any difference. When Grandpa had to leave—health—I was out and the daughter came in to replace me at $175.00 per month.

My next job was with Uncle Jack in the grocery store at $11 a week plus my lunch. While at the Bank I helped Bob Fuller in the IGA store after hours at the Bank and on Saturday night worked from 5:30 to 12:30 or whenever the farmers would pick up all their groceries. For this I got $1, which was big money. After work if the gang wasn't waiting on me, I would go across the street to Wilmer Lomax Tavern and usually eat two lamb fry sandwiches at 25 cents each and 2 glasses of milk at 5 cents each. At that time would eat every chance I got. Usually grab something at Uncle Ike's while on the milk route. Grandma McConnell was always glad to see me, clean up all her leftovers and that was always after eating at home.

It just came to mind, and has from time to time over years, those thresher dinners. Up till before the war, before combines, there was a thresher run. It was mostly oats and a little wheat. Each farmer would cut the oats with a binder. It would tie bundles with binder twine. A helper would stack 8 or 10 bundles into a shock. Then, when the oats were dry enough to thresh, the threshing machine would pull in and set. The farmers would all go together and help each other—called a thresher run. Ours usually had 8 to 10 farmers. Our thresher was Jersey Houser and he pulled the machine with a big Titan tractor. The crew to the west of us was Minnekus Visser and he pulled with a steam engine. The hayrack would go to the field and a pitcher would throw the bundles on the wagon with a pitchfork. There would usually be 4 bundle racks and 2 grain wagons. Jersey usually had Shorty McConnell (Dad's cousin) helping with the machines. Remember they both wore overalls, red bandanas around their necks and farmer cap. Shorty was usually carrying a squirt oil can. The bundle wagons would line up on each side of the thresher chute and pitch in the bundles. The straw would come out the other end and the grain would come out a chute at the middle. Each farm would take one to two days and then the tractor moved the thresher to the next farm. The thresher run would usually last about 3 weeks. We had the Shetland ponies and could get the job of water boy. I helped Jack and when he got old enough to handle a team, I took over the water. A gallon stone jug wrapped with a burlap sack and a corn cob stopper. There would be a leather strap on the jug to hang it on the saddle horn. Would fill the jug from the well, usually cool, and wet the burlap to help keep the water cool.

The absolute best thing about the threshing was the dinners. They would shut down and come to the house. A bucket of water was on the porch with a couple wash pans, soap and towels for cleaning up. Go in the house and dig in. Of course, there was no air conditioning, open windows with screens and there was always a problem with flies. Always fried chicken and another meat, mashed potatoes and gravy, homemade bread and home churned butter and everything else you can imagine. Finish with pie and or cake. Sometimes got 25 cents or 50 cents to carry the water, but I would gladly carry the water just for the dinner.

Ollie Harris and Velma Moore were the two best cooks on the run and probably Mother was just as good, but ate with her everyday. Remember coming home on furlough from the Service. Had been in Cadet training and really thought I was in the best of shape. Dad was baling hay. The tractor pulled the baler across the field. The baler would pick up a windrow of hay and tie into rectangular bales with baling wire 60 to 90 lbs each. A wagon was hooked alongside the baler and the bales would be kicked out on the wagon. Hey, this'll be fun! I'll load the wagon. That was the hardest work I ever got into. I wasn't about to give up, but didn't go out that night. After supper I fell into bed.

Bussey always had a 4$^{th}$ of July celebration and from the time I was big enough always worked the 4$^{th}$ and always peddled the milk. The first year I worked in the Bank, Wilmer Lomax was running the tavern and asked me to work for him. I can't work in a tavern—only 16. Won't be serving beer, just running the cash register. I could count money and the pay was $1 an hour. I sometimes worked at Bob Fuller's I.G.A. store and worked these mornings of the 4$^{th}$ and then across the street to Wilmer's at 12:00. He had a tent out the back to the alley with a bar, tables and chairs. Root Shaw (between 25 and 30) was the bartender, I was the cashier, and a couple girls to wait on the tables. Pharis Southern and his wife Lote had their picture taking booth in one corner. Pharis and Lote were pretty good drinkers and they were pretty much out of it by 10:00. I ran the cash register the first hour and then was doing everything. Root was a good guy and we were busy and got along fine. About 12:30 that night, the people had pretty much been drinking all day and were getting a little owley. Somebody threw a firecracker in the middle of our room. Thought I was shot and jumped under the counter. Root was already there.

One 4$^{th}$ while in the Service at the Sioux City Air Base, my buddy and I had been working extra at a shop in town. It was a little factory making pop guns. We had a stand at Riverview Park and sold the pop guns for 25 cents. We didn't make any money. Maybe it looked good on our resume. The buddy, Omar Fleshner, we called Hunkah, and I got acquainted with the guys that played in the band for the West Hotel Supper Club. Ken Granning played the drums. He had been with a big band doing stops across the country. They were in North Carolina traveling in cars. Ken's car got in a wreck. He buggered up his back and had to leave the road. Settled back home in Sioux City and played with this hotel band 5 nights a week. Plus with a bad back, couldn't get in the Service. He had put together a little wood shop upstairs at 4$^{th}$ & Pierce. There was a bandsaw, jigsaws, a sander and 2 drill presses. The gun would be cut from a 1" board, actually ¾". The barrel would be 6 inches long and the handle was cut from the board to resemble a gun handle. The barrel would be drilled the length. A smaller dowel would extend from the handle into the barrel, nailed to the end of the dowel was a leather washer. A cork on the end of a string was stuck in the barrel end. A pull and push of the handle would blow the cork out and create the pop. They were painted red with the name "Perma-Cracker" on the body. The help was pretty much Ken and high school kids. We spent most of our time there, Hunkah and I, and pretty much ran the place.

Ken was a good fellow, but if he had any money he was drinking. All the band did a pretty good job of drinking. One morning Ken got a package in the mail, about 3#'s of marijuana. His former band members had been playing in Texas and went over to Mexico—hence the package. Ken was pretty much in another world for about a week. I'm happy to say that Hunkah and I never even tried drugs. We did get into drinking, probably more than we should have. Ken paid us 75 cents an hour and high school kids 50 cents an hour. The problem was Ken hardly ever had the money to pay Hunkah and I. When we did get paid, would take him out and spend it all. Ken did treat us like family and took us a lot of places.

Out of the Service and in the Café at Bussey, took a little vacation and decided to check out to the old haunts at Sioux City. Looked up Ken's # and called. The conversation led to how you doing and then into money. He was trying to ask me for a loan. In the first place, I didn't have extra money and second place that would be a bad investment so Swede and I headed out of town and never contacted him again.

# 6

## *The Service*

Was in Chick's Place the afternoon of December 7, 1941. Chick had just installed a Howell's Root Beer Barrel he was real proud of. I was having a 5 cent mug of root beer. The radio was on and they started telling about Japan bombing Pearl Harbor. This sounded pretty serious—sinking ships in the harbor and quite a few people killed. My thinking right away, they already made us mad and in a couple weeks they'll be sorry they jumped on us.

The European War was going full bore. President Roosevelt had activated the draft about a year before and our buddy, Vernon Zylstra, was one of the first to be called up. We hadn't declared war on Germany, but had agreed to send troops plus to help England. Right away President Roosevelt declared war on Japan and this was getting more serious by the day. It didn't end in a couple weeks as I had thought. We were getting beat on every island we touched around Japan. This was really war and everybody was getting involved. It was either Service or something related to the War effort. I was to be drafted in another 6 months so I decided to enlist and maybe get something better than what they would give me from the Draft. The Air Corps Cadets seemed like the best deal. It would start out at $75.00 and upon graduation you would be an officer. The regular GI started at $50 and no guarantees.

Went to Des Moines the day before. There was 3 or 4 of us, can't remember who, but we would start on the test at the old Federal Building the next morning at 6:00. We stayed at one of the hotels in the area, probably Jackson or Kirkwood. There was a grocery store next door and we got a couple bunches of carrots. Was sure that would help our eye exam. We all passed the mental exam and they trucked us to Camp Dodge for our physicals. Was getting along real good and had passed everything so far. A buck sergeant made some remark to me and I gave him to understand I wasn't yet in the Air Corps and wasn't about to take any baloney from him. He said—Are you color blind? No. He took a thumb and flipped the book pages real fast. What did you see? Nothing. You're color blind and that was final. At the end the officers were going through the results and I told them what had happened. The Sarge's decision was final and nothing they could do about it. I would have to come back another day and hope I didn't get the same Sergeant.

I decided to try the Naval Air Corps, so back to the Old Federal Building. Passed the test and got into the physical. With the Navy I failed because of a ¾" overbite. In the Navy, they explained, with dive bombing that would make me blackout. My only option would be to wait a couple of weeks and try Camp Dodge again. This time held the cocky business and passed okay. The day was December 12 and was to go home and wait to be called up in a few weeks. On February 14 was called to report to Camp Dodge. They got us all organized and put us on a troop train for St. Louis and Basic Training at Jefferson Barracks. There were always stories, not the best, about Basic Training. About the first morning we were called out by the Sergeant, not nice at all, and I talked back to him. When he got through chewing on me, I was only about 1 foot tall. That was the final learning experience. I was meek and mild from then on.

We were put up in huts with a little cone shaped stove that burned coke. There were 8 in each hut. In our hut, 6 of the 8 were college guys from Minnesota. One of the fellows happened to have a pair of dice. I didn't know much about craps. I had about $15 to my name and that wasn't enough to make me knowledgeable. I decided right then that would be the last of my gambling. Of course payday was once a month and it would be a long 30 days. Wasn't about to write home for more money. There wasn't much a fellow needed to buy and would be more than a month before we got off the Base.

Basic training lasts 6 weeks and they just kept us busy from early morning till late at night. The first open post was on a Sunday, so a buddy and I went into town. St. Louis was real quiet on Sunday and somebody told us the action was in East St. Louis across the river. They were wide open. We got on the trolley and it made its first stop across the river. A fellow jumped on the trolley swinging a big knife (looked like a corn knife), probably 6 inches and the guy was drunk. Anyway, my buddy and I were trying to get under the seat. We rode the trolley back across the river and went back to the Base.

Basic Training was never supposed to be fun. It's supposed to change a person's thinking into a new World. A loose life of work and play into a structured play by the rules type of environment. It really was a whole different world. Out of the barracks at 5:30 to the loud hollering of a drill sergeant. Form a squad and march to the Mess Hall. You've all heard about the lousy food in the Service. The food wasn't too bad, in fact I ate good. At that stage in life ate everything that got in front of me and hungry most of the time. The cook got the best food available to start on and they did a decent job. Cooking for thousands and serving through a steam table leaves a little to be desired. They always had an insert of soup and good. From the days of K.P.—whatever the cooks were working with the leftovers were thrown in the steam kettle and that was the day's soup. The buddy and I were working on K.P. one day—pots and pans. Cook behind us yelled—Hot Stuff! The little buddy came up with Where? Where? Certainly served my share of K.P. Maybe the schooling from K.P. was what landed me in a lifetime in the food business.

One time at the Sioux City Air Base had a date with my girlfriend in town. She stood me up. Seemed to get that quite often. So, I decided to party and got into it a little too heavy. The M.P. gave me a ride back to the Base and I had a meeting scheduled with the Captain next morning. Guess I'll have to take that stripe. Can't do that, Sir. It's by act of Congress. How about 64 hours of extra K.P. duty? Yes, Sir! The Captain was well acquainted with my buddy & I.

Back to Basic Training—About ¾ of the time was taken up on the parade ground drilling. There was a parade to raise the flag and another parade in the evening to lower the flag. On Saturday we had a big parade like most everybody on the Base. Sunday was a little different. Think that loud drill sergeant took the day off, but there was plenty more guys around to holler at us. Anytime we lined up for marching, large or small, always the same—the tallest guy at the front left and he set the cadence. It came down until the shortest guy was at the back, which was mostly guys like me. Usually on the back line with my 5'5". That tall guy's small steps would still have us short guys stretching to keep up. Drilling on the parade ground was 50 minutes drilling and 10 minutes rest—smoke 'em if you got 'em. I didn't have 'em, so I got 'em. It was my first experience with the P.X.—Post Exchange. Found out it was about the best thing the service had to offer. They sold everything and very cheap. Don't remember how much the cigarettes cost but really cheap. Tried the cigarettes for a while but glad to say the smoking habit didn't take.

Glad to say we finished Basic. No graduation honors. The loud drill sergeant didn't even come to say you did a good job or glad to get rid of you. Think he was already hollering to a bunch of new recruits. We were veterans now and we got to whistle at the new guys just coming up. We were on our way to the troop train shipping us to the next destination. Our ride was to Michigan State College. That, like everything else, was controlled by supply and demand. S.A.A.C.—San Antonio Aviation Cadet Center was loaded up along with the training centers. There was a time after Pearl Harbor when there was a rush to get pilots and all the other units trained and into combat. By the same token the requirements were not as high at that time, about 10% of the pilots were washed out by the time I reached S.A.A.C. The rate was about 70%.

Our troop train pulled into Lansing, Michigan with about 900 eager and ready Cadets to be. The Air Corps brass were meeting us and instill in our minds strict rules. That was a little hard to do, but they definitely had the upper hand. This whole mass of words is partly from memory, some guess, some research, which is real sparse. Let's say I'm trying—hopefully getting close to the facts. When we unloaded from the train there was a 10 plus brass band making good music. That, I think, was made up of our group. It was amazing the talent within our ranks and, of course, there were a few of us with no talent at all. Actually we all dressed and looked the same. Michigan State is in East Lansing so we proceeded there. It would probably compare then and now to our Iowa State College. At this time there were 2,700 girls and about 500 guys. Most of the guys on the campus were in the Service. We were put up in a large dormitory complex at the East end of campus. You don't need a pencil and paper (before computers) to figure out the odds of available girls.

We were basically assigned 5 to a dormitory room. There were no phones in the rooms but every so often in the halls a pay phone. These started ringing when we walked into the building and never quit, mostly from the girls on campus. As I said, we were Cadets to be and the Air Corps officers were there to instill it into us. The food was a central kitchen and buffet and compared to Jefferson Barracks—Gourmet. I know you're thinking this young guy lucked out with gourmet living. You are right. How could I be so lucky? However, the rules were very strict. We had an hour of free time each evening and couldn't leave the premises. Saturday we were free in the evening and some free time on Sunday afternoon. The term gig: We would get gigs for any rule we would break like improper eating or sitting at meals, not standing up straight, inspection—personal or room. I don't remember any major rules broken. We all wanted to continue and get our wings, officers rank, etc.

At the time we got to Michigan, I had something like arthritis in my legs and could hardly walk. I roughed it out rather than go on sick call. I didn't want it on my record and it went away like it come. Enough gigs and you would walk them off on your Saturday afternoon free time. I can remember doing my gigs more than one Saturday afternoon in a triple tennis court. May I inject—Dorene (I sometimes call her Sugar or The Little Flower) just looked over my shoulder—Maybe you should call that a "fiction" book instead of a "true memoir." I was telling her a story one day and her eyes were straying. Would I lie to you? Always have!! She didn't hesitate a second.

Back to business at hand. Our studies related to what we were going to be doing. The math was tied into flying, another class about planes and how they got the lift, geography related to countries we might be going to, English was writing and speaking, even had swimming and to pass the course you had to swim the length of the pool and back without touching the end. I passed and don't know how. All I could ever do was dog paddle. We marched to class and everywhere we went (think our squad was 12). Our squad leader was Louie Pringle and really a nice guy. Can't say I had anything good to say about anybody else of authority.

We each got at least 10 hours of flight training at the airport with civilian instructors. The planes were Piper Cubs and one day we were shooting landings and I was at the controls. We would touch down and go back to the throttle and take off. I had set down and was coasting to a stop. He said—Let me have the controls and we'll go back and take off from a stop. He cut across the grass, hit a gopher hole, and nosed the plane over and broke the propeller. He wrote it up as my fault. His fault would have had to pay for it. I didn't really want it on my record, but went along with it.

Girls—there were plenty available and yes, we did go out with them when we had the chance. My buddy and I figured out right away the college girls didn't have cars. We found a couple with an available car and it worked out great. My girl corresponded with Mother and of course she was wonderful in her estimation. She really was a nice girl and her folks had me in for meals. This Heaven on Earth lasted about 5 months then we rode the troop train to S.A.A.C.

San Antonio, the Cadet Center, was a routing pool for Cadets. Now we're back to the real world of the Service and Air Corps. San Antonio probably had more Service Bases than any other city in the nation. Besides S.A.A.C., it was built around a huge Army Base and I believe it had the original flight training Base plus many others. I enjoyed the city and it seemed like they enjoyed the Service people. On the other hand, their economy had to be based on them. We were to take our final mental test and physical, then to our training base. In our barracks we had one fellow that was iffy 5'. The Cadets had quite definite dimensions. I remember the short figure at 5'. Before the physical we put this short buddy on a bare board for all night and everybody in the barracks took turns, one on each end, stretching him all night. Evidently it worked because he passed the next day.

You could make a choice what you would rather go for—pilot, navigator, bombardier. My first choice was navigator, which also demanded the highest score. I evidently didn't score high enough because was awarded Pilot. Was assigned to primary flight training at Vernon, Texas. Vernon was a nice little town, about 10,000, and 100 miles north of Dallas. A nice small air base about 400 bodies. The food was good. The smaller the base, the better the food and most air bases were smaller. Primary was ½ books and ½ flight training. Our pilot trainers were civilian and most of the ground school teachers were civilians. That was good and bad, but they were afraid of getting fired by the government.

I managed to get a girlfriend. She worked in a bank, which I could relate, and was Catholic, which I couldn't relate. Was off on a Sunday so made a date to go with her to Mass and was to meet her at church. Got directions, so many blocks left on the main drag from the bus stop. The church was where it was supposed to be—happened to be Lutheran. The Catholic church was the other way and, of course, I got there late.

My big worry in Primary was ground school. Was basically with a bunch of sharp, young college kids. Most had one, two, three years of college and I didn't. I worked hard on the books and did real good. The flying was the problem. To this day I can't explain it, but couldn't seem to do anything right. Maybe it wasn't supposed to be. I washed out in the mid-phase of flight training. I was devastated. Thought there would never be another happy day. A complete failure in life. Was given two options—airplane mechanic or radioman. I chose mechanic and was put on a bus with travel orders to Keesler Field, Biloxi, Mississippi. Had one day, but thought I better stay with the bus rather than do something silly. Came into my new home ½ day early.

Biloxi seemed like a nice little Gulf town. It was just barely and sure with the Air Base there it prospered and is quite a city by now. Checked into Keesler Field and was assigned to a barracks. I always had the top bunk because I jumped up there easier than most. As I remember, there were 8 barracks in the squadron. You could see right away that it was a bunch of misfits and washouts and I fit in. That was my thinking and your mind can really be pushed anyway you want it to go. It didn't take long to get acquainted.

My first bunkmate was Howard from Boston. A pretty good-sized rawboned Irishman. He was about 27 so we called him Dad, Pop, or Old Man, but he was really a great guy and did father us young guys. It didn't take me too long to get my heart straightened out. In this life you don't win every battle. I decided to do my best and really enjoy my time in the service. After it was over, I would put it all together and get back on track.

Airplane Mechanic (A.M.) school started right away. It ran in 3–8 hours shifts and our gang drew the 5:00 p.m. through 1:00 a.m. shift. Of course, form outside the barracks and march to class, same coming back. We studied every phase of an airplane, large and small. Of course it was all engines, radial and inline, and you remember it wasn't too long after the War jet's came into being. I just loved school and the airplanes. Learned right away that I would never be a real mechanic, but I could remove and replace with the best of them. Out of the 8 barracks in the squadron, ours could be voted most likely to be in trouble. Our physical training officer, we called him an "Eager Beaver," gave us P.T. 5 times a week. He could yell like the former drill sergeant. Maybe they had a school to teach that to those type guys.

Each barracks had a softball team and we played a schedule and then a tournament at the end. Loud mouth said the final team winner will get a 3 day pass to New Orleans. Our team had a pitcher that was unbelievable, had it all. I played right field and don't remember fielding over 1 or 2 balls. We won the whole thing and I said we wasn't in the good graces of the wheels and we never got the pass—always some excuse.

Biloxi was in oyster country and we were there in the "R" months and plenty seafood in the Gulf. Saved a dollar for a fried oyster dinner every open post. Dozen oysters plus the trimmings. Makes me hungry even today. Not too far from the gate was a diner type place that served waffles around the clock. A double waffle with a nice glob of butter for 35 cents. That was also a special stop for me.

Up the Gulf east about 15 miles was a ship building center called Pass Christian. Our day off was Saturday and Saturday night they had a community dance in the city auditorium. One Saturday night 4 of us hitched over to the dance. I was dancing with a nice looking blonde girl. The band was playing Sheik of Arabi. The dancers were all leaving the floor, heading for the stage. Looked up there and my 3 buddies were on the stage entertaining. Evidently it was working.

Had a buddy in the barracks, James Mazzoni from Kennett Square, Pennsylvania, known as the mushroom capitol of the world—grown in caves. Tall, dark, handsome with black wavy hair, a little mustache and blue eyes. He had it all, but couldn't talk. I took Jim to Pass Christian with me on Saturday afternoon. We walked down the street and right away he attracted some girls. I did the talking and we lined up a couple girls for the dance that night.

New Orleans was only 60 miles away and if we had any money, which didn't happen very often, we would hitchhike down there and stay over. Had a buddy that lined up 3 girls from New Orleans and me another buddy were with him for a date. This developed into a fun thing. They all worked and lived at home and actually all had boyfriends in the Services. On pay day we would take them out and the next Saturday they would take us out. For our first time we took them to the Blue Room in the Roosevelt Hotel. Johnny Long with his band was playing. An evening for 6 with drinks, dancing and a few snacks came to $57 and change plus a good time was had by all. One of the girls got her Dad's car. He worked for Standard Oil and was able to get a little extra gas. She would meet us at the bus station and we would first go to her house. We actually went to all 3 houses and they would each have food and drink for us and then we would head out for the evening. Looking back, really think the folks enjoyed us guys more than the daughters.

One weekend we would go to Bay St. Louis, a little resort town about half way to New Orleans. One of the girl's folks had a little summer cottage there. The 3 girls would meet us with an aunt as chaperone, and we would have a party. The girls would get us up at 6:00 on Sunday morning, press our uniforms the best they could and we would head to the little Mission Church for Mass. They would march us in and set us on the front row with them in the second row. Back at the cottage we would have breakfast and they would put us on the bus and back to the Base. We would go and be ready for school Sunday evening at 5:00.

One Saturday afternoon we were to go crabbing in Lake Ponchartrain. We had a row boat, string and tied bait on and throw it in the water. The crab would grab hold of the bait and wouldn't let go—pull him into the boat. Not really sure this was Kosher. We didn't catch any crabs or even see one, but we had a lot of fun. After this adventure we headed for the Crab House for six hard boiled crabs for $.50 plus 6 bottles of beer. At that time we threw the legs away and ate the body. Today it seems all you can buy is the legs.

One payday we had taken the girls out. We got a big idea—buy some liquor, take it back and sell it and have enough money for next week. The county in Mississippi was dry plus I believe they call that bootlegging. We brought 5–5 ½ of Three Feathers and smuggled it on the Base. We actually were in pretty early so we decided to invite some of our special buddies and drink one bottle. Our barracks captain had the room at the end of the barracks and the rest wouldn't know. You can probably figure out what happened. From 3 friends it started growing and we ended up finishing off all 5 and had the whole barracks lop eared! What a sad group marching to class that night. Another big money making venture gone South.

A.M. School was over and we were heading for Willow Run Bomber Plant. Usually in the war times, we had no idea where the troop train was taking us and that was probably for the best. Willow Run was a Ford plant out of Detroit and they were building B-24's, at the time our largest 4 engine bomber. We were at a small Base next to Willow Run with about 400 which again make for good eats. The kitchen was headed up by a great Chef from the area. One night we had breaded, boneless lamb chops. I had worked the grocery meat and had helped butcher the beef at Uncle Ike's for the store run by Uncle John. They were asking me and I had no idea what we were eating, but it was super good.

We were at Willow Run a month and went through the whole makeup of the B-24. We pretty much had Saturday night and Sunday free. Detroit was close by and as I remember, the Base ran a bus back and forth for free. The bus stopped and picked up at the U.S.O. downtown. On those kinda deals the pay day never caught up and most of us were always broke anyway. A buddy and I ironed two shirts for 50 cents each and that got us to town and back with money left over.

The U.S.O. in Detroit was a "take care of all the problems" type of place. Anything you wanted to eat was available free. In any area of Detroit you was going to, they had overnight facilities available. Usually church basements with cots and continental breakfast to send you off in the morning. From the U.S.O. you would get a slip to get you in this facility. The street cars were all free for Service people. There was a section behind 1st base at Detroit Stadium free at anytime for anybody in a uniform. I got there for one game and can't really remember who the Tigers were playing. Kind of seems like the Cleveland Indians, but can't remember the players. Of course at that time Bob Feller and most of the names were in the Service.

I don't remember ever paying for a drink at the bars. The bartender would look at the guy on each side and if they didn't offer to pay—on the house. One night a gang of us were at a hotel lounge entertaining some girls and had a round of drinks. Here came another round. Ten minutes later and another round. I told the waiter—Don't know what's going on but we only had enough money for one round. A couple of fellows at the bar had met up and talking over old times plus buying our drinks.

From Willow Run got a 6 day furlough and was to report to Lincoln, Nebraska routing pool. Was nice to get home and see the folks. Mom and Dad plus Ray & Velma Moore hauled me out to Lincoln Air Base. Ray & Velma were good friends of the folks and I sent Ray a box of Red Dot cigars when I had the money. The P.X. usually had cigars and they were cheap. At home cigars were almost impossible to get. From Lincoln we all figured on being assigned to a unit overseas, either the conflict of Germany or Japan. I was assigned to Sioux City Air Base. That, to me, was unreal. Right away I thought—Sioux City isn't war. If

I'm going to be in, let me be in the thick of it. On the other hand, if that's the verdict so be it. Somebody has to take care of the crews at Sioux City so might as well be me.

Sioux City Air Base was a B-17 Bomber Base that put together the crews to be sent overseas. I checked into the Base before midnight the day I was to report. Was assigned a bunk and assigned a B-17 on the Flight Line. 17's were sisters of the B-24–4 engine bombers. The only real difference, the controls were activated by electric and on 24's they were hydraulic. 17's were a mechanics dream to work on and I considered it a better plane.

By this time you can buy this statement—I can remember all the fun things we did, but having a hard time remembering work on the flight line. The 17's were lined up on the flight line, 4 to a line, and a plane was assigned to each mechanic. A flight crew was put together and assigned to a plane for the training—6 weeks. Then they would head for combat. It was the mechanic's job to keep the plane ready for flying. The new planes, as they came off the line, were sent to combat and replaced the ones that had seen combat, shot up, etc. My plane had seen some battles and bore some scars. They were flight worthy, but not too pretty. It was the mechanic's job to really mother the ship. There was a daily inspection—more or less visual. If the plane was scheduled to fly, you'd do a pre-flight, run up the engines, check out the instruments and controls. The crew would come out and your job was to see them off. The pilot and crew would write up any problem with the plane or anything that should be checked out. The line mechanic would take care of fuel and oil plus minor repair such as battery, spark plugs, starter, generator, etc. So many hours an engine would go in for overhaul and then so many would get an engine change. It was our job to say it was or wasn't air worthy. We worked an 8 hour shift, 6 or 7 days and around the clock every 3 weeks. Some shifts would be real busy and sometimes the planes would be out on a training mission. We all had a plane but worked together if one mechanic needed help

I had a little fellow from West Virginia crewing the plane next to me. He was a Mac too, not necessarily any education but a natural mechanic. He would usually do my trouble shooting. As I said before, didn't have any natural ability but really enjoyed the work. I was the greasiest and had the most coveralls chewed up with battery acid. In the Service with the close proximity living in the barracks, it didn't take long to get acquainted with everybody. We were, more or less, all the same and pretty much all good guys.

I mentioned before, Omar Fleshner worked in engine change and smaller than me. He was from Kansas City and a family of 5 with an invalid dad. At 12 he was trying, with odd jobs, to help the family and take care of his own needs. He followed a couple fellows around that had a jukebox—pinball operation and by age 16 had a route of his own. Of course at this time, the operators were real short of repair guys. Wasn't too long we were hooked up with the operators and were taking care of the machines at the Base. Hunka was doing the work and I got real good holding the tools. For a little guy he had a deep voice and made a lot of noise and of course I made noise too. We probably knew more people—especially the people running the joints downtown. There was usually a machine that needed a little fixing. We never charged for the work, but if we needed a favor they would be glad to help.

Hunka was a Good Time Charlie. We would go into a bar and there always was somebody he knew. Hi Sarge—set 'em up for all these guys—got any money, Gib? The Base was at Sergeant Bluff, about 5 miles from town, and they charged us a dime to ride each way on the bus. Many times we got to the line dead broke and there was always somebody there to give us a couple dimes—probably bought him a drink before. I wrote before about Ken Granning and the little Perma-Cracker factory. That took up a lot of our extra time. We were probably the two busiest guys in the War. I would go weeks at a time without messing up my bed, just grab a nap on the line while the planes were out.

Hunka and I knew a gang of young people in town. They would put together a party if we could be there. Remember one night we came in and everybody was sitting around the room talking. Wasn't two minutes and everybody was up dancing, singing, etc.

In our squadron headquarters was a bulletin board and part time job openings in Sioux City were posted. A bunk mate went in for a job emptying a railroad car. It was full of steel and it was really a heavy and a tough job. He explained that he was a big and strong looking guy so right away he gets on the tough jobs. Swift Pack wanted extra help for a span of two weeks before Christmas. A bunch of us went in. The big guys got the heavy work and they put me with the high school kids in the Canadian Bacon Department—not heavy and really kinda fun.

If I had a 3 day pass would head home to Bussey—happened about once a month. Catch the Milwaukee Road Hiawatha to Madrid, a stub train would take the passengers to Des Moines and somebody would pick me up. If the weather was good, could usually make better time hitchhiking. Everybody picked up the Service people and never heard of any problems. Had been at Sioux City Air Base about a year and hooked up with Hunka. We were working, partying, having a good time in general. We got to thinking—there was really a war on and here we are funnin in S.C., Iowa. Hunka and I went in to see the Captain in charge of our squadron. We want to transfer to Gunnery School and then we can get on a flight crew. The Captain was well acquainted with the two of us—both good and bad. In the first place, with your size, you would both be tail gunner and that's the first ones to get shot. In the second place, I need you on the line so get out of here and back to work—so work we did.

In the Summer of '45 the War was winding down. They shipped a bunch of us out. We were thinking we were to go overseas and replace some of the fellows that had seen heavy duty. I was shipped to Great Bend Kansas Air Base. They were mainly putting crews together for overseas replacement. I stayed around about 6 months and crewed everything from B-29's with radial engines, to fighter planes, P-38, P-35, with inline engines. In between they were trying to sign some of us up to reenlist.

I had met a fellow that could get me on with Bell Telephone and was thinking about that, had also thought about the G.I. Bill and college. Mom had sent me a letter before about the two ladies who had started a café in Bussey. It was too much for them and they would like to sell. Why don't I think about that? Want no part of the restaurant business. Finally they sent me to Jefferson Barracks to prepare for discharge. On February 14th of 1946 rode the train to Des Moines and caught the Doodle Bug home. At that point I started thinking—washed out of the Cadets and would finish out the Service to the best of my ability, but hang loose and enjoy. Also, when out of the Service was going to put something together and make it work. Already had one failure in my life.

# 7

## *Back Home*

Had made up my mind, I'll give this restaurant a try. Maybe can put together enough money to get me in college for fall. I really did have Simpson in mind. Before the War had checked Simpson out, but mostly had come to Indianola to check out a job. At the time Frank Ford headed up the Hy-Vee. Knocked on his door at home and two good looking young girls answered the door. Decided right then this was going to be my job. The War was heating up so enlisted in the Air Corps instead.

Home on Friday after the war and went to the bank on Saturday. The Uncle I had worked for before had to have Dad and Jack's signatures on the loan for $1,500. He evidently didn't have much faith in me. Closed the deal on Saturday and was to take over on Monday. Went in at 5:30 a.m. to open at 6:00. Had an old Majestic Range for the cook stove and a couple old ice boxes for refrigeration cabinets. Had paper, kindling and cobs to start the fire and then would use coal.

My first customer right at 6:00 was Minnekus Visser, an older widower. You got pancakes? Did you have pancakes before? Yes! We got pancakes. I found a griddle and threw it on the stove and started looking for something like pancake flour. Had no idea what I was doing but found the bag and directions—sounded simple. Put in a bowl and mix with water. Poured the batter on the griddle. Of course the griddle was still cold and it didn't do much. Minnekus (we called him Mink) got a cup of coffee and a lot of conversation and I was trying to make the cakes. Every couple minutes I would turn them and they were still looking pretty anemic. Finally decided they might be presentable and served them. Thought about it later and they had to be tougher than shoe leather. Mink ate them and never said a word of complaint. He was a good customer until he passed away—could be I hastened his going.

The ladies came by about 9:00 to see if everything was going okay and could they do anything to help. After a few days turned them loose and went at it on my own. Made a lot of mistakes, but had no fear. I could usually talk my way out of a big problem. The best thing I had going for me was I hired Mattie May to do the day cooking. Mattie had widowed with 3 young boys, husband killed in a coal mine slate fall. Her husband had been a hunter, trapper, fisherman and she could cook anything and make it good, plus she was conscientious and knew how to conserve. The two ladies before were good cooks and had developed the lunch business and Mattie was good enough to carry it on.

Mattie and I established our own menu. Monday—Soup beans and corn bread; Tuesday—Beef and noodles plus pork and dressing; Wednesday—Meat loaf; Thursday—Swiss steak; Friday—Fish. Monday's was always soup beans and corn bread, but the rest of them were not cast in concrete. Sometimes there would be liver and onions, heart and dressing, spaghetti and meatballs and occasionally chicken. There were hunters that would bring in different things. A trapper would occasionally bring in a young coon for a time and an older fellow brought in dressed domestic rabbits and in season, mushrooms. Occasionally on Saturday mornings it was a treat to have fried brains and evening was the time for mountain oyster sandwiches. Writing about all these makes me hungry. Mattie was a terrific cook. As we talk about food, along the way Jack and LaDonna married and I pulled out all the stops to get my feet under their table at meal time. LaDonna was and still is a great cook.

My hours for a few years were 5:30 in the morning and 11:00 at night. Hadn't been in business too long and I got a call from the Knoxville County Rationing Board. Had to go before the Board because I didn't have a menu or any of my prices listed in the establishment any place. They really had me scared. Thought I would end up in the slammer. I was just back from the War and didn't really know the rules. Had to have the prices listed so I wouldn't be able to gouge a new customer. About everything I used was rationed. This was a new business and didn't have a prior use list that purchases were based on. I had to more or less beg for everything I got. By calling me in, they were picking on a little guy when so many were running rough shod over the system. I decided right then if that's the way they wanted to play, I would learn how. It wasn't long before I was controlling my part of the area. Had an in to get quantities of coffee, sugar, meat and even had a supply of silk hose. With a little horse trading I could get anything I wanted or needed in the food line.

Equipment was needed in the kitchen and was really hard to come by. A cousin, Bill Hastings, back from the War, was running a restaurant in New Sharon. He had an extra commercial gas range which I made a deal for. Nutter from Central States Electric Company, our electric supplier at the time, had an electric refrigerator coming in his quota and he saved it for me. Those two items made the operation a lot easier. Woody (Virgil Woodard) had put together an old Crosley refrigerator for me. It sounded like a hyena when it started and a new person in the kitchen would do a little screaming and jumping for a few days.

The business was really pretty good, but had to figure how to make more money on the volume we were doing. There was a limit with 500 people in Bussey and what you could get from the surrounding communities. What really made the business was McConnvilles and their coal stripping operation. They had three open pits going. We also had Jim Richey based across the street in the old Beall Auto building. He had the contract for hauling all the coal from the 3 pits. Most of it was loaded on railroad cars by the overhead bridge north of town. Jim employed 65 people and most of them were in and out of the café at least once a day.

A little back tracking. It's real hard to think of thing 60 or 70 years past and every once in a while something pops in. Uncle Ike McConnell lived on the old McConnell Homestead which laid to the West. There was about 700 acres in all and we farmed together with horses and later on with mules. Leo Reed was Uncle Ike's hired hand and Tracey VerSteegh was ours. Tracey was my hero. Spent a lot of time following him around. I was always a baseball nut. Of course it was before T.V. and we just barely had radio. There would be baseball games on the radio and of course the newspaper—Des Moines Register and Tribune. We always took the afternoon Tribune. Tracey could list all the players on the roster for each team in the American & National leagues but of course, at the time, there was only 6 in each league. My favorite team was the St. Louis Cardinals—Dizzy Dean and Company. After we went to the World Series in 1938 it was the Chicago Cubs and still is. Think I have only had 2 winning seasons in all that time and one of those while I was in the Service.

Remember one time Tracey and Leo bought a coon hound and were going to make money selling hides. We had a good timber on the 80 North and it joined the Mehana 80 plus it joined into the Fitch farm. Of course Jack and I had to go along. Coon hunting is another experience. Somehow they had two hounds. Take the hounds out to the timber and turn them loose then wait for them to bay treed. First try I ran after the dogs and they had to put me on a leash.

Grandpa McConnell (Quince) was always a trader. Early on with horses and later with mostly sheep. Uncle Ike followed his Dad and become a full time trader. He would go to a sale every day but Sunday, mostly because there wasn't an organized sale on Sunday. He was a partner in the sale at Eddyville. There were 3 of them. Frank Reed was the auctioneer, Powell clerked the sale and Uncle Ike bought stock and brought it in. When I was about 12, Uncle Ike would have

Swede and I in the car about 5:00 on Thursday headed for Eddyville. We would help feed and water the stock plus slop the hogs. Our reward was to eat lunch (more like dinner) at Pyatts Café. They served all the sale people family style and I thought it was the best in the world. In the afternoon we helped run the stock into the ring. The sale was right downtown Eddyville next to the Des Moines River and the River Bridge. Pyatts was just a block up the street and another fringe benefit was Hattie VanLoon's ice creams shop just around the corner from the sale barn. A large cone was 5 cent plus Hattie had a good looking daughter I had my eyes on. Never did catch up with her and at the time was so shy she would have had to be the instigator.

Back to the McConnell Café. The candy and sundry items were mostly purchased from a small, on the road, peddler. He also had all kinds of punch boards. Ran into the same problem with him. He was saving most of his quota for his regular customers and being a new business, didn't really have an allotment. Wasn't long before I got that figured out with a little horse trading. Bought punch boards from the factory and cut out the middle man. There was so much profit from the boards really shouldn't have worried, but on the other hand that middle man didn't help me when I needed it. Punch boards were good—better than chocolate candy or pretty girls. They made so much money it had to be sinful which it was illegal.

Actually the boards came before the food. If a person sat at the counter I made sure a punch boards was in front of him. If a person sat in the front of a pile, arranged to spill them in his lap. If he didn't pick up a board and start punching, would get his order and move him out. I always had a lot of different boards—cigarette, always a fancy box chocolate board, cigarette lighter (Zippo) boards, money boards, pull tab, and usually had one with a radio or larger size. Had enough inventory that there was usually something new to look at. Cigarette board was a standard and sold out at least one of those a day.

Had a cigarette machine for a while, spin the reels with a handle and would pay what came up on the window—basically like a slot machine. Made me take that out because it was gambling. The boards were actually the same. Punch out a little paper and unfold it for so much money. This went gangbusters until 1950. In 1949 a lawyer was on the ticket of Attorney General to clean up the state. Much to my dismay, he was elected and took office in 1950. His story—afraid the Mafia was moving in to take over the gambling. The Mafia didn't have any part of my action unless you would call me the Mafia. Anyway, Sheriff Jim Van Hemert called me one Saturday and said the Attorney General was coming down the next week to check out the County. Put the punch boards away and I'll call you when you can put them back out. I'm still waiting for that call. So that was the end to the grand & glorious punch board era. It was really for the best because it was too easy and making a living should be harder than that.

There was always something going besides the food business. We were a Clothes Cleaning stop for Modern Cleaners of Knoxville. The cleaner was owned and operated by Ben Smith, a little younger than me and grew up in Bussey. We had a twice a week pickup and delivery. Also had a watch repair and would send them to Uncle Doc (O.R. Wilson) who had a shop in Winterset. He had also hooked me up with an overnight watch crystal service.

One morning the $50 a month guys were on the counter drinking coffee and solving the world's problems. After you were discharged from the Service you could get $50 a month from the Government for 6 months or until you got a job. A good percentage of them were sitting for 6 months. Merle Rouze had a '36 Chevy he wanted to sell for $240. Nobody came up with an offer. I got the check book out and wrote him a check for the $240. Now everybody wanted to buy the car. I absolutely didn't want to sell the car and gave them a dozen reasons. The price got up to $285 and I sold it. I made $45 without touching the car.

A drag line operator named Les roomed with Floy McClure and boarded with me had a very clean '30 Model A Convertible he needed to sell. I gave him a check for it and turned a $100 profit without even having it in my name. Another day Floyd Trinkle came in. He had Wayne Mick's '36 Olds and would sell it for $250. I gave him a check for $250 and went to the bank to sign over the transfer. He stopped in the store (Wayne at the time was running the grocery next to the bank) to tell Wayne he had just sold his car for $250 that he had just paid Wayne $125 for. The car's body was a little rough, but ran good and had 4 near new tires. I went down to Howard King's welding shop and gave him the story. You fix up the body a little and throw a coat of paint on it and we'll sell and split the profits. Within a month we had cleaned up the car and sold it to Tom Weldon (mechanic from Hamilton) for $750. Howard's bill was $150 plus my $250. We split $350 between us.

Uncle Ike was trading cars. He had a '39 Ford 4 door sedan and was getting a new '48. The dealer offered $500 on a trade. Jack Villont (was running the Sinclair station across the street) and I told him it ought to bring $900 and we would sell it for him. By this time everything, including cars, were a little easier to get and we got a little nervous. We about met our match. Finally we made a trade with Gerald Van Den Berg for an old Ford coal truck and 160 hens. We sold the truck to Tom Weldon for $700. We dressed the old hens (what a messy job) and put them in the freezer for the restaurant. Can't remember how we came out financially and how long the hens lasted (a lot of noodles). Probably don't want to remember, plus it was my last car deal.

We did quite a few special meals. If the McConnvilles had something they wanted to do for the community or for their help, we would take care of it. One time we fixed a turkey dinner for the Fire Department (Bussey) and their help, about 200 people. Served it at the Legion Hall. The turkeys were wild from Louisiana and the McConnvilles plus Jim Richey had got them on a hunt. They were New York dressed (the feathers removed and the rest intact). They had been frozen and an absolute mess to work with, but we got the job done and had a great party. Usually took care of Jim Richey at Christmas for his help. Did turkey or hams and sometime boxes of fancy chocolates for other occasions.

During the threshing season we had a number of crews that would come in for a noon dinner. There was usually between 5–8 and we served them family style. Don't remember the price, but we served them a good dinner. When they hit the door we had a glass of ice water for each plus a pitcher of water on the table. Next would come hot rolls and butter. Those two items helped cut the meat consumption which was the only expensive item on the table. Mashed potatoes and gravy was another that helped fill them up cheap.

In those days the secret organizations were going big—Odd Fellows, Rebekahs, Masons, Eastern Stars. The Rebekahs were having a big state meeting on a Monday. Allie Snyder was the ramrod and she convinced me there would be a world of people in town and would I help by serving them a nice dinner in the evening. The Methodist Church would be serving too and they would take what I couldn't handle. I bought Allie's pitch and set up for a full house. Brought in extra help and had all the food prepared. Even brought Nellie Thomas to help and as a consultant. Nellie was our $2^{nd}$ Mother from Chick's Place. About ¼ of the people showed up for the day's activities and, of course, we had no way of knowing that. Allie absolutely herded all the people down to the Methodist Church. We absolutely got not one soul from the Rebehahs. Even the regulars we would normally had stayed away to make room for the ladies. All evening the sum total of business we had was a drunk couple from the tavern. Maybe that's partly why I've always had it in for the Methodists.

Opened the Café at 6:00 and from day one had a pretty good following that stopped for something before they went to work. A bus that carried workers to the Big Six Coal Company Mine out on the Glen Rose property stopped to pick up Hjalmar Nylander at 6:30. Jum, as we called him, had always worked in the mines and migrated to Bussey from Buxton. Jum and Hazel were great people and think Jum was a second generation Swede. Jum, at the time, liked to play poker and drink. On this particular Monday he had gone from pay day Friday night to the card table and this lasted all weekend. I said—Jum, what did you have for breakfast? Tongue, nothing but tongue!! He was really a good guy and later quit drinking and card playing and finished out as a model citizen.

Digger Jones was a regular for breakfast and at the time worked for the McConnvilles. One evening I had made some mush and let it harden into a loaf to slice for fried mush and give the regulars a treat. Digger always had bacon, eggs, toast and coffee. I put a couple of nice slices of fried mush on his plate and served it to him. I always worked until 9:00 by myself and had just got back in the kitchen. What's this on my plate? (with volume) That's fried mush, try it you'll like it. I will not. Get it off my plate. I had to eat mush and soup beans growing up poor, but I don't have to eat it now.

Garrett Visser and Shorty McConnell were regulars and they would mostly eat anything I fixed. Shortly was a widower, my Dad's cousin, and mostly did my carpentry work. Garrett was a long time mail carrier. His wife Jean was a beauty operator and didn't get up early. Garrett had a dog, Julie, a cross between rabbit hound and something a little bigger and was with Garrett at all times. It was the only animal we ever allowed in the restaurant and everybody treated her like a regular customer. Garrett had a standing order for scraps. Would take them home for Julie and also fed most of the dogs in town. His saying—Might not have many people at my funeral, but will have a world of dogs.

Fred Van, another widower, lived by himself and took most of his meals with me. Fred was a guy that could do about anything. He finished up hanging paper and electrical. Fred had done the original wiring on the farm house when Iowa Power came to the country. Fred knew everybody in the world and had given me some good times on different occasions. He was a great dancer. Had a big paunch in front, but seemed to glide across the floor. In later years caught Fred one day. Do you still dance? Can't really move that good, but can get the lady out into the middle of the dance floor and hold her while she danced around me.

There was a time I caught Meadow Gold charging me 50 cents too much for ice cream cones. I'll show them. Bought a truck load, 25 cases, from Nabisco. Used about 3 cases a year. Did that make sense? No, but I showed Meadow Gold. Back to Fred Van—The load of cones came in and I would put them on top of the shelf that covered the south wall, still there from a grocery store before. Fred, I have a bottle of beer in the fridge if you'll help me put these cones up on the shelf. Fred helped put the cones up and we went for the bottle of beer—no beer. Somebody else had already got it. Fred hollered about that for a long time.

Scarlet (cousin Eleanor Doughman) was working at the Bank. I conned her into helping me on occasion and helping the rush at noon for her lunch. Kept telling her she was getting fat so she didn't eat much. I would promise to take her to a dance or an event which didn't always happen. One night she was working the kitchen when I didn't have anybody else. I had just gone back in the kitchen and very diplomatically told her not to put so much meat on the beef burgers. Five minutes later a fellow came in and I hollered back to the kitchen—Five beef burgers with everything to go. Scarlet fixed the beef burgers and out the guy went. Two minutes later he was back. A big, mean looking guy. What kind of a joint are you running here and he was mad. What's the matter? Scarlet had put everything but meat on the sandwiches. You told me not to put so much meat on. Sometimes I wondered, maybe I should get paid help.

Scarlet went to Minnesota with the Stones and some Knoxville people that had summer homes around a lake. She had been going with John Stone a little and had gone with the family for a week of fishing, etc. Right away people were asking—Where's Scarlet? I told everybody she went to Minnesota to get married. One day Uncle Ed came in. What you hear from Scarlet? She and John got married yesterday.

Swede, at the time, was working with Shorty as a carpenter. He would help me on Saturday nights. One night we had cold watermelon. Swede and I working the front and Dad was working the kitchen. The Raola Theatre was next door and I hollered out. The first person came in the door and I hollered (loud)—Slice of watermelon, then Swede hollered—Slice of watermelon. We had the joint full and everybody was eating watermelon just because we hollered. Dad was sitting them up in the pass thru window and had no idea what we were doing. Nothing could make more money or be simpler.

Over the years have hired a world of kids, etc. Mattie May could be considered a super hiree and Gloria Barnhill worked about 3 years while in high school and really a standout. Her Dad was a coal miner with a pretty fair sized family and they really didn't have much. Gloria ranked the best or close to all the young people that worked for me over the years. Her story is a Happy Horatio Alger. She married Harold Mick and they have done very well in Albia. Good family and good citizens. Harold and Gloria could buy me at least twice.

The Bussey restaurant never had a telephone. The telephone office was just down the street. Maxine Doad and Irma Neifert were the operators and if a call came in they would send somebody over to get me, plus they kept on hand all the numbers I might want to call. Did have a few girls on the string. Usually give the telephone girls a box of candy or fix them a dinner. I also think they enjoyed knowing what was going on in my fun life.

It seems like the Bread Man was always a good buddy and still pretty much true today. Eddie Bremhorst was my very first bread man from Lowenberg Bakery, Mary Jane Bread, out of Ottumwa. Remember when he first started. I had a few helps as a new business man and always checked the things coming in. We had a little bread rack up front and once in awhile sold a loaf of bread. Our total would be ½ dozen loaves and a dozen packages of buns. Ed let this go on for a week then—Gib, if I'm going to cheat somebody it will be with a big customer, with you it isn't worthwhile. I never checked him again.

Remember Grandpa Doughman saying for years if you couldn't bake it at home, you didn't have bread. Then Woody came in with the Bakery and you could get a loaf wrapped in a newspaper or naked. Now every business in town is selling bread but us and we're thinking of putting it in. Ed was kind of tall, gangly Dutchman and looked like there was no coordination in his body but he fooled you. Every move counted and he would line up the bread faster and better than you could see. Every day at 11:00 Mattie would set his dinner on the counter just about the time he sat down. It was her choice whatever she was cooking and I would usually eat alongside him. For quite a while the Wonder Bread man would eat with us. He would plop down and say the blessing—Good bread, good meat, good God, let's eat. One day our Methodist Minister happened to be sitting beside him—guess that was better than nothing.

Ed and wife Mary had 3 daughters and were very devout Catholics. In a couple years he moved on to Chariton as branch manager and then to Burlington. Some of the escapades with Eddie and Fred Van could be a book of its own. The commercial gas range bought from Bill Hastings was from a restaurant he had in Ottumwa. One day after lunch Fred Van and I headed to Ottumwa in a pickup borrowed to get the stove. Of course we had to stop in Eddyville on the way and a few other stops. Wherever we stopped Fred knew somebody and that usually led to complications. We got the stove loaded and headed towards home. Of course we had to stop and see Ed and Mary. We bounced into Ed's yard with the old pickup and the stove hanging out on all sides. We looked like a couple of vagabonds, but never heard about a repercussion from Ed's neighbors.

Did a few dances at the old coliseum on south side Ottumwa. It's still standing and the paper says maybe they will build a big new one. In a few years one of Ed and Mary's girls had married and moved to Phoenix. She was having trouble with her marriage so Ed and Mary (Ed was at retirement age) sold out and moved to Arizona. The other two girls soon followed. When Ed got down there and got the daughter straightened out, he got a license to sell real estate. Ed had always lived and never put anything away. Real estate at the time was very good and it was his niche. He made big money and it couldn't have happened to a better guy. In Phoenix, the girls put together a celebration for Mary and Ed's 50$^{th}$ wedding anniversary. I flew down to Phoenix for the party. While Ed and Mary were in Burlington and the girls were growing up, Mary and the girls spent a couple or three summers leasing and operating the A & W franchise from Wisconsin. Dorene and I had gone over to Burlington trying to interest Ed in being a partner in the wholesale business I had going. Ed explained to us after taking us out to the A & W how easy the root beer business was and how much money it made. That's how we first got interested in the A & W business.

# 8

## McConnell Winding Down

It was the Fall of 1948 and everything in and around Bussey was at the very best. The McConnvilles and their coal company were at the top of their game. The punch boards were going like gangbusters. A lot of things, including cars, were starting to come back on the market. At the time, Paul Bremhorst, Ed's brother, was traveling the country selling parts for Lamberson Ford out of Oskaloosa. Paul had lunch with us every Wednesday. On one of his lunch visits he said—Gib, what you need is the car in Lamberson's show window. Had dealt in quite a few cars, but never really had one to drive, still used Dad's. The car in the show window was a yellow '49 Ford convertible with the top down wrapped in cellophane with a big bow. The next afternoon after lunch, went to Oskaloosa and wrote Lamberson's a check for $2,500 and drove that convertible out of the showroom. That was the most exciting thing to hit Bussey since the bank robbery in the '30's. I was certainly the talk of the town plus all the girls were smiling. The girls would take one look at the new yellow convertible and say—I like that guy! The convertible didn't help the girl longevity, it was still 2 dates and out.

    I did go with a really great girl from Lovilia, Frances Sofranko before the war. Went with her quite awhile. Had a great girl after the war—Betty Klett from Rubio. Really had some great girls. Was it luck or good management that I ended up with the best of the lot.

    I made all the parades in the area—leading, carrying the marshal or queen. For the Attica Centennial I hauled the queen and her 6 attendants. The Bussey 4th was coming up and I was supposed to be in it. Grandma Doughman wanted to ride as a bathing beauty with 3 of her cronies as attendants. As I think of it today, that would've been the funniest entry but at that time I was into young good looking girls. Actually hauled Judy Duffy in a bathing suit. Grandma Doughman wouldn't speak to me for 6 months. My mother was in the parade as a professional wrestler. They had decorated a hay rack and Mom was squaring off with Laura Metz and they both had on long johns. The yellow convertible was great but there wasn't that many around and everybody kept track of me pretty well. In fact, I got blamed for quite a few escapades that I really wasn't involved in.

Had a real good 4 year run in the Bussey Café. In early '50's when they took punch boards away the profit, glamour and glitz went along with them and the Coal Company was slowing down too. I started feeling around for something to pick up the slack. A fellow, Sheriff Dwight Mateer's son-in-law from Oskaloosa, had just bought the Knoxville Beverage Co. The Mateers had started an independent bottling works in Oskaloosa. The fellow wanted to sell the Knoxville unit. It didn't take a rocket scientist to figure out the ingredient cost of a bottle of pop. The cost involved in bottles, help, and marketing was easy to figure out. My problem then and still is—jump in before you figure out how deep the water is. The bottom line depended on volume and marketing. I jumped in and bought this business before I figured out everything involved. In order to get space on a store shelf you had to have a real mover. At the time, Cola was the hot mover and I think it still is today. I jobbed Pepsi Cola from Arnold Muhl, Mahaska Bottling in Oskaloosa. The problem was Pepsi was the big mover and short on the profit end. I had a couple of good brands that I bottled myself—Masons Root Beer, O-so Grape and Orange. I bottled all the flavors and they were all good and very profitable, but it didn't add up if they didn't sell and they didn't. It took about as long to figure out this wasn't going to work as it did to buy it. The question came up real quick—how to get out.

Had a couple good fellows working for me, Bill Husted and Jim Speed. Jim was short and a little stockier than me, he had a little speech impediment and talked all the time. He knew and got along with everybody. I followed him around and soon knew everybody too. Bill would come to work clean and finish a hard day's work still clean. It took me about 5 minutes to get dirty. Bill moved on to another job and Jim Mitchell hired on. He was all personality like Jim Speed and also a good worker. I figured out a deal where these two guys could buy the plant, make wages, plus pay me off. It worked and they ran it about 3 years and sold to Arnold Muhl and also worked for him awhile.

In the meantime, a young fellow from Oskaloosa, Louie Pringle, had started a wholesale candy, tobacco, sundry business. It was an off the truck peddling business as you went. Louie was jobbing all his stuff from an outfit in Oskaloosa. Louie was trying to sell me on the idea to finance the thing and start a wholesale business of our own. Again, my eyes started lighting up and I jumped. The problem was the same as the beverage business—we had to sub job everything. If you could buy direct it could work. Of course, the dummy that I was hadn't learned yet. I established the business, McConnell Wholesale, along with the beverage company and after selling the beverage company moved around the corner into a building of its own. I bought a used International peddle wagon and started to establish a 5 day route in Marion County. Louie worked Oskaloosa and Mahaska County. Knoxville was working on their centennial celebration at the time and the order of the day was facial hair. I grew a handlebar mustache and a goatee along with a crew cut and I was really a funny looking guy. Was opening up new territory for the wholesale business and those new customers remembered me—maybe it helped.

    This thing was growing and getting along pretty good. Louie caught me on the road in Pleasantville one day. Louie had bad news. His wife had caught him with her sister. In order to keep his wife, they would move to Colorado and start over. Of course Louie didn't have anything invested so all he had to do was pick up and move. I was left with all the loose ends. Five days of routes and then on Saturday go to Newton to pick up the weeks supply from Newton Wholesale. We had a few candy bars plus a few odds and ends that we bought direct. Had picked up a line of gloves from Lambert Manufacturing out of Kirksville, Mo. I remember one day their salesman caught me at the warehouse. He took a look around. I bet you have learned one thing by now, Gib. It's easier to buy if you have credit than it is to sell. He was so right. The tobacco was the big item and real hard to get on direct. Louie's leaving put off half the volume so I got an idea. That was when Dorene and I went to Burlington to get Ed interested in the jobbing business. When Ed and Mary started telling about the A & W, another glimmer came into my eyes.

# 9

## *The Biggest Happening In My Life*

Went around to Willis Jones Barbershop one afternoon for a haircut. At the time, Willis was working by himself and Tom Wignall was in the chair. Gibson, I know a girl for you. Tom always called me Gibson. I was in my late 20's and everybody was trying to get me married off. She runs the store at Pershing and is the Postmaster. Hard worker, goes a mile a minute, good looking and I know she has $5,000 saved up. That 5 got my attention right away and I started figuring how to get acquainted with this girl. That same week the Meadow Gold ice cream man's truck broke down at the Pershing store. I was furnishing ice cream for the school hot lunch program and they started serving at 11:00. Dorene had the Meadow Gold man throw the ice cream in her car and she ran the ice cream down to me and saved the day. Right away, I started talking to this money girl from Pershing out of both sides of my mouth. She wanted nothing to do with me.

    I had bought the grocery store from Wayne Mick a while before and put Swede in to run it. Took Dorene to the store for a show and tell and she was more interested in Swede than the store. Swede wasn't really interested because he had a steady girl. I tried for a date, but that wasn't on her itinerary. Finally I got Scarlet and husband John Stone to go along. Tickets to the KRNT Radio for a show with Jack Benny and Phil Harris in Des Moines. She agreed to this.

    I went over to Pershing in my yellow convertible, my very best attire and bow tie. I went to the back of the store and knocked on the door. Dorene's mother came to the door and took one look at me and sicked the dog on me. She wasn't about to let her last daughter and best of the flock go out with a funny looking little foreigner. Dorene's dad and mother came over from Italy in the early 1900's. I took one look at the dog. It was a shepherd and looked like a lion but bigger. Took off around the corner—one bite, two at the most, and I was gone. I was in a strange town with a top down convertible. It so happened the poor old dog got around the corner and gave out and I was saved. Dorene talked her mother into letting her go with me. I also had a dozen roses. The florist had made it 13 and that created another problem. Mom was superstitious. Anyway, with John & Scarlet, we all made an impression on Dorene, maybe small, but she did have a good time and evidently decided I wasn't all bad.

It wasn't automatic but I eventually got on the good side of Mom. I'm sure she was a great lady in her day, but at this stage had a few problems. I usually didn't have any trouble talking a girl into a date. This one was different. She didn't buy my style. Maybe that was the reason it worked. She kept me on my toes trying to convince her. Never really figured out how I corralled her but happy I did. She did like the gang we ran around with and the restaurant, plus the ability to make money. I pretty much convinced her I would be a millionaire by 35. She should have kicked me out with the beverage and wholesale tobacco, sundry fiasco. They say you learn. It really was a little fun and didn't bury us. Back to courtship—this girl I kept a firm hold on with a whirlwind relationship. Could have been still thinking about the $5,000. It started in early 1950 and by Christmas we had set a wedding date for January 28, 1951. At the time, Dorene had two brothers and two sisters in Chicago and I had two uncles and aunts there so we decided to visit Chicago for a couple of days. On an afternoon when everybody was at work asked Dorene if she would like to go bowling. Never been bowling. I'll show you how. She beat me 3 times and we haven't been bowling since.

To back track a little, you never really know when something is going to pop into your head. Another girl I was going with before the war, Frances Sofranko of Lovilia, was really a nice girl and we thought of getting serious before I went to the service and I got to thinking that really didn't make any sense. She would be sitting home and I would be all over the world and decided to break ties. Little did I know the overseas duty would be spent in Sioux City. In the Bussey Café days I somehow got hooked up with this girl working in Des Moines. Her name was Betty Klett and she came from Rubio, a town or settlement of about 8 houses with a general store about 5 miles south of Keota. In order to go with her I had to round up a date for Jan. I enlisted Carol Visser and of course it took and it wasn't long before they got married and settled in Pella. About 6 years later Vis passed away. Later Jan remarried an old boyfriend and now lives in Humboldt.

Dorene and I went to see Father Albers in Knoxville about the wedding. He wasn't really enthused about turning over one of his favorite young parishioners to the likes of me. Father Albers knew me pretty well. He came in on occasion with the McConnvilles or Jim Richey. Dorene had helped Father Albers in his mission church at Pershing. He agreed to an afternoon service if I would take instructions. Sounded good to me. It was one evening a week for about 6 weeks. There were about 6 couples in the class and I was getting along just barely. Wasn't too enthused about the class, but on the other hand I didn't want to lose this girl. One night after class, the rest had already left, Father Albers looked at me—Gib what do you think the most of, God or the almighty dollar? Don't you answer that!!! At this time Father Albers and Gen are in retirement at West Point (southeastern Iowa). He is in his early 90's and until this last year has been real good. Until this day he is still amazed this union worked and did well. Think it helps his faith in mankind.

In '51 I was 29 and Dorene was 24. Had watched a lot of my buddies get married and of course there were many tricks played on different ones along the way. Knew there had to be a little payback. On the wedding day it was about 20 below. We had figured they would fix up our car, so we drove the convertible and parked it in front of the rectory. Dorene had her car, '50 Chevy sedan, hid in John Sims' garage north of Pershing. We also had it arranged after the reception that Gerald Smith would take us out to Johnsies in his car. As we thought, the gang had got to the convertible and engine parts were laying all over the ground. Dad and Mom had to drive it home and the gang was out there in the cold trying to put it back together. We were safely on our way to Missouri.

We took a few days at the Kirkwood Lodge near Osage Beach on the Lake of the Ozarks. Swede and I had vacationed there a couple years before and it was really a fun place. Swede and I had got acquainted with a group from Mississippi, typical Southerners. We had a big weekend and it was a Monday morning. The weekenders had checked out and now we were getting a new bunch checking in. The Mississippi people were sitting on the beach relaxing and Swede and I were running up and down the beach. Finally this Southern girl said—Swede and Gib, why don't you all sit down. You're just wearing us out running up and down the beach.

Dorene and I got back to Bussey to the little house next to the folks that I had moved in from the country and fixed up. The furniture and everything was in place and already to go. The first thing I did was go into the bathroom for a shower. The water was cold and finally figured out somebody had turned off the water heater. In the sheets they had put cracker meal and of course the clothes in the closet had a good going over—sewed up sleeves, things in the pockets, etc.

Dorene was still going to Pershing to run the store and look after her mom. Sunday was our day at home. The restaurant was closed on Sunday. Dorene went to early church in Lovilia and then she would fix our first breakfast at home. Right away she said—I make lousy coffee and really haven't made it much and really haven't done much cooking. She's a fast learner because she turned out to be one of the best cooks in the world. I took one drink of the coffee and couldn't imagine how it could be so bad but I wasn't about to say anything to this sweet little girl that was trying so hard. I drank the cup. Would you like another cup of coffee? No, only drink one cup. Was thinking might have to quit altogether. On inspection we found the gang had put chili powder in the coffee can. A couple of weeks later we decided to have a party for the gang, our feast as newlyweds. Dorene put the whole thing together and baked a nice big cake. On tasting the cake and frosting discovered the gang had put salt in the sugar can. We decided they deserved this and we served it at the party.

The next summer we took our honeymoon at the Dells in Wisconsin. We pulled into the area and looked around. The car in front stopped and of course I couldn't get stopped quick enough and hit him. It was an old Nash with a trailer hitch a foot past the bumper and this went through our radiator. This was a small village and the garage had to get a radiator out of the city. We were 3 days here without a car. It wasn't all that bad. We had everything we needed on foot—a lodge, store, church and the water.

Dorene was able to transfer the Post Office to another party before we married, but the store still had to be run and Mom had to be looked after. By fall she sold the store to Cooney Provenzano. She helped him get a loan for $2,000 from Eldon Job. Then she moved Mom to live with us in Bussey. My folks lived next door and my mother looked in on Nooney from time to time.

The going line has been—married January 28, 1951 and Pat was born March 4. Drives Dorene up a tree and then I explain Pat was born in 1952. My mother and Dorene's mother looked after Pat and when he got to walking, he was most of the time at the restaurant. Dorene was working the restaurant and I decided to buy the bottling works. Then came the wholesale business. This all came about in roughly 4 years. We were both working but if there is profit it's more fun. The last year paid income tax on a $3,800 net. That was with restaurant, grocery, wholesale and bottling works. That was when we figured out it was time to make a change.

Was familiar with the A & W's in Knoxville and Chariton. Called on them and sold them condiments and knew basically how a #10 can of ketchup related to sandwiches. I could see the profit plus how much easier and simpler it was compared to a restaurant. In the meantime the Maid-Rite in Indianola was for sale and the price was $2,700. We checked it out and they had a buyer from

Chariton, Byron Adcock. The sale was to be made the following Sunday. If Byron didn't take it we were next in line. This was known to be one of the hottest locations in the state. Byron took it on Sunday and we decided to go ahead and establish an A & W in Indianola.

We purchased the franchise in December of '55 and made plans to attend the National A & W Convention to be held in January at Peoria, Illinois. Dorene and I were in Peoria and we laid out our game plan. We would split up and try to hook up with the best operators and milk them. Don't remember who Dorene joined, but she did pretty good. The biggest operator at that time was Bill Rudy of La Crosse, Wisconsin and one of the biggest in Iowa was Elmer Rommel of Dubuque. The two were together and I joined them. It wasn't long before we were in the lounge. They were both good talkers and better drinkers and I couldn't do either that great and it ended up for me a partial lost cause of a muddled head. In spite of my muddle, the two of us did get quite a lot of information.

Plus the equipment people were there—Sargent Mfg. of La Crosse. We got an idea of what we needed then made a trip in February to La Crosse and ordered our equipment package. The total package was $1,200 and we were to pay $100, and the rest after we got open. The next week Dorene caught me on the wholesale route. I had written the check to Sargent for $1,200 and it came into the Bussey Bank with no money to cover it. What happened??? Had no muddle in La Crosse. I signed a note with Uncle Ed and things were then Kosher. I phased out the wholesale in March and we moved to Indianola first of April. We still had the restaurant and Verla Spaur would run it and we would come back to Bussey in the fall.

After Dorene had sold the store and moved Mom to Bussey, we decided there was no need for two cars so we decided to sell the cloth top. With the family coming along we didn't really need a convertible. Harold Mick was in the service, Korean Conflict. He and Gloria were married and he was stationed on the East coast. They bought the car and it made many trips between Bussey and the East coast. Was talking to him just this last year and he said if he could find a convertible like that one he would buy it and keep it around for old time sake. He said that was the best time of he and Gloria's life. It also has a ton of memories for me.

We had bought a double lot with a big old 2 ½ story house. The lot was 150 x 150 and a corner lot. The house took up 50' inside and I took the corner side of 100' for the A & W and lot. Shorty (McConnell) and Harlon Plum came up from Bussey to build the little plywood A & W—real simple. We ran a slab and put up a 2 0x 30 building. Leonard Utsler took care of the plumbing and electrical. When they finished I went uptown and asked Leonard for a bill. He knew I didn't have the money and gave some excuse of not having the bill figured up. This went on all summer. In the fall after we closed I went in and he let me pay the $1,200 bill. Leonard was one great guy. Years later we got partly even with him. He passed away and we furnished the food for relatives and guests.

The east side of the house was the west side of the lot plus a wood fence south to the alley. I had a big menu board made up and a sign painter had it all fixed up. One day Dorene was gone and I fastened it to the side of the house. She wasn't about to let that happen, but it was already up and she very reluctantly went along with it. Had painted on the sign—"T.V. Jumbo Box Popcorn—69 cents" with a big bag of popcorn painted along side.

Back in Bussey the theatre was next door to the restaurant and when it closed I bought the building and contents. Didn't really know what to do with it but bought it real cheap. A lot of salvage lumber and think Jack sold off the seats. I got it cleaned out and half of the building was made into a room for young people and cut a door through from the restaurant. Really didn't work too good. More trouble than it was worth. There was a big popcorn machine and I carried it to Indianola and put it out the south side window of the root beer. I had visions of selling a ton of popcorn. To me it was a natural and T.V. was the biggest source of entertainment at this time. The popcorn just plain didn't go. Sold zero bags of T.V. popcorn in all the years the sign was up. Even tried giving them a little tray of popcorn with their root beer and that didn't create any sales. St. Marys wanted to borrow it (machine) one winter (3$^{rd}$ year of trying to sell popcorn) and when spring came I let them keep it.

The first year we opened the A & W Drive-In on May 15 and closed in September after it started getting cold. We just had screens at that time and no heat. We had a full lot from the time we opened until we closed. Our total gross was under $20,000. That was in '56 with nickel root beer and 10 cent hot dogs, but we had to do better than that. We figured out pretty quick that we weren't turning them fast enough. So all winter we worked on speed plus quality and service. We also made a trip to Cedar Rapids and checked out Wally Luedtke. He ran, at the time, an A & W on 1$^{st}$ Ave. N.E. just a couple blocks from Marion and that year did $25,000 (a McDonalds is on that lot today). His biggest draw, besides root beer, was a big breaded tenderloin.

We also went to the national convention in San Antonio with Ed & Mary Bremhorst. Can't remember we learned much, but we had a lot of fun. Phil Price was the franchisee and had a couple A & W's plus he was also the distributor for Lone Star Beer. Our hotel, can't remember the name, was in the heart of the city. Our party the first night was at LaValita, a city park right in the center of town.

*The Biggest Happening In My Life*   53

We grabbed a cab and the cabbie questioned our destination. Yes, we wanted a ride to LaValita. He took us 1 ½ blocks to the park. Phil Price did a heckuva job with the party. Food, entertainment and a beer tap wherever you looked. In the nub of the evening we had been invited President Fran Loetterle to our room for an extended party after LaValita. We just got to the hotel room and a call came. President Loetterle called to let us know he had a full room and wouldn't be able to make our party. We had no party and about all we could handle was to get into bed.

The first year was a real learning experience. We had both been back behind the counter but this was a little different. We were trying to teach a brand new crew to do something that we were just learning and operating just barely. But we were both young and that does make a difference. High school kids are pretty much the same, ready and willing—just turn us loose.

We hired one older lady that came and applied for the kitchen. She had widowed, mid 30's with 5 little kids. Her husband had been killed in a coal mine at Summerset. She raised those kids with no help from anybody. No government help back then. She was about 60 when she came to work for us, lived in an apartment on the square and had married an old age pensioner a few years before. Florence Derrickson was her name and every day she came in happy with a cheery hello. Everything was just dandy with her and you knew she had more problems than anybody. She never complained and never missed a day of work. Her son, Bob Aubert, had cancer and the day he died she left work when the family came. The next morning she came in. We told her she absolutely did not need to work. She said it was better than being home. I've always said, and most are the same, sure don't want to see any of kids, grandkids go before me. We always considered Florence part of the family and she would fight anybody that said a bad word about me.

Florence didn't work for me. It was mostly for Dorene in the kitchen. I was a really lousy guy to work for. Always went full speed with 100% concentration and expected the help to do the same. No way the help is going to go full speed and the concentration is far from 100%. Larry said to me just the other day—no way you could work people like that today and he is right.

We had been in Indianola just a little while and the primary election was coming up. I told Florence we would go back to Bussey for voting but if we were voting here, where would we vote? You're Democrat. They don't allow Democrats to vote in the Primary, but we can vote in the General. You mean there are no Democrats in the city? Oh yes, there's me and the Godwins, and that's all she could really come up with. Florence stayed with us until she had a stroke about

1970. We tried to slow her down but we wasn't about to tell her she shouldn't be working. That was strictly her decision.

We opened in '56 with a limited menu and limited equipment. The menu: Hotdogs—10 cents, chilidogs—15 cents, beefburgers—15 cents, French fries—15 cents, orange and root beer 5 & 10 cents, plus a freezer with Meadow Gold hard vanilla ice cream that we hand dipped for floats, 15 & 25 cents. For equipment we had the 4 hole sink to wash mugs, mug chiller in water bath, Sargent root beer dispenser, freezer for the ice cream and we also had the orange in the freezer. The kitchen had a walk-in cooler and a fryer, two crock pots for hot dogs and beefburgers. That winter we went to Chicago and bought some equipment—a steam table, grill and another fryer. Anita and Annie had taken a fling in the drive-in business in Indiana, just across the line from Chicago, and it didn't work for them and they closed. We picked up their equipment—mainly ice cream equipment. They had a large batch ice cream freezer, malt mixers and related items plus a jet spray for orange and lemonade. So in '57 the menu expanded adding hamburgers, lemonade and cones. The batch ice cream machine had a gate to dispense the product in quantity, like 3 gallon caddies and almost impossible to make a cone. We did it anyway and had some funny looking cones and mostly too big. It did develop our soft serve business.

We were buying our hamburger patties and bulk hamburger plus shortening from Surber at the locker. Found out at the end of the season he was giving the Maid-Rite a better deal plus he was adding onto the shortening price. Of course the Maid-Rite was using a ton of product but I wasn't going to put up with it anyway. I had bought everything from Rath Pack the last 5 years at Bussey, but Surber had them tied up and wouldn't let them call on us. That was about the time we sold the store in Bussey and Swede had settled in Carlisle. Phil was teaching school and Swede was working with Rath in their little plant in Des Moines and of course we knew a few people with Rath anyway. So we managed to buy a used grinder and patty machine (from Joe) and put them on the back porch and were ready for business.

We had sold the Bussey Café to Verla and Toddy Spaur the spring of '57 and taken up permanent residency in Indianola. My Dad wanted something to do so he would come up 4 days a week and take care of our meat and then go back home. Shorty had stayed the first 2 years and did the odd jobs, and then decided he would go south a couple years to the Rose's in Norfork, Arkansas. Dad would grind the hamburger and make the patties. We would also buy strip tenderloins from Rath. He would clean them up and spat out tenderloins and we would bread them. This was an honest to goodness tenderloin. The people didn't really appreciate it. They were used to eating sandwiches made from shoulder and even fabricated patties. Dad stayed with us about 4 years until he wasn't able to do it. I never paid Dad anything for all his work but did buy him a 1960 Ford in the fall of '59. He was real proud of the car but he did drive too fast, but never had any problems.

The good hamburgers, tenderloins and coleslaw (by the second year), along with soft serve made us a pretty viable drive-in. Mr. & Mrs. Beymer lived just west of our big house and finished out our ¼ block. Lee and Lydia owned Beymer's Jewelry on the square and were Gerald's folks. Lee came to the back door one night and ordered two tenderloin baskets. We don't have baskets. You have sandwiches, coleslaw and French fries so just put them in a food tray. So simple but we had never thought of it. That was one of the biggest things we ever did and we always gave that nice old jeweler the credit. They were really nice people and after we bought across the street and tore down the big house they would sit out in the yard and watch the action.

George McVey had worked for Wonder Bread and about '57 he bought the A & W in Chariton from a couple that had come down from Wisconsin. George was a real good fellow but every once in awhile he would get his nose wet for an extended period. We visited back and forth plus traded a few ideas. We got our world famous coleslaw dressing from him.

The lot was rock the first year and in '57 we put down blacktop and marked off parking spaces with numbers. In the winter of '58 we dug a hole at the south end of the drive-in building for a storage basement and a chute to run the supplies down. A slab was on the top and that was our picnic area with a couple picnic tables. The little garage at the south end of our house lot also served as storage and the kids with their wagon would haul supplies to the root beer every morning. It was the winter of '58 when Bernie Grady came by to give us a demonstration of a chicken broaster from McCormack Distribution in Le Mars. Bernie was a great fellow and of course Dorene fixed dinner along with the broasted chicken. It was getting late and we talked Bernie into staying all night. He could sleep with Larry, about 2 at the time, and Larry wet the bed. Bernie has told that story 100 times and of course we bought a couple of broasters. At that time nobody had chicken and it was before K.F.C. We ran a couple specials and really did develop the chicken business.

# 10

# *The Catholics Come To Indianola*

Moved into Indianola spring of '56. A Catholic Irish Democrat and didn't have none of them here. Didn't really give out too much information on our background. It was a town of less than 5,000 with Simpson College partially funded by the Methodists. A large Methodist Church which had the largest church denomination with a membership of over 1,200 families. The politics was 90% Republican. We worked Saturday night and opened at 10:00 on Sunday so it was to early church. At different times we got to all of the neighboring Catholic churches, but Churchville's time in the summer was best. We were really almost orphans. We went to St. Marys Irish Settlement, Milo, Rosemount, Christ the King and even got to Bauer a couple times.

Father Hillary Gaul came early in '57 and started church and we met in the Legion Hall, a Quonset hut building, North 1st back of the Hy-Vee. He made it his mission to build a new church. The diocese loaned us $100,000 interest free. We bought the 9 acres from Mahlstadt, who was developing the area at the time and also happened to be Catholic. We dedicated the church in February of '58. Father Gaul had the contractor put up the building and he did most of the finish work. Gaul's people were woodworkers. His Dad and brother built the cupboards in the sacristy and all the work on the altar. His cousin, Margee Goode, and husband were living with him at the time. Margee's husband was working the territory with a magazine company. Margee did most of the painting. We closed the A & W in September and I helped at the church. Dorene would fix lunch for us every day for Father, Margee and me and Father's black Labrador. Remember it took Father and I a solid week to lay the floor tile in the basement. Margee also had a cousin's husband that did a lot of work. Don't know whether any of us people got paid. In any event, it wasn't much.

## The Catholics Come To Indianola

As the town grew the Catholics came. We even filled the courthouse with Democrats in 1960. At this writing, April 2000, we have 450 families on the rolls. In the mid 60's, Father Gaul moved on to West Des Moines to build a church at 15$^{th}$ and Grand. Father Burns came to take his place and mostly his mission was to get our note paid off. Father Gaul had told me once the hardest thing about being a priest was asking for money. Father Burns had a way of getting money and it worked.

When he first came I was afraid of him. We went to early Mass and I had been the Lector forever. Before the start he would motion to me from the sacristy. I just knew if I made a mistake in the reading I would go straight to the bad place. He got to be our best friend and ate most of his meals with us. Among other trips, he went to a couple National Conventions with us.

We had a convention in Disney World in '72, the year it opened. I was on the National Board at that time and Father Burns entertained the kids and Dorene while I was in meetings. He brought along his Mass kit and arranged a room for Saturday night Mass to hold 67. We got the word out and had no idea there were many Catholics—200 showed up for Mass. Even our President at the time and his family were Catholics. We were staying at the Contemporary in the complex. The next day was a Holy Day and I inquired at the hotel desk where the nearest Catholic Church would be. In the first place, they didn't much know what a Catholic was and second they didn't know of a church. Finally they located a church in Kissimmee. It was a mission church with nobody around to get information from so I missed that Holy Day Church. It was really quite an experience being at Disney.

We were there for the convention January of '72 and it had opened the summer of '71. Remember I got a haircut one day on Main Street U.S.A. When Father Burns came to Indianola it was in his head that people went to conventions to drink and chase women—usually other people's wives. Grant you that sometimes might happen, but I never considered it the norm. For years when the kids were growing up we used the national conventions as our vacation and always took the kids. The first night of the conventions we met at 7:00. I was busy during the day with meetings and entertaining the families. I offered to buy Father Burns a drink and he wasn't too sure it was Kosher, but he had one. We fooled around some and then went to bed. In the mornings we would meet at 7:00 for breakfast and I would head for the meetings, etc. Father Burns would head out with the kids and Dorene for a good time. In attendance this was the biggest convention we ever had. Normally there would be between 600 and

1,000 at our last night banquet. This one there was close to 2,000. Their largest banquet room would hold 1,000 so we had two of them filled.

The next year we went to Dallas, Texas and took Father along. Now he was a man of the world and he had hobnobbed with most of the wheels—board members, President, etc. Saturday night finished up the convention and before the banquet it was customary to have a cocktail. Father Burns spied our N.A.C. President and his party. He said, how about buying you a drink. It so happened our President, Jim & Adeline Gibbs, A&W Grand Forks, North Dakota, were strict dries plus the party with was his hometown Methodist preacher. It was a little embarrassing, but we passed it off okay.

The next day was Sunday and we were headed for home. One of the suppliers had agreed to get tickets that day for a Cowboys football game. He couldn't get more than two so we let Father have the one and he would take in the game and come home the next day. We hadn't been to church yet and checked the hotel church schedules—Mass at 9:00 and 11:00. The main airport at that time was Love Field which was pretty much downtown. The 9:00 Mass would give us time to catch our flight at 12:00. The church was only a block away and we walked there. Lo-n-behold the Mass schedules had changed with Mass at 8:00 and 10:00. 10:00 would be too late for our 12:00 flight. There were about 50 people there in the same position we were in. Father Burns said he would check with the Parish Priest and get permission then run over to the hotel and get his Mass kit and we could get the Mass in. There were a couple of fellows from Houston standing next to us—looked like oil barons. We're from Iowa and we carry along our own Priest. They were impressed. At the Mass at Disney the people wanted to take up a collection. Father would not have it. The McConnells are sponsoring me and I'm taken care of very well. This time the people wouldn't buy that story and he ended up with over $100.00.

That was a great thing for Father Burns. In the first place he had never traveled very much and never seen an NFL game. Plus, the Cowboys were riding high at that time. Father Burns was our best buddy. We did a lot of things together and he wasn't the average preacher-type guy. The average is always on the take. It was pretty hard to get ahead of him—always trying to pay back. I have always been a real chocoholic. At the time, and I think it is still there, Mrs. Drew made (Dexter) chocolates (good, fancy chocolates) down the Interstate West in her basement. If he had been out that way there would be a box of Drew's chocolates in the front seat of my car.

Father Burns passed away in 1996 with cancer. He was about 3 years older than me. The night before the funeral Mass they had a visitation with the body in the church. They had a little service plus a form of a roast by about a dozen of his good buddies. We enjoyed doing it and it kinda relaxed the family.

# 11

## *The Kids*

The kids had a good mom, but deserved a better dad. Family was the most important part of my life but it seemed I left most of the raising to Dorene. Of course, the first gets the most attention. Dorene was so positive and independent. Even today with her problems she works at finding ways to be more independent. During the first pregnancy, she had gone to Dr. Ralston in Knoxville on her own and I hadn't even met Dr. Ralston. She had gone to Knoxville in the afternoon and he had said tonight it is. I was starting to get excited and then when she said it's time to go—I lost it. It was snowing and blowing. The roads were starting to close. I called Swede and Jack. We started out with two cars. Over the hill and down to Tracey and hit 92. Figured the snow plows should be out to help us. Had called the doctor and he was to meet us at the Mahaska Hospital. We go about three miles out of Oskaloosa coming up this grade and the road was blocked. The car ahead of us attempted it and landed in the ditch partially blocking the one lane. I went running up to the car reading the riot act to this fellow blocking the road and us with a young mother about to give birth. Just who do you think I am? I happen to be your doctor! We put Swede in the driver's seat of our car to get it through the drift. He was the best driver and he made it through the drift. Put the Doc in the car with me and Dorene and on into the hospital we went.

It wasn't too long after we got in the hospital and Pat was born. Left Swede and Jack to get the two cars out. The snow plow was there by that time and helped them. They brought Dr. Ralston's car to the hospital. Poor Jack had always wanted a boy and of course had two girls. Along I came with a boy. Of course I was proud as a peacock. Can't remember all the details, but was uptown on South Market across from the Police Station eating breakfast and trying to tell everybody in the world. Back to the hospital and everything was fine so I came home that afternoon. Told Grandma McConnell. Where did she put it? I didn't know she was pregnant! By that time we had Noonie living with us and she and my mother kinda helped with Pat. When he was able to walk, Dorene took him to the café. Of course the coffee drinkers entertained him or should I say spoiled him. Jim Tucker was the worst. I gave him a hammer and nails and Pat spent much time driving nails in the wood floor that he couldn't hurt.

In 1954, March 26$^{th}$, Sandy came along. The second was a lot different then the first. It was 6:30 in the morning and not even any snow. To say I didn't get excited then was a misnomer—just as or more than the first but at least didn't upset the whole town. What a swell little black headed girl. I always thought she was cute like her mother.

I had bought and moved this mine house from 8 miles out in the country. It had been the Terrill farm home east of Bussey. It had a couple of rooms attached front and back, but we moved the basic square then finished it when we set it on the basement foundation. Back from the service had bought the café and lived with the folks. The business was going like gangbusters when I went in and I had added too plus put in punch boards. Was getting the coal workers money plus a lot of the servicemen sitting on the $50.00 a week the government was doling out for 6 months to get them established. About the second year the Chambers property, 80 acres that was the full boundary north of Bussey, came up for sale. The price was $16,000. I bought it and moved the folks into it. Dad had been helping in the café and now Mother could help too. They probably worked too hard, but I honestly thought everybody should go full bore.

Got the idea the strip east that fronted the park and was the old city semi-pro baseball diamond should be developed. So I platted it out for six houses and started on the first lot east of the original farm house. I had the house pretty well set when we decided to get married. It was really pretty small. Two bedrooms, bath, living room and a kitchen. It did have a full basement and I had added a full front porch. With Nooney and two babies it got right away pretty small. We decided to move Mom and Dad to the house and we would move into the big house. Mom was in her 80's and didn't really want to move. How can I have a big party in that little house? Mom, at your age, you're not able to have a big party. Anyway, they accepted the move but Mom never forgave me. Jack, in a few years, bought the 80 that laid north so we controlled the 160 that laid north of Bussey.

Sandy wasn't aggressive as Pat. More mother's little girl. She was two and Pat was four when we moved to Indianola. It was March of 1956 and I was busy trying to get that plywood A & W put up so we could get open. We opened on May 15. I had made it very clear to Dorene that she wouldn't be working in the Drive-In. Stay home with the kids. That lasted about two days, but she was pregnant and didn't cross the lot full time. On July 3$^{rd}$ at 6:30 she came out the back of the house and mentioned to me on the tap at the root beer—it was time. I went into orbit. Turned the A & W over to Shorty McConnell and got the car. We headed for the Methodist Hospital and I was getting more excited all the time, if that was possible. We got to the emergency entrance and they were waiting for us with the roll-a-way stretcher. They grabbed me. You have to go to the office and sign in. I wasn't about to leave Dorene. Two big guys convinced me I was going to the office. Had to fill out a bunch of papers that took 2 hours (actually it was only 15 minutes). I went storming up to the fourth floor and was getting ready to turn everything upside down. The fellow stopped me in the hall. Where are you going? I'm looking for my wife who is having a baby. He happened to be Dr. Porter and just delivered a son for me. Larry was born about 20 minutes after they got Dorene situated. Three days later was bringing Dorene and Larry home. At the time, Pat was 4 and Sandy was 2 and one of the biggest jobs of the car hops was to keep Pat and Sandy off the lot and kinda ride herd on them. We pulled up to the house back door. Carolyn McElwee and another girl were car hopping and Carolyn said to the other girl—Oh my God! Another kid to run after!

Tim came along February 10, 1962 at the Methodist Hospital. Dr. Trueblood was the doctor and I knew him previously. To say I didn't get excited worse than the first. The doctor made the remark Dorene gets along fine, but don't think you can handle many more. Dorene did have more female problems and that was to be the last.

We had help raising the other three. Didn't really plan any of them, but just in case the next one we would spoil ourselves. Might remark we did it pretty well. Shorty was around the first summer plus my Dad. Teresa came in 1958 to work and live with us. Teresa got married to Bernard Barry and left in 1964. It just so happened that I broke my ankle a couple weeks before Tim was born. Use the old garage on south end of lot for storage. The floor was dirt and uneven plus there were boards, etc. on the floor. I was on the step ladder and jumped off and turned the ankle—broke it in three places—so simple, so easy, so dumb. Snow was on the ground and managed somehow to drag myself to the house. Called Warren Chandler and he drove me and Dorene to the hospital. Put the ankle back together and put a cast on up past the knee and gave me a pair of crutches. Three days in the hospital. Like the three times before, Dorene got a long better than I did plus the crutches didn't help things. It was about two weeks later, Dorene gave the word—time to go. I went into orbit but on crutches not as wild. Got back home from the hospital about 4:30 and woke the kids up and told them they had a new baby brother. Sandy starting crying—Mommy and I wanted a girl! We're not going to bring it home. I said—Get up and get ready for school and I'll fix breakfast. They all said—We don't want any breakfast. We're not going to eat. What's the matter? Why don't you want to eat? Larry said—You're not such a good cooker like Mommy is. The Methodist Hospital entrance had about a hundred steps (probably a dozen). With those crutches, it wasn't really a given when I went to visit. Dorene really did a good job raising those kids.

# 12

## *Full Time A & W*

As I said before, we opened the A & W. Told Dorene she would be staying home taking care of the kids. She did that very well, but she also worked full time. The first years we had Florence working days and, of course, Dorene was there to help at lunch time. Teresa Klein came to live with us in 1958. She would ride herd on kids daytime and work nights. Remember we had a fellow from the start that would come to town every spring from Davis City and paint our signs. That last three years we had a typical sign painter that had grown up here and moved to Des Moines. He was to do our signs. Good enough guy but had a little trouble with the bottle. He painted the numbers on the lot one day—no #7. I called him on it. He was trying to convince me it was bad luck and no painter ever did #7. I let it go because it would be a major operation to change all the numbers.

By 1958 we were buying hamburgers, strip tenderloins, hot dogs and shortening from Rath Pack. Dad would get the beef ready to grind, clean the tenders, cut and patty them out. Dorene would normally grind the hamburger and make the patties. We had got the patty machine out of Joe's basement and repaired it. One early afternoon was working away and got a call from Dr. Trueblood's office. Would you check the grinder and see if you can find the tip of Dorene's finger? What?!? Shook up quite a bit. Found the finger and rushed it over to the doctor's office just a block away. They sewed it on and pretty much worked.

The first year we got opened May 15 and closed in September with just screens and no windows. That fall (1956) we were back to Bussey and ran the restaurant. The next year we put in windows and counters all around. We opened in April and closed again in September. That winter I went into Chicago to work for Joe. He had a hamburger joint in the loop, Clark & Lake, a block north of the Cook County Courthouse. Joe's idea—if he could get me into Chicago and see the big action I would stay. He had the idea I would run the hamburger stand and he would buy the tavern next door. It didn't take me long to figure out there was more potential for making money in Indianola than Chicago. Don't know whether that was the right decision, but have always been happy. At that time Anita, Tommy and Rena all had places in the loop. Before we left Bussey and were trying to figure out what to get into, Anita had told me that pizza was the hottest thing in the world and I should get into that. I told her pizza was just a flash in the pan and would be gone in five years. We all know how wrong that statement was. Nobody knows what might have been but in any event happy with our life in Indianola.

Working in Chicago the 6 ½ months was quite an experience. Stayed with Joe. He had a flat on Schreiber a block north of Clark & Devon about 55 north and 15 west of the lake. I would ride down to work with Joe in the morning. We would get there by 5:30 a.m. and have it open by 6:00. It was busy into morning with coffee, sweet rolls, hard rolls and full breakfast. Joe bought and served nothing but the best. He didn't worry about fixing the place up or overly clean. In fact it was cooler in his mind to give the inspector a payoff. A lot of people stopped in on their way to work. Stop for both the "L" and subway also street car on our corner. I talked to everybody. Actually said "hi" to everybody that came in the door. It took two weeks before got a response from anybody. They really couldn't imagine a person being that friendly.

There was another Jewish fellow that worked across the street and was in a couple times a day. Joe called him the "Blind Tailor." He really couldn't see too good and was quite cantankerous. The first day I served him—Where did you get this guy? He served me a ½ cup of coffee. I always swung the coffee around fast from the big pot and brimming full would spill. He wanted it brimming full and plenty of cream. The bigger percentage, about 90%, had cream and sugar in their coffee, mostly to get their money's worth. At Indianola it had always been about 20% use cream and sugar. One day the Blind Tailor asked me—Gib, what's the matter with you? Actually, quite a lot. Why don't you tell me? You're speaking to everybody and always happy. I'll tell you—one of their days I'll be going back to God's Country and that's Iowa. A big percentage of the morning customers would get a scratch sheet from the magazine stand on the corner, pick their winners, then come in and call their bookie on the pay phone. Place their horse bets for the day, then the day starts. Don't bother them before.

Joe's heart was bigger than his stomach. Great guy, but don't cross him. Every morning after the breakfast rush, Joe would say—Get your breakfast and eat. I would say—You, go ahead and I'll eat later. No, I'm not eating this morning—Going on a diet. I would have sausage, two eggs, toast and coffee. He had the best sausage ever and to this day day haven't been able to match it. About

9:00 a.m. he would be getting the noon special ready, come out with a big bowl of food eating with both hands.

On Wednesday night, Joe would go to the Legion in the neighborhood and gamble most of the night. I would open Thursday morning and Joe would sleep in. I caught the street car a half block from the door and ride straight down Clark Street to the joint—Took about 25 minutes. The highlight of the trip was Wrigley Field fronting Clark Street at about 40$^{th}$. A big muscular young Black did odd jobs for Joe and helped me open on Thursdays. We did have quite a few drunks plus down and outers. The hotel bar around the corner would kick them out and in they would come to Joe's. Sometimes they would be okay and other times cause trouble. Joe said—Don't fool with them, just thrown them out. Joe, they don't build them small enough for me to throw out, but don't worry we'll take care of them. I would be behind the counter giving the guy all the biz I had available and Rambo would slip around behind them and out they would go.

The night girl would come in about 5:00 and Joe and I would usually leave by 6:00. There didn't seem to be any organized meals at home. Of course, Gwen had no idea when Joe would be home. Sometimes we would stop at a restaurant and eat. A lot of nights Joe would order an extra dinner for his buddy that was coming later and then eat them both. Other times he would bring something home to fix.

Joe gave all the policemen free coffee so there was usually a policeman around. The neighborhood precinct was just a block away. There were quite a few Al Capone stories. Our block policeman was really a nice little Italian. His Dad had worked as a policeman before him and was in Capone's heyday. The precinct gave him papers to serve on Capone. He knew where to find Capone and approached him. You take this back to headquarters and tell them you couldn't find me and there will be a check in the mail every week for the rest of your life. He did as told and got a $30.00 check every week for the rest of his life. That was big money in the 30's and 40's.

Sunday the restaurant was closed and the family usually went for a ride. A few times to Milwaukee and visit relatives. I came home one weekend a month. I wrote Dorene a letter most every night. Rode the train, Rock Island, into Des Moines for about $20.00. One weekend Rena was driving home and would I like to ride along—save train fare. Between gas and meals cost me over $30.00. I wasn't one to take for nothing, but Rena didn't put up much of a fight or offer to split.

# 13

## *Sports*

At this point Dorene and I can't remember what went on first 10 years. We were both working night and day, plus doing with the kids. It didn't seem like we spent enough time with them, but again, I say Dorene did a good job raising them. My kudos—got the kids a good mother. Remember we hadn't been in town too long Pat (Age 4) came up from South Park and about six kids chasing him. He picked up a ball bat at the stand and chased the gang back to the park. Never did find out what the deal was, but probably 6 of one and half dozen of the other. Kenny McCoy lived in the neighborhood a block and a half south and came to the door one morning carrying Larry (age 8) and he was pretty much bruised up—no broken bones. He had been riding his bike pretty fast down the hill by McCoys and wrecked. We put Larry on the davenport and he wasn't crying, but hurting pretty bad. Where do you hurt, Larry? Everywhere, Dad.

Our old landmark school, Hawthorne, is gone as of five years ago. The half block now has a four plex plus Godwin Construction office. All four of the kids went to school there—kindergarten through sixth grade. Real handy like just across the street from the A & W. When the kids got to the $5^{th}$ and $6^{th}$, they would come over at lunch and help. The Elberts lived across the street a block over. The kids kinda grew up together. The Sapers lived right across the street. Marion was our kids' second mother. Chuckie Elbert was Larry's age and would come over and help at lunch. Chuckie worked for us until he graduated from high school. This year (2000) he is teaching at a Catholic school in Fort Dodge.

Baseball was always my favorite sport and thought with three boys should have at least one baseball player. When they were old enough for Little League, got them enrolled. They all played the two years and did a decent job, but it really wasn't their thing. Pat had very little interest in sports. The coach talked him into going out for football when he was a sophomore. He stayed with it two weeks and quit. Dorene and I were happy he did. Football was all right to watch, but rather not have my guys involved—too brutal. Larry was the best athlete of the three and his favorite sport was basketball. He tore up an arm pretty bad in pickup basketball when he was a sophomore and that pretty much ended his basketball career with high school, but he did play on town teams, etc. for a few years. Can still see Tim out on third base chewing bubble gum and blowing bubbles. To this day he has no interest in sports of any kind. Larry follows sports pretty good and has got me to a couple baseball games in Kansas City and also World Series in Atlanta which was the biggest thing in my world.

We pretty much always had a station wagon and it was really handy for hauling things. Most of the time when the station wagon started up to run an errand, it was filled with kids. Usually ours and their buddies. A fellow asked me one time—Gib, how many kids do you have? Only 4. Thought you had 10! Always a car load!

# 14

## *Cub Scouts*

In the 1950's when we came to Indianola, Scouts were a big thing. Mr. Bill Buxton was the overall Scoutmaster and John Parsons was the overall Cubmaster. Mr. Buxton was President of the People's Bank, the biggest and, of course, mostly owned by the Buxton family. Bill Buxton's Dad started the bank in 1919. (By the way—same year A & W was born). A Brenton Bank came to Indianola in the early 1950's and at that time only two banks in Indianola. We were still using the Bussey Bank when we moved and built, but when we opened we knew we needed to have a bank here in town. The Brenton was the most aggressive and was after our business which at that time wasn't much. We opened an account with Brenton. It took me about 2 ½ years to figure out the six employees of Brenton didn't compare with the 30 of People's in relation to potential customers. We switched all of our money to People's.

Back to the Scouts. The Scouts with the boys played out about the same as baseball. We got them in Cubscouts when they first could join—first grade (8 years old) and then at 12 they could join regular Scouts. All three of the boys served their time as Cubs and dropped the program when it came time for Scouts. Dorene served as a Den Mother for her group and I served as Cubmaster. Dorene was a great Den Mother and her den did a lot of different things plus she always had a good treat for them after the meetings. A couple of the boys still in the neighborhood talk about the good treats they had. As a Cubmaster, I didn't get as many kudos, but did get the job done. My job was to keep all the dens in my area happy and going. Once a month we had all the dens in our area for a show off and that was held at night in the gym at Hawthorne. I would run the meeting—a little motivation speech, awards, and sign a few songs. One of the boy's mothers played the piano and there was another mother that could really sing. I was leading the singing and said to her—I'm not too good at singing. Why don't you lead? You're not too good at singing, but you're loud. None of our group opted for Scouts. After the boys were through with Cubs, Dorene and I got out too.

Februrary was Scout Founders Day month and every year our monthly meeting would be the Founder's Day program. After I was out of Cubs, one year they asked me to be the program. I thought this would be a cinch. Have them all laughing in the aisles. I got into the speech and not even a smile from any of the cubs. I'll change over to serious—that didn't work either. I've done a lot of programs, M.C. and different things, but can't count that one as a success.

# 15

## *Building Houses*

In the fall of 1958 we closed the A & W again in the middle of September. Jack Green had lived four blocks east on Highway 92 in a little shack of a house with five kids. Jack worked for Pfeifers north of town on the farm. Things got a little better for him and he bought a pretty accent house on South First and moved the family. The former house on 92 wasn't too much on a 2/3rds lot. I bought the shack and lot for $1,000.00. Took the kids down with a sledge, crow bar and hammer and they used their excess energy tearing down the shack. Had acquired an old International pickup. Can't remember where it came from and used it to clean up.

    Had got acquainted with Warren Chandler, a farmer, lived north of town 65/69 West on the Evansville road. Warren was a handy do everything farmer. I made a deal with him. Would help him pick his corn and then we would spend the winter building a house on the Jack Green property. I would furnish the money. We would sell the house and split the profits. Warren had built a house for himself on the farm a couple years before so he pretty much knew how. Our tools weren't too sophisticated. I had a hammer, a crow bar and two hand saws. He brought a hammer and a square. We would build a three bedroom ranch. Got the basement done and got it closed in before bad weather. We farmed out the plumbing and heating and the kitchen cabinets. We did the electrical and everything else. Warren was pretty sharp, but we were putting in a three way switch and Warren got stumped. I had a little trouble wiring a one way. We went up town and Leonard Utsler showed us how to do it. Dad and the kids helped finish up the painting and cleaning in the spring before we opened. We were ready to put it on the market. Phil Anderson and his wife with two little ones were ready to buy it. They lived and owned a little house in Ackworth which we took in on a trade. We, in turn, sold it on contract and I know we only got half the money and finally gave up. The price of the house was $12,000 and it was financed through Chariton Savings & Loan. It was my first experience dealing with these kind of people and what upset me most was having to give points which really meant money out of my pocket. The Andersons were really a nice young couple. They built a garage and paved the driveway. His work was fixing business machines and after so many years was transferred out. They sold the house to the Wilsons. His father was a half brother of Uncle Doc's father.

Warren and I enjoyed building the house. We got to be pretty good buddies and many days something would come up more important than working on the house. Warren was a B-25 pilot during WW II and after the war had bought a used four passenger Piper Cub. I think he still has that Piper Cub and flies it south every winter and sometimes to Mexico. I never went south with him, but we did overnight in Kansas City one time. We had got to be pretty good buddies with Father Gaul finishing up the church. He was a licensed pilot and plane enthusiast. The three of us flew down, had dinner and a show and back the next day.

After we moved into the church, we had numerous fund raisers including an annual chicken noodle dinner put together and served by the men. Warren raised chickens and sold eggs. He had culled his hens and had a bunch that didn't lay. He would give them to the church for the dinner. Warren had a 50 gallon barrel. Put water in it and built a fire underneath. We scalded the chickens, picked them and dressed them in Warren's kitchen. Noticed Warren throwing all the innards (heart, liver and gizzard) in the bucket. We don't eat any of that stuff! We keep it and that's what makes the noodles good. About six of us brought in the homemade noodles. Dorene made my noodles, but most of the Parishioners thought I put this whole dinner together. Of course, I didn't tell anybody that I didn't and still today people think I'm a great cook. We did have a lot of fun making and serving those dinners. There must have been a little talent in our gang because the dinners were real good.

# 16

## *The Biggie Operator Years*

The A & W was too good, too prosperous and just sure I had to expand and take over Des Moines. As I recall, had my pick of 12–14 A & W's in the area. Had to go to the Big Town where the action was. Jack and Mrs. Iley had the A & W franchise for all of Des Moines with an A & W at 2556 East University he had built in 1949. They lived in LaCrosse and came down every spring to open and operate the A & W all summer. It was strictly outside with a little two room second story that he and Mrs. Iley lived in. They closed in the fall about the time school started and went back to LaCrosse. I went to see Mr. Iley. At first he wouldn't even talk. For some reason I was all bad. So I started figuring. The southern city limits of Des Moines at that time was McKinley and the settlement south was called Bloomfield Township. I contacted corporate A & W about a franchise for Bloomfield Township. It wasn't really Kosher, but they would figure out a way to make it work. They weren't too fond of Jack Iley. He had the franchise for all of Des Moines and had no intention of building more units. His idea was anything within 25 miles would take away from him. My idea was the more the better. We could convert the attitude to our way and we would all grow. I was young and aggressive. Dorene and I had gone to the National Convention and met everybody from Corporate. The President and Owner of A & W at that time was a good fellow, but no personality at all. In 1960 he hired Fran Loettetle to be President and Executive Director. He was all personality and into franchise growth. He took A & W from under 500 units to a peak of 2200 across the nation.

Anyway, I got the franchise for Bloomfield township. Had my eye on a location on Army Post road just east of Fleur Drive. I, in turn, hooked up with an Italian that had a grocery store close to Watrous and Fleur. He and I would buy 300 foot frontage on the north side of Army Post Road back east from Fleur. The Italian took the west 150 feet. It had a cheap gas station that wasn't too aggressive on the corner. I took the east 150 feet with a decent little stucco bungalo house on the east end. The total for the 300 feet was $28,000. I picked up $18,000 and the buddy $10,000. My end with the decent house also had a nice barn with a single garage in. The gas station on the other end was more of a liability than an asset. The property was 300 feet deep so it was actually 300 by 300. In the mean time I realized bowling was the hottest thing going and growing. West Des Moines didn't have one at the time. Rena was running a little hamburger stand that Tommy had set up for her in the Chicago Loop and it wasn't really too great. I contacted her and told her I would set her up in an A & W. I would let her have the location for the $18,000 and help her set up the A & W. Harland Plum came up from Bussey and built the stand. The house would take up 50 feet frontage and the A & W 100 feet. For the first couple of years Rena lived in the room built in the A & W and rented the house and later moved back from Chicago and lived in the house. She was open for about seven months and closed for the winter. Of course, there wasn't a week went by that she didn't call for me to come up and fix something. Rena did all right, but I never got more than a sparse thanks for the work and time given to her. That was really Rena's way. She thought everybody was out to take her. I shouldn't complain because I brought her in.

Rena opened in 1960. In 1961 trampolines were the hottest thing going. Did a hole and mount the trampoline on the ground. So she put a trampoline stop, six big tramps, on 150 feet north of the A & W joining the parking lot. This went like wildfire but only for one year. The problem—it was easy to break a bone and the insurance was astronomical. The trampoline business quit fast as it started. We bought a trampoline from Rena for $100.00 and put it in our back yard. At the time we were living in the big house along side the A & W. Our kids were the most popular in town and about all the kids played on the trampoline at one time or another. From early morning until we closed at night the tramp was busy. The positive side of this was our kids were usually in the back yard where we could keep track of them. Think we actually wore out three of Rena's trampolines before we quit. Rena put in a miniature golf course after that and I really think that went well for her.

Back to the bowling business. Got it into my head there was much money to be made with bowling. I started looking for a spot in West Des Moines. The spot where Val Lanes is now behind first of Grand was open but another guy had first option. I got my name in second if this fellow didn't exercise his option. To fortify my position, I went out to Railroad and Grand. There was a big roller skating rink on this corner and I could visualize 18 allies going into this building. I put a bid on this building and before I could get a commitment from these people the construction for Val Lanes was well underway. I backed off and dropped all plans to get in the bowling business.

In the fall of 1959 had closed on the Army Post property and had Rena ready to go with the A & W. Soon as we were able in the spring we started the building. It wasn't too complicated. A little grading and run in the sewer and water. Run a cement slab and then the building goes up. Had that settled and it was time for me to move on to something else. The bowling was in and out in about three months. The next step would be an A & W in West Des Moines. Dick Goldman of Goldman Real Estate and Insurance located in Old Town on 5$^{th}$ Street was an old Flynn Dairy man and friend of a friend. Purchased the West Des Moines franchise and went for a location. Dick talked me into buying a couple of houses on 5$^{th}$ actually where the West Des Moines Post Office is now. Had the two properties and went to the City Council to get my zoning permit. That night found out the U.S. Government wanted that corner for a post office. I wasn't about to give in and bought those properties and was going to put in a Drive-In. It didn't take me too long to figure out you can't fight City Hall and the Government is worse. They took over my properties and made sure the price wouldn't be a penny more than I paid. It took me three years to get the money for these properties and I was paying Central National Bank in Des Moines interest on the money in those houses. I jumped up and down and hollered, but nothing did any good. Dick really knew this was going to happen and sold these properties to me for the commission. I gave him both barrels. He was about my size and I should have clubbed him but just gave him all my vocabulary plus.

That spot was gone so went up on Grand to look for a spot. The southwest corner of 13$^{th}$ and Grand was open. A Shell Station was on one corner. A Citgo Station on the other and the small city library was on the other corner. The lot was on a pretty good slope and a ditch at the bottom. I visualized a walk-in basement and digging that would be about enough fill. The corner was owned by John Connolly II. He was with Connolly, O'Malley, etc. in the Royal Union Building before 5$^{th}$—6$^{th}$ on Grand—long since gone. There was easily 6 inches of snow on the ground and Mr. Connolly and I went out and walked over the lot. As I remember it was $100.00 a month. It was my cost to prepare the lot and build the building plus pay the taxes and insurance. We would have a ten year lease with an option for five more. That day on the lot we shook hands on the deal and he said he would make up the contract later. In all my dealings with John Connolly, there wasn't a sign of a problem. Connolly owned three of the corners plus the property west of the Catholic church and school.

We got the A & W open the first of May with a manager. He was a young fellow and his wife as a helper. I spent a couple of weeks getting him organized and then turned him loose. The young couple did a decent job and there was decent volume, but there just wasn't enough to pay a decent wage to the man. It was in the black, but not a great lot. In the meantime after I got West Des Moines up and running, I decided to go over and talk with Mr. Iley. By the time he and Mrs. decided it might be a good time to get out and they were about old enough plus I seemed to have a good line of credit and he might get his money. So now I'm a big operator with all of Des Moines and West Des Moines. This should have worked, but evidently I wasn't smart enough or tough enough because it was just not developing enough pay off to make it worth while.

This big operator thing went for over 10 years and looking back my biggest problem was with personnel. I just didn't have the money to hire good managers. I always had too much ambition and had to go full speed all the time and many things going on. My people were really all pretty good, honest and sincere, but just didn't have the full push to work like I did.

Had the West Des Moines unit going with the young couple operating it. So in 1962 had bought Des Moines from Mr. Iley. I needed an operator for Des Moines. It was at 2552 East University on a corner lot 150 x 150 and an old shed of a building. A friend of ours was on the police force here in Indianola—Joe Einstein. The history on Joe—he moved here a few years before from the New England states. Joe's dad had been the manager of a woolen mill (big money). Joe grew up like a rich kid, then the polyester and other man-made fabrics came in and the wool market went south. Joe was working at the mill and now was out of a job. He took a job with a mill in Des Moines. Hence the move to the Midwest. In about six months this mill shut down. Joe had settled in Indianola with his wife and family. Joe was a drummer and played with big bands and did this part time. Anyway, he dropped the older wife and hooked up with a girl 20 years younger. When he moved here he had a couple daughters 8 and 10. Out of a job, he got on with the police force and his wife got a job at Penney's. Joe was around our A & W quite a lot. Also went to church. We talked about managing the east Des Moines A & W and we thought he could handle the job. Joe approached the police chief that he was going to work for me. The chief was a nice older guy and had always lived in the county and I thought he was a pretty good friend of mine. He said Joe, does he know you're Catholic? Yes, and what does that mean? He's Jewish from Chicago. I had known the chief over five years and he honestly thought that.

Joe and I opened up the east Des Moines A & W the spring of 1962. He really got along pretty good and the volume was better than West Des Moines. I tried spending time at the two places at least twice a week. Bought some things in volume and carried them from home. The managers did a pretty fair job, but just wasn't developing enough volume. I was checking the bills in east Des Moines and found a bread bill for a week at $800.00. With their volume should have been about $90.00. Joe had no idea how or why the bread man swore he put it in. Went to the bread company and they finally gave me back $200.00. To this day don't know whether it was the bread man, Joe or both or maybe the help, but any way I was out of $500.00. I tried to ride closer herd on Joe and things got along. I paid the bills and gave Joe a wage with a little left. It really needed to be updated, but the question was would it really develop enough net to make for new facility to work. Cost at least, at the time, $200,000.

Back to West Des Moines. The unit wasn't developing like it should and the young couple, after three years, decided it really wasn't their thing. The fellow got on full time with the fire department and the wife was pregnant. It was still a seasonal operation and had a winter to find a new operator. Father Burns, our most favorite Priest and buddy, had transferred to Sacred Heart Parish in West Des Moines. He got acquainted with a nice Catholic family that he thought might make this work—Milo & Mary DePhillips. Right away this seemed right. Milo worked for the telephone company a long time and would be available nights and weekends. Milo's people, most of them, in the food business. Mary had been a homemaker and with seven kids that was a full time job. The kids were still in the nest, but youngest was 8. A lot of help available. Mary was an Irish girl married to an Italian. About the same as my situation, and just a sweetheart of a lady. Mary worked real hard trying to make it work. One day I was coming in to visit the unit and had a retired Methodist minister with me. This fellow had retired to Indianola and wanted a little tour of the A & W. He liked to tell stories and once in a while I got one in too. I asked him if he wanted to take a ride with me. We came in to the West Des Moines A & W and there were six nuns running it. They were from the Sacred Heart Parish School across the street. They explained that Mary was such a good person and was working so hard they just decided to give her a day off. That should have made the world news. That Methodist preacher came in and saw all those nuns. Don't know what he thought, but I know he was flabbergasted. He didn't ask any questions and I didn't tell him anything.

Mary stayed three summers and decided it wasn't working and just too much for her. She had a lady working for her that was pretty good and we decided to go with her the next summer as manager. Her husband was a heavy equipment operator in road building. He was one of those guys that could fix anything and a hard worker. He was out of work and they came to me. Maybe they could buy this and two of them operate it. The problem—they didn't have any money. We figured out a way for them to take over and away they went. This was 1967 and by 1970 they had enough. It wasn't working out and they gave it back to me. By this time I had enough. About nine years and this unit hadn't done much for me. There was about a year and half left on the original contract with John Connolly II. I went to him and he let me out of the contract and I walked away from it.

The east Des Moines unit was still getting along, but wasn't improving any and it needed a new everything. Joe was a good guy and was working at it, but the best thing was to sell it. Joe got a job working at the old Riverview Park running a ride. He kinda fit that—half carney and half good guy and was dependable. In May of 1970 we sold the unit to a younger Des Moines couple. They had a lot of go power, but didn't hardly fit. The couple ran it for a couple of years and gave up. There wasn't much money changed hands so they really weren't hurt too bad.

Back on the market and the area realtor guy bought in a buyer. They had gone to the University Iowa together and were good friends. This was in 1972 and Dick Wilderman was in the picture. He had gone to Iowa and was living in Iowa City. Dick had a wife and three kids and was trying to sell life insurance. He didn't figure on moving the family to Des Moines until fall or next spring. The first week the wife, Lynne, landed in the hospital with female problems so I took over running the A & W for a couple weeks. It was a little hairy trying to keep Indianola and Des Moines on a even keel. Dorene then took over Indianola. Did I mention I married well? I got the kids a good mother. Dick was a good guy, but that college degree didn't teach him how to use a hammer and screwdriver or the general things about running a business hands on. I told him one day—Dick, you don't know nothing. He was a fast learner and it didn't take him long to get the business rolling and grabbing the potential I knew was waiting to be picked up. He took over in 1972 and by 1974 had a new modern building plus paying me on the contract. Can't figure how he made the payments and built a new building. Must have sold it too cheap. When Dick came to me he didn't have a dime. A little equity in a house in Iowa City and an old Buick convertible. He would give me a mortgage on the car and what he could get on the house. I didn't really want to tie him up to that extent and possibly he wouldn't last more than a year. I said—Dick, I'll make a deal with you. I'll trust you and you trust me. Pay rent and a percentage this year. If you're happy and I'm happy, we'll do a contract and go on from there. The contract was for $47,000. and he paid it off in five years.

That pretty much sums up the era of my biggie operator years. Some people can make that multiple operator thing work, but it wasn't for me.

# 17

## *The Kids' Stats*

In those early years we worked day and night during the summer busy season and as I've said before we didn't have much time with or for the kids. How Dorene had time to do and work I'll never be able to figure out. The National A & W Conventions in January were considered our vacations and we tried to take the kids along. In all the years I think we only missed one convention. That was Cleveland in 1962. Dorene was eight months pregnant with Tim and I was afraid to take her. As the kids got old enough to walk we took them with us. Sandy didn't go as much. She didn't want to miss school and then college and she was gone.

I'll take a few pages for the kids' stats at this date (9/05/02) and also the grandkids. At different intervals have to remind myself—got the kids a good mother and never had got hold of that money. Pat graduated from high school in 1970 and married Lynn Coffey in 1973. Our neighbor at the time was the city sewer superintendent. He hired Pat the day school was out. Pat stayed with the job three years and then joined us at the A & W. Larry and Pat were partners in the A & W and Larry bought Pat out in 1999. Working inside wasn't really Pat's thing. He liked the outdoors. Pat and Lynn had bought an acreage (7 acres) on the southwest edge of town with a nice big old farm house that they remodeled. He started doing a little yard work, landscaping, snow removal so now he's doing that full time. They have two children. Megan is 22 and Ross is 20. Megan graduated from Iowa State this year (2002) and went to work for Better Homes & Gardens seems like the day after graduation. She has a boyfriend from college and they are making plans for a wedding in the fall of 2003. Ross is a sophomore at Iowa State.

Sandy graduated from high school in 1972. She enrolled at Coe College and finished in four years at Coe plus a CPA and has taken some courses at Iowa. I ran suitors off when she was home. No guy was good enough for our #1 daughter. She married out of college and after about eight years they split up. Sandy went to work for Collins and he was with the original Telecom USA. Sandy is still with Collins. She bought a little house on Elmhurst Drive behind Mt. Mercy College and right now she has it completely remodeled and very nice. She seems happy with her volunteer work for Y.F.U.

Larry graduated from high school in 1974. He pretty much liked that root beer business and seemed to hook right on. Our milk man at the time served the state fairgrounds and had a few connections. Jim Burken had always wanted a stand at the fair. With Jim's connections and Larry's knowledge plus vim and vigor, they got a root beer stand. They operated as partners and then Larry bought Jim out. As of 2002 it was Larry's 21$^{st}$ year and had six stands on the grounds. He works the fairs about four months and has been a pretty good thing for him. Larry married Jill Koelmoos in 1991 and they have three of our grandchildren—Anna 9, James 7 and Mary 4.

Tim graduated from high school in 1980. He could see right away there really wasn't any room for him at the A & W. Father Burns had got Larry interested in cameras and 35 mm. He developed this as a pretty good hobby. Tim picked it up right away from Larry and Father Burns. Mr. and Mrs. Eaton of Eaton Photography owned our local shop (Cadillac of the industry) and were at the age to get out. Tim worked with Mr. Eaton to learn the business and then buy. Think he bought in 1985 and it has been solid growth ever since. Tim married Shelli Netley in 1989. They have one of our granddaughters. Hattie is 8.

The guys didn't have time for college. Wanted to get into making money. I never pushed college and probably should have, but they have done very well plus the grandkids are super. The very best. As I have said before, there is no way Dorene can get all the credit due for keeping the family intact plus the business etc. As I have also said before, I always had a lot of go power. Wasn't the smartest guy in the world but got along. Maybe luck had a lot to do with it.

The Indianola A & W continues to grow at least in the early years. We updated. Did something every year. Starting with the little plywood building with screens. The second year we added windows and black top on the rock lot. The third year we added the outside electronic ordering system with a canopy south from the end of the building to the alley. Also dug a basement south of the building end for storage plus a work area and breakroom for workers with a toilet-wash room. The basement was capped with cement and that made for an outside patio and a couple of picnic tables.

In 1960 Noonie passed away. She had lived with us after Dorene sold the store about '52–'53. Noonie was a real sharp lady in her day, but had a brain tumor that affected her day to day living. Tony (Dorene's Dad) and Noonie split up after she had the tumor, but he was still around to call the shots. Tony was real sharp also. When you figure Tony came over here at 16 and worked for two years and had made enough money to go back over and get Noonie. They got married in the little village and he brought her over here. Think of all the obstacles they had to overcome that we normally take for granted. Tony ended up in Seymour with a little mine house on a double lot. We would take Noonie and go down to see him about every week. Tony had passed away the day before Noonie and the funeral Mass they had together at Knoxville. Sad but nice in the fact they got back together in the end.

In 1961 we bought the stucco house across the street north and moved. Then we started tearing down the big old house. It was an all winter job. The whole job was an old International pickup I had bought from somebody plus neighborhood kids with sledgehammers and crow bars. I furnished the tools and they let it all hang out. That gave us another row of parking up to 40 stations outside plus seating for 36 inside. The three story house was a little scary on the high part. Then we jacked up the little one car garage at the end of the lot that we had been using for storage and backed a small dump truck under it. We moved this garage across the street and put it behind the stucco house. Moving a structure like that required permits from the city and also the highway commission for crossing Highway 92. We just moved it and didn't tell anybody. If there had been a problem or we dropped it on the highway, we would still be paying. Saved time and money. Sometimes you luck out. We later tore down the little garage and incorporated it into a two car garage for the house. About 1982 Tim bought the photo business from Bob & Jean Eaton. He then decided to move the studio from uptown to a building they had built on the west end of the house incorporating the garage into it.

1984 had us moving to 304 West First which was the Criswell three bedroom ranch that we had bought at auction for $78,000 two years before. It was time for us to get into something smaller. Dorene's knees were giving her trouble plus the whole family was on their own. As of this day, 9/20/02, we are really enjoying this house.

# 18

## *The State Association*

Back to 1967. There was a state A & W meeting in Des Moines. I got the idea we should have a state association and time was right. McCormack Dist. (Broaster & Taylor freezers) were wining and dining us. Jim and Jackie Duncan had Ottumwa and Iowa City at the time. We had talked about forming an association. Jim was elected president, I was vice-president and Jean Barnhill was secretary/treasurer. I was to write a letter to all the Iowa A & W operators informing them of the new association. Our operator at Tama-Toledo was a lawyer and he was to draw up the by-laws. Dues were $50.00 a year and the money would be used to set up an annual state convention, form buying groups and advertising group. Wally Luedtke was one of our biggest operators and our second annual convention was in Cedar Rapids. The Association did a good job in the 1970's and 1980's until the fall out. We were the envy of the nation with our active association. In fact, we helped the states around us organize. Dorene and I went to Minneapolis and helped them get off the ground. We also helped Illinois get started. Missouri had the two—Fortner & Farrell at Springfield and they got things rolling. Nebraska was a little smaller in units and the eastern part joined with us. Our convention every year was quite a focal point. It was held after the National and we tried to bring in the highlights to our people who hadn't attended.

The newsletter (not because I did it) did serve a very good purpose—communication. It tended to get everybody on the same playing field. Through the years we never missed a month sending the newsletter and to this day (January 2003) it is still going. Our membership (A & W's) got pretty small, but thanks to Sid Feltenstein it is coming back up.

In 1968 I joined the Iowa Restaurant Association. In April of 1972 went to Marshalltown to attend Harker's 20th anniversary party. Harker's Wholesale Meats had started from a locker plant in Le Mars to three warehouses—Le Mars, Marshalltown and Davenport and employed 100 people. I was impressed with the company and with the party it had put together. I put together a writing of the party and gave it to Bud Proctor, editor of the Appetizer, the State Restaurant Association magazine. The party was a big success and my article in the Appetizer came off pretty good. Anyway, Marshall Abbe, Association President at the time, asked me to write a column every month. It was headed "Roll Down the Window Please" and supposedly related to the drive-in industry. This column continued through Peter Canakes (1967) and the reign of Les Davis, who was replaced in 1996. The whole association changed and Les was replaced by a couple ladies. The association changed and after a month the magazine was dropped. The one magazine they put out the lady changed my copy and wording. In the 25 years of writing before they had never changed a word or even corrected misspelling. One month I made a mistake and sent in a page of notes that didn't make any sense at all. That didn't mean that there weren't readers. It was proven my column was very popular. The restaurant association and magazine (January 2003) was a thing of the past, but still did the newsletter for the A & W's.

After we closed in the A & W with inside seating for 40, we started staying open longer in the fall. We later started closing a couple days before Christmas and we reopened a couple of weeks into January. That is still the operation with vacation time in January and that was usually the National Convention and I took the kids along. As I have said, the first convention was in Peoria and we tried to make it. The next was San Antonio and by that time had a year's operation under our belt and knew everything. For the life of me I can't remember much about the time from 1957–1967. The business grew every year and every January we went to the National Convention. Enjoyed the business and always enjoyed going to the conventions. The general public always felt sorry for us working so hard.

I considered it a labor of love and as I have said before we did something every year to improve while closed. If we didn't have anything constructive on the docket, we tore up something to make people think something was going on.

The monthly newsletter to the Iowa A & W operators started in June 1968 and haven't missed a month since. In July I started "Know Your Neighboring Operator." It was a write up about all the good things about one of our operators like background etc. Tried to keep our operators informed about meetings and current events. In 1966 A & W came out with a powder for French fries called "Super Fries." I took this on as my winter job to help operators get in the Super Fry business. The idea was great. The powder with no refrigeration and mix added to water and then dumped into a cylinder and then pressed through a plate into the hot grease. It was suppose to be the greatest thing on the market. It really never took the place of potatoes. As a product about 10% of the customers really liked it and the other 90% definitely did not. I spent a year working the state for A & W. We didn't really make any friends and after a couple years the product was dropped.

The newsletter gave a lot of service to the operator. We had a "For Sale, Wanted to Buy and All Items coming out of Corporate." We had figures for profit on ice cream (soft serve). We made up road signs available to our association members. Our convention also came up with a rotating or stationary sign. I took it on myself to get okayed for the state and sell the signs for my winter job. The signs would be sold to big business. I made the calls and sold zero. Maybe the selling job was not my thing. Couldn't make the wholesale business go and the normal person should learn from that. Will I ever learn? Probably not.

Had a lady call me in August of 1968 from Marketing Specialties of America, Inc. The company would send out 2,500 mailers with cards the customers would bring in and after $10.00 had been purchased would receive from me a push button index file. I would pay 10 cents a piece for the mailers ($250.00) and figuring 20% redemption they would furnish me with 500 index files. These would be paid for by pre-sold national ads on the card. If they got a check when they sold the deal they would knock off $25.00 I figured it was a good follow up for the A & W direct mail and would run it in October and let the people know we are open and figuring on staying open. The lady selling the deal grew up in my home town and I never thought but what it would be okay. Two fellows dreamed up this idea when they were in Sing Sing Prison. They would set up in a town, Des Moines in my case, get a bunch of money and move on to another town. They did this in quite a few towns and eventually going to head for the border but they did get caught. Fine. But that didn't get my $225.00 back. The moral of the story is don't be a dum-dum like your President. Glad my mother never saw this. She thought she raised a smart one.

Remember it was January in 1969. In the winter at our house it was a little slow and we had a ping pong table on the third floor. One night beat Larry 2 out of 3. Don't think this ever happened before so have to put it in print. The conventions were a big thing for us and always a lot of fun plus the learning experience. Fran Stupka, Davenport A & W, and I were appointed to the honorary N.A.C. (1961). We were appointed to help the convention with ideas for the operators. We lost Fran Loetterle in 1969 and it was a new ballgame with new President Weber. Dorene and I got to meet President Weber at our convention in New Orleans (January 1970). Our Iowa Convention was March 1, 2, 3 in Cedar Rapids. Two of our biggest operators were on the committee—Wally

Luedtke of Cedar Rapids and Roger Rommel of Dubuque. At the Cedar Rapids convention I was the toastmaster at the banquet and also ran the meetings. This job was with me till the end of time.

Our second Iowa A & W Association Convention was in Des Moines. Fran Stupka and I were trying to sell the national advertising. Found out at the New Orleans convention the celebration and parades start after Christmas and goes on till Ash Wednesday. There's a big percentage of Catholics in New Orleans. Everyone was supposed to bring their menu and any tips they could come up with to the convention in Des Moines. We always had a sing-a-long at the Iowa Conventions. Fort Dodge was the site of our third Iowa Convention. Had a lady playing the piano. Thought I would be a nice guy and buy her a drink. Evidently she had already been there and that put her out of commission. At the time of New Orleans convention, Mike Mazerky was our T.V. commercial guy. Mike found out I was from Iowa and asked about Babe Sharkey (that was Babe Bisignano's wrestling name) as they had wrestled together. He was happy to hear Babe was doing well.

It is 1970 and I got hold of a weapons carrier wagon from the second war. It's four wheel and very substantial like the government would build it. Installed a Dole Director (3 faucet), built a counter, cupboard and installed a sliding window. The drinks were root beer, orange and cola. We did farm sales and town sales that were pretty large. Last Saturday had Junior Hereford Association meeting in Indianola. The kids ran this and took in $90.00. Not bad figuring the profit margin. Had one casualty. Tim stepped in some cow stuff. These city kids.

That little sale wagon served a lot of sales, celebrations, etc. All three of the guys were involved to start, but Tim and Pat phased out. Larry kinda took and enjoyed doing it. I got him his first big job at the 4$^{th}$ of July celebration in Bussey. As you remember, that was my start. With Larry it took and has been his life to this point. He does fairs in Illinois, Iowa, Nebraska and ends up in Oklahoma City. I try to visit the fairs with him as I can. Got to Oklahoma City this year (2002) to finish. The Oklahoma City fair is 20 days. Most are 10 days. Dick and I drove down on the last Friday of the fair. Dick came home on Sunday and drove one of Larry's vans with whatever Larry needed to bring back. I stayed and rode home with Larry on Monday. Larry let me work the counter. He had two units at the fair. He only sold three sizes of root beer and floats. A lady at the counter put down three dollar bills for her purchases. I picked up the money to put in the cake pan. There were two bills stuck together. I turned around to give the lady her extra dollar and she had walked away. I called her and she came back and thanked me. As she was walking away I heard her say to her buddy—I can't believe that carney gave me the dollar back.

As I said before, was appointed by our company president (Weber) as an honorary member of the N.A.C. (National Advisory Council) and then it was formed for real and the members were by a national election. I was elected to serve on the first board and then was re-elected to serve a second two years and then I opted out. Thought the job should be passed around. The N.A.C. served the A & W operators well and really a pretty good thing. The N.A.C. along with the newsletter helped the individual operators a great lot. While on the N.A.C. I served as Public Relations guru and had a column in the News Dispenser and wrote that until the N.A.C. went out of existence. The Burger family came into and onto the national scene in the early 1970's. Mama, Papa, Teen and Baby Burgers and it was super. I honestly think it should be still around and part of but went out in the late 1980's.

I started this book in 1998 and catch it in my spare time. Now it is 02/03/03. The biggest problem is I can't remember what I wrote. There might be a little duplication but hope I get a small snicker out of the second time around. The A & W was and has been our life and working there was a labor of love. Been in the food business since 1946. Some people think I have to be a great cook and other people know the truth and other people know that I have a little trouble boiling water. Now I can work on this book full time and still slow. I'm the homemaker with Dorene's condition, but at this data we are getting along fine.

The Iowa Association Conventions and all the other fellow operators made it a great life. At this date in time (1972) it is our $5^{th}$ annual A & W Iowa Convention. The first year we had our convention in Des Moines (1967). The thing started with registration and cocktails on Sunday night. Monday and Tuesday were meetings and banquet on Tuesday night and then home. On Sunday night we announced a cocktail party which would probably run up to $400.00 and our Association with no funds it was a little hairy. I scouted around and found out Jerome Paulsen, Fox Products, (ice cream toppings) had a three room suite to display his product so I real fast sent everybody up to his display. He didn't know till five years later that he hosted the Association's first cocktail party. Everybody had a good time at our conventions and we usually had visitors from other states. At this point, of course, a lot of those people are gone (2003). Irish Kelly from Waukon was the Big Irishman and I was the Little Irishman. We did more than our share of entertaining.

In thinking back from today, February 2003, I'm at year 1972 with the book. Was writing the newsletter, A & W News Dispenser and restaurant association

Appetizer, and working hard at the A & W. Now the Dispenser and Appetizer were gone. Does that mean me??? No. No. No. It was a lot of fun over the years.

Back to 1972. Pat at the time was working for the sewer department. He was down a manhole and overcome with sewer gas. His two co-workers pulled him out and gave him mouth to mouth resuscitation until the ambulance came. It was close and scary but the next day he was back to work.

Joe Einstein managed east Des Moines until we sold it. He got a job running a ride at Riverview Park. That fit him pretty good. One day he took Tim and couple of his buddies and gave them a free pass for the rides. I'm sure they thought this must be heaven. Larry and I went to Pella for the grand opening of their new Phase II. Norm and Neoma were great people and charter members of the association. Fast forward to today—February 2003. The A & W has been gone three years and we buried Norm last year.

Did the Harker party last month plus the Appetizer column. In July started the first column of "Roll Down Your Window, Please" (June 1972). As I said before, the writing is a labor of love. Sometimes people ask—Where do you find the stuff to write? No problem. That kinda stuff keeps rolling out of my head. It might be good if something constructive would roll out of my head. We have and have had a lot of great people in our food industry. Stub & Vi Johnson of Spencer. Stub was one of the greatest promoters. For years had full sized windmills in the country around Spencer. He was big with the Coffee Day for Retarded and he started Ride for Crippled Children. The Horse Clubs of Iowa, on the certain day, would ride around and collect money. Their big thing was to set up at intersections and shake down the cars. Also the same at drive-ins. In the Restaurant Hall of Fame, Stub will be second following Babe Bisignano. The Wingas in Washington, second generation now, and their restaurant started in 1928. As the story goes, when John wanted to start a restaurant (in the 1920's) he went into the local bank to borrow some money. They turned him down flat. At this time (1972) he is serving as President of the Restaurant Association and Chairman of said board. Ermal Loughry, Carousel in Coralville, one of the great characters of our industry.

A little side track. We had built the church and dedicated it in 1958. I had helped Father Gaul and Dorene had fixed lunch all winter. Then they moved Father Gaul to West Des Moines to build a school and Father Burns in to pay off the $100,000 debt. Father looked real stern on the pulpit and actually scared me. I filled in as Lector at 8:00 Mass about every week. Our gang filed in the church, fourth row from the front on the right hand side. I would get the motion from the sacristy to come up and be the Lector. I had told him before if I would be bet better than nobody to give me a call. I'm on six weeks in a row and beginning to think the people had me pegged as an apprentice for the Big Guy in the Sky. One morning I wore my new N.A.C. outfit—brown jacket, white pants and A & W orange tie. Father Burns came on with—If there is anything to do here I'll do it. You work your own side of the street.

From day one I've been an up guy and start everything with a smile. Everything is good until proven otherwise. Dorene is mostly a downer and everything is bad until proven good. The National Convention was a big event for us and even bigger when I was on the N.A.C. Our convention was at Disney World (1972). Disney World had just opened the summer before. Sandy had shipped off to Coe College and Pat had gone to full time work. Larry and Tim were having fun with us at Orlando. Looking back I would say the Disney World Convention was the biggest and best ever. Disney World was brand new and our hotel, the Contemporary, was brand new and in walking distance from the main gate.

Pat was married in 1973. The first for us, but we did it up pretty well. Our house was just a half block from the church. In fact, we were right in the middle next to three churches. No wonder we were religious! Dorene fixed ham, roasted chicken, potato salad, etc. and homemade bread. I was in charge of the beverage department which was also adequate. A new life for Pat and different life for the family.

As I say over and over again, the A & W was certainly our life and the National Convention was our yearly vacation. Usually tried to do an extra few days. The State Association Convention was the peak of our life. J.C. Glover, Electro Hop., and his hospitality suite was usually the most popular. At that time Coors Beer wasn't available in Iowa so that's what everybody wanted. J.C. would load up on Coors Beer on his way in from Texas. His bath tub was always full of ice water and Coors Beer. When Coors moved into Iowa, I haven't drank a bottle of Coors since.

A lot of working and fun with the Iowa A & W Association. We brought in wooden nickels for $16.00 a thousand. To write this book I'm trying to reference my mind plus the newsletters, News Dispenser and Appetizer. Again I get a little mixed up sometimes. Those columns have pretty much been our life.

The hot air balloons came to our town in 1970. The word around town—what is a hot air balloon? I think there were nine balloons that first year. Everything went so well they decided to schedule another event in 1971. That year (1971) they fell in love with the people and community and decided Indianola would be the home of the annual National Balloon Championship. In

1973 there were 50 balloons. The Simpson football practice field was the balloon field. Tim was about 10 and he hooked up on a chase crew. He settled with a balloonist from Minnesota and was right there chasing for the whole event.

Father Burns (1972) went with us to the Disney World Convention. The next year (1973) was Dallas and we took him along. By now he had visited with and practically knew everybody which included the President and the N.A.C. Board. Father Burns was brilliant and had studied many different subjects and could carry a conversation in any field. His one fault, I used to tell him, he couldn't make it on the outside with his every day personality. In his mind, conventions were for getting drunk and chasing women (other people's). After his first convention, he figured out we were all pretty legitimate. We were at the cocktail hour in Dallas before the banquet and Father spotted Jim Gibbs and party (our N.A.C. President from Grand Forks, ND). He went over to them and offered to buy a round of drinks. Jim and Adeline were strictly dry and his party was his Methodist Preacher and wife. A little embarrassing, but Father got over it. Father Burns passed away with cancer a few years ago (1992?) and we do miss him. At the Dallas convention our program was Abigail Van Buren. Abby and Anne Landers grew up in Sioux City and Abby received her proposal for marriage at the A & W—4$^{th}$ and Jackson.

The Little Flower came up with a classic the other day (October 2003). We were talking about my writing. Sure you come up with something occasionally but you have to eat so much baloney to get to it. Irish and LaVerne Kelly from Waukon in the 1970's were on our "Most Favorite People" list and we did more than our share of entertaining—the Big and Little Irishmen.

The Disney World Convention in 1972 was the greatest in A & W history. Our 2,000 registered with 1,442 for the Saturday night banquet. The banquet rooms had a max of 1,000 people so we broke it up and had two banquet rooms. I was on the N.A.C. and the first big A & W function that we had handled. Our hotel was in walking distance of the Disney World gate. Tim and Larry had a hey day along with Father Burns.

The best thing the Catholics have done in the last 400 years is put the song books in the pews. Tim and I along with a neighbor went to early church this morning. We were in the middle of a song. Tim reached over to me—Dad, you're on the wrong song. I sing pretty loud.

# 19

## *The Early 70's*

With three sons I thought maybe we could have one athlete. They couldn't get it from me, but their mother had a lot of those qualities. Got the guys into Little League and after their two years they were out. Pat did not care for athletics. He was more into game hunting. Larry was the potential athlete. He banged his arm when he was a sophomore playing basketball and ended his high school athletics. Tim didn't care or know anything about athletics. He did his run of Little League baseball.

The State Restaurant Association was getting more time in our lives. I was elected to the Board of Directors before we were acquainted with the A & W people and now was getting acquainted with all the restaurant operators. Winga's at Washington was a landmark restaurant that was started in 1928 by John Sr. and still going today with John Jr. I'm not sure about the third generation. They have a son and daughter and they have gone different directions. In the industry Winga's would rank near the top.

(April 2004) If I could keep going on the writing it would be so much better, but seems like I get out and don't get back for six months. Back to September 1972.

The new thing in this era was pressure fed ice cream machines. The selling point was that you could adjust the air going into the final product. With the gravity fed machines it was always about the same and with enough profit. Of course, I had to have one of those pressure machines. It had twice as many parts and that meant twice as many problems and the product wasn't really that great.

Now the kids are back to school and Sandy shipped off to Coe in Cedar Rapids for her first year in college. Tim built a soap box derby racer by himself and placed second in the demolition derby. That was really quite an accomplishment.

Back to pressure fed soft serve machines. Dairy Queen has always used the Duke? pressure fed machines. I could say that their product wasn't the best, but they are more successful than we are so what do I know.

My Mother (Mabel McConnell) passed away October of 1972. She was a great lady and put up with a lot from me. She always found something funny about any and everything. Dad (Byron) had passed away a few months before. They were the greatest and we never really gave them credit for the job they did for us.

Up to February 1973. Dorene had major surgery and got along fine. She has so much will power and takes pain like you can't believe. I broke my ankle about 10 years ago (1961) and it was repaired with a screw pin. Over the years it was working out and got infection. So the doctor said come into the hospital and we'll work on it. The doctor came in with a nurse, one intern and four nurses' aides. I'm thinking this will be quite a show. Good for 15 minutes at the P.T.A. I felt a needle go into that raw flesh and something was said about a screwdriver and I started grabbing for the bedrail 'cause is has to hurt. The doctor will see you tomorrow afternoon at the office. Aren't you going to do anything? All done. The whole deal all of 10 seconds.

Dorene and I were the guests of honor at the Y's Men monthly in January. We donate to the Y's Men half of our lot for their Christmas tree sale. They made a flowery speech and presented us with a framed used Colonel Sanders wrapper they had found on the lot. Have to put this in—Larry gave me a McDonald's coupon for Christmas.

Pat and Lynn were married in 1973. Found out real quick that dad of the groom isn't really too important at this function. Sandy was a bridesmaid and Dorene and I agreed she was the nicest looking of the whole gang. Lynn changed her name to McConnell and then she was #1. Our home was a half block from the church. In fact we are in the middle of three churches. Probably the reason we are so religious. Of course it was about three steps from the church to our house and Dorene hosted a nice dinner after the wedding. Broasted chicken, ham, potato salad and fresh baked bread. I was in charge of the beverage department and a good time was had by all.

The restaurant and A & W association were our entertainment and mostly was our vacation including the conventions and different meetings. It was actually a bunch of good people and they all talked our language. Tim and Larry traveled with us to the conventions a number of years. Sandy was pretty much in college. Pat, of course, was married with a job. The A & W convention was our highlight. In the peak we would entertain a couple hundred people. Every year the officers moved up and the meetings would be in a different location. At this time we peaked out at 102 operations in Iowa. Jim Duncan was our first President and then Wally Luedtke. At this time Wally had been in the business 23 years. He was really quite a promoter and gave us all quite a few ideas. The breaded tenderloin was probably the biggest.

1972 was the first year for Tim in the Little League. None of the three cared for baseball and cared for nothing about sports. Tim came in after his first game. Hi Mom, we won! What position did you play? What's the one between 2$^{nd}$ and 3$^{rd}$? Shortstop! Yeah, that's it and I made three runs. Home runs? Naw, struck out twice and walked three times, but I got a foul ball and that's how Mickey Mantle started.

This year we brought in wooden nickels among other things. It was really quite a good promotion and just the other day (2004) I ran into a box of wooden nickels. Kinda fun to pass out yet. In 1970 I sent out the first letter to the N.A.C. members as I was on the first appointed (by the President) N.A.C. Board and then on to the first elected board. The board is still active today (2004) and more important than ever with the merging of five fast fooders—A & W, John Silvers, Pizza Hut, Kentucky Fried Chicken and Taco Johns. The newsletter is still important. I served two elected terms and then opted out. Thought it was important that most should be active and be involved and with new people maybe new things would happen.

The Iowa Association and N.A.C. was our focal point many of these years. I've always felt the Iowa Association was real important and still is today. With me on the sidelines (retired) it's a little harder to keep abreast. I was appointed by President Weber to our first National Advisory Council. It was really kind of an honorary job and we didn't have any authority or involvement. Then came the elected N.A.C. I served two elected terms (two years each) and then opted out. Honestly thought everybody should take a turn and everybody should be involved. We had committee meetings and then a state convention. Our state convention was after the national convention which was normally the first part of January. This was to get the ideas to the operators that didn't make the national convention.

In October 1972 we got Norm Ruffridge (Pella) to run for the N.A.C. and I stepped down. Norm and Neoma ran a good operation in Pella. Scandinavians from the north in this totally Dutch town. I've mentioned it before in this book, but the N.A.C. was and is the best thing that ever happened to us. As franchises (this just came to me) back in the 1960's and 1970's, we had a group of 12–15 operators in the Southeast. We would get together and have a relaxing party and would take turns hosting. Our turn came in June and for a little pizazz I gave them a choice—the opera at Simpson or a ball game at Sec Taylor. Everyone opted for Sec Taylor.

By this time the Iowa Association was in full swing and the newsletter kinda kept things together. Included was a letter from our Association President and the N.A.C. happenings plus any news that I could put together. We peaked out with about 102 operations in Iowa and think this was our peak time (1973). The Iowa Restaurant Convention was a winner in November 1973 and we had an A & W Association meeting too. Our National Convention was in Dallas—November 15, 16, 17 of 1973. Would have to say President Ed Weber was one of the best things that ever happened to A & W. It was the first elected N.A.C. and got a new contract for Phase II building.

#3 son Tim was along at our Dallas convention. We really tried to take the kids if they were available. Tim, in 1973, was 11 or 12 and went along with us. We really worried about him having a good time. In the big hotel in the middle of Dallas he and I went to breakfast every morning and then he was on his own. Every once in awhile throughout the day he would pop up and say Hi, Dad! In the morning we were getting ready to leave and he had to go down to the lobby to say goodbye to all his friends. He knew all the hotel personnel and the maid on our floor who said, Hi, Tim! Father Burns had come along with us. He was a great guy and could visit with anyone and get acquainted with the whole gang. Tom Cooney (operator from Pueblo, CO) gave Father a ticket to big league football—the Dallas Cowboys vs. the Philly Eagles. He caught a late flight home. We caught the 12:30 out. We took Father's bags and his little bag with the Mass kit which was a carry on. One of the bags beeped the beeper as we were going through the security check. They opened the bag and it was the Mass kit. The fellow didn't say anything, but you could see what he was thinking—Priest, family, oh my.

Our entertainment for the banquet at this convention (now I can't remember their names) was writing names Abby & Anne Landers, sisters that grew up in Sioux City. They were both journalists. Abby was our banquet program. She received her proposal for marriage at the A & W on 4$^{th}$ and Jackson. Another side track—one of our balloon people lives in Dallas and the promotion company he works for has an A & W and Father Burns flew the balloon over Dallas with the A & W logo. Maybe I didn't mention that Father's hobby is balloon flying and he has a pilot's license.

Mabel Miller owned and operated the Hotel Manning and the hotel restaurant in Keosauqua. The only lady President of the Iowa Restaurant Association (think in the 1970's). Later she married a D.N.R. man (I called them "Blue Jackets") and moved to Indianola. She sometimes went to meetings with me and Dick. A real good lady. Keith and LaVerne Kelly stayed with us while doing this convention. We were best buddies. They had a nice operation in Waukon. Kelly passed away in the 1980's and LaVerne in the 1990's. They made all the state conventions and meetings, but never the nationals. In his hotel room he always had deer sausage and all kinds of beverages. A real hunter. I think it was a tall gallon bottle of Jack Daniels that sat in the corner of their room. We were known as the big and small of Irish vintage. The year was 1974 and it started out good for me and Kelly. January 1st headlines in the Des Moines Register—Irish are #1.

It's all history and gone now, but the Association was the best thing the Iowa operators had going for them. I started the newsletter in 1967. I think it was in 1972 when it started going out every month. Still going out every month. Still the same. There was time when it was a news and helper communication. Now it is a "maybe" in 2004. The 1960's through the 1980's were the boomer years and it was a helper. The 1980's and 1990's were the problem years and the letter helped get our side out. Then in 2003 we had the merger of five—A & W, L.J.S., Taco Johns, Pizza Hut and K.F.C. Who knows what will happen now.

November 1972—Tony Prochello of Des Moines was a beverage promoter and was putting together a trip for the Restaurant Beverage Association. In January 1975 they were going to Spain. The Little Flower and I signed up. Then The Little Flower enrolled she and I in a conversational Spanish class at the high school. For Dorene (has the smarts) it was pretty Kosher. Not for me. The teacher looked at me and thought—teach this dumb Irishman and he hasn't even accomplished Irish yet! Anyway, I didn't go back after the first night.

The hot air balloon event was very successful so Father Burns and I had a deal cooked up to a buy a balloon. Should work. I'm a hot air balloon specialist and he's a sky worker. The Little Flower got hold of this and put the kibosh on it right away.

We're doing a little catering and the County Republican Fund Raising Committee came in and asked about us serving dinner. What's your politics? Republican. Got the job and served the dinner. Also serve the Democrats dinner. Had always been a registered Democrat. No discrimination in our camp.

A side light—Dick Wilderman had come in to buy the east Des Moines A & W in 1970. He had no money, but a run down Buick convertible and a little equity in a house in Iowa City plus a wife and three little kids. I'll make a deal with you. I'll trust you and you trust me. You run the A & W next year on a percentage basis. If you're happy and I'm happy, we'll sign a contract and go from there. I found out they came from West Bend and assumed they were Catholic. Lynne's mother was there helping. She informed me in no uncertain terms they were Methodists and they have the biggest congregation in town.

Built the West Des Moines A & W in 1962. Had different managers working it and couldn't get the potential going. Got a couple that moved here from Sparta, Wisconsin which had produced so many good operators over the years. Frank and Bev Taylor had four daughters. They would operate the first year with the option to buy the second year. They increased the volume 40%, but still wasn't enough to make it viable. Sold it a couple more times and finally gave the leased property back to Joe Connolly II and walked away.

So the state fair is on and The Little Flower gave me tickets to the Bob Hope show. We took #2 and #3 sons and had an absolute ball. Bob's Pollack jokes were real good, but thought his Irish jokes were in bad taste.

About this time they put the song books back in the church. We filed into church Sunday at 8:00 Mass. Fourth row from the front right side. Took up most of a pew with four kids. We got into the first song. Tim was next to me—Dad, you're on the wrong song and I sing pretty loud.

It was a great time raising the kids. You might say growing up with them (3 boys and one 1 girl). I get a little confused at this stage. Think Pat graduated high school in 1970, Sandy in 1972, Larry in 1974 and Tim in 1979. In a conversation with #3-Tim: That's what all parents do. Trick the kids into eating hamburgers and they do steak.

With the N.A.C. (National Advisory Council) we had about three meetings a year plus the convention and it was really important that we be involved. At one trip we pulled into the L.A. International and our meeting was at the Marriott at the fringe of the airport. Someone from the hotel was there to meet us and a little lady hopped out and said, "I'll take that bag." If I hadn't let go I would have been in the trunk with the bag. Yes, the ladies are moving up.

Bud Proctor was editor of The Appetizer (I think he was a Professor at Drake for his real job). Anyway, I would see him once a year and evidently thought I could do no wrong and did relate to the operators. It was 1973 and the annual restaurant convention was at the Savery. Our President was Francis Kapler. He had Henry's Drive-ins. Had a sing-a-long with words on the screen. I was really into it with a buddy. Isn't this great? Yeah, but evidently we're the only two that think so. Rest have gone to eat.

This year was Kelly and LaVerne's 25th wedding anniversary. Of course The Little Flower and I had to help them celebrate. It was snowing and blowing and off we took. At Dungey's at New Hampton 25 miles away decided the weather was too bad. We really didn't have any trouble. Started off with an anniversary Mass. You would have been amazed at the nice things Monsignors said about Kelly. I've known Kelly for years, but really didn't know anything nice about him. Big crowd coming and going all to the K.C. Hall for dinner and dance also lost count the number of Priests. Kelly stuck a pack of cigarettes in my pocket. Never did really smoke and I never bought, but would bum. Kelly said he didn't want me bumming from his guests and relatives. Kelly and LaVerne had a world of wealth in friends.

Our January convention was at the Adventureland Motel. They had quite a nice area to dine and also the pool was in the area. It might have been too close. We had a couple in the pool with clothes on.

First started the article in Appetizer in April 1972, so I was just getting started. Pete Canakes had taken over as Executive Secretary and he thought I was too windy. Took up too much space. Went to President Kapler for permission to continue the Appetizer column. Kappy said I can sum up your column with one word—Bologna (sometimes spelled baloney). Keep it up! It's great!

The Spain trip was great. There were 10 A & W operators along. The Little Flower had mastered a little Spanish. I had one word—Cerveza. Arriving at the hotel my first order was a Cerveza. Of course the waiter didn't understand. Finally he said—bet you mean a bottle of beer?

Our national convention was at the Fairmont in Dallas. We took Father Burns along mostly to cover my tracks. I went in a week early to help set up. Finished up on Saturday and caught the plane home on Sunday. We were just a block from the Cathedral and we could catch the 9:00 Mass. We thought Father could take a holiday and listen to another. There was about 30 of us waiting for the church to open and a nun came. This Mass was changed to 10:30. Most of us had a plane to catch at that time. Father Burns went back to the hotel for his Mass kit. There was a couple of Texas oil men waiting and they were impressed. I know you people are big, but we carry our Priest along just to take care of our needs.

Had a letter from Stub Johnson with an ad for the Appetizer: Considering our energy crisis, I will lease or loan horses or reasonable facsimilies of such and equipment and tack all in good condition—no older than I am. They have been with us for some time so want assurance they are going to a good home. Most are smooth mouth and moon eyes (the corn and hay should be ground. The Hobart Chopper does a nice job). Send inquiries to: Stub with Horses, Spencer.

Hats off to Mable Miller, one of our greats in the restaurant industry and only lady President of the restaurant association.

I use Father Burns from time to time to pan in the Appetizer. He got hold of a copy the other day and looks like I'm headed for the bad place.

Coffee Day for the Retarded promotion from the I.R.A. and this year I'm President. Have worked it for years. Good cause and something the industry will gain respect.

About the Spain trip, it was great. We traveled around with Gerry and Sue Adams (Creston). There were 10 A & W ops and we rented the little Fiat sedans. There were five Fiats traveling Spain. The hotel had a fully grown lion on a chain in the yard. They got it as a pup and it was real tame and the people played with it but I'm not really to fond of cats so it wasn't on my play itinerary. We had 249 on our Spain trip. Filing through the gate of customs the Spanish official announced 251. Probably a couple of beverage association guys trying to smuggle a couple of the flamenco dancers aboard. Our hotel was real nice and new. Just built last year. Spain was beautiful—mucho mountains. No radio or T.V. in the rooms. Wouldn't be able to understand anyway. Three significant things: Their toilet paper would sell very well in our market as fine sandpaper, toothpicks were non-existent and you had to buy the matches and they were hard to find.

We did get up to Kelly's 25th anniversary. I never knew anything nice about Kelly. LaVerne—yes. Went to their anniversary Mass and the Monsignor actually spread it on with flattery. Kelly must have paid him pretty good.

Larry came through the A & W decked out for the sports dance and mostly in my clothes. Why didn't he ask me?

How about Hank Aaron and his home runs. Now on my big people list with Babe Ruth, F. D. Roosevelt, Joe Louis and Mel Ott. Babe was finishing up his career when I was learning to read. Hank has been around 21 years and I didn't even know who he was until last year.

It's Italy next January. The Little Flower and I already have that on the schedule. Dorene will tutor me in Italian. Maybe Jimmy Lacona (Noah's Ark in Des Moines) can fit me with a new name. McConnell doesn't fit.

In 1967 Nebraska Concession opened the Des Moines warehouse which makes it super for us. Used to call in the order. Maybe it was raining or snowing and it was always beautiful on this end. It took her a year to figure out I might be stretching the truth a little.

# 20

## *1974*

It is 1974 and our N.A.C. meeting was held in conjunction with the National Restaurant Show. Biggest restaurant show in the world. It takes about two days to visit all the booths. The set up is at McCormick Place, a complex for conventions and shows on the outer drive south.

Dorene and I got out to visit the north and west—Humboldt, Webster City and Clarion. Caught Forest City and then to Ottumwa and Mt. Pleasant then back to Oskaloosa. All of these units have been remodeled or gone to Phase II. Between 1960's and 1970's of A & W years were probably the very best.

Jean Barnhill pretty much turned her new A & W into a restaurant serving breakfast then into lunch and dinner with mashed potatoes and gravy plus homemade pie. Dorene and I have been that route. We left a full service restaurant to this limited menu fast food. The money is better and work is less. You can't altogether let your customers run your unit. You have to use a little common sense.

At this time Indianola Hot Air Balloons is going full bore and Father Burns is in his glory. The Great Root Bear was also a big feature. First the company had one we would rent. Then six of us from this area bought one and then eventually everyone bought and had their own. I'm not sure where it is at this date (2004). Can you imagine the Bear holding a six week old baby while grandpa snaps a picture? Had to put this in. Kelly was having the 25th anniversary celebration and had the Bear for a little publicity. A little problem—some of the guests mistook the Bear for Kelly's brother.

Tim is 12 and he was doing an extended telephone call. I inquired what it was about. Just talking to some girls. You're too young to be fooling around with girls. We're not fooling around with them, Dad. We're just sitting with them at the show. I told that as toastmaster at our Iowa Convention. I was eating breakfast on a Saturday morning and the gang was watching cartoons and Tim says—Don't say anything while Dad is around or he'll get up in front of a whole bunch of people and tell it.

Really was a great time when the kids were growing up. We'll say this again. Somebody asked Larry—Larry, it had to be fun growing up with your dad. Larry just said—Well ... I was really a tough guy. The boys do everything that boys do—sports, hunt, fish. We had pheasant and quail in November, rabbit through the winter, fresh fish in April and then came the best of all—mushrooms. They haven't brought anything like wild hickory nuts yet.

Went for an ice cube in the refrigerator last night. They were all grape. Doesn't go too good with a warm glass of beer.

We're like dyed in the wool Democrats and found out the other day Father Burns is a registered Republican. I said—Father, I'll say a prayer for you.

Next year it's going to be a trip to Italy. If we're going to Italy I will have to learn a little Italian. Don't think Cerveza will work. Jimmy Lacona was commissioned to get me an Italian name. In a ceremony (wouldn't let them crash that good bottle of wine) my spaghetti name is now Gibba Maconelli.

Now is the Des Moines summer festival of Opera at Simpson Blank Performing Arts Center. We gave money from the A & W and should really make an appearance. Dorene wouldn't go with me. Afraid I would embarrass her so I took Sandy. Rather this wouldn't get around, but I went to sleep in the first act. Woke up before the lights went on at intermission so there wasn't too many knew. Stayed awake through the second and third and enjoyed but really think I'll stick with Guy Lombardo.

It's time for the National Hot Air Balloon Championship. Pilot, Father Burns, with our A & W balloon took our Governor up for the first flight. It was a little windy, but Father corrected that. We use the guy for a lot of things.

Hope to break ground for our new A & W Phase II. Took a side trip with the contractor down to Mt. Pleasant to check out his just opened new unit. Coming back we were stopped by a patrolman. Clocked at 59 and he proceeded to give us a warning ticket. As he left he said, "May Hiram guide you safely down the highway." I said to Gerry—Who is this Hiram? He gave me the Mason-Shriner business and I said—We got Hiram and St. Christopher riding with us and if they don't get into a fight we ought to make it. Was watching the Shriners North-South High School football game and a little Catholic girl was crowned queen.

November 1974: Our new A & W to be has broken ground. Have to be going at the start of next season. October 1974: Held the A & W Iowa Association social at Babe's in connection with the Restaurant Association Convention. Most of the people call me the Italian in the family instead of Dorene. We're getting ready for the trip to Italy. Found out some of our V.I.P's were using stuff to take or cover the gray head. Got a bottle two weeks ago and it's not working. Then my scalp started breaking out and did away with the miracle bottle.

Back to the Iowa Restaurant Convention. Pete is back and he got the grand welcome. Betty Ahrens in the office and Stub Johnson (Spencer) and Ed Kotz (Clear Lake) and all the funny looking guys with beautiful wives. Think of Babe's from the WW II days. W.A.C.s had induction training at Fort Des Moines. Babe's was the W.A.C. downtown headquarters and it was truly a jumper. Any serviceman on leave made it their headquarters too.

# 21

## *Rome*

January 1975: I've said it 100 times already, but our life centers around family, A & W ops and the Restaurant Association. This year our early itinerary is: January 13–17 A & W Convention at Las Vegas, January 22–30 trip to Rome and finish with Iowa A & W Convention at Adventureland. Curt and Florence Jante: Curt is President of the Iowa A & W Association this year. The board had a meeting at his farm home. Would you believe he had about 50 muskrats in his basement that he had trapped.

The new A & W is coming along. Deb Stevens (Keokuk) gave me a squeezing rock. It's getting a lot of use and may not see me through. Asked Deb to send me another just in case. Deb is a Laplander and is a little different. Keokuk is Ke-kuk.

Ed Weber has resigned from A & W. Was with us about five years and one of our better ones. I was President of the Iowa Association in 1968. Had our convention at Johnny & Kay's in January 1974 and I was leading the program at our banquet. I got up and started taking off my shirt & coat. Everybody, including Mr. Weber, got excited. Is this a stripper? I had on a balloon T-shirt and wanted to let them know about our balloon fest.

Our Las Vegas convention in January 1975 was the family's first shot at Vegas. We took Tim and Larry and also Father Burns. Father was in a sports jacket and the security guard asked Tim if that was his dad. No, my Father.

Back to the Iowa Convention. At our Monday night cocktail party we had a Calcutta. Can't really explain it but everybody gets too much champagne. The next night at our banquet we had Beanie Cooper for our speaker. Beanie was the very successful football coach at Sioux City Heelan. He had us all laughing in the aisles. Our new Corporate President is Mr. Berkley and I should mention Bill Capehart our regional A & W man and basically from Missouri. Forgot to mention the Vegas convention beat the attendance at Disney World by 100. There were 1,430 at our banquet. Can't seem to remember everything in the proper sequence, but Father Burns had the A & W balloon up on Sunday night at Adventureland.

About got Berkley broke in and in jumps Jim Lynch as our President. So many different heads and staffing of people under them led to many problems for the operators. Our state association and state conventions were the envy of most of our neighbors. Had at our conventions members from Nebraska, South Dakota, North Dakota, Minnesota, Illinois and Missouri. At this time we also had a summer social. It was a break in the busy summer for a nice dinner out.

Yes, I do get mixed up. (I doubt if that gets much better.) Have been thinking we first opened the new unit on May 15, 1975. From the newsletter it happened March 12$^{th}$. From the Iowa Beef Queen: Cows are cuddly. From #3 Tim: Anyone caught stealing good money from the company will be prosecuted to the fullest extent of the law. He's a money collector. Another from #3 Tim: Mom, you know those two things I sleep between on my bed? You mean sheets? Yeah, they are really soft this time. Don't ever change them.

Tony Prochello, our guardian angel, put together a trip to Italy for the operators (we were wannabe Italians) in January 1975. Of course I had to be Italian. We were in Rome which is a little south of center. I just didn't measure up. Looked the part (one native asked if I was Sicilian). The size is right (they are little people) and talking with my hands is natural, but the dialect blew me completely out of the water. The Jim Ackerman's (Starlite Village, Fort Dodge) brought along Monsignor Tolan. He will be remembered as the benefactor of athletes for many years at Fort Dodge. Don't really believe the guy could keep the Big Plane riding the clouds, but sure if it did go down he could speed up the transition.

We took the train from Rome to Bussoleno (500 miles). The last of Dorene's mother's sisters and there were a lot of cousins on her dad's side. The auntie was 90 years old and just a sweetheart. A school teacher daughter lived with her. The auntie took a liking to me and thought I should have a glass of fresh squeezed orange juice before I went to bed. I don't really care for orange juice, but I drank it right down. Best in the world. Dorene speaks enough of the dialect to get along and the three of them were chattering like at the chipmunk convention. Of course in Rome we had an audience with the Pope. Us and 5,000 others in an auditorium. He came down the main aisle on his chair and stopped right beside to the salute of the army choir. Last line from Italy from Auntie when we were getting acquainted with me using hand signals she said, "I like him. He's simple." Dorene agreed with that.

By May of 1975 really enjoying the new A & W News Dispenser. Les leaves (KFC and Dinner Bell). He just got married. His first wife had passed away. Les is a big guy and I'm a small guy. Has its advantages. You're a little dummy sounds better than you're a big dummy.

Another item from Italy came up. Larry came along and asked if he might cramp our style. First day we introduced ourselves to a couple—Okay, you're Larry's folks. This happened about three times and then: Hi, we're Larry's folks. Larry got acquainted with a Jesuit Priest from California studying in Rome. A light complexioned red head and a first generation Sicilian. He gave us a great whirlwind tour and was standing on the steps of one of those beautiful Catholic churches 40 steps up. Have hardly any fat people here. Probably running up and down the mountains and all those steps. We saw a tank truck stop in front of a house and run a hose into the basement. Asked a Priest—Fuel oil? No, wine. You actually use that much sacristy wine? No, we drink it. Water is for washing and wine is for drinking.

Back home and at Mass was listed in the bulletin for a Lector next week under Big McConnell. Jimmy Lacona—does that have anything to do with Italia and the family? At Sunday Mass in Bussoleno in a small church (our St. Thomas could fit inside with plenty room to spare), a little older lady with a game leg was hobbling around for the collection. Is that women's lib gone overboard. Next year there is a Caribbean cruise on the docket.

With the new A & W (1975) we put in a computer for order taking, in fact two, and also a time clock. That was the best move of the century. With the new unit we were up 41%. Maybe it was worth the $130,000. Dorene is making strawberry pie plus a cream pie and they are going like gangbusters.

Coming back from Italia we stopped for 30 minutes at Shannon, Ireland airport and got off the plane to maybe get a little Irish conversation. First tried a big Irish cop. Three grunts. Met a little fellow with conversation named Mike Sweeney (spelling)—gotta check on this Gaelic.

Back to our state convention. Our current President James Lynch is pretty much gung-ho and ready to go, maybe a little too much for our sleepy organization. He actually was born in Valley Junction. He came to our meeting alone. Usually there are a half dozen company reps along. Dutch Strootman and Del Stevens were complaining they were so busy it wasn't fun anymore. Never had that trouble myself. When we were busy and making money, I could go on forever. Back to Father Albers. When I was trying to marry one of his favorite parishioners, he looked at me one night and said Gib—What do you think of the most of—God or the almighty dollar? Don't answer that!!

Had a note from Gary Leiran (Decorah). They were having their Octoberfest with a visit from Gustav VI. Not sure but think it's some kind of beer drinking expo. Irish and I are putting together a song and dance routine. We call it the Irish jig. We're already booked into Emmetsburg for St. Pat's. About this time everybody is getting uptight about A & W Corporate marketing canned and bottled A & W root beer.

Got into trouble with the Decorah thing. It was King Olaf visiting for the Nordic fest. Right now I'm trying to get back in favor with the Nordics. St. Pat is the only saint we can get through to and I'm not sure he is Irish. Our Lutheran minister is second generation Norwegian and a good buddy of mine. Not sure if that is good or bad.

The annual Restaurant Association Convention is coming up at the Savery on November 3, 4 and 5$^{th}$. Monday the third is set aside for the drive-ins and we have a good program lined up. Hormel will present the Ground Beef Story: Product & Profit and that kinda tells the story.

This year a father's dream has been fulfilled. #2 son Larry has made it as a carney. He worked a concession spot at the Iowa State Fair like a veteran. He put together a new root beer trailer this year and it worked.

What a nice write up in the Big Paper about one of my favorite people Mabel Miller. Mabel is a great one and the only lady President of the Iowa Restaurant Association. Hotel Manning and Restaurant was named to the National Register of Historic Places.

1974: Right now we're getting excited about the Caribbean cruise. These ventures in January are great. We are taking Tim and Larry (they are loose) and other operators bring their families along. Tony Gaetano (Tony's Little Italy in Ames) is bringing his 12 year old daughter along (about Tim's age).

I am the Executive Vice President of Gib's A & W (Little Flower is President) and I have a lot of decisions to make. Every morning at 7:00 I shake myself out of bed 5 ½ steps to the bathroom and shower, shave and then comes the big decisions. Brylcream, Arrid and aftershave. What goes where, why and first. About once a week it goes on backwards. Any of you other executives have big decision problems?

One of the greatest personalities baseball has ever known passed away last month.

Had a letter from Stub Johnson. Two young guys from Spencer have enrolled at Simpson College. Send a commission check every month. Yes, Stub, I'll put that check in the mail. Have to start getting ready for the cruise.

Part of Lowell Sharp's gang from Creston (Falstaff Distributor) stopped in the other day. We spent an hour laughing about the fun we had on the trip last year.

Went lame last month. The flat feet I've had for 53 years riled up. Got some built up shoes and back on the go. They say the way to tell a true Irishman is check the feet. All Irishman have flat feet. Think how tall Kelly would have been with regular feet. News: Gerry and Sue Adams had a new baby in November, a girl (no other particulars). A very Merry Christmas is in order.

In 1975 with the new unit revenue was up 41% over the year before. The total we estimated at $75,000 with extras that we added finished up at $175,000 cost but believe it was worth it. A first class place to do business. Time for New Year's resolutions: 1) Change name to Gibba Maconelli. Be the bigger guy and join the family. 2) Learn a new word every month. For this month—differendum. (Rhonda's note to Gib-I don't think that's a real word) Don't know what it means but a nice big one. 3) Go to the State Restaurant Convention. 4) Say nice things about everybody: Ed Kotz (Clear Lake-Barrel Drive In), Stub Johnson (Ranch Kitchen & House of Plenty-Spencer), Irish Kelly (A & W-Waukon). We'll send a Peace With Love every month.

The other day I was helping The Little Flower clean chicken and in a real bad mood. The fellow came in with our hamburger. I started hollering at him and then feeling ashamed ducked out. The guy said to The Little Flower—Is that some kind of Italian? Yeah, he's some kind of Italian.

Tim got the flu at school. The nurse called at 12:00. Could we come get him? Tim came up with—They'll murder me for calling at noon!

Next comes the cruise on the Mardi Gras in the Caribbean. Not sure what they do on a cruise, but whatever it is you can be sure I'll be doing a lot of it. Missed the National A & W Convention, the second ever. It was 1960 and we were real close to a new baby.

# 22

## *The Bicentennial Year*

February 1976: Gibba Maconelli is my name and glad to get out of the minority group (Irish). The frames of my glasses were getting a little wobbly and the seeing was a little erratic. So, I went to the eye man. New metal rims. #3 Tim says—Are you trying to be a groovy dude? Most of us Italians are groovy dudes.

Went to Sandy's last performance with the concert band at Coe College. Four years at Coe and we finally made one of her performances. Of course it was great and a choral group in between. One girl and a mallet (percussion) hit the bells three times in a whole number. Would say she is eligible for unemployment.

Father Burns and his strippers are all done with the pews and they are beautiful. This line was in last week's bulletin: "Please dust off sitters before depositing same on our newly refinished pews." Not sure what response he got that time.

The farmers had a very good 1975 and as the farmer goes so goes the nation. The Caribbean cruise was super great. The word was don't wash your face and hands so that the tan will last till spring. For the ladies a feather duster will keep the face presentable and the men a worn out razor blade for shaving will help.

Don Manning of Club Café and Catering of Le Mars rode the ship during WW II. At that time it was Empress of Canada and a troop ship between Canada and Algeria. Had Larry and Tim along and we had a great time.

At this time Bob and Leona McGurk had the Motel and Supper Club, Iowa City. They were the very best in every respect and we had a lot of our meetings and shows there.

Had our little A & W state convention held every year (about 200 people). At this time there were about 100 operators and we had a fair attendance from our neighboring operators. Finished up with a banquet and speaker. This year it was Beanie Cooper. He was the football coach at Sioux City Heelan and a whole family of solid Catlics. The words of Beanie—start and finish everything with a smile.

Had a promoter come in off the road with a coupon book. The greatest promotion in the world. Of course I bought it hook, line and sinker. It turned out as a monster with him sucking up all the money and leaving town. I was up in arms and got my picture in the paper. Neoma said I looked like the Pope. Is that good or bad?

The N.A.C. comes into the picture. Big corporate is getting a little iffy and trying to take away some of our rights. Dick Christensen, our A & W Representative, is doing a great job fighting back. Break in to add the Ames A & W float came in first in the Viesha parade.

Our new President Jim Lynch is sitting on our 1% advertising money and the canned and bottled thing is in the middle. Jim Lynch is making our little company (or trying to) into more canned and bottled. More money can be made easier in canned and bottled. Thank our lucky stars for the N.A.C. and Dick. On a little less serious note, Dorene looked at my head and the thin spots and said, "I believe one more tube of Brylcream will do you."

Our operator in east Des Moines that I really didn't think would make roll call the second year opened their new Beta 60 and are going like gangbusters. Dick and Lynne are super and we're lucky to have them.

From the Restaurant News—Fish-n-chips had the hottest growth last year and Mexican was second. Might be something to think about.

The Bicentennial Wagon Train stopped in our town over the weekend (April 2, 3, 4). The wagon train started in Washington State last June and hopes to be in Philadelphia July 3rd. Got the information from a 12 year old girl that hooked up with the train last December and has her school books along.

Yes, we did the Caribbean cruise. Down to breakfast the second morning Tim said, "Well, I did it again. On my head this time." Tim slept in the top bunk over Larry and that first step was a long one.

First stop was a nice peaceful little island. The cruise as a whole was peaceful. Dorene was enjoying the sun. I was watching, visiting and found a few drinking partners. Do you remember reading about the Farmer Millionaire-Iowa Style? It was written about Grundy Center and also mentioned Jim's Jolly Popcorn. Jim and his family were on the cruise. In fact, it was Jim's little guy that was breaking all the clay pigeons in skeet. The whole trip was beautiful and the people were the greatest. About 1,200 on the ship and about the second day we knew most. Sat down by Jerry Sullivan (first generation Irishman from Sioux City). Did we exchange a bunch of lies. Back at Des Moines in the airport and spoke with two young ladies from Dubuque that were on the trip. Did you have a good time?

One's eyes lit up—Yes, and he's coming to see me in April! Don't really know which and didn't ask.

The problems with Corporate are heating up. Dick Christensen and our N.A.C. contract is keeping us in the ballgame. They want control of the 1% money for advertising and do away with the N.A.C. It won't happen in either case. Our problem is the corporation changing owners and they automatically think they should control what they own. We just get a President broke in and they change. The Bear came in and is one of our best items and relates to root beer.

Hot news—Steve and Laurie Waskow of Independence had twins. Laurie did the work and Steve did the stewing plus the bragging.

Father Burns and the hot air balloons are heating up. He and the Bear did Iowa Falls on June the 27th. Clear Lake is hosting our summer social this year. Super outing for us South people on dry land.

Another line: There are many ways to smile, try one today.

National Convention time in Chicago. Can't go but Bobby Crouse was to bring back a report. Two pages of night life and four lines about the show.

Clear Lake Summer Social: Had 30 for dinner. Les Davis and Roe Roof did the catering. Had all the water things like boats, skiing, swimming and sunning. Had three young guys, two from Eagle Grove and one from Hampton, see a group of girls around the corner and they were gone like a flash. Even did a little volleyball with J.C. Glover no less.

Father Burns wins the Minneapolis Balloon event. The guy takes everything too serious. A serious sky worker and balloons are one of his lines. At one time this year we had 230 registered and 183 airborne at one time over Indianola.

Our restaurant association summer outing this year was at the Amanas. #3 Tim and I got in on the second day. We took the village tour. Tim hadn't been before. Said "Hi" to my buddy at the Ronnenberg—Bill Oehler. Sampled the wine, bought the bread and summer sausage. Oohed and aahed at the $3,000. grandfather clocks. Had a nice visit with Carl Oehl. They have the Colony Market Place, Colony Kitchen Foods and horseradish that you see in the market. Carl had redone an old slaughter house, cellar and smoke room. Even had an authentic wishing well. Even took some of Tim's money. Results? Didn't ask. Carl and Bill were along on the cruise last winter.

Bicentennial Birthday party at Bussey 4th of July. Tim took it in. Came back with more money than he took—sold some firecrackers. Smile is the same in any language. Use it wherever you are. Think I have written it before. The kids were selling firecrackers out of our little garage and I never did catch on. At this time it was our warehouse in the summertime and they would bring down the supplies in the little red wagon. We never really locked up anything. A lot of our supplies were out by the back door. Another happening on that 4th of July was I dropped a CO2 tank on my big toe. I said "Glory Halleluiah" among other things. Went to the A & W meeting with one shoe, one slipper. Now the toe is well and have a pair of slippers to sell—one hardly used.

Another line from Bobby Crouse and the big convention in Chicago: One night we made it to Rush Street. We were leaving this joint and the lady said, Bobby, see you around. Yes, I'm sure. He made a few impressions.

Spent many years writing in the Appetizer. Always good copy from Stub Johnson, Spencer (NW), and Irish Kelly, Waukon (NE). In August Stub comes in with—The horses are in good shape and the threshing machine is all greased up. Kelly sent a report on the deer population. Guys, this is a food magazine and I can't really handle the stuff not related.

Iowa Association is going good. Raised the dues to $70.00 from $50.00. Held our meetings in conjunction with the Restaurant Association Convention at the Savery. Big trouble with A & W Corporate at this time. They have the advertising money tied up. I say this about every page: The N.A.C. was the best thing that every happened to us.

Hot news—Irish Kelly has sold out. I'm in a state of shock plus depressed. I'm advertising for a new N.E. correspondent. No qualifications needed. Kelly didn't have any. Back to the Convention. Dick W. arranged the social and group—Beautiful Beat. In fact, my head had that beautiful beat for days.

Did the drinks (root beer and lemonade) for then Governor Carter when he was on the campaign trail. Known as the peanut man. It was peanuts and lemonade and root beer. At least I didn't have to pay for the peanuts. It was in a pasture at Scotch Ridge.

I'm a little mixed up but think 1976 was the first year for Larry at the State Fair. It was always my wish from day one. I didn't want to be President of the United States. I wanted to be a full fledged Carney—a Pitch Man at the State Fair and, of course, have a stand at the Iowa State Fair. I didn't make it, but did get number #2 son Larry at the high pinnacle.

In trouble with Father Burns. Was to be Lector at 8:00 Mass and overslept so now I'm back on probation. Back to our Carter party. Father is mostly Republican, but he did help carry water for the Carter party. Rio is the next big event. In between is the I.R.A. Convention. Took #3 Tim and a couple of girls to the banquet. The ballroom was full of like Who's Who's in America. I had the navy pinstripe suit with the vest. Always wanted a pinstriped suit and this is the year. The clerk said, "Blow up the hair on top of your head and you'll pass for Godfather #1." Don't believe those eight hairs would cause that much of a rumble. A wide brim felt hat could make me an Irish-Italian.

Jim Huss, Iowa State Extension Service, came in to be our guide in the business. Jim was a welcomed helper plus knowledgeable. He was a past Bolton & Hay manager plus operating his own unit on the west coast. About this time soy flour was coming into the market and Jim was giving us the pros and cons. Keith Johnson (Executive Director of Iowa Beef Council) had already given us all the cons. Stan Dollemore came on with the A & W—N.A.C. story. Stan was an executive from the N.A.C. and helper with the A & W battle (or bottle???). Finished with the 1 ¼" pork chop for dinner and then Ted Weems and his band for dancing and playing the Golden Oldies. Dick Christensen made the remark in his letter: The Democrats are in now and we can all go on welfare. (What's that?)

#3 Tim's teacher called to see if I could speak to the restaurant group for career days at the college. I could do it if you can't get anybody else. Already tried everybody else. Get a lot of work that way.

Lynn Schlutz was elected Iowa Beef Queen—daughter of Bob & Marilyn. Bob is head of about everything in our world—Board of Directors of Iowa Restaurant Association. Had a number of K.F.C.'s and also Happy Joe's. Bob and Marilyn are for real. Had a question about spelling of his last name—it's "lu" instead of "ul." Never got the reason.

Sandy is out of college interviewing for her first job. How'd it go? Sure wasn't impressed with one place. Two fellows owned the business and they were both old as you, Dad.

Jim Ackerman was elected President of the Association and they had along Monsignor Tolan. Monsignor was and is a great Priest. His biggest go is working with schools kids and athletes, etc. Had a great gang at this time. Mabel Miller, Keosauqua, Stub & Vi Johnson, Spencer. We had the spread in the Sunday Register about Stub and the Chuck Wagon Races at the Clay County Fair. They call Stub the "Marlboro Man from Spencer." A good year and the Cincinnati Reds beat the Yankees in the World Series and we won the Big Election plus I got the peanut franchise for all of Warren County. Next it's fun and sun in Rio.

N.A.C. and A & W advertising and Jeff Rogers comes into the picture. He was supposed to be working for us, but actually working both sides of the street. Working only for the money. Canned and bottled added to the turmoil. That actually gets out on the shelves and in the homes. Adds up to the same. Tap beer at the bar or homemade chili—us against commercial. Plus—get ready for Rio and Portuguese.

# 23

## *Rio de Janeiro*

Our state convention and #2 got into the act taking tickets, etc. We had the 20 day Rio trip and back home the Las Vegas Convention was starting. The Marshalltown Moores and us were traveling together. Marge and Dorene were down, but Dick and I were ready to go. Actually, our reservations for room and show were already made. Dick and I made quite a stir like we were hooking up with the show girls. It didn't happen but most thought it did and that was the idea. Beth, Dick's Ames Manager, reported he was sick on the way home from drinking the water. I certainly didn't drink any water. The people went to Rio with a couple of suitcases full of money and came back with the cases empty and fingers full of rocks. Myron and Laura were showing off the big stones. The market was supposed to be the best and cheapest. The Little Flower and I didn't partake. Dorene is allergic to any metal and I'm too tight. Rio was probably our best trip ever. Best bunch of people to travel with. Big, beautiful hotels fronting the most beautiful beach in the world. Right behind the hotels was the worst poverty you have ever seen.

Sandy is out of college. Her first job was with an accounting firm in Des Moines. She came to me with—Dad, do you know Ike Harris? Yes, St. Louis Card's Football. She had one on me. Three of them were doing an audit of a firm in Des Moines. Ike was big and Black. Sandy pint sized and running the job was an Oriental. You couldn't really say that job was overloaded. All American 6' white males.

In my frail mind Rio keeps popping up. The Airline Varig-Brazilian was the very best in every respect. There was a little trouble getting our rooms at the hotel. They had oversold as most do if they get the chance. Finally got a key. It was a meeting room with no furniture. As we had waited we were entertained by Bill & Anne, Tavern in Bridgewater, plus Lowell and Betty Sharpe, Midwest Beer Distributor in Creston. Everything in Rio was pretty much Portuguese. I had two words "Brahma Choop." Suppose to mean a glass of beer, but that didn't hold true at this juncture. Back to the room. A call to the front desk got a maid with two folding cots. Another call netted three straight chairs. Again the call—"If you're not happy with that room, we'll assign you to another." This time we hit pay dirt—a beautiful room. Had a lot of funny things in my travels, but that beat all.

For Sunday Mass we had our own Monsignor Tolan and Father Jang (Breda). It probably took two priests to cover the tracks of the 69 wild Iowans loose in Rio. We did have a good time on these trips and made a lot of solid friends. Who in the world could be better than a restaurant-beverage operator? Jack and Gen McNeil of Valhalla Supper Club, Clermont—Jack is about 2/3 Irish, but that shouldn't be held against him. Stub and Vi Johnson, Spencer—these people could be called top Iowa characters. They have agreed to send news for the Appetizer column.

Another bit from Rio: Our good neighbor to the south—Osceola Best Western and Byers Restaurant and their two daughters. One of the daughters met an old schoolmate she hadn't seen in five years. Lorraine Gracey writes for the New York Times and also in Rio on vacation. Plus I got to meet a real journalist. Don't get any bigger than that.

Dick's report in the newsletter: Corporate and the operators' conflict is pretty much coming to a head. A & W Corporate is bound to take our advertising money and run with it. Dick and the N.A.C. is still doing a good job. Right now this tussle with Corporate is taking up time that should be used to create business.

Another sidelight (more sidelight than actual meat): Dick graduated from Hayfield High School. That sounds like selling the Brooklyn Bridge to the man on the street. There can't possibly be a Hayfield High School. Looked it up—the school is now Garner-Hayfield. Dick's dad still has the farm up there. Dick and Peg were automatically crowned National Couple of the Year representing Iowa. At the banquet I was presented a trophy for my dedication to the newsletter. I graduated from Bussey High School. Everybody has heard of Bussey. It's the capital of Marion County.

Our summer outing will be at Clear Lake South Park. Our unit plus five other units bought a bear costume. The state should have at least three. That, today, is one of our biggest promotions. It really creates quite a stir at your unit. The little guys with the Bear—some kissing and some crying.

That Monsignor Tolan never fails to amaze me. This year at our state basketball tournament he was in the center of the floor passing out trophies.

Another item from Rio—Races (horse) are held year around on Sundays and holidays. We were there on a holiday and everybody was going to the races. The Private Club was letting in dignitaries (visiting) for free. That's us. Would you believe about three of us with shorts weren't allowed in—Lowell Sharpe, Dick Moore and I. We had to sit with the peons in the grandstand. It was probably more fun any way. We went to the window for betting. The money in Rio was really deflated—about 15 to 1 American. Of course I won in the 7$^{th}$ race. A stack of Argentine money about three inches high. So right way I'm buying the house. It didn't take long to spend the big pile. About two rounds and it was gone.

We took a trip sight seeing out in the country. It was beautiful, but too much poverty. We stopped at a roadside banana stand and I hopped out and bought a stalk of bananas and passed them out to everybody on the bus. Of course, the story goes I bought the banana concession and was trying to make enough money to cover my expenses.

Seems to be a lot of new franchises and independents starting. That happens when the economy is too good. The Restaurant Association is planning another trip—Octoberfest in Austria. They know how to do Fest—rates right up with the Irish and St. Pat's.

Read in the Big Paper other day—flat feet can be helped with ballet lessons. Dorene and Vi got together and enrolled Stub and I. From Vi and Dorene—they are both flat footed and clumsy and maybe ballet lessons would help. Will hit on Mr. Pete to let us perform at the convention.

The N.A.C./Corporate thing is healing up. It's for us older operators to follow new rules. We've been independent too long. The fight is on. Canned and bottled is coming in. We're trying to get a stipend for each case put out plus absolutely not allow fountain syrup-post mix. We did get the post mix stopped for now. This, again, is where our State Association comes in. We are organized as one and do have respect.

Back to advertising. The Bear Straw was probably one of our biggest promotions of all time and bringing it back. Then this summer the Bear Glass and Pitcher comes in. That has to be a winner.

The family is coming along. Pat isn't interested in books too much. Girls and hunting (not girl hunting—gun hunting). Sandy is school (books) and music (saxophone). Larry is pretty much all athletics. Tim is maybe a problem. School books not too popular. Athletics doesn't seem to be his bag. Couldn't make the second team of the B squad. Then the 9$^{th}$ grade class play came along. Tim played Huck Fink in Tom Sawyer and he was enthused, excited, motivated and besides he did a super job in the play. Think he has found his calling.

Things are going good with the business. Dick and the N.A.C. are doing a good job. Was up to Garner the other day. His Readerboard read: If the Colonel had our chicken, he would be a General. Russ Nichols was a sharp guy and good operator, but he didn't last long. Published some good lines for the Readerboard in the Newsletter: 1) Miners really dig our food. 2) Lawyers buy our goods by the case. 3) Prospectors dig our Golden Fries. 4) Our hot chocolate will warm your heart. 5) We fry harder. 6) You can get hooked on our fish. 7) A & W—The Wizard of Ahhhhs. 8) Tennis players love our service. 9) January is a Chili month. 10) Keep Iowa Green—Bring money. 11) Our fries sell like hot potatoes. 12) Voters elect to eat here. 13) Live longer—eat here. 14) Eat out—the wife you save may be your own. 15) Customers wanted—experience required. 16) Watering hole for thirsty travelers. 17) Burger Bank—Transfusions Urged. 18) Values for millionaires with little money. 19) Franks for the memory. 20) Our cook gets a day off. Does yours?

Did you know the ice cream soda was first made in Philadelphia in 1874? It's my favorite soda fountain item. Almost as good as an A & W root beer float. An item of interest: I'm getting pretty good with the ballet lessons, but Stub is having a little trouble getting up on his toes.

Had a good time at Clear Lake at the A & W Summer Social. Red Hauser, Mason City, and Doc Dostort, Hampton, had four people in the area with boats giving rides. Verl Harness had a pontoon boat. Some of these people, evidently, have time to play.

Did you catch the article in the Big Paper? Flying Father from Indianola wins the Minneapolis Balloon Event. He's an experienced sky worker and hot air is one of his lines. At our last balloon event Father tethered and gave rides. Keeping Father Burns in the air costs a little money, but believe it is worth it.

Dick Christensen and the N.A.C. are keeping us abreast of Corporate and all their beefs about the N.A.C. Advertising mostly, but everything else is involved. We're very fortunate to have Dick and the N.A.C.

The Little Flower and I didn't make the Restaurant Association Summer Social this year. Had many good reports. Evidently Mr. Pete did pretty good at the card game. Didn't get a special assessment letter.

Had a little squeezing problem this week. I got a tube of Ultra-Brite toothpaste and it's a little hard to squeeze, especially early in the morning. Next comes Brylcream (a little dap will do you) and a real easy squeeze. So I'm all revved up for the Brylcream squeeze and I get a whole handful of cream and my hair is a little scarce like the strip farmer in strips where there's no crop. Ever try to squeeze

Brylcream back into the tube? Roe Roof was badgering me about banana concession in Rio. Think I will send him a tube of Brylcream for Christmas.

Not to brag, but I was named #1 Hot Air Propulsilator at our Balloon Fest. Quite an honor. Bobby Crouse was runner up. Russ Reel (La Pizza House) was inducted into the Softball Hall of Fame. Our Mr. Pete is also in the Hall. Put it in writing—Stub and I are for ISU—Ames at the interstate play off. Got a block of tickets for Wrigley Field and the World Series. Let me know if you would like a seat. Newsworthy: Al Formanek (A & W-Britt) was voted Honorary Hobo King at their fest. Helping the judges' decision was his high school diploma from Hayfield High School.

Dorene and I didn't make the Octoberfest with the Restaurant Association. The convention was in the Veteran's Auditorium for the first time this year (100 booths). Our A & W National Convention is in Hawaii in January and we're planning on it and hope to take along Larry and Tim.

Woody and Mary Diehl came into meet with Dorene and me. President Carter was coming to visit the state and was to stay on the farm at Diehl's. Mary wanted Dorene to come out and fix breakfast for the big occasion. I mean BIG occasion. It was to be bacon, sausage, eggs and coffee. Dorene and the neighbor ladies made fresh rolls. We came sliding into the back door at Diehl's about 6:30 A.M. and there was President Carter sitting at the table. Had it not been raining he would have probably been out looking over the farm. We got the handshake and Dorene and I a picture with the President. I was so awed by this was speechless for five minutes (and that's an all time record). Dorene happened to get a tape of this silence and calls it the most blissful five minutes of her 25 year marriage. It will probably reign as the biggest event of our life. Kinda grew up with Mary Diehl in Bussey. It seems a lot of big people came from Bussey.

A letter from Dick (for the Newsletter) about the settlement. Now maybe we can get back to something constructive. We both won, but we both lost. Now let's all work together and move forward. I would call it a good settlement. Our business is up about 12% so much better than being down. Think we have been up every year since we started in 1956. Plus we are also moving forward with the Association. The Association has been better and done more for the operator than the wildest dreams of me and Jim Duncan.

Did Career Day at Simpson College again this year. Gets a pretty good list of people to work. Tim was Santa Claus at our A & W Christmas party. I did the library thing. Our Santa suit gets a workout.

The Balloons and our National Balloon fest are a part of our community. The natives try to dress like Balloonies and the Balloonies try to dress like natives and a good time is had by all.

The question—What do you do when the computer stops working? I drop to my knees and say three "Our Fathers" and three "Hail Marys" and then into the blankety blankety blank. Works for me. Dorene and I couldn't make the Octoberfest trip, but Deb Stevens brought us six bottles of German Octoberfest beer. Yes, I can see how they get into that polka.

Tony and Pauline Prochello are putting together, Hawaii, Hong Kong and Tokyo. Sounds like a Biggie Goodie and starting to sweet talk The Little Flower right away.

Jim Huss, Iowa State Extension Service, has come in to help us at our meetings, etc. and is really okay. The Convention at the Veteran's Auditorium was awesome. The people remarked about all the open room and one remarked the air is even better. The tobacco smoke usually gets pretty thick.

The visit from President Carter at the Diehl's went super good. President Carter is really good, down home country. He is morally good, honest and sincere. Hope he can hold his own with those thugs in Washington.

Some more lines for Readerboards:

1. Let our restaurant become a family tradition.

2. Don't go by. Come buy.

3. Quiet—hospitable zone

4. Status symbol—quality

5. Haven't we met yet?

6. Friendly service—flavorful food

# 24

## *The Orient*

Now into 1978. The weather was bad and the crops were worse. The farmers are down and will reflect on our next year's business. Dick Christensen has a great Iowa Convention all set—Hawaii Luau. Roast pig with all the trimmings and, of course, it's poolside. Getting all set for the National in Hawaii in January.

Our National A & W Convention is in L.A. with a visit to Disneyland. A good family convention. Disney does everything right. It will be one of our bigger crowds and now to the State Convention in Des Moines.

The Cotton Bowl Parade had Steve Waskow's Independence High School Marching Band. #2 Larry and Beth from Ames were in attendance. Atlanta is also home to the Varsity Drive-in, the largest and oldest in the nation.

Next 15 days is a trip to the Orient. Usually pack an underwear change for every day. The Little Flower right away pops up with—You don't have 15 sets of underwear. There were five A & W operations represented on the Orient trip and we did have much fun. We got back from the Orient for the A & W Iowa Convention. Added thought—We married in 1951. I have never said anything or been serious in my life. Doubt if Dorene ever picks up on that.

Yes, to the Orient. Started in Des Moines at 7:00. Three hours to L.A. then to Tokyo for 4500 miles in 11 hours. It is a completely different world. The first one I stumbled over getting off the plane. Agnes Formanek, Dick's Country Inn-Hayfield. Yes, there is a Hayfield, Iowa and there wasn't anybody from Bussey getting off. Do I count? I was in my glory. They are neat, clean well dressed (most all wear a suit and tie to work) and possibly change to a uniform, but any way they look and are very sharp.

It took two days to catch up on the jet lag business and with my timer it was even tougher. Forty-three of us on the trip. I move pretty fast normally, but these people were like on the run and all business all the time. Beautiful, big hotel. Spent the first two days getting lost. Tokyo has 11 million people in an area not much bigger than Des Moines. Of course, it helps they are smaller. We sat on the plane by Roy and Catherine Isaacs. She was a sweet smaller lady and he was a big guy. Must have looked like a giant to the natives. I would look straight ahead to his belt buckle. Eating: The big thing with the Japanese is raw fish (actually it is a certain kind of fish). If I didn't know, probably would be okay. The food was good but compared to Chinese is a slow second in every category.

The first night we headed for the Land Mark Restaurant and specialized in same all prepared in front of us—rice, vegetables, oysters, etc. Then came the bill. It cost an arm and leg and made me cry (Won't write the price here. Afraid of breaking up). Japan's economy is really booming and everything is very expensive. The exchange rate was $2.40 to one yen.

The second day we headed north. They have two basic religions—Buddhism and Shintoism. They are very similar with beautiful temples made of wood. Some over 300 years old. Would you believe there was four inches of snow, but not really cold. The same breed as our snow and with pigeons that make the same kind of mess as in Iowa.

In February 1978 it was our 11$^{th}$ annual A & W Association Convention. Big snow storm late Sunday night and some didn't get in until Tuesday. It was a Valentine's Day affair and there was a carnation for each lady and bouquet at each table. Dolph Pulliam, Drake's basketball big center on their final four team, was to be our program. He entered the wrong date on his calendar and we're left in a lurch. Dick gave his President acceptance speech and I gave them ten minutes of nonsense and the op's thought they had a program. Next year the National Convention is scheduled for Hawaii on January 3, 4, 5 of 1979.

This is the year #3 got his driver's license. We live across the street from the A & W and Tim is now driving to work.

In the Newsletter, Dick Christensen writes a note from the N.A.C. and a little news: Al and Barb Formanek's daughter Lori was married at Duncan Catholic Bohemian. That, in my book, would be a real wedding. One of Hayfield's most celebrated alums, Peg Christensen, won the free throw contest at Ellsworth Jr. College.

Had a Restaurant Association board meeting. Our President, Virgil Abbe. Griping is a way of life with Virgil. I had breakfast with Virg and his wife. Virg picked up his bill—Too high! What did you have? Mrs. came back with—If you can't afford me, divorce me. Too high—give me another option.

Hardees opened in May 1978. It gets a big play for a month and it settles back down to business as usual. If they run a good operation it brings in a bigger customer base. Hardees is on a good run right now and will shake up our clientele for a while.

More about the Orient. Japanese ladies aren't considered too important—second class citizens. Seiko is the Seth Thomas of Japan. Toyota seems to be the Henry Ford. I still remember Pearl Harbor and it really is hard for me to like anything about Asia. After watching these sharp little people for seven days, I wonder how we won the war. From Kyoto to Hong Kong, had a chance to read the book I had picked up on Japan—"It's Not All Raw Fish." I laughed till the tears ran down my face. The author was Dan Maloney, an executive stationed in Tokyo.

Hong Kong is altogether different. Melting pot of the world. It was Saturday evening and we needed church. The bell captain got us in a cab and to church with no hitch. Mass was in Chinese. Coming back to the hotel from Mass was an experience. It took ten minutes to get through to the cabbie that we wanted to go to the Sheraton. I was in the front seat trying to make small talk and the cabbie slammed on the brakes. Don't know what I said or what he thought I said. It took much arm waving to get him started again and then my lips were sealed.

Hong Kong was controlled by the English with 90% of the population Chinese. It was the melting pot of the world. Every nation was represented in a given time. Across the street from our hotel was the Peninsula Hotel, one of the finest in the world and still the best service. Remember the "Call for Philip Morris" on T.V. and had a lot of those little guys running around. It was another country—don't drink the water. San Miguel beer was very good and helped the liquid problem.

In Hong Kong the thing was to have at least one suit tailor made. I got the suit, two shirts and a pair of shoes. Dorene got a leather coat, suit, purse and shoes. It took three days to have them made. Then we bought a couple Seiko watches and the serious shopping was done.

At the time our A & W Representative was George Johnston. Young and probably needed help for his social life. He brought in his date last week. She had a 40" bust and an I.Q. to match. She thought the Ford Foundation was a new kind of girdle. The Association continues to help the operator often with volume buying. The problem with Corporate hasn't got any better. Our biggest hang up is changing of Presidents. Seems like a new one every year and they all have different ideas.

We're getting tuned up for the Hawaiian trip. The Convention is on January 4, 5, 6th and everybody is figuring at least a two weeks total to do the islands. Hope to take the kids, probably Larry and Tim.

Back to the A & W. We had a coupon mailing for the month of March. Those who used the coupons had a 23% increase, without 3%. Must have worked.

In April Virgil Abbe passed away. He was to be President at the I.R.A. next year. Spring comes—we had dandelion greens, asparagus tips, fresh mushrooms in butter with spaghetti, fresh bullheads from South River and topped off with rhubarb pie and that is the ultimate in eating. #3 Tim went fishing the other Saturday and came back with the exciting story—got 11 bullheads and one was a monster—¾ #!

Leftovers from Hong Kong: Hong Kong is off the tip of China. We toured to the top of a hill and overlooked the river and the Bamboo Curtain, the patrolled entrance to China. Many rice fields north. Water buffalo still used for farm power. Many pens of ducks that must be used for Peking Duck. Quite a few chickens. Rhode Island Reds, but here they are Chinese Reds. Fortune cookies didn't exist. They supposedly originated in San Francisco. The only thing that looked like a Chinese laundry was hanging in my bathroom after 12 days out and that was run by a cute Italian lady.

This is June and boys and firecrackers are synonymous. Haven't found any around, but sure if we have a house fire before the 4$^{th}$ it would sound like the Third World War.

From spring in the Newsletter. Must be summer. My neighbor just returned my bottle of cough medicine I loaned him and borrowed some sun tan lotion. Dick played a round of golf with A & W Representative George Johnston. Dick's word—If his social life is anything like his golf game, I can see why he's in trouble. He once missed a hole in one by only five strokes.

At this time a lot of new operators and change of ownership. We try to get them to the Summer Social which is at Adventureland in July.

Then up comes Sandy and Mike getting married next June. Father Burns wanted the new last name for the church bulletin. I gave it to him—Scia. I had headlined the newsletter: #1 daughter Sandy married a four letter word. Four years and I didn't even know the spelling—Scaia.

Still talking about the Orient trip. Rice is their main crop and a lot of things are made from it. Mats on the floor from rice straw, fine writing paper, rice cracked (served as a snack on our plane). All of the buildings had lower ceilings and risers on the steps a couple inches shorter, chairs smaller and lower to the floor. Yes, this is my kind of people and country, but that Pearl Harbor will never get out of my mind. One of our side trips was to Macao called the Las Vegas of the Orient. Dorene and I aren't too much on gambling, but did notice the trip back to Hong Kong was lighter. That's Mr. Pete's main thing and a few others that win more every time. Wonder if they go to confession regularly?

Our guide was 20 and real sharp. Dad was Portuguese and mother Chinese and he spoke four languages. How did you learn English? Mostly from watching Baretta on T.V. Too bad Dizzy Dean isn't still announcing baseball games. He could learn real English.

On the 14$^{th}$ day we loaded up for the trip home, us by way of San Francisco. We're four hours out in the middle of the ocean plus the movie. Flash of light and a loud KABOOM. This is your Captain. We are experiencing engine difficulty and we are diverting to Honolulu. Everybody was getting a little edgy and I was trying to comfort them. After all, I was a ranking officer during the #2 World War. The Little Flower made me qualify that—made P.F.C. by act of Congress. Three hours and forty-five minutes from Honolulu. Hail Mary. Come in, Father Burns. Full of grace. Come in, Father Burns. The Lord is with you. Where are you, Father Burns, when I need you??? I'll go direct—Give me the Hot Line to the Big Guy in the Sky. Yes, we landed in Honolulu and then on to San Francisco. The story is easier to tell now.

# 25

## *The end of the 70's*

Yes, June 24$^{th}$ was the wedding of Sandy and Mike. It was going to be a bowl of cherries walking this girl down the aisle in the new suit, etc. Started out with the Big Smile and ended all choked up with tears running down my face. Father Burns did his usual fine job and would have to say that was the prettiest bride ever walked down the aisle at St. Thomas. Only one thing—seems like there were a lot of funny looking people on his side. Come to think of it, the same thing at Pat's wedding.

This year Balloon Days were the biggest and best ever plus the B.F.A. voted to make Indianola their permanent home. Father Burns was head of the weather committee and really did a good job. Can he really control the weather? They were only grounded twice in 8 days. It was like Las Vegas. Nobody was getting any sleep, walking around monkey-eyed. Sandy and Mike were down the last two weekends. Is it just loading up on food? They also said they were trading cars. If it is a truck we are really in trouble with the food category.

Bill Capehart is leaving A & W. Think he is the last good guy from the old guard. He was really a dedicated employee. One of the best ever for the operators and also Corporate.

Again I say as in the past, the Newsletter is more of a visiting piece and if I can get one smile it has partly served its purpose. Dick Wilderman is our new President and is getting his letter out even before the first of the month. Don't even have to call and Dick Christensen (N.A.C.) is also super. These are two of our younger and better operators.

Got a call from Dick W. He's been reading so many bad effects of smoking he's decided to quit. He's also going on a diet. Have known Dick since the early 1970's and every meeting he's giving up smoking and starting a new diet. His words—I've read so much about the bad effects of smoking that I'm either going to give up smoking or quit reading.

#2 Larry had the Great Root Bear at the State Fair for three days and I'm sure it did a tremendous public relations job for the whole state.

New competition is the big thing this year. The new guy takes about a month and then the business settles back but growth is harder to come up. The Tuesday Coney dog (29 cents) is up to about 650 and creates traffic. Our insert started on 9/06. It came out in the afternoon and we took in 68 coupons. Thursday, a full day, 115 and the average sale per coupon was $3.00. I consider that pretty good.

#3 Tim and I made it to the State Fair one day. The Toby Show (tent) and Old Shaffner Players. We sat on the front row, hollered and laughed all the way through it. Couldn't be a better place for me than Iowa corn and Indianola Hot Air. Father Burns is being transferred. That is a big blow to us. Who will handle Balloon Days and fly our A & W balloon?

Wow-wow-wow. The Little Flower just came in a Honda Express moped. I can see it now. Next will be the black leather jacket and then the gang (tattoos), etc., etc., etc.

Our State A & W Convention is coming up. Bob Schlutz, fellow Restaurant Board Member and owner of K.F.C. plus a couple of Casey's, will try to explain how computer cash registers can help us in our business units. The high tech is changing and sure that will continue.

Stub and Vi Johnson (Spencer)—House of Plenty and Ranch Kitchen—Stub would be classed #1 on the character list. He and I are exchanging a little work. I went up and pitched bundles for the Old Time Threshing. He's coming down to chase our balloon. With his hot air there will be no trouble getting it in the air.

Just got a note from Agnes Formanek, Dick's Country Inn, Hayfield. Hayfield High School's girls beat Bussey 1 to 0 in state softball. Did she really have to write and tell me that?

It's the eve of Balloon Days. A strategy meeting with Father Burns and the balloon crew. If you place in the top 10, off comes the head. Not really because we have to use that guy for so many things.

This is the year Stub Johnson wanted me to help with the Chuck Wagon Races at the State Fair. I squeezed out of that one. Al Formanek (Britt) was in the Hobo contest and finished last. Anyway, he finished.

Mrs. John Winga Sr. gave me a plaque at our last board meeting. Wingas are celebrating 50 years in business—1928 to 1978.

When my mind is a little vacant I like to think about our time in Rio and the beautiful beaches. Beautiful sand, pretty water, nice breeze and other things. I like to look at the other things best.

I'm using my writing of the monthly Newsletter and columns in the Appetizer to bring my mind back to the happenings. Below is a passage from the Appetizer in November 1978: #2 son Larry (he's the carney) and I took a fast trip to Oklahoma City. That's a long run for one hitch at the wheel. The Oklahoma State Fair was on plus ½ dozen A & W's to check out. Pulled into Oakie City at 3:00 am on Sunday. Had a reservation at a motel and conked out for about six hours. Out of bed and down to the lobby and checking on a church nearest to the fairgrounds. Bell boy has all the information. Turn left on Meridian and follow to Portland. Take another left and follow the bingo signs to St. Pat's. Larry was taking care of all the bills, but I said—I'll take care of the collection plate. It starts coming down the aisle and I pull out the billfold. The smallest was a $10.00. I'm fumbling and the plate is right in front of me and in goes the 10er. Out of the church and I was still sobbing and Larry—Thought you was cracking up.

It was 12:00 and there is going to be 200,000 at the fair. We were following directions and a sign said: Fair—this way to Gate 26. We drove right up to the gate with no traffic and parked within a ½ block. Walked right through the gate with the attendant saying—Good mornin', how you all? Within two hours we had all our fair business finished and visited the A & W's What I'm really trying to say—all of you non-believers that St. Pat was really taking care of us.

So we had the Iowa Restaurant Convention. Big attendance with full house meetings. Had a good representation of A & W's and, of course, we are getting ready for our A & W Convention in February. At this time Dick W. is President of the Iowa A & W's ops. and Dick Christensen is our N.A.C. Representative. Dick has now sold Iowa Falls. Still has Ames. He is 39 and set his goal to retire at 40. That is the farthest thing from my mind. Working the A & W is my enjoyment. Guess I'm really put together different. Plus the National Hawaii (A & W) Convention is January 4, 5, and 6 and the Iowa Convention is February 11, 12, 13.

Wow-wow-wow. The holiday season is upon us. Have to dust off the Santa Claus suit. As I've said before, I love to be Santa but some of the kids are bigger than me. Dolph Pulliam (Drake basketball great and big) also plays Santa Claus. Wouldn't that be a hoot if we were working the same block? The kids would really be confused.

A little add—we were selected to be #1 broasted chicken outlet in the state of Iowa with a Golden Chicken for our trophy case.

Our Restaurant Association Convention was a record breaker. Stub is our cheerleader, but doesn't jump too high on that last rah. Jack McNeil will have running interviews with all the V.I.P.'s. Stub will work the bar along with cheerleading. Jumps will phase out early and no profit expected. Al will interview the ladies. It will have to be verbal because he only writes in Bohemian and I can only translate Irish and Italiano. It didn't work out. Jack lost the pencil by 7:00 both nights. Stub very faithfully stayed behind the bar and not sure that was good. Al did not show up! The Little Flower thinks those guys are bad influences on me. After three days my nose started getting red.

A brand new year 1979. Looking for it to be the greatest. I take the oath January 1$^{st}$ (doesn't everybody?). I solemnly swear to do everything in my power to bring a smile to your face every month (taken from the January Appetizer). I'm apologizing right now. Should have more family news, maybe?

Business was down about 5% last year and with inflation it was realistically down about 12%. Problems: Added competition, labor up 10%, fixed costs up 2%, meat up about 15% and all goods and supplies up 7% plus the menu prices couldn't keep with the costs. Our years in 1977 and 1978 were exceptionally good and hopefully things will level towards end of this year.

Our new Restaurant Association President from one of the minorities, Tony Helling, from Dubuque (Irish Catholic). Vice President is Dave Heaton, Iris Motel & Restaurant in Mt. Pleasant. Dave used to be 5 x 5 and has now slimmed down to 5 x 1 ½ and as Mother would say—Isn't he a handsome young man? Mom thinks everybody is good.

So, the Restaurant Association trip is to Greece. The A & W National Convention is in Hawaii, so we elected to go there. Stub went to Hawaii last year and is loaning me his grass skirt. He's also trying to teach me the free action hip movements. Really a good crowd for our Hawaii Convention. Larry had the Iowa Bear pins made up and the Iowa ops were the envy of all. There were about 20 of us (Iowa ops) in Honolulu New Year's Eve. Actually a block off the beach in the second floor of a cheaper hotel. Windows even opened. Fireworks are legal from 6:00 pm to 2:00 am on New Year's Eve. The natives (if you could find one) suggest we hole up because it gets a little wild with the fireworks. It was really something. Out of this world. The next morning firecracker casings were six inches deep in the streets. The evening was just starting and in came Tim with two big bags of fireworks. A rope of 2800 firecrackers for $8.00. (I didn't ask how many ropes he had.) Yes, we arrived back home with our sun burned faces and snow falling to cool it off.

So, moving right along. It's February 1979. We have our new priest, Father Klein, and we are gradually getting him broken in. At my first greeting (my greeting is always—How's business?) he said—Mr. McConnell. Very formal at first.

Your pants don't show any wear at the knees. We'll change that. Think he's taking us right back to the basics and it might not even hurt.

Yes, got too much candy for Christmas and I can't leave it alone. Of my many weaknesses, that's right up near the top. Plus high powered after shave. Gonna have to water it down a little plus it tends to get me excited and a girl might grab me before she realizes the grab wasn't too much. Borrowed Stub Johnson's grass skirt and hoola hoop with a mirror. So far the action is improving my looks.

Sunday morning, December 24$^{th}$, had a little skiff of snow and #3 Tim has a few jobs cleaning and scooping snow. Up at 5:30 so he could get back for church at 8:00. He got the clothes on sleepily and was putting on the boots on the back porch and leaned up against the door bell. He goes back through the house and opened the front door. In the meantime The Little Flower had rolled out of bed.

Next comes New Year's Eve. For some unknown reason we didn't even have a drink. Inflation is till heating up. Wage and hour moved from $2.65 to $2.95. That means the overall gross will have to rise to keep us afloat.

Our A & W Association election has John Rotjer as President and he should be good—100% numbers man. Dick Wilderman was one of our better Presidents along with first Lady Lynne. Dick and Peg Christensen have moved on and we wish them well. Our State Convention is history and was the very best. John is trying to educate us about gross, profit and volume. With John, the Convention had a lot of meat to chew and devour plus an ample amount of funnin'. Of course, I take notes of the meeting, presentations and things of interest for the Newsletter. Haven't made it through a Convention yet without losing the notes. Good thing I have a little memory left.

We were trying to establish a mini-promotion and Dick as Secretary/Treasurer is working on the by laws. I was on the program to present numerous plaques: Ted Malone for his good work with the operators; Mrs. Rommel for their many years of good operation in Dubuque; Marge & Dick Moore, Marshalltown, for 40 years of continuous operation. Marge took over when Dick went to the service in WW II.

Dues for the N.A.C. ($100.00) are due and payable and also the election is coming up. The menu changeover is on the front burner. To me the Burger Family was the best thing ever and is now being dumped. Coffee Day is coming up and we're trying to get the whole state involved.

Had a beautiful Easter. Business seems to be going along good. It really shouldn't be that way, but our life is dedicated more to business then family. Part of our wish—it takes money to raise the family and I guess everything evens out.

The A & W does give the whole family a job and think that is good. Experience in the business world is real important in growing up.

#2 Larry is into real estate among other things. Bought a house in the area next to the college (north) and next to the Phi Beta Phi sorority house. Can you imagine that? 22 and single and my, my. He was the "Golden Arrow" Man of the Year away this year. #3 Tim was awarded a trophy as most valuable theatre person at the high school honors assembly.

The Summer Social will be at Adventureland on July 16$^{th}$. Also have a coupon coming up in October. Business is a little soft. Seems the customers are a little more price conscious. As the saying goes, the rich are getting richer and the poor getting poorer. The middle class are getting smaller and that's the area that makes business go. The rich are the tough ones. Bury that money.

The Maid-Rite corner on 65/69–92 with Ken and Sandy Newell have moved into a new building and calling it the Cottage Inn. Maid-Rite is and has been a very good franchise and a positive money maker and a third easier to operate than a restaurant. I found that out real quick coming from Bussey. Some of the not too good operators on the corner is a boon for us.

More about Hawaii. #3 Tim, our chauffeur—on the 11$^{th}$ day we put him on the plane headed back to school. Beach, to Dorene and I, is not a great thing. The one thing Dorene and I agree on we're not too fond of water. We did grab a sandwich and drink then laid on the beach for a half hour. That was primarily to take home a tan. The natives like the four wheel drive pickups and on Sunday all get on the road then stop along the side, sit on the tailgate and drink beer.

Then came the highlight of the Des Moines social season—Babe Bisignano's roast. The #1 power in Des Moines was John Ruan. To me the #1 good guy and successful business man was Babe. I'm not a writer, but it would be easy to write a book about Babe's life.

St. Patrick's Day: Had a busy day on March 17$^{th}$. Brought in 1A and 3A for the Catholics at Boys' State Tournament. Heard by the grapevine the Catholics will have their own class next year.

This has to be a landmark after all these years. I'm voting Republican this year, at least on the state level. The Democrats are trying to give away the farm. The visit of the President at Diehl's was a big biggie. Probably biggest in my life. Received a new shipment of pictures—President Carter, Little Flower and me. Call for a copy.

Back to Hawaii trip. Remember the Little Italian girl that did the Chinese laundry on the Oriental trip last year? Same thing this trip. We checked in at Kona Lagoon Hotel. Made reservations for dinner. They had a nice club. The sweet young lady at the desk announced our name. M-A-K-A-N-O for dinner. Have answered to every other nationality and Hawaiian isn't bad. Europe will be our trip next January and we will try and make it.

With our A & W being in a neighborhood, it's a continuous job to keep good relations with the neighbors. In 1956 when we came to Indianola, the P.T.A. of the elementary school across the street circulated a petition to keep us from coming in. This spring the P.T.A. honored us at their dinner with a plaque for being such good neighbors over the years. Needless to say, we're very proud of the plaque.

George is doing a good job for us. He was with Dick at University of Iowa. When I first met them didn't think either would make good operators. It just goes to show you first opinion doesn't always cut it.

Had a letter from Frank Sonoc, Sterling, Illinois. He is serving on the N.A.C. now. He was interested on my take on the new menu. Answer—positive. All our units are up and that tells the story. Frank is a good solid operator and family man. Remember the last convention and Frank's family. Wife is a sweetheart and three daughters ages 6 to 12 and dressed to a T and Frank's wife had made the clothes.

Our Summer Social was at Adventureland. We did the park for the young 'uns and a city tour for the elders that were interested. Dick and Peg were guests and used their beautiful van for the tour ending in Old Town West Des Moines for ice cream. We also found out we had some pretty good increases over the year.

Had a little confrontation with The Little Flower. Why is it when you write or tell a story you always have to stretch it just a little? I can get by with a little stretch, but when it gets by that Father Klein calls me in. Besides that The Little Flower hid the Easter candy on me and I didn't find it until Easter morning. She was buying chocolate bars that she shaved for the top of chocolate cream pies. She started buying bitter chocolate and there was no more trouble. Then Father Burns would come in and say—You know how lucky you are to have that lady? Actually, The Little Flower gets sweeter every day. Italian ladies and wine are the same—get better with age. Father Burns is coming back to fly in the balloon event.

A few weeks ago Dorene and I took an afternoon off and headed for Lake Rathbun. We kinda planned to end up at the Green Circle to eat (Centerville). Paying at the counter, the food was real good. Are you the owner? Yes, Mrs. Sacco replied. I read you in the Appetizer every month. That makes a total of 10 readers I have.

On the evening of July 17th, Bobby Crouse came in with a 50 cent cigar—It's a boy! Bobby was really pumped up. He could have put up a balloon without the fan. There will be pictures, dimensions, specs, etc. at the same address for Carter pictures.

The Little Flower and I made our first summer outing. It was at Tony Helling's new facility in Newton. Beautiful snacks at the cocktail hour and the dinner was gourmet. Dorene and I try to sit at a table with people we don't know and get acquainted: Jim and Karen Rastrelli of Rastrelli's in Clinton (a landmark family Italian pizza place and Jim is second generation); Bill Warneke and Ginger (a sweet redhead) of the Executive Inn, West Des Moines and also a second generation fooder; Henry and Betty Holman of Clinton House; John Murphy new owner of Duncan's and the Dairy Sweet across the street in Monroe and a bar in West Des Moines. A capsule write up of John would have to be in book form. Jim R. and I broke bread for the group as ranking Catlics.

Again the Des Moines Metropolitan Opera was a great success. Had Stub and Jack McNeil down for one opera. Jack made the remark—Best he had ever seen. Probably the first and only. Babe has agreed to serve on my editorial staff for the Appetizer.

The Balloon Days is a keeper. A single day total of $3,800. The three day weekend—Friday, Saturday and Sunday was $9,200. or $3,006.67 per day. Yes, the Balloon Days will continue. A & W at this time is on a roll. A newer unit in Omaha (we halfway call it in Iowa) did in excess of 75,000 for July. John Rotjer reports on the new menu. Food cost at 30.6. Business is good, but more competition is certainly moving in.

Yes, about the Papal visit and my entry in the September Newsletter. I have been appointed a distributor for the official papal visit lapel pins at $5.00. For the Big Operators (spenders) we have a special—12 for $60.00. Send your checks to this address. They all have the Polish Blessing. For the Irish-Italian Blessing it will be $1.00 extra. For the Bohemian Blessing—just can't do that from here.

Been eating crow since the game between Iowa-Iowa State.

Did give the great Sky Pilot (Father Burns) an ultimatum—#1 this year o you'll be a free agent. Well, had to back up because we use that guy for so many different things.

Into baseball season. Our #1 sport has taken a turn for the better. More interest and better crowds. The most significant thing about baseball, most of them chew: Red Man tobacco or bubble gum. The bubble gum concession must go for pretty good money. I really think the farm system is to teach the young players how to chew and spit. The game would be more enjoyable if they would outlaw spitting.

The other night a neighbor lady came in and wondered if we had some left over chicken for her casserole. You bet. About this time #2 Larry came in. Want you to meet this important fellow and have dinner with us (during our little fair). The handshake, time of day, where you from? Hayfield. How could anybody important be from Hayfield? Don Greiman, President of the Iowa State Fair Board. He was judging cattle at our fair and we had the honor of him eating with us. August 12$^{th}$ is the second Chuck Wagon Races at the State Fair and I'm trying to get on as an out rider. No go.

So it's time to book one of the annual Restaurant Association trips. An Italian was handing out Italian propaganda newspapers and he couldn't get anything out of me. More later about the Rome, Italy trip.

We had our 47$^{th}$ annual Iowa Restaurant Association Convention at Veterans Memorial Auditorium. It gets bigger and better every year. Over 100 booths. Our Honorable President Tony Helling (Newton Motor Inn) brought in the Polish Cowboys for our entertainment and dancing pleasure.

One of the girls in the neighborhood (18) we helped raise and she worked for us a couple years. She took a sabbatical and went to build a Baptist Missionary unit in the Caribbean with a group of young people and adults. The poverty there is unbelievable. They live in the Baptist house. It and the Catholic house were the only buildings with floors. The people took cans of food along. The native diet was rice, poultry, fish, bananas, etc. The language is Creole and the people are basically happy and fun loving. The basic major religion is Catholic. It gives these people from the U.S. an idea how lucky they really are.

#3 Tim took me to the Big Fair one afternoon. The first thing—we went to the Toby Show (Shaffner Players). We sat on the front row, laughed and clapped all the way through. Ran into the Wingas. Mrs. Winga went to school with Jimmy Davis' (Toby) father. Jimmy now owns the show and it was with Mrs. Winga's recommendation that the Shaffners hired Jimmy 20 years ago.

Got the "Hi" from the cute little 4-H girls. Took me all afternoon to figure out they were giving Tim the "Hi."

Looking forward to the Pope's visit next month. Our gang hooked up with Decker Davis Catering in Des Moines (Berwick). We checked out Living History Farms and possibly put up some easy stands to work the crowd. We looked it over and by some unknown reason decided to back away. It was one of our better decisions. Hy-Vee went in full bore and lost about $100,000. We would have lost about $20,000, so we figure we made $20,000. The people came and went without eating.

John Rotjer was A & W President in 1979/80 and did a terrific job. He took to the Newsletter like a hen with a whole flock of babies. Our Convention was in October 1979 at the Fontaine Bleu, Miami Beach. The new menu is still the biggest thing on the table. It has to be implemented by January 1, 1980. With A & W as a franchise, we have been free to go our own way too long and hard for some to take instructions. Also we have a new road sign. Larry and I bunked with John at the Fontaine Bleu. A stable one with two maybes. It was okay in the daytime, but they would slick up and put on the smelly stuff and there was fire in their eyes. I was trying to take it easy. I sat and talked to Dale Rudy for five minutes and he kept looking at me out of the corner of his eyes. I'm recuperating from an operation. Thought there must be something wrong with you. The longest I ever saw you sit still.

The food is always high in the hotel so we usually go around the corner to the coffee shop. Here there was no coffee shop and no corner to go around. The best deal was a good bowl of soup for 90 cents and oysters on the ½ shell for 20 cents. If you didn't like oysters, you was in trouble. It was a ritual with me every afternoon putting oysters away. Dick Moore and John didn't like raw oysters and were amazed at me putting them away.

Everything about the convention was positive. Myron approached me—You write about Irish-Italianos-Bohemians and you never write about Germans. I don't know any Germans. I'm German. That gave me an opening for about three pages and he does look like Sgt. Schultz in Hogan's Heroes. Maybe there is a story there. We had a fifties dinner and dance. I bought a stock of Brilliantine. Don't tell but I moved the price up front 10 cents to 15 cents.

Dick was putting all the past Newsletters in a hard bound book inserted in plastic covers and he borrowed my copies to have them all. Six months passed by and no Newsletters from Dick. I'm a little concerned. It comes Christmas with a nice big package from Dick. All the letters in a nice book. Father Klein, I take back all the nasty things I was saying about that boy.

Another super Restaurant Convention goes into the books. Dave Heaton is our new President (Iris Motel & Restaurant in Mt. Pleasant). I'm a little slow. Just a week out of the hospital. My committee did a good job. Jack gave me this report. Everything went super well. Was he lying or just stretching the truth? Made it too good. Sounded like a nunnery party.

The results of the poll taken from "Operation Hernia" were 468, 6 maybe and 3 spoiled ballots. I do feel obligated to give you the highlights and it shouldn't take more than three issues. Was to check into the hospital Thursday afternoon. Kissed The Little Flower goodbye and she had a glint in her eye like I'm going to be the Head Honcho now. #1 and #2 didn't ask any questions. See you later—that means you're really not too important in the joint. It's expensive, but the accommodations are out of this world. Private room with complete bath. The stand by the bed had more controls on it than the Big Mercury.

Thursday afternoon went by pretty fast. All the testing for getting ready for Friday and then the flush out. Friday was about 2/3's lost. Got up early and did the bathroom chores (operation scheduled for 8:00). Got the sleeping pill at 7:00 and then onto the flat roller bed and down to the operating room. Backed into the waiting stall and then into the cutting stall. Bright lights and a blanket separating me from the knife and more shots. At about that time Doc sticks his head over the blanket—How are you? Never felt better and then four more hours before my toes would wiggle so I could go back to my room. Arrived back at 4:00 and was super glad to see The Little Flower. A lay person came with the communion and I wasn't interested in nourishment of any sort. They have closed circuit T.V. from the chapel. Mass every afternoon at 3:30 and they bring communion to the room. Could use that at home on Sunday morning. Will speak to Father Klein about that.

Babe Bisignano's wife Catherine passed away November 5th. Long bout with cancer.

Cheeseburgers originated in Kentucky in 1934. Sunday, November 4th, was the 100th anniversary birth of Will Rogers (died 1935). You youngers who don't remember him missed one of our great ones.

Went to the Jefferson-Jackson day dinner. Shook the hand of young Joe Kennedy. Youngest son of Ethel and has the Kennedy charisma. Yes, we're on the band wagon for Carter. Can't really buy Ted Kennedy. And a Ho Ho Ho for Christmas!

# 26

## *1980*

It's January 1980. Hey, it's a winter without snow. Not sure about North. Of course those dummies pray for snow. At this minute it's snowing and blowing. The mailman is trudging through the snow with the mail. A card—southern Texas—poor girl in a bikini. Wish you were here. So we're happy, happy, happy and thinking about the fun we'll have and lies we can tell January 20–21–Seven Villages Restaurant, Williamsburg.

Hernia operation on Friday. Felling pretty chipper on Saturday. Did the shave and wash thing in bed—not the handiest. Got the foam lather for shave. Figured it out and would you believe I put the Colgate toothpaste on my hair. It certainly gives you that slicked down look. The nurse came in—Why don't we leave this bath and shaving stuff by the sink?. Nice way to say—this little old guy is clear out of it and she not far from right. Dick Wilderman stopped by Monday with a box of Cherry Chocolates. Had to eat fast to keep ahead of him. In the conversation Dick said—I've never been in a hospital. Is it really a lot of fun?

Father Klein, The Little Flower and I attended the wine and cheese premiere of the Papal Pilgrimage (V.I.P.) film. The film was introduced by a Jewish gentleman who introduced Bishop Dingman who introduced a Methodist. Can't get any more ecumenical than that. In one mixed sentence—$5—Lapel pins, $6-Commemorative Book and saw the Cornets play their first game. Better get the order in. The Pope things are going fast and supply is limited.

We're into January and The Little Flower plus Sandy and Larry left for Europe. Maybe if I'm good they might take me along next year. As a bachelor (been in the food business since 1946) the cooking leaves a lot to be desired. Dorene left enough cooked wrapped in foil, etc. to last a month.

Back to the Hernia thing—On the 3$^{rd}$ recovery day was supposed to walk the length of the hall. Ran onto a little Irish Nun (50 years as a nun). She retired from teaching in Des Moines Parochial schools—Sister Carlotta. In conversation we covered city, state and national politics, religion, Ireland and the Pope in 5 minutes plus a lot of Blarney (from both sides). Then we also had a Flannery from Albia down the hall. In years past I knew everybody from Georgetown and I'm telling Flannery how much fun I'm having. By the same token it's about time to leave this good life and get back to reality.

This paragraph is on the Q.T. In the Service we called it the "creep in crud." In the hospital they have a big name for it but we'll just call it fungus infection of the crotch. In the two days bandaged from the operation this fungus got in. The next time you see me I'm walking like a cross between a bowlegged cowboy and Charlie Chaplin. Yes, still have it.

Back to the Cornets girls game. Rick Hodson (Senior at Iowa State) was covering the game for U. of I. I fed him root beer as a babe in his mother's arms. He said—Gib, could I ask you a question? How old are you?

I wrote our Honorable Editor Frank DeFazio a letter. Could I pay you a commission on the Papal sales from the column? No. Send it to Mr. Pete. I obligingly sent Mr. Pete 79 ½ Hail Marys.

The other morning The Little Flower and I were exchanging a few words. She said even at your funeral you'll figure a way to get in a joke. Again I say The Little Flower deserves better.

Dick and I made it to the Minnesota A&W Convention. Gary Rudy from La Crosse, was at the Convention (3$^{rd}$ generation A&W Family). He turned in his Franchise and is going independent. Thing are getting rocky with the Company. Every state has lost operators. Last year Larry was with me and this year Dick. People thought he was one of the #'s. Stopped in Fairbault on the way home at the Lavender Restaurant. Started about 25 years ago as a hamburger stand. I inquired of Mr. Jensen about Ray & Agnes Unser. Ray is an A&W living legend and helped many operators get started. He was also an innovator of root beer equipment. Ray still has one of his original root beer machines. Heard Agnes run the stand. At this time they must be in their 70's and Ray still flies his own plane. Two very fine people.

The Little Flower, Sandy and Larry had a great time in Europe. Now it's the Iowa A&W Convention, February 17–18–19. We invite all our neighboring states. A lady from Minnesota asked—Why is it Iowa gets all the national publicity. Sit down here. It'll take 2 hours to give you all the reasons.

Next coming up is Coffee Day for the Retarded. This is the #1 event that the Restaurant Association sponsors and good publicity for the food service industry. Dave and Carmen Heaton are serving as President & First Lady of the Restaurant Association this year. Dave is young and aggressive operator from Mt. Pleasant—Iris Motel & Restaurant. We have one of our better A&W operations there.

The name has left me. Could come back any minute. A little side—basketball. The game announcer Al McGuire coached at Marquette. More fun to watch him than the game. He's also a real good banquet speaker.

It came to my attention that ladies' hose is seamless now. Really thought I paid attention to that sort of thing and what do you know—here comes a lady with seams. Is she a new "In" or an old "Old"? The sighting was in Old Town West Des Moines and that could explain it.

Economy is rising—gas prices are up and it's cutting into travel. Minnesota was down 20 % in tourism, etc.. The banker said, restaurant, coal mines and soft drink bottling plants have the highest mortality rate. I'll add a coal mine to my holdings and really go down in a heap. Larry & Mary Mayberry were two of the brightest lights in our industry. Graduates of Iowa State Restaurant, etc.. Established one of the first restaurant filling station stops of the interstate at Williamsburg. Things were going great for them and Larry got cancer and was gone at 27. Such a waste of a great talent.

At our last A&W Convention it was a 50's theme and dance with appropriate dress. #2 Larry came on with a 50's A&W uniform as a girl car hop—white wig, saddle shoes, and professional makeup. Needless to say he brought down the house. Next dance Larry had 3 girls on the floor and I grabbed an older fellow and said, let's help this kid out. Would you believe I ended up center stage in a wipeout. Larry said—That's my dad. Get him out of there before he dies! That's the problem—older people just don't know any better. The boys just have a terrible time keeping me straight.

About the Europe trip. The Little Flower and #'s had a great time but couldn't get any wild stories out of them. She says that I don't really lie but switch the truth along quite a bit. Been sorting out classifications. Would ethnic group mean Bohemian & Irish or would those two be classified under endangered species? Promised to write about the happenings at home while the family was in Europe. Will have to refrain from the grounds it might tend to incriminate me.

State News—Congratulations to Al and Britt girls—State 2A Champs. Al's #2 daughter, Cathy is a cheerleader. Dick's Melanie is a mascot for East High. A couple of dandies. Cheerleaders are my favorites. I would rather watch the Dallas Cowboy cheerleaders than football.

Coffee Day was up about 20%. Drafted a couple fireballs as County Chairman, #2 Larry, Bobby Crouse and Lute Olson as State Honorary Coffee Day Chairman. President Carter had to be $2^{nd}$ or $3^{rd}$ choice on the T.V. Friday, March 4. Iowa was playing Syracuse in the N.C.A.A. and the girls in the middle of basketball State High School run off.

The Little Flower and I have an agreement that we try to make an appearance at social functions. She goes to the weddings and I go to the funerals. Last week she went to the Isaac Walton Fish Fry and I drew the inauguration of Robert McBride as the 19th President of Simpson College at the Methodist Church. I had to get special dispensation from Father Klein to attend. A very prestigious affair. I wasn't a reserve seat participant, just general admission. President McBride and I have quite a few things in common. For starters we're on the same page in the telephone book.

Meet Grandpa Gibba Macanelli and Grandma Little Flower. On February 7, a little re-haired Irish girl came forth. Name: Megan Joy. Dimensions: 20 inches by 7 lbs. 10oz.. The proud parents are #1 son Pat and Lynn McConnell. Pictures are available at this address and will be up dated by the week.

Thanks to the young lady from Corporate, Jan Perez, for helping put together our Iowa promotion. It certainly worked for Indianola. Of course the positive results are in direct proportion to the local promotion and work put in.

You all and our kids think I'm an old foggy but last week helped with a pig roast and rode a Gold Wing 1000 Honda and you can't be any more in than that. Some of you remember Joe Einstein, our manager of East Des Moines A&W. He passed away last week with a heart attack and many other problems. Joe was like a kid and never grew up. He was closer to my boys than me. Bet right now he's not sitting with Sr. Citizens. He is with St. Pete's fun and games.

Al Formanek is our Association President this year and has a column in the Newsletter. Got from Al this month—This is not your Bohemian President, but his ½ Bohemian daughter Kathi. As his Father's Day present I will write his message this month. She gave all the kudos about being the daughter of an A&W operator and all the fine people associated with plus the fun and education from. Ended the letter with—Now I have to get back coercing Mom & Dad into taking me to the National A&W Convention at Reno.

The Little Flower and I along with 106 people had the honor and pleasure of attending the gourmet dinner served by the Food Service Program at the Area Community College in Ankeny. A little different from a Fast Fooder. A four courser would be hamburger, French fries, coleslaw and root beer. Add ice cream (soft serve) for a five courser. To add to the glamour, at our table Bob McGurk (Highlander, Iowa City) and next to The Little Flower was Jim Spear of Chi Chi's (West Des Moines). Next to Bobbie was Ken Johnson of the program, so we also had a play by play. And we say again the Food Service Industry program is the greatest.

My schedule is getting a little tight for rest of the summer. July—Old Thresher Days, Stub at Spencer, First of August—Britt for Hobo Days. Then it's Hot Air Balloons at Indianola. Then we'll finish up at Valhalla Supper Club. Jack says if it is too quiet we'll start something.

Father Burns (our Balloon Pilot—among other things) stopped by with a 3# box of Mrs. Drew's fancy chocolates. The Little Flower hardly eats chocolates and I might self-destruct.

For the first time in 25 years a lady was entered in the Kentucky Derby—Genuine Risk—and she takes home all the marbles, As a side—I graduated cum laude in "How to Spoil Your Grandchild" and I'll say it again, "Grandmas are nice."

It's hot—hot—hot in July, but business is a little flat. We were up $300. for June and with inflation that makes us down 10%. We're working harder. Kissing the ladies. The young guys grab the good ones leaving me with the little older ladies.

Talked on the phone with Joe Cimono, Wimpy's, a landmark restaurant across the river south. Terrible location, but did a ton of business. All men waiters starting in 1931 (Just bordering on 50 years). Wimpy had been in the hospital, out and back to work. After two weeks he gave up and closed the restaurant. He relates, the hardest thing about it all is realizing he couldn't work any more.

This week had a little mouth problem. Lost one silver cap (half my tooth). Took a month for a dentist appointment. We should have it so good. So, I'm eating smooth mouth. Barb related that Al is having mouth problems. With him it is the noise that comes out.

Told Pete my mind is getting shaky and might have to quit the column. Pete would like to get rid of me because I take space and he has to add pages and that costs money. He tries to cut me down every month. It all relates to money.

Our Summer Social was one of the best ever. That's in July and next will be the Restaurant Convention in October. These breaks make it enjoyable. The restaurant people are fun people and A&W are all super. I'm not a golfer so it's my job to drive the beverage cart at the morning golf outing. There were 36 for golf and over 75 in attendance. They accused me of picking up pop cans out of the ditch. A nickel is a nickel. We also had Bingo. Borrowed a set from Father Burns. Their old set in the garage. They have electronic equipment in their hall. Don't know if it's Gospel, but the word is Catholics are #1 with bingo. Al Formanek is doing a good job as our Association President and writing a good column in the Newsletter plus youngest daughter Kathy is heading to Iowa State this fall.

For the Restaurant Convention, Mr. Pete made a ribbon of 100 $1 bills for the ribbon cutting ceremony. The ribbon cutter, Governor Ray, would then give the ribbon to the charity of his choice. On the last day $300 was given away. It did help last day attendance. Really think Mr. Pete has completely lost it.

At this time The Little Flower is trying to domesticate me—washing dishes, clean, vacuum. Sure it's not going to take. Sent Betty the Appetizer column last week. Betty called and I had sent her an empty envelope. She thought I was playing a joke on her. She doesn't realize I do dumb things like that all the time. She's laughing and I'm crying for wasting the 15 cent stamp.

In the Newsletter column from Al: A couple from Bussey are working in the Bank at Britt. That should bring Britt up 100%. Yes, Al, I grew up with their folks. It was Pinky Avon and wife. Treat them good, Al, because all Bussey people are good. Think they will fit.

One of our lady customers belonged to the W.C.T.U (Women's Christian Temperance Union). She thought I might be interested in the W.C.T.U. State Convention. I can tell you how to get there. Go to Lucas, turn right at the Tavern onto Jericho Road, past the Memorial Home of John L. Lewis to Jericho Hill and you will see the Christian Union Church Camp. I'm not all bad and certainly not up for Sainthood, but that was a little beyond me.

Our new A&W Representative is Harry Ayres. We've had quite a few different Corporate Reps, but Harry rates as one of the best. He is knowledgeable and willing to help. As a side, we had a milk man at this time. An introvert and he would try to come early or late to miss me. I was always into a story and trying to make him talk. Once he said—Gib, if you've been every place you said and done everything in your stories, you'd have to be 150 years old.

The A&W in Fort Dodge closed up and had a sale. Dutch Strootman was the first operator and ended up in the hospital with a heart attack. Larry was our Representative at the sale and bought his share: two van loads. Things did go too cheap. Hope Dutch gets along okay.

Jim Huss, Iowa Extension Service, has been helping us and is really doing an honorable job with some government help and very welcome.

Right away I found out Dorene's priorities. #1 Pat was going to the Ozarks for a few days and Dorene got out before I woke up and left a note: Gone to baby sit our red headed granddaughter.

The Iowa Restaurant Association Convention has grown to be quite a nice show. Over 100 booths at the Veterans Memorial Auditorium. The Convention has grown similar to the A&W's growth. We started out with an orange crate-type unit, rock lot, and then came inside seating. In 1975 we moved into the new unit seating 82. Any improvement has paid back with extra volume. A not too shabby volume. Double within two years with the new operation. At this time

I've been accused of having an A&W tattooed on my chest. A report just came in: Dutch Stroolman is in intensive care at hospital in Rochester. Our thoughts and prayers are with him.

Got a note from Al. He is ready for the Reno Convention (National A&W) and has the Iowa Hospitality Suite already spoken for. Our Fall Social is coming up October 27–29 in conjunction with Iowa Restaurant Convention. We'll all get together for a social hour and supper at the Mandarin then back to the show for Las Vegas night.

Our A&W State Convention will be February 15–17, at the Hilton on Fleur across from the airport. The theme will be "Carnival" with clowns, etc.—get the clown suit ready. We have quite a few members that won't need a suit.

Dorene and I have been out visiting. Made it to Clarinda last week. Good unit managed by Steve Strong and second in state volume. Gene Benolken is getting along fine and out of the hospital. Stopped to see Doug & Lois Ward, Cedar Rapids A&W. My directions are mixed up in C.R., but to me it is on the S.W. side. Had a nice visit with Lois but hard to converse with a Bohemian (Doug).

Four people stopped in the other day and I helped them locate some relatives. They stopped by the next day and were looking for the little old guy that helped them yesterday—Oh my!

Our Hot Air Balloon Championships—Father finished with the also ran. I was ready to give him an ultimatum—either give up the part time job or else. He presented me with three beautiful pictures of him greeting the Pope at the Airport. I got all gushy and picked up his option for another year. It was Father Burns' honor to greet the Pope because he landed in his Parish at the time—Christ the King

Went to the Big Fair with #3 Tim. Definitely the biggest boar in the world. Stared at the Malt Liquor Bull. Tim is definitely a city boy because he was worrying about stepping in pig and cow stuff.

For Balloons, WOI-TV was down doing interviews of how we liked the Balloons (both business people & visitors). They caught me and my answers were all affirmative. After all, I had to get overload springs for my "Brinks Truck." It really was our biggest week of the year.

Took a day and went to the Farm Progress Show in Nevada. It ran 3 days. Our bank ran a bus and I snuck in on the second day. It was 80 acres of farm displays, equipment, etc. I covered the whole area and didn't step in any pig or cow stuff, but plenty dirt from a 30 m.p.h. wind. Farmers aren't too different from food operators. Truth stretchers from a different time. It was really well organized. The food stands were run by area churches. There were 9 food stands all laid out the same. Four serving lines for each and two fast food lines. The drink stands were manned by 4-H groups. There were about 150,000 people in attendance on my day. I would say each stand had $15,000 gross a day and probably netted $20 to $25,000. Better than passing the collection plate twice. I bought a book for The Little Flower on homemade bread and autographed by the editor. "The Country Parson" was there and bought his book of one liners. Every big implement company. had a free show—real entertainment. I bought my dinner at a Methodist Church stand—$4.40—my ecumenical contribution.

The economy is down big time. Our people are still doing good but tightening up a little. Curt Jante ordered his new Cadillac and had the dealer leave off the chrome bolts on the license plate.

Did I mention #2 Larry has a nice big house in the college area next to a sorority house? He is 23 and single. What does that add up to?

# 27

## Here Comes the Big Mac

Our State Restaurant Convention was a little sparse. It started off with a 7 inch snow. Just a thought—at our conventions we sample food all day and big dinner at night. How about a fertilizer convention or better yet, our neighbor who is head of the City Sewer Department? Yes, we are fortunate. I was also elected to the Executive Board. Proud to be elected to a 1800 member organization. One of the largest state organizations in the nation.

January 4$^{th}$—7$^{th}$ went to Las Vegas for the National A&W Convention. Stayed at the Imperial just around the corner from the burned out M.G.M.. Did a little relaxing—that for us means still moving but half speed. Checked out the hotel casino and went to Saturday evening Mass. A nice little church on the Strip. Big see-through collection baskets and they passed them twice. The good Father made it very clear they would accept chips, slot slugs, credit cards, even I.O.U.'s. Most people put extra money in and figured St. Pete would give a little edge when they hit the casinos. Didn't work for me. Had good attendance with over 400 licensees registered and over 1,000 bodies. The program emphasis was on remodeling. Al & Barb were mostly hosting the Iowa Suite. A & W President Frank Dwyer & wife were surprise guests after the Wednesday night banquet. Larry and Tim were the official photographers and Larry won the Disco contest on Tuesday night. Got that talent from his mother. We happened to get an Early Bird Suite. Big round mirror in the ceiling and wall. I woke up in the middle of the night and looked at the mirror and said, "Hi!" Don't really know because that is for older type peoples. Al's Kathy, now at Iowa State, asked dad if Gib & The Wild Flower were going to the convention. Al is now elected to the N.A.C..

This is start of New Year 1981 and mucho Republicans. On my list of New Year's resolutions: 1. Listen to Republicans. 2. Be kind to Republicans. 3. Fraternize with Republicans. 4. If in a crowd where not well known, be a Republican. This may well be a change for me. I went to Father Klein, could I include these in my nightly prayer? Permission pending.

Had one of the best Iowa A&W Conventions ever. Betty Stevens is our new Iowa President and Cliff Heinricks was elected to the N.A.C.. The clown night went over great and my forever wish to be a clown was fulfilled. Had a lot of great suits and our Gary Edwards from the school system painted the faces. Hollered so much at the Carnival lost my voice. Thought I wouldn't be able to be the toastmaster at the banquet. A little raspy but made it thru. It actually cleared up for the banquet and then was raspy again. No, it wasn't the Big Guy in the Sky helping. Lost faith in him when he let Notre Dame get beat in the Super Bowl. Back to A&W—Our advertising including the Wuppets was the best of all time. Have a fellow coming to spray paint our pagoda. The price was $800. It was kinda worth the money.

With the Iowa Restaurant Association Bob McGurk is our new President. He and Leona are two of our finest people and the very best operators. Of course Bob is all Iowa and we in Central Iowa are more Iowa State. Bob brought the Hayden Fry T-shirts and they didn't go over that big. Besides, #2 Larry can get us a better deal at the Big Fair. Now with Larry and his stand at Iowa State Fair our family is 2/3 carnies. #3 Tim and I and can do our share at the stands.

Catholics are making a comeback with Pope John Paul II coming over here. Then he sends that Polish quarterback, Jaworski, a medal he blessed. Where was he at the Sugar Bowl? An add—getting a little hard of hearing. May have to advertise for used hearing aids.

Our life changes. Being a Grandpa isn't all a bowl of cherries. New Years Eve and were babysitting. #1 son Pat & Bride came home at 3 a.m.—"Thanks, Dad." Doesn't even offer mileage.

It's March of 1981. Our fine Appetizer Editor, Bud Proctor, asked if I could write an article—"Know Your Neighboring Operator." I chose Shorty Cox of Shorty's Steak House in Pleasantville for the opening article. Shorty was a real character. When they first started he had a partner, Blacky Gilderbloom. Blacky was also a pretty good character. Shorty was the cook and Blacky worked the front end. Shorty, at that time, came over to Indianola every Monday to get his liquor supply. He came to the A&W first to have a beefburger, but mostly to haggle me. One Monday he came in and bought Blacky a new suit—no pockets. Shorty's son Denny & wife also helped. Denny was also the Pilot of Shorty's Hot Air Balloon and he was enjoyed by all of us ballooning. Shorty started his business career with a small grocery store in Swan. Brother Art started as a stock boy for Mr. Dahl in his original small store in east Des Moines. Art retired last year as President of Dahl's 9 stores. Only in America do these things happen.

For 1981 Betty Stevens is our Iowa A&W Association President. She is really taking it to heart and going all out. It's different than a guy and change is sometimes good. Now our numbers are down and not sure what that is about, but things seem to be getting together and moving ahead.

On January 18 the McGurks hosted the Restaurant Association to a gourmet buffet. The line was beautiful and the food was fit for the upstairs people. Can you believe two kinds of shrimp, two kinds of mushrooms, escargot, chicken tetrazzini, something Chinese, frog legs, smoked salmon, small BBQ ribs, small buttered buns and a young lad carving a baron of beef, plus numerous items that I forget. Later, coffee with an after dinner drink. I will say it again, Bob & Leona McGurk are the very greatest.

Now we have Coffee Day coming. Lute Olson has agreed to be our Honorary Chairman again this year. It's really super to get together with our business people once or twice a year. Shake hands with some, rub noses with some, tip a drink with some, and tell lies with most all. Said hi to Dan & Shirley Ales' daughter, Sharon. She didn't really recognize me at first. Oh yeah, you're Larry's dad. Mike Dorland came by with a "Hi, How's the Wallflower?" Stub Johnson sat down in the middle of the floor and Becky Mariet pulled off his boots. Stub forgot his boot jack and Vi couldn't handle the chore.

As a side—President Reagan can't be all bad He uses Brylcream. The Pope loses the Super Bowl after blessing the Medal of Jaworski.

Yes, we'll have a Big Mac—plans to open May 1$^{st}$. As I've said before when I came to town, a lot of people said the Big Guys will come in and blow you away. Hardees blew us away for a month. In about 3 months it gets back to about normal. A good operation brings more business to town and we seemed to get our share. But it does take away the profit margin (at least tightens).

Can I mention that Betty Stevens is a good example of Women's Lib? In fact she's been liberated for some time. Yes, Betty does the Newsletter column and she is long winded. When Delbert says "Ke-kuk" us Northerners says "Ke-O-kuk."

At this time we're losing some of our old time and good operators and operations. Frank & Virginia Stoner spent the winter in Texas. Dutch Strootman passed away in May. Gene & Margaret Benolken retired 1$^{st}$ of January. Dick and Peg sold out. Jean & Bob, Oskaloosa, also sold. The first thing in conversation is Big Mac. We will overcome. Our business was down less than 2% and we had visions of being down 40%. Guess that's a winner.

A new buddy comes into our lives. Rocky (Rocco) Lavalle of Rocky's Pizza, Iowa Falls. He was raised in Greenwich Village. He met the love of his life, the

Norwegian girl at La Guardia Field, Beth Larson. After the War in 1949 they married and by 1952 decided to move to Iowa and Rocky went to work for Beth's dad and then into the pizza business. Rocky and Beth had 4 children. The youngest, Tom, is working in the business. I asked—married or otherwise? Tom said not married and the good looking young man handles the otherwise very well.

We have a dandy softball team. Good guys but they don't win too much. Had a couple of our team drafted by the Cubs. They fit. Used to losing. At this time only have 300 pictures left with President Carter, me and The Little Flower. Sure they'll be collector's items.

Yes, Big Mac is running and isn't hurting although I cry quite a lot. Right now I'm President of Indianola Community and trying to find a home for Humane Society Animal Shelter. That's a tough one plus Chairman of Fund Raising for Balloons. We invite you all. Bring money.

July 5th and baseball strike is on. One good point—my Cubs aren't losing. In Des Moines they are into Ugliest Bartender Contest. Think Babe will win it hands down. He has my vote. Jim Huss (Iowa State) has been helping us (from Iowa State College and can say your tax payer dollars are well spent). He is now writing a column in our Appetizer.

The Summer Outing at the Highlander was a world beater. I'm making a motion that we keep Bob as President at least another 5 years. The very best in hospitality from the McGurks—super food and drinks. The cowboy hats for the Texas-Mexican theme were a real topper. I don't think The Little Flower is going to let me buy a horse.

We used to call "shacking up" is now "cohabitations." Would you call that education?

There was no joy in Mudville. It rained out our big weekend for Balloons. Also Stubs Old Fashioned Thresher Bee plus the Hobo's at Britt. Could it be that Father Burns isn't getting through to St. Peter? We christened a new Balloon with a 30 foot Great Root Bear on it and never got it out off the field. Al, Stub and I went to Pete for a little subsidizing from the Association.. Think he is still sputtering.

#2 son Larry just corrected my vocabulary. We don't call independent concessionaires on the road "Carneys." They are "Roadees."

In our day today the A&W glass and pitcher promotion didn't go good as anticipated. The glasses will keep and maybe another time.

Another year at the State Fair. Spent one day at the fair with Dick. We were eating triple decker ice cream cones and Dick made the remark, "I really like the smell of this cow stuff." Isn't that a city guy for you? But don't think it will be that great with sugar and cream. Had the Great Root Bear at the fair two days. Went down the Giant Slide and the Bear had to be between me and the Queen. Also did the children's ward at Blank Memorial Hospital. We had a sticker: "I hugged the Great Root Bear today." A lot of rewards for that day. Mr. Pete asked Dick, Les and I to a V.I.P. breakfast at the Budweiser Tent sponsored by the Des Moines Chamber. Pete left right after to pick up delinquent memberships. We ran into him a half dozen times and he was always talking to good looking ladies and they didn't look delinquent to me. A side—Dick is taking guitar lessons the last couple months and he almost has chopsticks mastered.

Yes, the ladies have been liberated and this lady President Betty Stevens, is a world leader. Her Newsletter every month is like a book. She really did a fine job at our convention. A couple of good speakers and then dinner at Spaghetti Works. Jim & Joanne Huss were honored guests with 54 in attendance. From Betty's words—Ask Gib to return thanks before dinner—Good bread, good meat, good God, let's eat. It sounded a little strange to me but evidently that's a standard with Catholics.

With our problems at Corporate level they have cancelled the National Convention so more emphasis is placed on our State show. We really have been getting good play from states around.

Got an official type call—You're not employing minority. My answer—I'm an equal opportunity employer. In fact, I'm Irish Catholic Democratic and you can't get any more minor than that plus half my help are slow—slow. No, I'm referring to your work with the Appetizer. You have three men columnists. I have a snoozer Stub Johnson, a Bohemian (Bo-Hunk) Al Formanek, and a shanty Irishman, Jack McNeil, plus me and that all adds up to negative talent. The gist was no woman. So now we have Mr. Pete interviewing for a woman on our Board.

49th annual Restaurant Show (Iowa) was one of the very best (1981) with 146 booths. In the Veterans (spacious) Auditorium it continues to grow. Stub was in rare form at the bar. Couldn't catch Jack in between dances and Al was hitting at Black Jack. Bernie Grady was inquiring—Where was I at the banquet? I was at the head table behind that large bouquet of flowers and by the same token I don't sit too high in the saddle.

On November 21st our great state was born again: Rose Bowl bound, greatest thing that ever happened. At this time yours truly is figuring on being at the game. #2 Larry (he's the Roadee) has a friend that does concessions at the Coliseum. If on T.V. you see a little old guy in the lower section of the 50 yard line peddling lemonade, that'll be me. It's not what you know, it's who you know in this world.—So, I didn't get to the Rose Bowl. Mostly because I was too tight to come up with the money.

Now we have a lady on our Appetizer staff. Wanda Abbe, The Colony Club, Waterloo. Her acceptance speech—What an honor to be chosen to work with very talented gentlemen. Doesn't she say nice things? We may just get along, All the losing participants for this position will get a picture of me and former President Carter.

Have a retraction—Dick didn't really say he liked the smell of cow manure. It was cow stuff: Milk, buttermilk, cottage cheese. I don't really buy that.

So I don't get to the Rose Bowl mostly because I was too tight to come up with the money. The Little Flower backed out on the trip to Europe. Think may be she saw my add in the paper for a live-in housekeeper.

Our guys #1 Pat, #2 Larry & #3 Tim are into snow removal business and, of course, they are praying for snow, (we'll see how good their connection is). Their connection is better than I thought—We're getting much snow. So everything is slow and peaceful this particular night so #2 & #3 and I went to Pete's. I don't get there too often so I got the bill. Set 'em up, Pete, and threw down the Big Bill ($20). Pete counters with—The tab is on me. Next time I talk to St. Peter, take another look at old Pete. He's not all bad. Our big Iowa state A&W convention is coming up. Our hotel will be the landmark Savery downtown. President Betty was giving us a run down of all the extras in the Newsletter. Spa, massage for $10. The word is a massage north it is a lot higher. Will check it out and let you know.

Now it's time for Coffee Day and Lute Olson has agreed to be Honorary State Chairman along with me as State Operator Chairman. Lute is a foot taller than me and for the photo had me standing on a box. Plus I'm predicting this will be the biggest ever.

Just finished the year with the Methodist lady and it was a real struggle. The new President comes in—Steve and Laurie Waskow, Independence. Started out—What's your religion? He started stuttering—Let's drop that subject right now. N.A.C. Representative was bragging about his E-Hawks—2A Champions again—Cliff Hinrichs, Emmetsburg. At present we are down to 53 stores. Future doesn't look too bright.

#2 Larry was at the state tournament (Vets) selling T-shirts with Carp. Cliff was impressed with their operation. They really do a ton of T-shirts. The state wrestling is best. They are macho. Next is girls' basketball.

Our State Convention was really super. A lot of the credit goes to President Betty Stevens. Held at the Savery Hotel and that's a grand old hotel. Charlie's

Show Place for dinner and show—great. Then the banquet at the Savery Penthouse. The Savery Penthouse was the home, in the past, of Ed & Mrs. Boss. Mr. Boss, at the time, owned about 14 landmark hotels. Old, classy.

For many years it has been the Rose Bowl Parade plus more parades and many games and usually it is with a headache. This year The Little Flower filled me with spaghetti. My apologies to the drink operators, but think I've paid my dues in that department. It was a great day of games, but our Hawkeyes lost. But it was a great season anyway.

Bits and pieces: Got a call from Les and Pete. Les is working with Pete trying to learn the ropes. Executive Secretary of Arkansas Restaurant Association along with Miss Arkansas will be in town for promoting Arkansas tourism. Wow, sounded good to me! Called Dick. He could decoy the Executive and I would give the queen the royal treatment. Dick and I did our P.R. work, but no queen. Should have known Pete and Les wouldn't have ducked out if there was to be a queen.

Yes, I married one of the best cooks in the world, but I still have the 32" waist. Okay, but it hangs under that 36" bulge. Sad day at our household. Our family member for 18 years, our dog Butter, went to St. Pete's Dog Heaven.

Important news—at the Britt 81st Annual Hobo Convention, Al was installed as an Honorary Grand Duke of Hoboes. Tell me we don't have class in the A & W ranks.

Now we have the Iowa Cubs at Sec Taylor in Des Moines. No longer will be have to travel to Chicago way to see them lose.

Coffee Day is coming up and Lute Olson has again agreed to be our Honorary State Chairman. There is still a lot of hubbub on the National level. Not sure Taubman is good for us, but we'll see.

Of course our N.A.C. Representative was down with the E-Hawks for their second in a row 2A Boys' Champs at State. He had been making fun of us and Larry as a carney. He was amazed at their T-shirt operation at Vet's and envious.

A new heir apparent to the Indianola A & W throne. Pat and Lynn had a boy on April 14th—Ross Michael. Was holding out for Lute, but what chance does a grandpa have?

One of our best area men, Harry Ayres, is being transferred to Phoenix. He will be missed.

We ran the float promotion with the Bear glass last two weeks of February and first two weeks of March. Got rid of about 10 cases. Consider that good. We ran the Papaburger Pop for three weeks. Average 52 a day and also last month there were 69 calendar coupons redeemed. All of these things help to bring our volume back. Roger Rommel, Dubuque, had their sale middle of March. Rog was second generation and Dubuque had been one of our best for a number of years. One of our best in the state is gone.

At this time our dispenser was foaming. My thought—has to be a leak. Went through the whole system. No leak. Harry came by. Replaced the Thomas valve and it did the job. Harry, before you leave the country, come by. I want to kiss you.

I've done some big things in my life, but making that Coffee Day commercial with Lute Olson ranks right up there. He's a cool 6'4" and me—let your voice fall after 5'. For the photo I was standing on a milk crate and was still a little short. An addition—Had Father Klein praying for the Hawks with their N.C.A.A. bid. Also used him for Coffee Day. The Hawks went down, but the Coffee Day broke all records. One out of two isn't bad.

When we had President Carter, there was peanuts on every table and with President Regan it's Jellie Bellies. At this time it's in between. Basketball season is over. Now for baseball and it's a little ho hum. We'll have a couple season tickets to the Iowa Cubbies. Come on in and we'll enjoy. We haven't asked Mr. Pete for the ticket money yet but sure he'll give. He's such a sweetheart.

March 31$^{st}$ was fun in 5 Seasons Center in Cedar Rapids. Had the Big Ten going against the A.C.C. Most of the A.C.C. didn't show up, but they will next year. Al McGuire was coach of the Big Ten and Billy Parker for A.C.C. Dick Enberg did the announcing with Bobby Knight and Lute Olson for color. A full house of biggies and had to be a lot of fun.

Can tell The Little Flower has a mad cow when I have baker's bread for breakfast. Glad it doesn't happen very often. If you haven't been to the market place for awhile, there are no hand adding machines or calculators. Everything has gone electric and high tech. Us older guys are already behind.

How about April 4–5$^{th}$? Went from 79 degrees to a wind chill of 22 below. Must have been for the snowbirds to let them know what they missed.

The captain of the All State Girls' Basketball team grew up in Indianola. Grandpa lives in Milo and was right there with the Big Smile.

Got the very big "NO" from Pete about the Iowa Cubs baseball tickets. How about sending out a special bulletin for the birth of my grandson? Another big "NO." Mr. Pete did make a small concession. Gave me three ball point pens. One from Babe's, one from Amalgamated Spirits and Provisions, and McGarvey Coffee. Plus they all work.

Our advertising inserts were a disaster—like a 20 a day average. The neighbors, Osceola and Creston, were about the same. Des Moines were the only stores fairly good. Reported 70 average.

At our meeting we decided to hook up with Minnesota for conventions and alternate every year. Our numbers are down to 49 operations. Dick's college buddy, Nile Iles, and wife have taken over Emmetsburg. The Little Flower and I motored up north last week and stopped at Emmetsburg. Seems to be doing quite well. Very clean and neat. Help seemed good and Nile is happy.

#2 Larry and I got out south last week and stopped at Creston. A new Big Mac had opened in December. At our visit Dennis (A & W) had 10 cars and Big Mac had none at 3:00 in the afternoon. Possibly we're just getting the in between business, but it is encouraging. Cliff was sold out at Emmetsburg and Dick will serve the remainder of his N.A.C. term. Nile Iles had gotten out of Emmetsburg. Too much work. Cliff had taken it back over.

Our Summer Social is set for Adventureland. Sure the kids can have a ball at their expanded park. Let's call it a Disney World look-a-like in miniature.

I did remember Mother's Day with The Little Flower. Have a deal with the flower shop. She has a list of my important dates. Have The Little Flower fooled so far.

Had word from Roger Olson, Strawtown Inn. Thought we could trade a little work. I would help him at Tulip Time and he would help me at Balloon Days. We got blown out right away. The Burgermeister says—we, neither one, look close to being Dutch. Would you call that a major compliment? Picked up a bad case of writer's elbow. Not much sympathy. It is the left arm and I'm a rightie.

Dick and I on our annual state visit. Sheldon is making a splash—Art & Dorothy Peterson. Have a super location and have added inside seating for 78 and 38 outside stations. A beautiful salad bar, broasted chicken, homemade pie and dinner rolls plus coffee and cinnamon rolls in the morning. This could be A & W's new trend and we are happy for Art & Dorothy.

Iowa is hooking up with Minnesota for a joint convention. This year at the Hilton Inn in February and Summer Social in July at Adventureland. I broke down and bought a pair of white plastic Florsheims. Tim and Larry hit the roof. Dad, nobody but preachers and undertakers wear white shoes. They threatened to have me committed.

Remember Pete with his consolation? Three used pens? Shorty Cox felt sorry for me and sent a box of Shorty's Steakhouse pens. Pete isn't all bad. He doesn't charge for the space I use in the Appetizer.

The Little Flower and I got down to Keosauqua which is Mabel Miller's old territory with Hotel Manning.

For sale or trade: A pair of slightly used white plastic shoes. Would consider a trade for a double breasted suit or used hearse. Also have ball point pens for sale. The word from Sheldon is great. 16 cars on the lot after 9:00 p.m. Plus The Little Flower and I got to the opera.

Summer outing: Harold Schurer and his Chuck Wagon buffet with roast pig and all the trimmings. Borrowed cowboy boots from the roadee (#2 Larry) and bought a cowboy shirt and pants. Told #3 Tim I'll make a good looking cowboy. Dad, you'll look funny. You look funny in anything. Dick and I were bunking together. He snores and rocks the house but with my poor hearing it doesn't matter. Was looking for the room key the next morning. Found it sticking in the door outside. What if a Woman of the World had come in? Maybe one did. One look and said it isn't worth the hassle.

Bought a nice brick house at auction. Maybe Dorene is getting the reward I promised her 40 years ago. Looked up and the A & W balloon is flying over and here comes the chase crew with Crew Chief Stan Woeste (Head Methodist Preacher). I'm thinking they are carrying this ecumenical thing too far. On the other hand, Father Burns may be hedging his trip tickets.

Our summer outing for A & W in July at Adventureland was really a fun thing for the young 'uns. It was a good time, but the sad part was a going away for our good buddy Harry Ayres. Think everybody was sad at losing him.

The Taubman purchase is good or is it bad? We'll see. They seem to be taking the acquisition real serious. We sure do need direction and on the other hand the operators have been independent so long it will be hard to follow—all the same way.

Yes, The Little Flower and I made it to the opera on Indianola night. Dorene and I thought it would be great to rub noses with the Biggies. Turned out most of them were Smallies like us.

The State Fair: I look forward to that every year. If I was in charge there would be at least four fairs every year. This year The Little Flower and I got to the grandstand for the Dolly Parton show. In educated circles they call that a "Visual Experience." If she was a Warren County farmer, she would be flat busted.

An all time first—a baby shower. It was in house for a young lady with us for about six years. On my "Want to Do List" that would rate along side the opera.

Wore the white shoes as Lector at Mass during Balloon Days. Wanted to show Balloonies were a class act.

An article in the paper about senior bird watching. I would rather watch girls. Hope that doesn't change.

Here it is October and we get snow. Cold, not really fair. The State Convention was great. Now to get a little rest and we'll head for New Orleans. Is that an old guy talking? I've always thought New Orleans should be added as the 8th Wonder of the World.

Les, Dick and I got to the Missouri Restaurant Convention. We bunked in one hotel room. Les was paying. To say "conservative" for Les is putting it lightly. Dick snores, shaked the whole hotel. I flood the bathroom and Les hollers at both of us.

The economy is bad to worse. Business was down about 3%. That's bad because we are usually up about 10%. Kinda makes you cry. Now we get a call from Dick (N.A.C.). They have cancelled the New Orleans Convention mostly because of poor response. That is honestly my favorite place. That makes two cancellations in a row. Down in numbers is beginning to make a hurt. In between I was again State Chairman of Coffee Day. Bigger and better.

Hooking up with Minnesota for our State Convention. Dick and I along with Larry and sometimes Father Burns. Have visited three of the last four and really enjoy. Now it's time to bring all the Minnesota people south to Iowa. Every time in Minneapolis would wake up to 6" of clean new snow. Won't be able to match that in Des Moines. Our weather can be Minnesota one hour and Florida the next, but that's not all bad.

Now it's the I.R.A. Convention at Cedar Rapids. We would stay over with #1 daughter Sandy. She met us at the door. New carpet so take off the shoes. I can live with that. The 50th anniversary of I.R.A. One of the biggest conventions in attendance ever. Our show was blessed with the attendance of Monsignor Tolan (Wall Lake). On the real bright side, Sharon Ales (20ish) and the three fine daughters of Bob and Leona McGurk. The Rastrelli's of Clinton have the second generation in charge and doing fine. Would you believe the two sons married Irish girls and the daughter has a boyfriend with an Irish name. Of course, The Little Flower married an Irishman and she has real good taste plus it gave her a full time job.

# 28

## *1983*

Here we go into a new year—1983. My New Year's Resolutions: 1) Treat The Little Flower as the queen she is. 2) Be better to lady candidates. 3) Say my prayers every day (request from Father Klein) 4) Release my two Cubbies cheerleaders, Wanda and Shirley, from their contract if they get a chance to go with the Dallas Cowboys. 5) Look in the mirror every morning and smile (not hard for us handsome guys.)

The Iowa Restaurant Convention was a winner. Jack Laughery, President of Hardees, was our opening day speaker. Couldn't talk with Jack that good, but his folks from Grundy Center were in attendance. His dad, Gerald, was a former auctioneer sale barn operator and order buyer. Had a good visit with Gerald. Mike Darland was at the convention. Beautiful wife, Barbara, was home with new arrival Jacklyn Michelle. Fringe benefit of the Rose Bowl.

The Little Flower came up with an allergy that makes her sneeze. I'll be in big trouble if she's allergic to me.

Our National A & W Operator count is down to 800. Last hurrah for Steve Waskow as Iowa Association President. He had to end the banquet with a hit at me: Gib made a pass at a cute young thing the other day. She came back with, let's get it on. I was just kidding. Checking to see if I still had it. The cute young thing was probably a grandma. Our buddy from Hampton passed away in December, Doc Dostart. Quite a good operator and super guy.

The Wildermans and McConnells attended a surprise birthday party on Jerry Tooley (60). Jerry is the owner of Village Supply and was really surprised. Ray Marshall put this together (about 250) and did a terrific job.

At this time #2 Larry broke his arm playing basketball. He really likes basketball and this will throw him back for the high school team. Larry told Dick somebody stepped on it. I didn't think Larry was that short.

The Little Flower and I had a little R & R in Florida (10 days). In our book, that's a bunch. We had dinner one night with Dick and Peg along with Wally and Sharon Luedtke. They have supposedly retired. Dick is trying to recoup raising milk cows. Wally has bought some apartment buildings to keep Sharon busy. A good time was had by all. Big stories—lies?

Now the A & W Convention is history. Think we gave the Minnesota operators a good convention. Everybody was happy with the attendance and our neighbors to the north thought we were great hosts. Got a kudo from Bob Loughman as a good toastmaster. Our numbers are down. Eight Corporate Presidents in 12 years and that's a big part of our problem. Bob Loughman took over as our new Iowa A & W Association President. Bob and Cindy are really doing a good job. Operator of the Year award from A & W Corporation also Business of the Year award from Albia Chamber of Commerce. A quote from George Allen (Washington Football Coach): A winner is a problem licker. A loser is licked by his problems.

Into my second year as State Coffee Day Chairman. Have added the Pork Producers and a pork sandwich at a fair price and at the A & W we have gone from $200. to $600. for the cause so it definitely is a keeper.

A late addition—On our convention city tour we visited the Botanical Center. Asked the older lady the cost and her reply—Are they all senior citizens? No, they are all young'uns like me. Foolish me paid full price. After all, I'm a young 60.

It's a little late reporting, but I had a good haul at Christmas. Notre Dame jacket, shirts, scratch pads (I scratch a lot). Father Klein had asked me to be Lector at midnight Mass. Help was either hard to get or he was setting me up for a favor. Anyway, I call it an honor.

Yes, Dick is in his first term as N.A.W.F.A. Rep. He was away five days for his first meeting. Back at work and was waiting on a customer at the counter. Connie, she looks familiar. Yes, she should. She works here. Five days out isn't that long. Are you slipping a mite?

Have been writing in the Appetizer since 1972 and Pete on more than one occasion has told me not to take up so much space. Now I have Dick and Bob Loughman. Both windy. Might have to cut them back. So far it is really great working with them. With our Association we have a new President every year and everyone is different.

Our Coffee Day for Retarded this year is March 25th and with the pork sandwich it is making a difference. The problem is to get the whole state into the pork thing. We want to sincerely thank Lute Olson for being our Honorary Chairman a second year.

The Little Flower and I had a nice 10 day junket to Florida in January. Caught Ozark round trip for $200.00 bucks a piece. The plane had no first class.

Guess we were all middle class. Did you ever have shoes stuffed full of paper without a hole in the sole? We carry money on a trip and the object is to stow it in many different places. Yes, I had a shoe stuffed full of $20 bills. The weather wasn't great. Saw the sun twice on 10 days. I got to wear my Christmas Notre Dame windbreaker. Florida natives, like California natives, are a little hard to come by. After five years they give you Homesteader Status.

Things are getting better. The bike promotion is going very well. We also gave a check to Variety Club, which is a very good cause. Norm Rufferidge has had a double by-pass and seems to be getting along good.

Would you believe a Waterloo station lost the commercial Lute and I made? Cut another with Lute and ran it. We have the Pork Producers and Pork Queen set to go.

I've reached the ultimate plateau. My own personal barber and she makes house calls and the price is right.

Got a call from Barb Formanek. The Summer Social meeting is at Sister Sarah's in Algona. I'm a good card carrying Catlic, but an evening out at a nunnery? Anyway, The Little Flower and I did the meeting. Sister Sarah's is a family restaurant with the décor early American to an expresso machine on the back bar. It's a Summer Social at the Great Lakes. Seems like the North is taking over. That's Iowa's vacation heaven. It will be in conjunction with the I.R.A. Convention at The Inn.

A letter from Dick—I'm on a diet, trying to quit smoking, got hit with a softball from a 13 year old girl in the eye, plus the #2 son demolished the family car, plus it hasn't stopped raining in two weeks. Any complaints, call Gib. My slate is full. Oh my, we certainly feel for you, Dick. I've known Dick for over 10 years and the line is always the same about diet and smoking.

Now I'm getting flak for setting up a statewide pork sandwich promotion on a fast day during Lent. I actually did it for the Protestants. It's fair to take money from them any day and now our buddy Lute is heading for Arizona.

Would you believe Dorene had dandelion greens on March 6th? If you're going to be a cowboy, start before 60. I have new boots and can't make them go. Don't even work walking bowlegged.

It's May 1983 and we now have 43 stores and 36 are paid members of the Association. 33 participated in the bike promotion. Next is the helmet promotion. Yes, it is the Lodge for a Summer Social in Okoboji. The first mistake I ever made.

Will there be life after Lute? He and Bobbie are in Arizona. Now we have George Raveling. From his first performance looked like a fun guy. Between him and Johnny Orr next year should be a funner.

Iowa is #1 in pork production and the Eskimo Pie was born at Onawa in 1922. We cleared $500.00 for the Retarded on Coffee Day and already shooting for $1,000. next year. Have to say Gerald Knoll, K.F.C., was a super helper. Even had a helper from McDonald's and that's a first. They are hard to get anything out of.

I'm in a happy mood and usually am (Dorene would have to study that statement). Actually Dorene is a downer and I'm an upper. Has worked for a number of years. We meet in the middle. How could anybody have it so good. Run a big A & W Restaurant and the rent's paid. Live in the best town in the world. Have a brick house. Drive a big Mercury. Have The Little Flower with a great family. What I'm really saying is think positive with a smile.

Dorene and I got the Good Guys Award at our neighborhood elementary school program. When we first moved here in 1956 we weren't too popular in that department.

Our Strawtown Inn and our I.R.A. board member Roger Olson got 4 ½ stars from the Grumpy Gourmet. Edna Borkowsky, Hamburger Shop in Audubon, moved up to 3$^{rd}$ from 7$^{th}$ for state's best cinnamon rolls.

Forgot to mention, from above, have white church shoes. Yes, I'm a member of the peer group. Indianola Balloon Days is going great and, of course, we're known as the Hot Air Capitol. In Hot Air I'm #1 just barely over Bobby Crouse. Pete Seiler has his moments, but Ken Newell is a distant 4$^{th}$.

One of most famous operators and only lady President for the I.R.A. is Mabel Miller. Mabel has moved to Indianola in retirement. She had many appointments over the years from the Governor. She sold the Hotel Manning and Restaurant in Keosauqua. She came into the A & W—I would like a small volunteer job. I got the word out and she reports the phone never stops ringing. Your fault! Could be.

Stub Johnson and Jack McNeil are coming to our Balloon Fest. The other member of our group, Al, is busy with Hobo Days in Britt. The three of us (or 4) are short on smarts but long on hot air.

The helmets are in and we are averaging about 10 a day. We finished up the Bear glasses. Had a few preachers and bible school classes happy, plus the weather is hot and business is rolling.

It's August and they are redoing our street and our front drives are out. A plus—we are feeding the workers. Les took me to the Kraft Show and enjoyed stopping along the way. Have to enter this—Betty Holtz of Avoca, Park View Drive In and Coffee Cup Café, was ecstatic that the writer of "Roll Down the Window" would stop to see her. That makes two fans I have plus she will be President of my fan club.

Our Summer Social was great at Iowa Great Lakes, but was disappointed in the number of A & W's. Not too great. Dorene and I are neither big water people, but we thoroughly enjoyed. Had the scenic boat ride and enjoyed the food. They are full house in the summer. Need to develop something for the winter.

I was elected President of the I.R.A. Quite an honor. I've been writing in the Appetizer since '72 and Pete is running a pretty good ship plus we have a chunk of money in the bank. Long as Pete's around nobody is going to waste it. It was really a great atmosphere around the area and Lakes. Had my annual gin martini and Les came around. Take you to dinner? Didn't know Les that well, but he was tight on the purse strings like Pete. It was after 9:00 and most places close at 9:00. He took us down to the K.F.C. and got a barrel of chicken besides the K.F.C. was owned by our good friend and fellow board member, Jim Miller. An insert—Les Davis was one of the first K.F.C. franchises located at Mason City. Les was with the Colonel many times and was considered a friend. Les only let me have two pieces of chicken, then to the Dairy Crème for a hot fudge sundae. That menu suited me.

The next day got on that big wooden roller coaster. Was in the last car. About did me in. Then there was salt water taffy and nutty ice cream bars.

The balloon event this year was the best ever. Hot, hot, hot. Fun, fun, fun. Bank, bank, bank. Just about wore me out carrying money to the bank. Stub didn't make it down, but a brother, Johnny, from Texas did. Good guy and not as windy as Stub. Al was busy with Hobo Convention.

Had an invitation from Al & Barb—25th wedding anniversary. We couldn't make it. Had a couple of big catering jobs. Al & Barb had over 300 people for food, drink and dance at Duncan. Al, maybe we can make your 50th.

At the Iowa-Iowa State football game, Brian Cooney put a banner behind a smaller plane—"Kevin Cooney says Go Hawks!" Kevin is a graduate of Iowa State. Brother Brian is a graduate of Iowa and they are nephews of our buddy and operator Tom Cooney of Pueblo, Colorado.

Our Iowa A & W Association President Bob Loughman from Albia is playing with a baked potato with various toppings. It has been going good in Missouri—15% of their volume. My thinking—won't put it in at this time.

The I.R.A. show this year is October 30 thru November 2. Plus I'm President of the I.R.A. this year. At the Vet's with over 200 purveyor booths. Win Schuler, long time Michigan restaurant operator, is lead off speaker on the 31$^{st}$. We were also able to get Joe Lee, President of the National Restaurant Association, for our Fast Food meeting. Mr. Lee heads up Red Lobster and York Steak Houses in our vicinity. He will give—Today, Tomorrow and Yesterday. We'll also have Susan Clarke. We picked her up at the Missouri Convention. She is a motivational speaker—Spirit of Service. She is on loan from the Missouri Restaurant Association. She actually works for a franchise out of Kansas City. Our group dinner at the Sea Galley and then back to the hotel for "Pete's Roast." I'm not on that program, but could come up with a ton of material for a Pete Roast.

Salad bars are coming into being. John Rotjer and also Lindsays at La Porte City have great ones. Dick is also thinking salad bar or maybe already has it in. Another job for Connie, his right and left arms. We're thinking, but I'm against it. Why? Not sure. It seems to me like a lot of waste.

It hasn't been announced yet, but Dan Gable has agreed to be our Honorary Coffee Day Chairman. That sounds great! He will also be Olympic Wrestling Coach in 1984.

Every year about this time I have a birthday. A year past 60. Yes, life begins at 60 but you really better figure on beginning a little sooner because it takes a little longer.

Les, Dick and I got over to Omaha.—Association business, convention, etc. plus we had to have a Runza. Roger and Betty Kubic—soft serve ice cream and a villager down the road. Rog is so-so, but Betty makes up for it and a couple of daughters. Nice family. Margarite Goodenow ran the Granary. She was liberated before the term was established.

The 51$^{st}$ Iowa Restaurant Association Convention—biggest ever. Was that last year's line? Win Schuler, landmark restauranteur from Michigan, was our leadoff speaker. Governor Brandstad cut the ribbon. The President of the National Restaurant Association, Joe Lee (Red Lobster Inns & York Steak House), was also on the program.

Got to one day at the Nebraska State Fair. Think Big Red Machine and Runza are equal in popularity. Nice fair, but small compared to Iowa. Now to think about Iowa-Minnesota Convention at Registry Hotel in Bloomington—"A Touch of Class."

Our ranking in the Tastes of America Favorite Restaurant Chains: A & W ranked 28 out of 34. Not all that great. Another new President—Howard Berkowitz. Every time we think maybe this will turn us around. There is nothing new in the world. It's all stolen from someone (Bob Loughman). Now, we have the Christmas Spirit. How about keeping that year round.

Started a collection of A & W mugs. It's real surprising how many different A & W mugs have been around. Dorene just informed me I would have to dust them. It just doesn't seem to be as much fun now.

This year is the 25$^{th}$ for St. Thomas. Seems like yesterday we moved to Indianola (1956). Catlic, Irish, Democrat and then dedicated the church in 1958. Turned everything around but the Irish. Think that is an endangered species. I changed the name to Gibba Maconelli.

It was my privilege to pick up N.R.A. President Mr. Lee at the airport. His job is President of General Mills Food Series Group. He stepped out of the company Lear jet and said—Iowa with its 10 feet corn and they send a five footer to pick me up. Mr. Lee, we are in the era of compacts and I'm a pioneer in that field. I had a nice packet for him. A balloon pin for each member of his family. I happened to hit a soft spot since he's a balloonie with a Red Lobster and Good Earth balloon in their stable. Who says there are no fringe benefits in these jobs.

Our Betty was chauffeured up to the front door of Vets in the rain by Dave Palmitier. What a nice bunch of queen candidates and the four finalists at the banquet were super young ladies. After the banquet I went around to congratulate the four finalists and Shelly Doyle, our new queen, said—You have to be Irish. My answer—Nobody knows for sure.

# 29

## *President Gib*

Took my favorite sister-in-law to Osceola for the Amtrak the other night. The train came in and Lily Tomlin got off and I got to welcome her to Iowa. Yes, it is great being the President and living with the First Lady.

Time to lay 1983 to rest and gear up for 1984. New Year's Resolutions to make and break: 1) Have fun. 2) Be a good I.R.A. President. 3) Treat The Little Flower like the First Lady that she is. 4) Not make fun of Les's big feet. It's guys like him that put alligators on the endangered species list. 5) Keep a low profile (and that's the story of my life—short guy). Yes, life is good in the brick house. So we lost all three bowls (Gator, Rose, Orange).

Bob Loughman is winding down his year as Iowa A & W President and has become one of the best. Plus we have a new A & W Corporate President. More problems? At least he has a background in food service.

Had a good Christmas. Too much candy as always. New ping pong table and set plus an old fashioned alarm clock that ticks and really works. In between we did a complete remodel of the A & W dining room. Got rid of all the dark—the dark plywood to light wallpaper. Counters and booth tops are white with all the trim new oak, new curtains—wow!

Iowa-Minnesota Convention is coming up at Minneapolis. Don Baum is our new State President and should be super. He seems to be a go'er and is making many changes. The bulk of our operators have been independent so long. Sure there will be a lot of fall-out. The first thing—change the hamburger names back to hamburger. I really favor keeping the Burger Family names, but what do I know?

We salute Northwestern—Orange City, NAIA Division II football title. The McDonald All American Band (are those dirty words?) is made up of two members from each state and one each from outlaying states. The Iowa Reps this year—David Lang from Dubuque and Karin Corbin from Indianola who grew up as my neighbor. On New Year's Day The Little Flower enjoyed the parades and I cried through the games and I'll still vote for Nebraska as #1.

We lost Monsignor Luigi Ligutti, champion of the poor. He established the Homestead plots in Granger and came back to Granger to be buried.

As President of the I.R.A, I'm a little short among other things. Not too many can buy bootie pajamas off the rack and one of very few wearing overshoes carrying a real handkerchief and would be lost without Vick's Vapor Rub. Now I've bared my soul.

We have a new celebrity—Susan Clarke. She is a motivational speaker. She came up through the ranks and is on loan from a restaurant group in Kansas City. Her talk—"Spirit of Service" and is super. She has headed up our I.R.A. Convention.

Yes, life is good. Live in a brick house, drive a big Mercury plus the Presidency of the I.R.A. About this time Anita is having problems in San Diego (physical). Dorene was supposed to be gone about three weeks and was back in five days. I didn't even have time to get in trouble. Anita is in the first stage of Lou Gehrig's Disease. She will clean up her affairs in San Diego and possibly come back to Iowa and stay with us.

Think living in the brick house is going to be great. We put in a new kitchen at the brick house. The dishwasher looks like the instrument panel of a B-17. The refrigerator seems simple and thanks to Joe DiMaggio was able to make coffee.

In the first part of January Les asked me to meet him in Cedar Rapids and help him make some calls. We were treated to V.I.P. dining at Ron Godwin's Winifreds. Very good, but for the most part these people are go'ers with a capital "G." They start on drinking and the party thing early and finish up late. I learned real fast to start with that Shirley Temple. Great people, but a little too fast for me. We did manage to get them back with the I.R.A. We finished up at the King Tut Lounge that evening. Brenda, a nice young lady bartender, said—Gib, are you sitting on a low chair? Even in Cedar Rapids I get no respect.

In mid January the people of Pleasantville had an appreciation dinner for an ailing Shorty Cox. They served over a thousand. A good community gesture for one of their great ones.

#2 Larry and I rode up to the Minneapolis A & W Convention with Dick and Lynne. Their theme—"It's a Class Act" and that it was. Everything you can imagine in food and drink. Even had a 30 pound box of mixed nuts, the kind with no peanuts. That's class. Proud to say 27 out of 37 franchises got to the Minnesota Convention.

The Convention really was a class act at Minneapolis. At registration the guys were in tuxedos. Don't look at guys that much but the ladies were all dressed to the ultimate. At each of our doors the following morning was a Wall Street Journal. That is real class. Not that we have operators that even know that paper.

Our I.R.A. summer outing with me as President is June 10–11 at the Highlander. Nobody does it better than Bob and Leona McGurk. We're looking forward to a good time in June.

Worked the Variety Club Telethon again with Les by helping to feed the workers at Adventureland. Chuck Hunt did the Great Root Bear. Would say very good mileage and on national T.V.

We were up in February and down in March. Weather is partly to blame plus the economy is in the tank. The farmers have to get well and that won't happen over night. It's the big Cubs in the World Series. Anyway, they won their first game. If you need tickets for the little Cubbies see me or Southside Myron. We're on the inside.

In that last big snow, ice, rain, snow, ice, I fell down three times and did something to my right knee. Having trouble getting up and down. That spells trouble with us Catlics. Might have to change to another church that doesn't do up and down. We'll check the Methodist prices with Betty Stevens.

On a four day trip to the Southwest, The Little Flower and I had a day over in Phoenix. We went to a 10:30 brunch, a 50$^{th}$ wedding anniversary of a good buddy of mine. My first Bread Man in 1946 and one of the greatest guys in the world. We were actually headed to Reno for our National A & W Convention. Had a two hour lay over in San Francisco which is also the Eighth Wonder of the World. Definitely different people of every nationality squeezed into a little area. Predominantly young running from freakish to square. Iowa is still the best place in the world.

Hard for us South people to believe the Great Lakes—April 6$^{th}$—are still frozen over. Didn't actually see this. Got the info from Stub Johnson. It might not be gospel. Could call Monsignor Tolan. Don't really know if he's Irish. If he isn't, he should be. He has all the symptoms. Besides, business is good. Even sold 52 gallons of root beer last week. Got a call from Don Baum. He hid all the Easter eggs Saturday night and Sunday morning there was 6 inches of snow.

Got all the A & W operators participating in Restaurant Day (former Coffee Day for Retarded) and this year raised over $50,000 state wide. A great raise from the 3 to 5 thousand the state used to raise. The Iowa Licensed Beverage Association and the Iowa Restaurant Association have merged and we'll now be known as the Iowa Restaurant & Beverage Association which moves me from in front of the bar to behind the bar. Went with Les to Dubuque for a local Association lunch with John Hall of The Bridge. Had ham and boiled cabbage, mashed potatoes and gravy. Then we ended up in Amana to check out the Barn Restaurant and get them in the fold. It was brats and sauerkraut. A lot of cabbage for one day.

With Berkowitz and A & W changing the names of the burgers back to hamburgers that bacon cheeseburger has picked up 100 fold. Plus the labeled jugs are a winner which is kinda bringing the bulk sales back. Business is looking pretty good, but Hy-Vee is opening a newly remodeled store this fall with deli-restaurant-catering and cheap. Tough business to fight.

Right now working on 5$^{th}$ annual Balloon Championship. It will open Sunday with the Great Root Bear Balloon and Father Burns taking up Governor Brandstad and they will have A & W caps in hand as T.V. cameras from all three networks roll. This opens the National Competition and that's a biggie.

The float promotion is in conjunction with National Dairy Month plus the thermos and mucho refills. The Metro Opera is in town and they are really good root beer drinkers.

Haven't had a bicycle wreck for over a week now. At my age with a few parts wearing out, glad the hearing was the first to go.

Can't believe I missed a month of the Newsletter. The good part was busy-busy. County Fair and then Balloons were both the biggest and best ever. That County Fair is always good. Father Burns and the Governor kicked off the Balloons with their opening flight plus one of our girls sang the National Anthem. Yes, we are involved plus it is the best week of our year.

Back to business at hand. We are doing a good job with the ½ gallon jugs. In between Dick has gone on a diet and quit smoking. Is it every week he does that?!?

We really had a great Pork Cook Off on Restaurant Day. All the food people were working together and amazed a lot of the business people that we could work together. We definitely had the City Dads confused. We raised $1,590. in three hours for the cause.

It's count your blessings time and for me it's knowing the upkeep on us little guys is ½ what the bigger is. Shorts are pedal pushers for me and those over the calf socks very nearly cover my knees.

Had a nice outing with Les at the evening Regional Beverage Association in Dubuque. When you belly up to the bar with those pros, you better sneak in an occasional seltzer with a twist. Actually tipped glasses with a bunch of great people and we are part of the greatest business in the world. For frosting on the cake, I did a marketing presentation about franchise operations for a class at A.I.B.

The Little Flower and I took in the National Restaurant Show in Chicago (1984). As President of the I.R.A., we were honored guests at a reception. Yes, that's a biggie. The total answer in life is if what you're doing is fun and taking care of your needs and family's. The food business seems to have done it for us.

Bumped into Ron and Cynthia Friedhoff of Ross's Restaurant in Bettendorf. Ron is second generation and we were at a party in the Crescor Room. I was trying to do an interview while watching a belly dancer and that didn't work at all. On Sunday out for 8:00 Mass on North State Street. Nobody out but the dogs and the Catlics. We did have a super turnout at the National Restaurant Convention.

Back to the Summer Social at the Highlander. Bob and Leona McGurk are the very greatest. They also have three sweet daughters. One has already left the nest but 2 were there to help entertain us. Stopped at the Wingas on the way home. They introduced me to a lady. She had to be in her upper 80's and one of Dad's first waitresses. She had just stopped in for her morning coffee. I know she thinks the world was created by the Wingas. The Wingas are the very best and super representatives of our industry.

On July 6$^{th}$ The Little Flower and I went to Tony Prochello's funeral. Tony was a great guy and had more miles than his age. He started out early in the restaurant business at Sioux City. As we knew him, he headed up Iowa License Beverage Service. Tony put on our trips in the 1970's.

A typical day at work. Business is pretty good and at 2:30 I went to the hall at the bank to help a Milk Maid Magic contest and got to visit with the State Dairy Princess from Plainfield. Then at 6:30 went to the Cubbies for a baseball game. Beer, Polish, popcorn and we won.

If you thought there was a brouhaha between me and The Little Flower, it actually was a bicycle thing. I was showing off and rolled the bicycle on cement and grass with a few welts and scratches. Dorene swerved to miss a couple of little older ladies and got scuffed up pretty good. #2 Larry, the spokesman, called a family meeting. Okay, we cool it with the bicycles or they go to a museum.

In the Big Paper, a divorce settlement in Nebraska. Big Red tickets would go to each every other year. In Indianola, we've been around so long some people think we Homesteaded and they built the town around us. Bill Knapp and his wife's first business venture was a restaurant in Allerton and they couldn't make it go but look what he has done in real estate.

## President Gib

And now we're into August of 1984. The Balloons are heating up and the Cubs are in first place in the Eastern Division and business is good. We should book into Chicago for the World Series. Sure Less will pick up the tab as an Association function. On the other hand, I couldn't get a nickel out of him for the parking meter.

Yes, the Democrats have a lady candidate for Vice President—Geraldine Ferraro, a second generation Italian Catholic. I'm an authority on second generation Italian Catholics. Married one 30 years ago. A couple questions and answers from my experience: Is she smart? Comes up with the answers before the computer. Can she be sweet? Could melt butter in a freezer. Can she be firm? Ever get caught with super glue? Is she conservative with the money? Would rather try to get money in the middle of a lion's den. Is she a competitor? The only game I've ever won from her when she said "yes" in front of Father Albors.

Hey, it's Balloon time. People everywhere. One thing I'm concerned about, I'm Chairman of the Finance Committee and on the Balloon Board, and one of our sponsors is General Motors and they have 20 of those little Chevy pickups running around and I'm still on a bicycle!!

Was giving the Nazarene Preacher's wife (my neighbors and beautiful people) a pretty good story the other day. Gib, would you lie to me? Mrs., that's the reason we have confession. What in the world do you Protestants do?

The new menu plus our extra advertising and float promotion has the volume stepped up pretty good, but there is a little trouble with the bottom line. On a fun note, Dick, Les and I did the State Fair one day. We actually took Les along to pay the tab, but he paid nothing. The weather was super this year for both Balloons and Fair. We put Father Burns in charge of that department. The Methodists couldn't seem to cut it.

We have an Octoberfest tied into the I.R.A. Convention. The Fort Des Moines Polka Band and some entertainers, brats, sauerkraut, beer, beer garden, etc. Monday night we'll bus to Charlie's Show Place for dinner and show. Also had a good program. Our keynote speaker was Don Smith, restauranteur from Michigan and big on motivation. Also Walter Conti, gold plate speaker with a good message. Susan Clarke is bringing in "Selling Front and Back." Chef Louis Sather, Chicago-north side, will head up Monday's program with his pork demonstration.

The Restaurant Association is going pretty good. Kappy Kapler is doing a good job in the field and Les seems to be working good in the office. Having Betty around is a blessing.

Up comes the 62$^{nd}$ birthday. I don't really feel that old, but the years are moving up. Plus I moved out of the President's office. It was a great time and experience with a few extra speeches and appearances. It is a let down. Don Baum is doing a super job as President of the Iowa A & W and Sherry is an absolute sweetheart. He writes—On the last insert there was an 83.1% add on. Very good. Ours was a little less. Don also met with the Minnesota operators to help them form an association like ours. Dorene and I had helped Illinois form. Missouri has done pretty well with Ken and Dan of Springfield. Don Baum is complaining about turning 40. Wait till 60. The past has been. Hey, I'll be retired by then. The older (anyway this guy) you get, the more you want to stay the same.

We were all stunned by the passing of Bob McGurk on October 6$^{th}$. He was a special friend of mine and did me many favors the last of which was hosting a super social for me as President. I considered Bob the #1 operator in the state.

The Iowa-Minnesota convention will be February 3, 4, 5. We just got word from Wisconsin and they would like to join us. A tri-state convention in 1986?

The theme of our convention will be "Nostalgia" in keeping with the Corporate marketing theme. Our by-line will be "Allen was Wright." Monday night will be early drive-in: Sloppy Joes, coleslaw, baked beans and dress will be 1900 to mid. Then comes the auction and after we'll dance to the Old Dudley Band. Chuck Offenburger will be the program

Les and I were guests of the Mississippi Valley Restaurant Association. Les was the program and he did a pretty good job. It was held in Davenport at the Blackhawk. Great dinner. Chef Tony is a protégé of Chef Louis and even looks like him.

After 60 you don't have to make decisions. The offspring (I call them #'s) will make them for you. It comes as a suggestion. Dad, will this work? Les got the idea I'm getting senile. Not so. Have always been this way.

It was a sad surprise to go to Bob McGurk's funeral Mass. There were 10 priests on the altar and the bishop sent his regrets. It was for a special buddy, friend or benefactor. Bob had touched all those priests in some special way. I'm a pretty fair Catlic and there would probably be 1 ½ at my funeral. After the services everybody was invited to the Highlander for a spread only Bob could have put together. He was a class guy and he will be missed.

Yes, there is life after the presidency plus the Convention was the best ever and Dorene was with me. Three nights in the Presidential Suite and that's right up there with the Big Biggies. I had volunteered to pick up our keynote speaker at the airport and Les showed me a picture of a clean shaven executive type guy. Here I am at the airport watching the people getting off the plane. Nothing like the picture. Before I could panic this guy hollered—Les, Iowa Restaurant Association. Close enough? He had a full beard which threw me clear off. Got to give him a city tour plus a key to our city and talk about A & W (A & W Balloon pin is my key to the city). Motivation is his game and for me it was a fringe benefit of being the President.

Our magazine editor and a professor at Drake is totally amazed that we put the program together on a brown paper sack and an hour later we're doing it. Everybody has a good time and it works. At Drake it has to be rehearsed and by the numbers. A lot of it has to do with—hang loose.

Time to don the Santa suit and do the Ho Ho Ho. I have about three gigs I do and it's the most rewarding job in the world. Of course, some of the kids are bigger than me. One of my 6 year old buddies said, "I'm almost as big as you." Next year you probably will be. He came back with, "Next year I'll be bigger than you."

Always have to watch the legislature. They meet and they have to do something. Pass to a few bills to let their constituents know they are doing something. For us it would be better for the most part if they would do nothing. They picked up the smoking bill last year and we informed them we cold handle this on our own.

# 30

## *Northern Italia*

In January 1985 we had three weeks in Italy (Northern—above Torino). Dorene gets along pretty good with the northern dialect and I smile a lot. Actually, I don't even do good Irish. The hospitality was super. In fact, I was so full of hospitality I doubt if I could have handled another week.

The trains were great—clean, courteous and on time. We spent three days in France. A cousin lived in a little ski resort on the French Alps. It snowed 4 out of the 5 days we were in the area. The cousin had a little French car. You've seen them drive in the movies. In real life here it is the same. Try riding up and down the mountain with them. That'll make you squeeze the juice out of the Rosary Beads. Only dummies would go to a cold country on vacation from Iowa. The relatives informed me right away that high class Italians don't pinch ladies. That's just the Southerners. Figured out right away that water isn't considered on the menu. It's wine and beer.

We flew out of Des Moines to Chicago on Christmas Day. Plane was loaded and quite a few buddies going to the Freedom Bowl. Air France to Paris. Beautiful Christmas dinner on the plane and then a movie. I'll have a Coke and then coffee. The stewardess says, "You'll have white wine with the turkey dinner and then coffee." We had a five hour lay over in France. Then we jumped over to Torino and a couple cousins met us at the airport.

Bought an Italian cup. The relatives informed me right away the high class Italians don't pinch ladies. That's just the Southerners. Figured out right away water is endangered. Drink beer and wine. No, I didn't pinch the ladies, but between you and me—wanted to. Yes, we had a super great time.

Added to my collection Larry Station personal message and autograph on 1984/85 Hawkeye football calendar. Larry made first team All American linebacker.

Restaurant (Coffee) Day is April 12th and got started putting it together. The pork patty thing is growing pretty good. First the gig of Santa Claus. Asked the little granddaughter who do you like the best—Grandpa or Santa Claus? Without hesitation, Santa Claus. You find out right away where you rank with the grandkids.

Sandy had been on vacation and went through Switzerland and got me a nice pocket watch. Sandy, pocket watches are for old people and I'm still a swinger. Yeah, Dad, but an old swinger.

The President's Ball in Ames was a beautiful Hawaiian setting for very special royalty-rock and Beth Lavalle. Our compliments to George Larson and his staff. Rocky and George used to be partners in the pizza business. Mabel Miller and husband Bob made the remark that it was the nicest President's Ball she has ever attended. Mabel was our first and only lady President of the I.R.A. and now retired and living in Indianola.

It's February 16$^{th}$ and #1 Sandy lined up, with a friend from Cedar Rapids, tickets to the Iowa-Michigan State basketball game at Carver-Hawkeye Arena, 3 pm game time. The friend, Bob, did stats for Iowa and the seat was in the press box. Best seat in the house plus got to go down the tunnel at half time and have a hot dog along side Jim Zabel and Mac McCausland. Was at the urinal alongside Bump Elliott. Rode the elevator with Brad Lohaus and Al Lorenzen. Carried a paper and pencil and the multitude probably thought I was a big time writer. The end result, Bob sells hearing aids and he would line up an appointment in Des Moines. Now I have two hear plugs. That was a biggie from Biggiesville. Of course, I lost my money clip on the way into Carver-Hawkeye arena. Had 35 cents to my name. That takes me back when I had the candy-tobacco jobbing business and bummed cigarettes at the functions. Found the clip on the car floor when opening after the game.

The Restaurant Day with the pork producers went over big. From 11:00 to 2:00 sold 1,500 and cleared about a thousand dollars for the cause. All the Indianola Restaurant operators were working together on our lot and the general public was amazed at our togetherness.

Our Iowa A & W Association President, Neoma Ruffridge, is right into the thick of planning our first Midwest Regional Convention—Minnesota, Wisconsin and Iowa. An A & W rep met with our guys. Nov. 4, 5, 6 are the dates. Not official but our lady says we now have 100% membership in the Iowa A & W Association.

Right now our advertising is with inflatable floats. A little different and it makes it better. Plus, Dick makes his monthly report: Lost 11 pounds. Is that after a gain of 22??? Dick reported he catered for 30 Methodists, friends of Betty

Stevens. Reports were all good. Afraid for me, that would be considered sacrilegious.

A bit of news—Les and Sue Kotz are marrying June 1$^{st}$. Congrats are in order. The appreciation dinner for the legislators was a success. Dave Heaton was all smiles. Usually he's pretty serious. Caught Bill Leischenring and fine wife just weeks away from heir apparent to the Old Yoke Inn throne. Bill is new with me at this point and I called Bill "Tom" at least three times. Bill, if I can't get my head programmed would you consider your name to be "Tom"?

The Little Flower came home with 6 bottles of Skin Bracer. Said it was on sale. Evidently she's figuring on picking up my option for another 5.

Brian David of Kuemper Catholic, Carroll, Iowa, signed to play for Lute Olson at Arizona. Brian comes from Templeton. Growing up I thought Templeton Rye was the community name. It seems every village has a celebration. Sydney has Dandelion Days. That's different plus I hear Doug is making dandelion wine. Will check that out and let you know on my next visit.

Our Association President, Neoma, has put together a Summer Social. A Race Off on July 17$^{th}$ at Ak-Sar-Ben. May have to get a little extra money from The Little Flower for Horse Money.

From Dick—Myron has been under the weather and went to the doctor. He was living too fast and should give up wine, women and song. Myron gave up singing.

The Little Flower and I did an overnighter last week. Went out on a P.R. tour for the I.R.A. plus get a couple interviews for the Appetizer. Ended up at Irish Kelly's in Waukon. Kelly is a big wrestling fan and lives in the hot bed of wrestling in the northern tier of counties and especially in the northeast. His most prized possession was a picture of Dan Gable and Russ Nichols. Can't get any bigger than that.

This year our Summer Social was on July 17$^{th}$ at Omaha (Ak-Sar-Ben). Have to sweet talk The Little Flower out of a little money to feed the horses. Good time, but sorry to say my horse didn't come in.

Les and Sue Davis were married June 1, 1985. Les is Board Chairman of the I.R. & B.A. and spokesman for our great family. I continue to get the fun things in our world. The dairy ladies asked me to be a judge at the Milk Maid Agri contest again. We had first and second at the State Fair last year. Maybe I do know something or maybe it's my helper. Had 35 entries and that's a lot of tasting plus I'm a big helping taster.

Father Kenkel celebrated 25 years of ordination (August 1984) at Dowling. A real class party. Catered dinner for 350 and then Mass in the gym for over 1,000 and a reception after. 35 priests assisting with the Mass and we got to sit with our newly to be ordained priest from our parish. The good news is that Father Burns has been reassigned to Indianola on July 14$^{th}$.

Our Italian trip continued: Next time I'll take an interpreter. Probably need 3 or 4 because they all talk at once when they get excited. Every Monday in the little mountain village of Corio they had a complete market on wheels. They would set up at 8:00 and fold up and move out at 12:00. It was really a nice service for these people.

They really fed us good. Palenta with rabbit and tomato sauce, vino, cheese, fruit-ooh, la, la. We also had bunget every meal—carrot tops, garlic, anchovies chopped in oil.

We also visited the cousin that has a hog farm with 5,000 from farrow to finish twice a year. Quite an operation. They also had a variety of chickens and a rooster that crowed and woke us up every morning about 4:30. If you're wondering, the pig stuff smells the same as at home but the squeal is Italian. Didn't see a single labeled cap or jacket. That market is wide open.

The Little Flower brought home a tube of Brylcream that I had ordered and was complaining about the $3.50. Just charge it up to maintenance.

I was an invited guest to a B.H.S. 1950 class reunion on July 5$^{th}$ in Oskaloosa. It was held at the "Hull House" (actually Al's Steak House). Al came to work for the Hull House as a manager when Mr. Hull bought it and after he passed away he purchased it and he's doing a nice job.

The Restaurant Association helped the legislature pass a bill to make it mandatory for the schools to open after September 1$^{st}$.

Our County Fair was good and Balloons were super. Father Burns is back—our balloon pilot and sky worker. The State Fair is heating up. Got up one day and another to serve dinner to the State Charolais Youth Group.

Have sold 18 of 25 cases of root beer (nostalgia) mugs. A root beer with the purchase of a mug. Minnesota is getting our tri-state convention in Minneapolis in November 1985 ready to go.

My lady for typing and printing the Newsletter sacked it up and my new lady is having a time deciphering. She has Dick as "Doug." If I can't get that changed, might ask Dick to change his name. Doug sounds better anyway.

Got Volunteer of the Year award from Balloons this year. Don't do that much, but guess the seniority kicked in. Anyway, it is a nice honor.

I'm the M.C. at our all school Bussey High School reunion. That plus bringing in the food at the Policeman's Rec Hall in Pleasant Hill. It's every two years and this year 165 in attendance.

Yes, I have the hear plugs and it is the look of distinction for the mature man. My first love is The Little Flower. She still has that original $5,000. Second in line is that I thoroughly enjoy writing in the Appetizer. Our editor, Frank De Fazio, is our unsung hero. Would give Les credit, but don't want him to get the Big Head. Had to do over I would go Italian. Beth Lavalle said the same thing. The Cubs are winning. See you at Wrigley Field in October.

Have been traveling with Dick quite a bit. Really thought he would never make it in A & W, but turned out to be one of the best. Dorene and Lynne couldn't make the Summer Social so they turned Dick and I loose. We finished up the afternoon (Clear Lake) in the lounge telling stories. Mike Corso (windier than me) from West Des Moines was telling as a boxer in the navy sparred with Mohammad Ali and I told of Joe Louis and Sugar Ray Robinson visiting our camp with a boxing exhibition (WW II). When we were getting ready for bed, Dick came up—Did you really spar with Sugar Ray? I do spin a few stories, but in my wildest dreams would I be in the same ring with Sugar Ray? Dick was in the middle of a story and started snoring.

The next morning he related. He found himself on the floor above in his briefs, evidently sleep walking. How did you get back in the room? The door was wide open. I said—What if a woman of the world had come in? How about me walking the halls in my briefs! Yes, it's the chance we take in the Big Hotel.

Speed Herrig (Cookie's Barbeque) grew the beard for the Wall Lake Centennial in 1977. First met him at the 1977 Iowa Restaurant Association Convention and he still had the beard. Our college librarian moved to Washington D.C. a couple years ago. A great fan of Cookie's BBQ and won his club's do-it-yourself BBQ two years in a row before they found out he was cheating with Cookie's.

School is back in session and guess we're lucky. Had a good season and the rent is paid for a couple more months. Iowa Restaurant Association, at this time, is pretty much our life. Kappy (Francis Kapler—fieldman for I.R.A.) came by and I climbed in with him to make some calls. Stopped first in Pleasantville. Kappy wanted to get his ducks in order. Come into Bare Drug and I'll buy you a cherry Coke. The lady said—Gib, we haven't had a fountain for 20 years. Then comes Shorty's Steak House. Denny Cox invited us into his house (the son of Shorty) and there was the fountain and back bar from Bare Drug.

Mentioned that Father Burns is back. We have a young parish. Dedicated in 1958. Three priests and a re-nun.

Our Summer Social and first time at Ak-Sar-Ben for Dorene and I. Reported back to #3 Tim. I had won—two sixty. Dad, I know it's $2.60 and also know you're not about to get into big money. Yes, won $2.60 and lost twenty dollars.

Now it's our 53$^{rd}$ annual Iowa Restaurant Association Convention on October 27, 28, 29, 1985. We again had Don Smith as our opening speaker. One of the best as an operator and speaker in our industry. He is now with the School of Food Service at Michigan State College. Also the college of John Winga. Of course, I went through there in the war thing.

We had Last Vegas night on Sunday and on Monday night was at the Ingersoll Dinner Theatre for dinner and a comedy. Tuesday we brought the Convention Committee to Indianola for an inflation of our new balloon. Our good Father Burns was taking up Chris Brandstad. I protested but you don't get to antagonistic with the guy that's punching your ticket.

The Big Fair was good. Weather was perfect. It was a little cool for the lemonade guys but #2 Larry did fine with floats and elephant ears.

Amana was at the Fair this year with an exhibit of their products plus a restaurant pretty much put together by Carl Oehl. Plus Carl gave me a V.I.P. tour. It was a great addition to our Fair.

Missed the Newsletter last month. One of the few missed in 20 years. Neoma (Pella) is our A & W Association President. The Ruffridge clan do a good job in the Pella A & W. We get a lot of business from the Pella people when they come to town with H.S. or Central. That means the A & W name is good from Pella.

The A & W Army Post Road (Rena's) is going out. Taken over by the F.A.A. for airport flight path. Myron and Laura will probably move to southwest Texas and I imagine Rena will eventually follow them.

There are quite a few A & W's changing hands and we're losing a few with the new regime. I'm knocking on wood. Haven't had a bicycle wreck for over 6 months. Did blow a bicycle tire the other day, but I managed to keep it under control and at the speed I go that's tough. Plus, I'm still saying bad words at the hearing aids.

We have to be proud of our football. October 1$^{st}$ we had three (Iowa) #1 ratings. Iowa Division I-Northwestern; Orange City; Division II; Ellsworth Jr. College, Iowa Falls. That's a bigger biggie. There's a few people in this nation that don't know Iowa from Idaho, but we're correcting that with those numbers.

The big I.R.A. Convention is coming up. Don Smith is our lead off man again on Sunday. He is #1 motivator and if you can't get motivated listening to him, might as well call the Digger.

Les and I got to Lincoln for the State Convention. About a 1/3 of the size of ours because of population. The National Restaurant Association President Ted Ballasteri was the feature speaker. Good draw. A part time executive and no magazine for the Nebraska Association. They have got one thing going for them—Big Red Football. Red is my favorite color, so....

At our Convention my office will be at the McGarvey Coffee Booth. Don't tell McGarvey, he might want me to pick up part of the rent and my perks don't cover rent.

It was the final demise of the K.R.N.T. Radio Theatre in Des Moines. Back in the 30's and 50's era it was theeeee place in Des Moines—plays, shows, barn dance frolic. On my first date with The Little Flower, picked her up with a dozen roses and the bow tie in the new 1949 Ford yellow convertible. We went to the Big City to see Jack Benny and Phil Harris at the Radio Theatre. Don't you think for a minute that I didn't sell that cute Italian girl a bill of goods.

At our Convention's Sunday afternoon meeting I was presented with a plaque—Honorary Board Member of the Iowa A & W Operators Association. Quite a year. Volunteer of the Year award for Balloons and an award for Outstanding Service to our County Retarded Citizens Home.

Things are a little iffy with the economy. Not too stable and Corporate also iffy. Got the word from Berkowitz: The Ames unit should be open in March or April. Our year was down about 7% from last year.

Things aren't all bad. #3 Iowa is headed to the Rose Bowl. Chuck Long is on the run for the Heisman. Dan Gable is revving his troops for another national championship. Johnny Orr and George Ravelling should be in the top 20.

We lost the National Balloon Championship. Battle Creek doesn't play fair. They brought money to the table. 1986 will probably be our last so we'll go all out to make it the greatest.

Congratulations to John and Carol Winga as our new I.R.A. President. John's dad was president 15 years ago. Maybe this is the first father and son as President of the I.R.A.

Presented Glen Gulsvig, V.P. sales McGarvey Coffee, with our personal balloon pin with a 5 minute pitch of its importance. He came back with his Gold Coffee Cup pin. You can't get a head of those salesmen.

Now it's time to dust off the Santa suit. Les volunteered to go along on my visits and be an elf. Some of the kids were bigger than me and they absolutely couldn't figure out Les.

Just got word, Iowa is now open to the outside world. Bridge is open between Keokuk and Illinois. I'm not sure whether it will be Iowa escapes to Illinois or Illinois escapes to Iowa. Of course, that means Delbert and Betty can now escape to the outer world.

Did the Santa again at the Isaac Walton family party. A great thing for a great bunch of people. Nothing in the world as rewarding as playing Santa Claus.

Just got the word Anita is in the final stages of Lou Gehrig's Disease. She had retired in San Diego (cream of California). Dorene went out to San Diego for a couple of weeks to help her settle up her affairs. Then she brought Anita back to finish up with us.

# 31

## *1986*

We're going into 1986 with the economy down and we're hoping it's the year for recovery. For the business at hand we'll get into the New Year's Resolutions:

1) Be sweet to The Little Flower and sign a new long term contract. 2) Cut down on the serious time. 3) Watch more sports. 4) Say my prayers every night and remember Hayden Fry, Chuck Long, Larry Station, Ronnie Harmon, George Ravelling, Larry Bird, Walter Payton, Mike Ditka, Joe Dimaggio (to be continued on a later page). 5) Needle Les at least once a week to keep him on his toes. 6) Say nice things to The Little Flower. 7) Help with George Ravelling's prayers to keep Roy Marble healthy and bring in four more just like him. 8) Visit Dubuque. Did you know John Hall of the Bridge Restaurant and I are two of the biggest little operators in the state? Don't believe it? Just ask us!!

9) Clean up my act in the bathroom. Les has mellowed a fraction since the wedding, but still tough on my water splashing.

Might have to get professional help for those prayers. Is that a job for Father Burns? On the subject of going up or down, our old buddy from Oelwein, Don Pirillo (longtime exhibitor for Smokarama), has arrangements for the final in Oelwein and that's what you call "Love My Hometown."

Have had the privilege both years to haul Don Smith to and from the airport. He is an outstanding gentleman in many ways and never stops talking.

Governor Brandstad has brought in the "Homecoming 1986." Sounds far fetched, but tourism business would be like money from home.

A & W is at the very critical stage. We are down to less than 500 from a peak of 2,300 plus. Dale Mulder is now to be our Executive Director. We have to follow our faith that Dale, as an operator, will be totally on our side. A & W has to be turned around or we're down the tubes. Dick is telling me faith and prayers will do it (he isn't even Catlic). Maybe my faith isn't that strong.

A little trivia. Remember Bill Veek? He passed away a couple weeks ago. Bill helped make baseball fun. When he owned the St. Louis Browns he hired a midget to pinch hit and, of course, they couldn't pitch to him and he walked. Takes me back to high school before I got my growth. Coach used me the same the first two years. I did letter four years in baseball.

The economy is still in the tank and it's important that we work with Up, Up, Up which is also the theme song of our Hot Air Balloon.

Yes, we've lost the National Balloon Championship. Battle Creek came to the table with money and we can't combat that. We won't roll over and play dead. The museum will be built and a permanent field for launching the balloons is now being readied. We will stage a balloon event that all Iowa can be proud of. Let's overcome and make '86 a banner year.

A little trivia from the 1930's: A good customer, Lefty Weddell, handled the telegraph for Dutch Regan's (our Honorable President Regan) sportscast at W.H.O. Also in the 30's, I was growing up on the farm with no electricity or running water with an outside three holer. The first change of times was when Sears Roebuck went to slick pages in half their catalog.

Iowa was sad again in the Rose Bowl but the parade was great with Erma Bombeck. Another highlight was Iowa's float—"Homecoming 1986."

With Neoma as our Iowa A & W Association President, she managed to get 100% membership. Neoma and Norm have always done a good job in Pella. Our new President is Red Hauser and I'm sure he'll do a fine job. Our Regional Manager, Chuck Hunt, had a little trouble with his checkbook. Checks left and no money in the bank. Chuck was a good guy, but didn't have it all together.

I'd like to say business is great, but Father Burns has raised my ante and I can't afford any more trips to the confessional. Plus the B.H.S. girls are going to State so the world isn't all bad. We're all set to inflate the A & W Balloon inside Vet's if the Bussey girls win State, of course with Father Burns at the controls.

We are into "Homecoming '86" plus Restaurant Coffee Day is on April 11$^{th}$ and Hayden Fry is our Honorary Chairman. Hopefully we can get more of the counties into the pork patty thing. That coffee thing doesn't generate enough money.

The President's Ball honored the Winga family at the McGurk's Highlander. We can all look up to John Winga representing our industry. It's a move up. The last two Presidents were shady at best—Gib and Rocky.

Now we have Dorene's sister Anita at our home and getting along fine. In a conversation with Father Burns—You realize Dorene is wearing a halo around her head for living with you for 35 years? No answer!!!

Getting in a little round ball time. One morning caught Phil Donahue interviewing a covey of strip teasers. Would give up A & W for that. It was art at its best.

Stub and Ed Kotz stopped on their way to Missouri for goose hunting. Who in the world would believe that venture story?

A real newby—doing Junior Achievement Class at the high school. Teach class one day a week for 12 weeks—social studies. Really a fun thing. Good class and everybody was responding. More fun than Santa Claus, but that's enuff. Back to root beer. The first four weeks I taught the kids and then they taught me.

We always have fun at our meeting and convention. We work along with the greatest people in the world, second only to our customers. From Dick and stories from the past: Ron Kubly won the volume award and asked Wendell Peck how much he did. Pat Thul pushed Red in the swimming pool. Steve Waskow is giving swimming lessons in Minneapolis and more stories about Gib than I have paper for printing.

Every Sunday Father Burns calls me from the pew to be Lector. This Sunday, no response. It so happened I was in the wrong month. It's good that I'm the only dummy in St. Thomas Parish. Plus our boys and girls both got to the State.

The Crouse family hosted a gourmet dinner as a fund raiser for Balloons. The Crouses make us proud to be a part of the food industry. They raised $5,000 and that's not small change. Crouses have always done more than their share. Have to keep those balloons flying in Iowa. If it gets really bad I'll call in my people from Chicago. As a side, Kansas City Royals headquarters is in Lenexa, Kansas and also the spinach capitol. (I wouldn't be too proud of that) and also the world's largest bumper sticker factory.

Had the whole gang in step for the Coffee-Pork Sandwich Day. Made $1,450. in about three hours. At this time there are only 26 A & W's in Iowa and the whole thing is looking shaky. Plus it's time to get out the white shoes. I think it's amazing that I'm one of the few wearing white shoes as classy guys are a thing of the past.

The Taubman group has put A & W up for sale. That could be bad or good. We'll certainly hope for the best. Business is still hard to come by. It was like a breath of fresh air to see Harry and Jean Ayres this summer. Harry is and has been the very best fieldman.

Had another successful Restaurant Day. Did 1,350 sandwiches in three hours. Even had Big Mac involved for the first time. Plus we delivered in the K.F.C. van. Also had Hy-Vee Deli.

Invited Les in as a guest lecturer for the Junior Achievement teach. It went well until he tried to give away K.F.C. coupons. I put my foot down on that.

Yes, we talk about inflation. A little girl was showing me a dollar the tooth fairy left under her pillow. In my day it was a nickel and we were just as happy.

The candy shakes are going gangbusters. Really think it's the overflow from Dairy Queen, but every bit of business is welcome. Business is slow to slower. The Company hasn't sold a franchise since 1970. Everything is a little shaky and hopefully it will turn around.

The Cubs are doing a good job. Looks like they are a shoo-in for the pennant. The #'s got me a Cub's cap and jacket for Father's Day. I'll go ahead and order a block of tickets for the World Series.

Got The Little Flower out last week for an afternoon and evening. Headed south to the Rathbun area and ended up at the Pale Moon for dinner. I told Dorene I knew a shortcut on 10 minutes of rock. 10 minutes we got into a rain and I got turned around and we couldn't get off this rock road. The Little Flower got me to stop at a farmhouse. We are at least 20 miles in the wrong direction by Russell. The farmer got us to the hard road—#34. That was like when I was showing our visitors the country church where the Pope had said Mass. I was completely lost and pulled into this farm lot. The lady said—Hi, Gib! Husband even hollered from the lot. Always was kinda lucky.

Pat figured our partial redemption for sales tax—gas and electric used for cooking. It was a little time consuming, but will save us about $20.00 a month.

Did my yearly gig as a judge for the Milk Maid Magic Cook Off. One of the judges writes a silly column for the Newspaper and the other lady is the County Home Economist in the Extension Office, and a good time was had by all.

Had a super Summer Social at Clear Lake. Got a tour of the Winnebago plant. Quite large and in Forest City yet. No wonder we have so many Winnebagos on the road. They have done a tremendous job plus it's in Iowa. 275 units—to me that's big. Had a great time reminiscing with Dick and Marge Moore. Think they go back to the 1930's. The menu was root beer, hot dogs, popcorn and candy bars. $50.00 a day was considered a good one. Every item on the menu was 5 cents.

Was making the rounds doing interviews for the Appetizer. Do this on my own for fun—no pay. Does it show? Did an interview from Dubuque and Ottumwa. Took a number of good pictures for the Appetizer with no film in the camera.

The Little Flower's inheriting a little money. Maybe we can move up to slab bacon rather than that sliced in the package thin kind. Nothing changed. The inheritance must have been light.

It's the 4$^{th}$ of July and I'm standing at attention saluting the flag. It doesn't mean much to the younger set, but for us 3$^{rd}$ or 4$^{th}$ generation Americans it meant liberty and even chance for success. Most of us were in World War II.

Got the Quality Assurance report and it was bad. Waited 10 minutes at the counter for a bacon cheeseburger and the bacon was over done. That will be corrected.

Another bicycle wreck. The bicycle is in the shop. I'm not in the shop and getting around just barely. The Summer Social this year was at Dubuque. We had lunch at The Bridge with John and Teresa Hall. Teresa was into her third score birthday so on the boat we rocked with the Happy Birthday song plus a super prime rib dinner. Governor Brandstad was the speaker and he hit a winner with the "Homecoming '86." We love to pick up that foreign money from our plush visitors. We rode the cable car and bought caramels from the Trappistine Nuns. John Hall wants to be my reporter from the Northwest. We'll have to see if he can write.

The fool proof camera that the photographer (#3 Tim) loaned me—make a mistake and it beeps to me in Japanese. Tim forgot to tell me it doesn't beep if it isn't loaded. Called Betty and told her about forgetting to put film in the camera for Dubuque and she was laughing so hard she couldn't talk. She was still laughing a week later.

Word of Monsignor Tolan's last bash held at Ida Grove. His passion is getting money from Protestants. He claims this will be the finale. He has a lot of those under his belt plus a passel of years.

It seems like every month there is a convention. I call it a perk. We don't think about it but our conventions are for eating. #1 Pat's first job was helping our neighbor at the city sewer plant. Need I say more. This year our Iowa Restaurant & Beverage Association Convention is on October 26, 27, 28, 1986. Over 200 booths at Vets.

The balloon event was perfect (weather, that is). Cancelled only three events for the weather and that gave barely enuff time to rejuvenate the body. In fact, we got all the pickle buckets full of money. The Iowa State Fair was also good weatherwise plus the people were spending money.

Joe Guidicessi (Christoper's) has been at the Fair for 18 years. Carl Oehl was drawing beer at the Amana stand. Think that is new this year. Top of the hill by the Arts Building. Bob & Marilyn Schlutz were working the K.F.C. stand and #2

Larry was all over the place looking after his four units. After 6 pm, getting into the Fair is 2 for 1. I came in one evening and a young lady said—You and I can get ½ price at $1.75. So through the gate she said—So long!

One of my most favorite things is fancy chocolate. I maneuvered a box some way and my standard line—will hide the chocolate so I won't eat them all. I hid them and it actually took me 3 days to find them. Gospel!

When I'm not writing it's reading or sports. Cubs, Celtics, Vikings. If those words don't mean anything to you, you're not a sports fan. Then comes college, high school and, of course, Lincoln, Nebraska along with Notre Dame football. Was watching baseball playoffs and Gene Autry was sitting in the stands. Grew up watching him in the saddle and singing. I think of all the things the youngers have missed.

We are down to 25 operations in Iowa. Dale Mulder resigned as Director of the NAWFA and is now President of A & W Corporation. That should be a good move for us. We are definitely fighting for the survival of our company. Burr has resumed as Director of the NAWFA. Dick suggested we get Harry Ayres. I'm not a fan of Allan Burr and think Harry would be super.

City of Des Moines has bought the A & W on Army Post Road and are in the process of bulldozing it. Myron and Laura came out smelling like a rose. That A & W has been a cash cow for Rena and her gang.

Did get out to Lincoln and an overnight with #2 Larry at the Nebraska State Fair. Checked on the Spencer Fair and Stub Johnson. Stub bought us a cup of coffee at his cafeteria. Larry was checking the fair out for a location. He decided it was a little late in the season for lemonade. Flew down to Oklahoma and rode back home with him on Monday. Larry sent a couple of cute young ladies to pick me up at the airport. They put on heavy lipstick and grabbed me with the big smooch. We created quite a stir, but sometimes those Oakies need a little stirring.

Had an A & W Advertising Committee meeting at Forest City. Curt and Florence are the greatest and Curt's forte is hunting, fishing and a little nip. Curt had got a moose (maybe in Montana) and Florence had prepared the moose and invited half the town. Even met Ma and Pa Brandstad.

The Convention at Wisconsin represented over 12 states in the Midwest and was held in LaCrosse. The Wisconsin operators did a tremendous job plus it is central. The Iowa ops will have it next year and voted to hold it in La Crosse. The Wisconsin people had a sing thing and the Iowa gang didn't do too good. Dick can't carry a tune in a barrel. Don Baum might be worse. Larry and I aren't great, but the best of the bunch but couldn't carry over Don and Dick. The Convention was super and I thoroughly enjoyed sharing the McGarvey Coffee booth.

Had to apologize to Russ Reel. Betty read it in my notes as "Reeland." My writing is just barely and most of the time not that good. My typing is worse, sooooo. A lady from The Lantern in Ainsworth pinned me with a pin—"A perfect example that nobody is perfect." Bruce Lamport's daughter was along with the Lamports. I introduced her to #2 Larry, but it didn't take. Also tried Monica Stence, our Miss I.R.A. from last year, on #2 and that didn't take either. Les called on me to introduce our new President and Les shoved up a chair for me to stand on. Governor Brandstad got up to give his presentation and I was bringing up a chair. #2—Okay, Dad, cool it.

We're coming up to Christmas and I'm not sure Santa, Confessional, and Father Burns will all mesh. I was informed they are completely different operations. Plus I stepped on The Little Flower's sore toe on the dance floor. Trouble, trouble, trouble.

Just got a letter from Big Al's Wet Goods in La Crosse and he wants to book the Gibs Brothers for next year's Christmas party. At this time the Santa suit and a Ho Ho Ho to all.

# 32

## *Down Under in Australia*

The Little Flower and I are leaving December 31$^{st}$ for Australia. Les is sending us on an all expense paid trip to do an article on their food industry. If you believe that, there is a new bridge south of town you can buy!!! It's summer down under and wish you could see my tan. Just back from Australia and had a great time. Signed up for the tour from a flyer which included 120 medical doctors, 1 banker, 2 restaurant ops (that's us). The doctors had an average age of 75. It was really tough breaking them out of their shell. They never really learned how to be regular type people. There were 6 young couples and we hook up with them. Great!

Now it's 1987 and 1986 was my 40$^{th}$ anniversary year in the food business. Of course, I started in 1946 and The Little Flower joined in 1951. If I was to start again tomorrow, it would be in the food business. There'll be no resolutions this year. Us older guys get special dispensation plus 10% plus, sooooo.

The Little Flower and I both enjoyed the visit to New Market. That is former coal country and we both grew up in that environment.

Last year at Thanksgiving (always at Bussey), I was singing praises of the dressing. Yes, it was Stove Top. This year with oysters yet.

#2 and #3 took a fun trip to San Francisco and I'm figuring at least a bucket full of Ghiardellis. They are into this healthy thing—not too much chocolate. They brought me a pin—"Got Any Chocolate?"

In between, the word "senile" came up. I'm not getting old. It's a graceful aging process that sometimes creates a void. Bob Loughman and I are working on a bike promotion with the Iowa Association paying 2/3 of the tab. Need that Association money to get working.

Had a letter from Betty Stevens. The bridge is in so they can now get here from there or something like that. Besides, The Little Flower and I got out for a visit with the operators. Ended up in Iowa Falls and Rocky was entertaining the kids with balloons, etc. One of the little girls said—Are you Rocky's daddy? That took the wind out of my sails since we are about the same age (within 10 years).

Yes, we are into a new year and it's inventory time. 1) The business wasn't too bad and take it from this one, will be great. 2) The Cubs won a few, but not the World Series. 3) Larry Bird won it all. Johnny Orr is packing them in. 4) The Little Flower gets sweeter all the time. 5) The Arts—had a big time at the Des Moines Metro Opera in July. On December 21$^{st}$ went to the Des Moines Ballet—The Nutcracker. It was a present from the gang at the A & W. Yes, for me it was iffy.

#1 daughter Sandy had the family Christmas dinner this year. Mom & Dad had to go a day early because Mom had to supervise. Beautiful Christmas dinner. Now it's time for midnight Mass. That little foreign car, whatever, is going to take 6? The Merc did it with room to spare.

The wedding band wore through and dropped off in November. The Little Flower got me a new one. That's pretty serious. Probably a long contract extension.

Had a little warmer type weather. Get to thinking dandelion greens, bullheads, mushrooms, Cubs and then comes reality. It's not really spring. Plus I visited the eye doctor and those five year old plastic lenses were history and now the fog has lifted in Indianola. This pair might run me in.

Have the bicycle promotion to go in May. We put together a 32 oz plastic cup promo to go later. Red Hauser has been our President the past year and has done a yeoman's job. Was in Mason City and stopped to see Red. He was closed and the neighbors didn't have any idea where he was. Stopped in at Chuck Shills' Maid-Rite. Les and Chuck were buddies. Red and Doris were spending a few days in Florida. Asked Chuck to borrow a little money and he ran out the back door.

Our "Know Your Neighboring Operator" for the March Appetizer was from our trip to Australia. The Australian people are hang loose and fun. They do quite a bit of drinking. If you're in a neighborhood and can't see a pub, you're probably standing in one. Most all had a band. In our pub was a six piece band—trumpet, bas sax, trombone, guitar and piano board. The hostess was called a Public Relations Person plus the band was playing my kind of music and the hostess grabbed me for a dance.

The next venture was run by a family—man and wife and two sons—12 and 14. They have a cruise launch that takes customers up the Hawkesbery River to their homestead for a sumptuous BBQ. They also work boys camp and girls camp and plus other various groups. On the launch they serve hors d'oeuvres plus beer. Arrived at the homestead and had rib eye steak, grilled prawns, baked potato and extensive salad bar. Beer was served before and a nice white wine was served with dinner. This was topped off with pecan pie. The family pretty much ran the operation. The homestead is hardly accessible by anything but boat. Two neighbors helping were Sawley (Sally) and Di. Back on the launch, a nice cup of coffee was served. The beauty of the landscape and wonderful people we met were the real highlights of this sojourn.

The Australian trip was one of our very best. It was kind of a second honeymoon too, but will bypass the mushy part. It was a tour we received through the Iowa Bankers Association. We figured it would be a group of bankers. Out of 200—one banker, 120 medical doctors, 2 restaurant ops (me and Dorene) and the rest were assorted. The average age had to be 70 which made us youngish. Remember at one juncture an older doctor with a camera wanted a picture and his hand was shaking too much. I offered to help. What scene did you want? Just point and shoot.

Took off December 31$^{st}$ to spend New Year's Eve in San Francisco. Took the cable car (Powell and Market) to Fisherman's Wharf. Ate fish with a couple of bottles of beer. Did the street scene to Ghiradelli Chocolate then headed back up the hill on the cable car. Checked out the old St. Francis Hotel then to our Hilton Union. Went to our hotel room when the swingers were starting their go at the new little guy—1987. The hotel book said Mass on January 1$^{st}$ was at 7:00 a.m. As usual they were wrong—7:30 a.m. We got there two minutes before 7:00 a.m. (2 blocks) and just stayed and visited. Quite a few got the wrong information. Not sure the $5.00 I dropped in the collection plate covered our escapade of the last few days.

Will get back to the Australia trip later. Our business was up about 12% for February. Menu prices accounted for 3% and super weather was the rest. The economy is still iffy. On the positive note, the Hawks had a good season and could go to the Final 4.

Our Restaurant Coffee Day is still building with the pork sandwich and we are happy. This year we cleared $1,000. from our A & W and that's up from about $300. before.

I visited the beverage show in Cedar Rapids. Said hi to our hostess with the mostest Monica Stence from Jerry's Alibi (Elkader). Monica, I'll run #2 Larry by again. Will you give him another chance?

We are heading into middle of the year and things are looking up just a hair. Even see a farmer smile once in awhile. From the beverage convention our legislator from Carroll informed us that Templeton Rye is still alive and well.

My balloon pilot, Father Burns, celebrated his 40$^{th}$ year of ordination in March. He had a beautiful Mass and we all filed down the hall for a nice dinner. Two minutes before the festivities were to start—You're the M.C. Father, happy to do it, but maybe somebody else would be better? Asked Dick and he's down in the back. You're it!! The lady in charge of dinner said—Gib, aren't you scared? Sure, this guy has my ticket punched and if I blow this I may have to go Methodist and I don't trust them at all.

Went to John Rotjer's sale. The Waterloo economy plus competition did him in. Bob Lindsay was sold out the day before. Road moving had something to do with it. Verle and Louise Harness have retired. Had word from Evelyn Lewellyn. Verne passed on about three years ago. They had been in Casper about 10 years.

Our Summer Social will be in Keokuk this year. Fixing that bridge opened that country up. Delbert even sent me a fishing cap. Maybe some day

Yes, I had a little problem last week. Was heading to Des Moines for the A & W meeting. Got pulled over by the local police. Had forgot to renew the car license and my driver's license had expired 9 months ago. Besides the embarrassment, had to take the written test. Used my one phone call to tell President Florence I wouldn't be at the meeting. Bought the new car license and next day took the test. Stopped in at the Police Chief's office. Take me off the Bad Guy List. I'm clean. The kids have a good mother, but dad is a jail bird.

We got the bike promotion in and it went very well by all reports—24 of 25 billed and 23 of 25 were in the plastic cup promotion.

Australia trip continued—On our overnight in San Francisco, The Little Flower laid her glasses on the bed and then rolled over on them. It popped a lens out. The next day is New Year's and we are on our way to Sydney. I tried to fix it for 5 minutes, no luck. Next day Dorene was relating this to one of the ladies. Helen's husband can put that in. took him 10 seconds.

The plane trip was 19 hours. Stopped in Hawaii and changed planes. Then another stop in Aukland and 2 hours on to Sydney. Three meals, three movies, drinks plus a little sleeping. Arrived in Sydney at 2:30. Not too sure about the day. Crossed the dateline and the watches get pretty confused. New Zealand and Australia are beautiful. After all these years we find we are doing most everything wrong. Drive on the wrong side of the street and that relates to walking, escalators, etc. Down under the sun is directly north at high noon. The water gulps out of the sink in a left hand swirl. The Little Flower and I were walking down the street in Sydney and I was trying to get my directions. Asked the gentleman coming down the street—Which way are you going? He thought about 5 seconds—I'm going the right way.

Back to business at hand. The big question on our fronts—Should we have this tri-state plus the National Convention? A ton of different answers. Our Summer Social at Keokuk is July 13$^{th}$ and that's a go. Sure Betty has a great afternoon arranged for us in that great river town. Betty is a mite churchy. If there is a choice between, I'll take a "girlie show" over church.

A few years ago we had a little social thing, abut 15 operators in the Southeast. Have a party or something in a different unit every month. The time at our place the choice was an opera at Simpson or 3A baseball at Sec Taylor. Every vote was for baseball.

For Father's Day the kids got Jack and I three tickets for a Cubs game. It was actually with a tour group. Into Chicago on the Amtrak from Osceola on Friday, Wrigley Field on Saturday and back on Sunday. There were about 28 in our group and we really had a good time. Jack was the ring leader and really entertained. When we got back to Osceola and said our goodbyes, they all said it wouldn't have been the same without you. Jack said—What did they mean by that? They weren't hugging me.

Our Summer Social will be at Keokuk. The rooms aren't too plentiful, but Betty says not to worry. She has pup tents and you can pitch them in the Methodist church yard.

Had a call from Florence and our #'s are down to 23. Maybe we can have an alumni gathering to get the crowd up.

The Restaurant Day Pork Cook Off was successful and fun. Had the whole town involved. Had Mabel Miller in charge of the money. Netted just under $1,000.

Back to the Australia trip. I could fall in love with Sydney (as in Australia). Of course, I already have a love. Drunk driving laws are very strict—.05. They do a ton of drinking. Really hang loose. Great people. There are many different kinds of football. Lawn bowling is quite popular. Very popular from the English background. Esky is a picnic. Shandy is ½ beer and ½ lemonade. M.Y.O.B.B. means Mind Your Own Bloody Business. B.Y.O.B. is like our country—Bring Your Own Bottle. Take away food. Give away at intersections. Good Die, Mates.

August 1987 and a really hot summer. The whole balloon show was great. Our first show at the new field in the country. #2 Larry got Volunteer of the Year this year and also last year.

Dorene and I had to miss the Summer Social in Keokuk. From all reports it was a real winner. Nobody does a better job of hosting than Delbert and Betty.

For Mother's Day the #'s gave mom two tickets to Cats at the Civic Center. She was to take her best boy friend and I was hoping she had a hider. Told the guys it was great.

Didn't get to the opera. In fact, on opening night Jack and I were on the Amtrak heading for Chicago and Wrigley Field. More about the game—The Cubs were getting beat and in the 8$^{th}$ inning it started to rain. What do you think, Jack? If they can play, we can watch. You can only get so wet and then it starts running off.

So on Sunday morning had to catch church—3 blocks from the Palmer House. Jack is Methodist so he didn't have to go. We had a couple hours to kill before the train ride home. A foxy little older lady inquired about a cab to take her to church. I was trying to explain the church was only a block and half away. That's fine, but I happen to be Episcopalian. Oh, my! Jack and I headed for the Sears Tower with our Cubs caps on. A couple of workers with their brown bag lunch popped up with—Tinkers to Evers—and Jack says—Yup. Let me give you a couple of stories. No, no, no. Got to get back to work.

The Little Flower gets sweeter and I am five years past—life begins at 60. Balloons were great. The County Fair President asked me to be a judge at the County Fair Cookout so we missed the dinner train. Got to Waterloo just as the train was coming back. They had a good time, you could tell.

This is the year for our bi-annual Bussey High School reunion. In 1985 I catered the dinner (165) and gave the opening prayer and was the M.C. The committee decided I was doing too much so they had a preacher (one of the alumni) do the opening prayer. Brother Jack was a 50 year grad we were honoring and I was telling the grads I thought he was the funniest guy ever and vowed to be just as funny. Jack pops up with—Bet Mom wished we had a few smarts, don't you, Gib? They presented me with a plaque—Best M.C. Ever. Don't know what they were comparing to. Only one they ever had.

Second honeymoon Australian trip continued: We had two days in Sydney. Dorene had a cousin there. Migrated from Des Moines plus we had the parents of a concession buddy of Larry. These two gave a good tour of Sydney plus it was too bad we didn't have more time with them.

After Sydney we went down the coast for a day in Tasmania and then on to New Zealand. We lived on our cruise ship (Viking Star) good. In fact we didn't have to move our underwear every day. Our cabin was on the third level and three doors from the laundro mat. Eight washers and 3 dryers. With 750 passengers, it was the busiest place on the ship. We were close enough to catch it at odd times. I solicited the customers and Dorene did the washing. In the trades they call that "laundry pimping."

The second day out Dorene got a heckuva cold and next day I got it too (probably snuggling too much). There were 20 medical doctors in our group. One particular doctor buddy asked me what I was doing for the cold. Hall Cough Drops. Guess that beats my Vicks.

One of our stops was to view the yacht races. A passenger, Amy Connors, was mother of Dennis Connors the pilot of Stars & Stripes.

We had a day at the State Fair planned and it rained out but we got together (Dick, Les and I) for one afternoon and evening. The Little Flower did her annual dinner for Larry's buddies and fed over 100. A farm couple from Swea City got in and apologized for finding out and offered to pay. Larry told them they were very welcome and just sit down with those carnies. You might learn a new trick.

Now it's the I.R.B.A. Convention October 25, 26, 27 at the Savery. Good old hotel plus Guido is doing the food which is super good. It's 200 booths at the Vet's and back to the Savery Penthouse for our banquet. Curt Jante is our A & W President and he and Florence are great hosts. The seminars are great for learning and smarts, but I come for fun and socializing.

Had another fun weekend. Flew to Okalahoma City to help Larry button up the Okey State Fair. Was down there the weekend the Okey guys were beating up on Iowa State. Larry sells a quart plastic jug and it took me two days to figure out the natives were saying—"Give me a jug." #2 Larry put me up first class in a Best Western!!! There were four of us in the room.—three guys and a grandma cat. Large bar of soap (remember hard water Castile). After 2 showers it was either skin transplant for the face or different soap. Hey, it's a Midwest World Series with St. Louis and Minneapolis. I'm picking the Cards, but next year it will be the Cubs all the way.

Back to the I.R.B.A.Convention. A lot of good seminars, but I'm mostly into the socializing and fun. McCormack Distributors with Taylor Ice Cream machines and salesman Bernie Grady as one of the great ones. The first time he called on us in the afternoon was with a lot of conversation and had a couple of drinks and he stayed all night. Had a big old three story house and four kids and a couple ladies (workers) staying with us. Bernie was to sleep with one of the little guys. Bernie had a cast on one broken leg plus he was a big guy and wasn't too mobile. The little guy wet the bed and fixed him up pretty good. That enters into the conversation years after.

Plus the Cubs won the last game of the season. No place to go but up.

It's October and another Oklahoma State Fair. Flew down to the Okie City to help Larry finish up (wasn't that much help but enjoyed the Okeys). Here I am serving root beer to these guys and their brothers are in Ames beating our guys to a pulp. A friend of mine was working a jewelry stand with real gold rings. Take these home to The Little Flower. Haven't done anything that bad. Besides, it's time to get started on my letter to Santa Claus.

Sent my copy in to the Appetizer. Dick and Les pulled it out and put in a write up about me. When St. Pete calls and I have to get my things in order, Dick will get the job of writing my resume.

McDonald's is hurting my image since they started hiring old ones. People now think I am just another little old guy off the street.

Had our Tri-State Convention at La Crosse on February 14 & 15 at the same hotel as last year. It was Iowa's turn to host and Wisconsin makes a great setting plus good people.

Yes, turned 65 and we start getting blessings instead of working on resolutions. Thankful I'm ¾ Italian by association, the brick home, the Big Mercury (we're aging gracefully together), The Little Flower (she gets sweeter all the time especially since she got that inheritance), my job, Australia, New Zealand, Cubs, Hawkeyes, Johnny Orr, Stub & Vi Johnson, my foster son Dick and bride Lynne, the Civic Center (The Little Flower and I are getting big in the arts), Balloon Days and all the State Fairs.

Have a Big Wedding in the family planned for January 9th. #3 Tim is marrying Shelli Netley, the girl he has been going with for 7 years. Still have #2 left and he might be a problem. Monica Stence (little queen and eligible), operator at Elkader—Could you and I get together and talk about this? Another great year and I vow to have more fun than last year. Enrolled in Retirement School, but flunked out.

Father Burns has been in the hospital. The Methodist prayers must have helped because he's well on the way to recovery.

The National Convention in Orlando was a huge success. We took the grandkids down to have the run of Disney World for a week. Great service for us and also the kids. Next the 2nd annual Tri-State at La Crosse. Our numbers are getting small so we need 100% participation.

I was involved in the Iowa Restaurant & Beverage Convention at Cedar Rapids. Those beverage guys are a tough bunch to keep up with. They start about 8 o'clock in the morning.

We're into the holidays. Hayden Fry is taking the team to the Holiday Bowl and winning. He will get my write in vote for President plus C. Vivian Stringer for Vice President with her Lady Hawks. We're also thankful for George Perles, Michigan State, who restored a little credibility for the Big Ten with his Rose Bowl victory. The Wingas were in the stands. John is a 1956 graduate and played with their band in two Rose Bowl parades.

Did the Santa Claus gig and the grandkids (5 & 7) figured Santa Claus out, but they thought it was a funner anyway. Plus we were in a holiday party at Christopher's. It was 5 stars all the way. The Little Flower is a sweetheart even if I never got my hands on that inheritance.

On our social calendar the Restaurant Association was our life. Now it was time for the President's Ball at Newton with Tony Helling as President. Tony is the greatest as host along with his girlfriend. The theme was country western cowboy. A lot of bowlegged cowboys. The cowgirls were normal. My legs started bowing at about 11:00.

The next night was our annual Appreciation Legislative Dinner. Our 3 lobbyists were mingling and everybody seemed to be enjoying. Soft sell all the way and Les managed to hand them a list of our priorities.

# 33

## *The Last of the 80's*

Then came #3's wedding. Good to have boys. Supposed to be cheaper. The rehearsal dinner should be a breeze. The guys said—Hey, it's a party and Dad's paying! Ended with and cost more than Sandy's whole wedding. The wedding was beautiful. That's what the ladies always say. I was more into the dance. Tim's in-laws, Howard and Sharon Netley, are really swell. Sharon asked me to dance 3 times. Howard is a nice guy, but I wouldn't care to dance with him.

Yes, the Tri-State Convention was a real winner. The Committee did a super job. 11 of our 23 units represented. Dick and Lynne rode over with me. We were on I-90 with the snow blowing and me with both eyes on the road and Dick as co-pilot. Dick was into a pretty good story with the punch line coming up and he stopped. I looked over and he had gone to sleep. Dick gets real excited when he's telling a story. At our banquet the theme was the Roaring 20's with the Committee ladies in flapper dresses and guys in Al Capone suits. Then came the auction and they gave me the job as ring man. Bid in a few things and lo & behold bought 10 Nebco coffe cups. Guess they were reselling any way and got home with 4 cups.

The next morning the Committee served coffee to the guests with 3–10 gallon thermoses on dollies. Knocked on a door—Jeanne Chapman came to the door and gave me a peck on the cheek. I'm going to bid on that job next year.

Did the Bike Promotion again this year. W.L.O.C. put the bikes together and delivered to the participants. Then came Coffee Day-Pork Patties. This year it is after so that gets me off the front burner.

The Beverage Convention in Cedar Rapids was next on the agenda. Great bunch of people, but too fast for me. They are on the sauce by 8:00 in the morning. The Mayor, Don Canney, (good Irish Catholic) gave the welcome Monday morning. Welcome to the smells of Cedar Rapids—Roses, A.D.M., Pencik Ford or Quaker Oats. Alburnett got the nod for best dancers in the state. The Pohlmans and Mahoneys won with George Seffrit and Daisy a close second. One of my favorite young ladies won the Pool Tournament, Monica Stence from Elkader. There was a question—How many sweaters Dick brought? It was 12 and he wore every one of them. Chuck Gordon, Sherrie's Place, Sioux City, was the #1 entertainer. He sat at our table and we were laughing all the time.

The Pork Patty Day did $900.00 and the Co. did a total of $1,900, against a total of 3 or 400 before.

At the National Convention I won a blazer-slacks from Angelica and a little green bill cap. Will be a great outfit for St. Pat's Day.

Yes, we lost as of 1989 the National Balloon Championships. They moved on and I'm not crying. Could be better for us. The plan is to have a balloon event of our own.

It's time for Coffee Day again. We're getting a few more into the Pork Patty thing all the time. It takes longer to set the traps, but it pays off. Our old buddy Mabel Miller is helping this year to take care of the money. Nobody is more qualified for that job. She is the absolute greatest.

Through the year I can be Greek, Italian, Jewish, etc, but on St. Patrick's Day it's back to Irish plus a break from Lent. Yep, it's write in for President—C. Vivian Stringer and V.P. Larry Brown. Plus it's the year for the Cubs—tied for Division $1^{st}$ place after the $13^{th}$ inning win August $4^{th}$. Besides that it's time for dandelion greens, bullheads and mushrooms.

It comes to mind now, we had the bacon cheeseburger (Teen Burger) 25 years and it was far and away our best selling sandwich before the Big Guys caught on and put it in. Now they are bringing in bacon which is a good idea.

The Bike Promotion went real good. Hardees are taking over the world. Opened this week in Indianola. They don't really have a come on. McDonald's had the 15 cent hamburger, we have the root beer and they have ho-hum, but so far they are doing it.

News from beyond—Bill Leischenring was elected to the Board of the National Restaurant Association. Bill took over the Ox Yoke Inn (Amana) in his early 20's from his parents. He's also this year's Coffee Day Chairman. Jim Duncan was also honored. He has been the voice of Drake Relays since 1951 and this year the track was named the Jim Duncan Track.

Aside—went around the corner too fast. Feet went out and went down the stairs on the back side. Was a little sore for a week but got along. Plus we are into a dry spell pretty much all over the state. Root beer floats, which is a natural for us, are going well.

The national election is coming up in November. We're voting for the people that will help us and we have Bill Leischenring with the N.R.A. to take care of our needs there.

Now The Little Flower's bike breaks down. A 1950's vintage Gambles bike that just plain got tired. We have a picture of the Pope on the wall above the cash register. Fellow inquired—Is Gib Jewish? He has a picture of the Pope on the wall. Can't really hook that up but whatever works.

Greg Johnson and his fiancée were at our Summer Social (Austin, MN). Great couple and are joining our Association. This Clear Lake Summer Social had to be the best ever. Plus the Okoboji meeting was super. Maybe the Great Lakes do have something to offer. Our last National Balloon Championship is coming up—August 4–13, 1989. #2 Larry will be President of Balloons next year. I've been Finance Chairman since day one. We hope it works. The County Fair usually precedes Balloons and the pre-fair party for all the county 4-H'ers on Friday night and we help put the party together.

#2 Tim's bride, as of January, a graduate of Iowa State in Home Ec and went to work for Better Homes and Gardens (Meredith Publishing) as a cook book editor. I offered to give her writing help and she never did give me an answer.

September 1988—Business is still rolling along at a nice clip—good summer. We have a nationwide drought that will eventually catch up with all of us. Our little County Fair was one of the best ever and Balloons were super. Fair ends on Thursday and Balloon registration starts on Friday. I change from a Fairie to a Balloonie overnight (might want to change that wording).

Dick Wilderman's dad passed away. Les and I got to the services in West Branch to pay our respects. John Winga made the front page cover story of U.S.A. Today on July 8–10 about Washington and the drought. Wingas are celebrating their 60$^{th}$ business year. Cedar Rapids T.V. had a program about John and the restaurant business. More publicity. We may have to call him "Stub Johnson."

Les and I judged the Milk Maid Magic contest. We had our white laboratory coats and the ladies thought we knew what we were doing. A few years ago I taught a 8$^{th}$ grade Junior Achievement class and last year #3 Tim taught the class. I offered to come in one day as a guest speaker, but never got the call!??!!

Been promising Les a balloon ride for years and this year got him scheduled in the morning when the air is cooler for more lift. Another reason smaller is gooder—I can be the Lector at Mass and fill in as altar boy and nobody would know the difference. The Balloons were a complete success. If you need money we are loaded up. Will even furnish the pickle buckets to carry out the money.

Had a casualty at our house Monday. Dorene fell off her bicycle and broke a hip. I was out on a sojourn with Les and they caught us at Central City. Les and I got back to Des Moines at 9:00. They put in a plate. Right now she's doing fine at Mercy. She has more guts than the average 10 and stands more pain. She is now giving orders by telephone. In case you didn't know, there is more to operating a household than running a vacuum cleaner. For instance, how do you run a dishwasher, microwave or a washer-dryer? Plus I put an ad in the paper for a live-in housekeeper. Rather you wouldn't mention that to The Little Flower.

Dorene was in the hospital five days and home 3 days and asked me to take her to work. I ignored her, but she called #1 Pat and he took her. She gets around on a walker and sits on a stool to do chicken and onion rings. Her mouth works real good giving orders, etc. She did get a little mad when she caught me selling her plants.

Ed Kotz stopped in Sunday. Had been to Missouri dove hunting. I'm not sure that guy hunts, maybe just getting away. This time it was young Ed. Sr. is home taking care of the new bride.

Did the World Expo Show at Amana. All night at Sandy's and the train down to Middle Amana. Then ride the train back at 5:00. Sandy went along and we really had a good time.

News—Greg and Kristin Johnson (Austin, MN) were married 10/16/88. A couple of nice youngers and we wish them the very best. Plus Greg has joined the Iowa Association. Kristin is a nurse at the local hospital.

We're having our A & W meeting with the I.R.A. Convention on October 30th. Our A & W Group had dinner at the Kaplan Hat Factory on Court Avenue. Then back to the I.R.A. masquerade and dance starting at 9:00. Some of us don't need masks and for others it's a good chance for one night of glamour, plus we got that hour back we lost last spring.

The Little Flower is gradually getting back to full swing. Still one shift instead of two. The cards, letters and flowers were much appreciated. For a household hint, before putting clothes in the washer, separate the dark from light and if you have a red velour blouse hide it in the closet or better yet, sneak it into the Salvation Army box.

Back to the Ag Expo—A farmer asked what I thought of the foreign plows. Didn't really see any foreign plows, but observed the parking operations, the $2.00 charge at the entrance, the food operations and general layout of the show. The farmer laughed. That wasn't what he saw at all. We also saw the Toby Show. I laughed more than anybody and Sandy laughed at me plus Toby was wearing white shoes just like mine.

Another year of finishing up the Okey State Fair and riding home with Larry. I almost understand those people now. Another year and I can probably pass as a native.

It's Thanksgiving coming up and we all got to Bussey for dinner at Jack's. With that gang it is almost as good with the cooking as my girlfriend.

Have to put this in. At the I.R.A. Convention, Pete Harmon was our lead off speaker. Peter was running a little drive-in in Salt Lake City and got acquainted with Colonel Sanders at the National Restaurant show in Chicago. Later the Colonel was on his way to San Francisco and stopped over to see Pete. The Colonel cooked them his complete chicken dinner. The next week decided to put the chicken on the menu. Pete was also a part of naming Kentucky Fried Chicken—K.F.C. and Pete signed up to be the Colonel's first franchise. The Harmons have over 200 franchises in the West at present.

Also at the Convention, Hot Dogs & More have come into being. We're supposed to get a letter from Paul Neirzwicki (names like that is the main reason Smith and Jones are so common). The Taste of Elegance by the Pork Producers was followed by the ball. Would you believe two Santas showed up? One of them had to be an imposter. Dick was in good form with his backless suit—striped shorts yet.

A perk for my Restaurant Association work. Went with Les to the Iowa-Ohio State football game. Rained ¾ of the game plus cold but nothing really matters when you are having fun. Plus Simpson beat Central for the Conference Championship and that's the first time in 20 years.

Update on The Little Flower—still holding onto the walker. Her broken left hip is still tender and right knee is less than good plus arthritis kicks in once in awhile. She fired me from all household duties plus a few other things. She was actually broke down one day and stayed in bed.

At our after convention board meeting I was appointed to get the Christmas lists of our operators. Our President (IRA) is chicken and our Chairman of the Board is chicken. From Kappy—Put "I do" on the ownership as in. Yes, I want to belong to the IRBA. Betty would like a Palmer writing course for Gib and a 10 speed for riding to work. For Stub Johnson—Get a contract with Santa to use llamas instead of reindeers. Bob Schlutz—Want to trade a new Santa suit for a used one. Don't want to make the rounds at Christmas looking like a rookie. Dick Wilderman—Need a new back for my go to church suit. Rocky—Maybe you could change me to a nice, lovable little Irish guy like Gib instead of Italiano. Bill Allen—Mr. President, I want to be a Big Chicken like Les or a 5 pound gavel for the IRBA meeting. Bill Leischenring Jr.—Need a couple more meeting dates.

# The Last of the 80's 197

Every so often I have a day with nothing to do but work. Carl Oehl—Tourism is my bag. Send a couple tour buses thru Iowa. For Carl I will send a load of Balloonies. Patty Maas—A present for each kid in Eddyville. Bring a present for that very special lady. Frank Clements—Four conventions for four times the fun. Dave Hammock—Bring a bag of votes and tell my people I am a good guy.

Right now we're trying catfish on the menu. Cook it 9 minutes in the broaster. I'm a fish guy and to me it's super. Later on it will be once a week on Friday and eventually it will probably wear out.

Had a good Christmas. Four boxes of fancy chocolates, shirt, tie, sweater, pressure tank to air up my bicycle tires and a couple good books—Lee Iacocca's second book and George Burns and Gracie Allen a "Love Story." From Kappy—Not everybody has "I do" on their lips for the IRBA member. Stub Johnson did get the llama contract for Santa's sleigh. Gib's writing hasn't improved but Betty did get the 10 speed bike.

Now it's contract time for writing in the Appetizer. Money isn't mentioned. That word makes Les real nervous. I get 12 balloon commercials, two ball games, a Christmas party and at coming out parties I get to kiss one third of the girls.

It's January and count your blessings time. Dick and Bill Leischenring have agreed to be Co-Chairmen of Coffee Day. We asked C. Vivian Stringer to be Honorary Chairperson. She is one my favorite people and probably the best girls' basketball coach in the nation.

News—Dick's mother passed away between Christmas and New Year's. His dad had left us last year. Good, solid people. At this stage you don't confide in the parents, but when they are gone you really miss them.

Our National A & W Convention was in Las Vegas at Caesar's Palace. Think we had 10 Iowa operations represented which is really pretty good considering our numbers. It's a good time in Las Vegas. The Little Flower and I got in a couple shows. I got excited over the topless in jubilee plus a little gambling and a few drinks. Just living the good life and it gets no better than Caesar's Palace. The Little Flower and I drove and figured on being out about three weeks.

In between I flew home for Father Burns' retirement party. Dick Van Aernam was to be the M.C. and ten minutes before the program started he went down in the back. Father Burns caught me and said—Dick went down in the back and you're the M.C. No made up program or anything written down. In the trade they call that "Winging it." Yes, I did it and got a lot of compliments so maybe I pulled it off.

For Father Burns' retirement party, Mass at 3:00 with the Bishop doing the homily, reception at 4:00 with cookies and punch, then dinner at 5:30 for about

250. Father was our balloon pilot from day one and also on the pulpit. I called it "Double Exposure."

I sat at the head table, the Bishop on one side, Father Burns on the other. It was a funner. A little hard to come up with things about the average Priest so I had to story a little. Would say didn't really get my ticket punched with that exposure.

Father Burns really was a good buddy and traveled to a lot of conventions with us plus vacations and meetings. That Caesar's is bigger than you can believe, especially for a country boy from Iowa. Dorene was in a wheelchair and, of course, everybody was pushing her and I lost her. I'll get one of those poles with a red flag on it. It was a 3 week vacation-type thing. The old '78 Merc is a trooper and still demands respect. We actually visited friends all over the Southwest.

#2 Larry drove his mother to Phoenix and we spent a few days there. Then comes the Tri-State in La Crosse on January 29–30. Dorene and I won't make the Tri-State. Have a Legislative Dinner on Monday night. Pretty important for our I.R.B.A. Larry will be there and represent me plus he's more fun anyway. From a few of the stories I wasn't missed that much. At a meeting it was decided to drop the Tri-State (each has hosted) and put the emphasis at the National in Phoenix. We'll bring the individual state meetings and bring back the national program for the ones that didn't make the National at Phoenix.

At Phoenix had a nice visit with Harry. Didn't tell him but swiped enough tangerines to last all winter. Also stopped overnight in Alama-Gordo to see our old buddies—retired and younger than us. Isn't everybody?

Have the Bike Promotion again and also the squeeze bottle is quite popular. The bike thing gets a lot of publicity and isn't that expensive. Too bad there is only one winner—actually 3—ladies, men, kids.

Some people go thru life without doing anything dumb. Gosh, it must be boring. I did 3 important interviews for the Appetizer and shot 12 pictures. Open up the camera—no film.

Bob Greenfield, Mabel Miller's husband, passed away Christmas night. Can you imagine a worse time? Les and I attended the funeral in Keosauqua.

Last week (March) Iowa Tourism and Development was sponsoring a show for the State Legislature at the State Fair 4-H Building. The object was to make the legislatures aware that more money was needed to promote tourism. Every area of the state was represented. #2 Larry was manning the Indianola Balloon booth. Larry is President of the Balloons this year. On one side was Emmetsburg promoting St. Patrick's Day. Sac County was on the other side promoting popcorn. Across from us was Speed Herrig and Cookies BBQ Sauce. Speed was telling us our old buddy Monsignor Tolan is not too good in the Sioux City Hospital. Father was set to retire next year. All the booths had about 8 people, but probably Larry and I got more talk in than any of them.

Was talking on the telephone to Dick. A table full of customers had driven off and left a 2 year old son. Cute kid but Dick wasn't interested in 2 year old kids at this stage. A half hour down the road they missed the little guy and came back. Dick was glad to see the mom running into the A & W.

Pork Patty Day is coming up plus have Dick setting up downtown Des Moines and also have Ames going.

Dorene and I received the Community Service Award. The inscription on the plaque read "The McConnells organized the annual 'Restaurant Day' for the mentally handicapped in the country and then promoted it statewide thru the Iowa Restaurant Association." This was presented at our annual Balloon fund raiser and, of course, I had to catch bids at the auction. Like always, I got out of hand and spent about $500.00. My voice was gone plus The Little Flower grounded me. No more auctions.

Snuck in last week for one evening of the Girls' State Basketball Tournament. For lunch I usually have a Polish, but production was a little slow. So I settled for two boxes of popcorn. Keeps me from eating the program.

The Little Flower is making progress. She's down to two canes and sometimes only one. I think she's improving but she does get discouraged doing the exercises. She's so independent. Won't take any help unless there's no other way. She does keep hold of the money. I'll never get hold of it and that's good. Took her in Monday, February 28$^{th}$, to remove the plate. A screw had worked out and pushed into the ball socket.

Our old buddy Frank Clements of Frank's Place, Springville, was named Iowa Beverage Person of the Year. Frank was a fooler. Actually you'd think he couldn't put one foot in front of the other. At the function here comes Frank in this big new Cadillac sedan.

In January 1989 The Little Flower and I stopped in Phoenix to see our first bread man from 1946. Ed and Mary Bremhorst retired and has a condo next to a golf course. Guess all breadmen and restaurant people retire in the chips.

Last year The Little Flower and I won the Community Service Award. We were in Florida at the time so they presented it this year at the Balloon fund raiser. The kicker was the inscription: "The McConnells organized the annual 'Restaurant Day' for the mentally handicapped in the country and then promoted it statewide thru the Iowa Restaurant Association." Les didn't even realize that. They call that "King in Your Domain." Actually that's the way it should be.

Ask somebody in Washington and it would be the Wingas or in Spencer Stub Johnson, both great guys and I imagine both of them have sold a little I.R.A. stock in their days.

With Father Burns retired will we have to get involved with the Methodists? No, no, no. Plus Curt and Florence sold Forest City and moved to their lake home at Clear Lake. If we could put together a party at Clear Lake it would be Al & Barb Formanek, Curt & Florence Jante, Ed Kotz and, of course, have it at Ronnie Newlin's Waterfront.

Art and Dorothy Peterson have sold Sheldon to Cliff and Nancy Heinrichs. Sheldon is and has been our biggest volume operation since they rebuilt in 1977. Don and Sheri Baum have also sold. Sheri was and is a sweetheart. It's going to be a Summer Social at Prairie Meadows July 26$^{th}$. Prairie Meadows is really alive and well and I haven't checked it out. Looking forward to it. We'll have our own private room for our party. Creston also has new operators. A couple ladies. One is Bill's wife from the Windrow.

Dick and I are scheduled for the National Restaurant Show in Chicago. A joke from Dick—The Prime Minister of Japan was forced to resign. There were irregularities. Noboru Takeshita.

Had a little trouble with a knee couple weeks ago. I couldn't bend it. First I swore then I smiled. Seems to work. Think that knee was rebelling. Thinking I was going on RAGBRAI.

Our gardener is heading to the nursing home and the yard mower moved. Got my neighbor to take over the garden and a buddy to do the yard. The knee immediately got better. Plus I went to the doctor and he gave me some pills. Plus I haven't had any mushrooms yet.

Was telling a story to a fellow the other day and #2 Larry popped up with—That isn't the same as you told it last time. It loses interest for me if I don't change it from time to time. Worked the Arthritis Foundation thing again. Good cause. Father Burns would be out of business if there wasn't something for the confessional. Got word from Father—he spent 2 ½ months in McAllen, Texas and doing real good. He got hooked up with a large parish short of priests and even helped with a building project.

The Little Flower has advanced to one cane and working full time. I'm trying to get out of work. Everything seems to be getting along good. Michigan winning the Rose Bowl. Then they beat poor little (and Catholic) Seton Hall in the NCAA Basketball Championship. Cubs are out of chute first. Looks like it's on to the World Series for the Cubs playing Kirby Puckett and his gang.

Babe Bisignano's bash on March 25th brought back a lot of memories. There's few from that area that doesn't have a Babe story. Sometimes I wonder if he didn't give away more drinks than he sold.

Our Restaurant Day Pork Cook Off was a couple hundred bucks better than last year. Gross of $625.00 and with our donations makes for a good net. So now we'll figure out how to do it better for next year. Plus we also sent $615.20 to the Arthritis Foundation. Hopefully our work and results from these causes don't go astray.

The Little Flower has a lot of problems. All of her joints are bone on bone plus the arthritis gets in. Sometimes I think her physical problems out weigh the problem of taking care of me.

Our Summer Social at Prairie Meadows was on July 26th. Have our own private room to view the races plus another room with machines to take care of our money. It does have good points. The food is good plus reasonable plus the drinks are cheap.

Story from Dick—Reggie Jackson said when you play baseball 10 years, up to bat 7,000 times and get 2,000 hits it means you've gone 0 for 5,000.

While me and Dick were in Chicago for the National Restaurant Show, we went to see the White Sox play plus we went with Les to the Hard Rock Café. A real good time plus things to see and learn at the Show. Former President Reagan was the lead off speaker. A lot of stale jokes but with his charisma he pulled it off. In two days we ate and drank our way thru 2000 booths in 3 buildings. One booth had a Polaroid camera with figures to stick you head through. I was a macho man and Dick was a bathing beauty. As a guy he won't win any prizes, but he really makes a cute girl. Also Steve Mazerak and "The Doll" doing pool shots. A close up with the Doll was worth the price of admission plus Dick lost his name tag the first night. I loaned him an extra which, of course, made everything Gib and I got a ton of somethings in the mail.

Father Burns stopped by. He's mostly in Columbus, Nebraska. His brother, the M.D., has a spread out there and his son works it. Doubt if Father Burns will ever make a farmer, but they did get him converted. He was wearing red.

Back to the Convention. The Cresco party was in our hotel so we took in the belly dancers and a real good polka band. Then a German lunch with brats, sauerkraut, potato salad, baked beans and draft beer. Makes me hungry again writing about it. Our next stop was the Hilton ballroom for the Johnny River's concert. Les was trying to look after me and Dick. Les introduced me to Fred Samson, the Restaurant Executive of New York State, and he started telling me things I had written in the Appetizer the last 15 years. Right away I can tell this is the top executive in the nation. Also compared notes with a lady from New Orleans.

Dick and I are a pair. He snores and I mess up the bathroom. I have an advantage because at night without the hear plugs I don't hear much. Monday night we went out to Cominskey Park and watched the White Sox get beat and then rode the "L" back to the loop. From there to Ed Debevick's Diner (50's) for mashed potatoes and gravy, meat loaf, etc. Had to stop at the Hard Rock Café. Sweatshirt for Dick. Three days of funning with Dick and forgot about the knee. Maybe I'll have to do funning full time.

Gonna be a good time at our Summer Social at Prairie Meadows. Dick has been out talking to the horses so it should be all winners for us. Plus Adventureland, plus visiting with the operators.

The Little Flower popped the ball out of the hip socket at the President's outing at Clear Lake (IRA) Sunday night. Sitting on that straight chair and it had to be painful. We got back to Des Moines Monday morning and the D.O. popped it back but now we're back to square one and she is wearing a brace for the next six weeks. Housekeeping is not my long suit but hopefully I'm getting better or a housekeeper is a second option.

Our new Priest came middle of June. Youngish in his 40's. He even makes house calls. He stopped at our house to see Dorene. #2 Larry stopped in. Yeah, Dad is pretty good with stories and tends to be a little creative with numbers. Remember when the kids were growing up? You got a little nervous when company came. They might tell something they weren't suppose to but this kid is 35.

Our old buddy Monsignor Tolan had to pack it in. He retired January 14th at St. Joseph's in Wall Lake. He was set to retire in the fall, but a few mechanical problems forced him out. He has been the greatest. Besides, who's gonna keep Speed under control?

The Little Flower got a new hip the middle of June and so far getting along pretty good. Next comes a new knee, shoulder. Sometimes I think her physical problems outweigh putting up with me.

Monday, August 14, and I am depressed. The Balloons just finished. We were sweating it out. First year without the Nationals. We had over 100 balloons registered and actually was the best event ever. #2 Larry was President and running the show plus handling the concessions. The Great Root Bear was in the parade plus worked every night at the Balloon Field. He was known as the Classic Good Will Ambassador plus we gave three cases of root beer suckers.

Had a letter from Al (Britt). Hobo Days were the best ever (August 11–13). It even made the Minnesota Star Tribune. Had a picture in the paper of the

Hoboes in a pickup coming to the A & W to eat. Said they were tired of Hobo Jungle Cooking.

Curt and Florence have sold to the Dierks from Gladbrook after 33 years. Now we need a new A & W Association Secretary. The Jantes certainly will be missed.

Back to our Summer Social at Prairie Meadows. Curt learned that you can't make a fast buck on a slow horse. Never bet on a horse that went 1 ¼ mile in 2 minutes but when they took him out of the truck he didn't do so well. Belmond bet on a horse so slow he was arrested for loitering. Larry Hansman bet on a horse they had to photograph the track to find him. Actually it was the first Summer Social I ever missed. The gang figured I was probably filling in as a jockey. Lynda Dembowski, Franchise Service Manager, attended our Summer Social and is getting us a report on curly fries. Our IRA Convention is coming up and the Park Inn is the host hotel. It isn't true that all we do is go to the conventions and play. No, but it seems like it this time of year. Plus Al & Barb are building a new house at Clear Lake. Think we should open our next convention there. Maybe even surprise them. Dancing, skating, ice fishing, snowmobiles and finish up with snowball fights.

Have a new Bear that sells for $3.95. Should be a good stocking item also ½ green aprons. Sometimes I ride out in the country with Les. I enjoy writing in the Appetizer. Quite a few out in the country-type dinner houses. They have very few problems with help. A lot of time with housewives for something to do and earn a little money.

Always nice to hear a compliment. Dr. Breedlove's Nurse (Dorene got a good report) said they go to the A & W on the East side and really enjoy. A nice young couple running it. Always get compliments about Norm and Neoma from the Pella people. Had a $30.00 order from a John Brummit customer and told them I would send John a commission check. John, that won't happen. Our Simpson men's basketball coach grew up in Cedar Rapids. He went home to see his mother and took her to Doug Ward's for dinner. Had high praise and only complaint they didn't have a root beer frosty. I make those on the malt mixer—root beer and ice cream.

Have a new Health Insurance Trust for IRA. No way you can figure the intricacies of any insurance contract. I rely on the salesman after I research him pretty good.

Our first annual National Balloon Classic is now in the history books. Actually went over better than we thought it would. Les was down one night and called that he lost a pair of shoes—Reeboks. The old people call running shoes.

You don't lose something that big. Like losing a 747 in a Wal-Mart parking lot. With feet that big he could stamp 6 times more grapes than the average foot in Italy.

Marjorie "Marge" Sharp passed away August 28$^{th}$. She was a good buddy and a partner with her sister in the Derby Restaurant. She rated 3 columns and pictures in the Big Paper. The Derby Restaurant is known nationwide for its down home cooking. It is unique by today's standards. No can opener, microwave or air conditioning. Sister Gusta, "Gus" Flack started the restaurant in 1958 and Marge joined in 1960. Marge was 78 and Gus at 75 says she will continue operation of the restaurant.

The Bussey High School Reunion was on August 20$^{th}$. We fed 186 and I think that's amazing. I brought the food and it was my 50$^{th}$ and as I recall there were 6 or 8 from the 1939 class. Plus had the M.C. job and they could have done better.

Life is beautiful and we're part of the greatest and largest in the world (restaurants). The Cubs had a good season. Been my team since 1938 and second winning season.

Mabel Miller passed away with cancer September 23$^{rd}$. She was a landmark restauranteur and really super lady. She ran the Hotel Manning at Keosauqua for many years and the first and only lady President of the IRA.

Took The Little Flower for an outing in the Northeast. My excuse was to see the turning of the leaves. My main mission was to visit the restaurant people. Our first stop was Guttenberg and then to Marquette and then to Waukon to see LaVerne and Irish Kelly. Of course, we had to have dinner and stay overnight.

IRA Convention was at the Savery and always a good time and an A & W meeting. 120 operations represented. Curly fries seem to be the big thing at present. Good to have something nobody else has. It seems we have them in every operation at present.

Cec Meinecke passed away in November with cancer. Cec at one time owned Britt, Garner and Webster City. Besides he was a good fellow, nice family. Florence took care of the flowers for the Association.

The new Junior Cook Book from Better Homes & Gardens with two grandkids, Ross & Megan, gracing the cover. #3's wife Shelli put the book together. Everybody should buy at least one copy. Think they are cheaper by the dozen. For your information, bible is the #1 seller in the nation. The red checked Good Housekeeping Cook Book is #2 and the Junior Cook Book is #3. While we're into statistics, grandpas rank ahead of Santa Claus in the under 5 vote.

The IRBA Convention at Vet's was a winner and get better every year. Banquet was at the revolving top of the tower. Park Inn plus I got to sit by Lynda Dembowski. Will have Megan and Ross in attendance and they have agreed to sign the cook books. I was awarded a nice clock plaque for my work on the Appetizer. For me it's a labor of love. At the banquet we had a number of students from Emmetsburg Community College and their sponsor spread them around two at a table. They were all envious of the two at our table because we had more fun than the rest. Michael Lavalle hollered at us coming down the aisle with his beautiful wife as of September. Sanita Mancuso grabbed me from behind with a big smooch and I said "Hey, let's do that again!"

The Iowa Pork Producers' recipe contest was again won by the Godwins. Pete's Steak House in Hartley was second and Pete is also a pork producer. #3 was Paul Wendl of "The Port" at Lake Panorama. All good buddies of mine.

On our way home from Keosauqua Les and I stopped at Albia. Bob Loughman bought the noodle factory. Don't know whether to help pay the rent or another job for Cindy. About that time Cindy came in and Bob said, "Hi, Neva." Neva's Old Fashioned Home Made Noodles. She had just broke 60 dozen eggs.

Towards the end of '89—Christmas letter, family picture and get out the Santa suit. Actually have quite a few stops. Sometimes the kids are bigger than Santa, but nobody has more fun.

Joke from Dick—At the race track a priest was blessing a horse. It won. The priest blessed another horse and it won. The man saw the priest praying over another horse. He rushed to the window and put down a hefty bet. The horse came in last. What happened? The priest asked the man, "Are you Catholic?" "No", the man said. "I thought not", the priest said. "You don't know the difference between a Blessing and Last Rites."

# 34

## *1990*

Now 1990 and that's a big number. The first order of business is New Year's Resolutions. Our Honorable President of the I.R.B.A., Carl Oehl, decreed he is near perfect and doesn't need resolutions. First Lady Fern's version of that answer was different, but we better not get into that. From our Fearless Leader Les—I resolve to go on a diet and do it every Monday. From our man on the road, Kap—If I could just have the good people say "Yes" as in joining the Association. As for Betty—I resolve to help the above with their resolutions. The Little Flower resolved—I was such a sweetheart, change nothing. Now off to confession.

Restaurant/Coffee Day April 6th. Jerry Krause, Mileport Café, Clear Lake, is our Chairman and is working the pork patty or any extra thing that will develop more money. We're hoping.

The Little Flower reads a cook book like I read a joke book. We had a younger priest filling in one Sunday. I was to be the Lector along with the two wine servers in the sacristy. The priest—Is this too much wine for the glasses? Cut it back. If there is any left it will just go down the drain. I piped up—Don't worry about it. I'm an old wino and it won't go to waste. The priest started stuttering and the Bread lady said, "Father, that's a joke."

National A & W Convention in Phoenix. There were 8 in our party. Convention was up beat and great plus the facilities couldn't have been better. Every time you would turn around there were three guys trying to help you. Marketing sounds good. Promotion for every month.

We have the Bike Promotion in the hopper. All members will pay $80.00 and the Association will pick up the 200 American Ross Bikes. The bikes will again be assembled and delivered by the retarded.

The Nationals went well. Eight Iowa A & W's represented. I got a plane ticket at the last minute and went. The Little Flower had to stay home. A new knee as of December 27th. Our grandkids had a great time. At 9, Megan thought the horseback ride plus riding around in the mini-van Uncle Larry leased was really cool. Ross is 7 and he thought missing 1 ½ days of school and seeing Rawhide were the neatest things. I think swapping lies with the operators you see once a year plus kissing the ladies. Don't tell The Little Flower.

Wally Luedtke stopped in. He and Sharon have retired to mid-Florida. Used to have 5 units in Cedar Rapids. He still comes back every year to sell Christmas trees. Had a letter from Curt Peterson. He has sold his unit in Freeport, Illinois.

So it's New Year's 1990. Three parades and 7 bowl games. Think there is a few more but all I could handle. Our Honorable President and Father Protector, Carl Oehl, is a champion of our Visit Iowa Promotions. If he had his druthers, there would be a bus load of tourists in every member's lot. The Little Flower is back on a walker. She got a new knee December 27$^{th}$ and was to come home January 3$^{rd}$. That morning I came down with the 10 hour flu. This is when you discharge from both ends with fury. After 2 days at home she got it. I could at least run for the bathroom, but with her there was a few problems.

A friend of mine, Drake Wresting Coach Lonnie Timmerman, asked me to do a little gig for his Take Down Club that meets for lunch once a month. I'm a sports fan, but know very little about wrestling. It worked.

Back to the Convention in Phoenix. I invited Jean and Harry Ayres to the banquet. Of course, Harry had a nice present for me and I made a thing of it as M.C. and unwrapped it with a flourish. A K.F.C. snack (chicken)—plastic no less. Also got to see Ed and Mary Bremhorst. He ended up in Phoenix to take care of a daughter with family problems. Ed got into real estate sales and made it real good.

Bag O Burgers was and is a good promotion plus business seems to be pretty fair and also there is a lot of snow this year. The guys are all in snow removal. They are the only ones happy. From Dick—George Halas, ex-Chicago Bear Coach, said, "I knew it was time to quit coaching when I was chewing out an official and he walked off the penalty faster than I could keep up with him."

Our gang decided to retire me as of the first of the year. I'll work about 20 hours filling in. I don't like any part of it and don't think it will really take. Right now I'm working to make Pork/Coffee Day the biggest and best ever. Time seems to go faster all the time. Does age have anything to do with that?

We just got the lady of my life all pumped with a nice sweetheart bouquet for Valentine's Day and along comes St. Pat's Day and we blew it. Business as usual is best, but it hardly ever happens that way. The Super Bowl overlapping the President's Ball (I.R.B.A.). Our President and Queen, Carl & Fern Oehl, are the greatest. Then they said—Let's sing "Happy Anniversary" and I came up with—To who? It was The Little Flower's 39$^{th}$. Back in the doghouse.

I did the little gig for the Drake Wrestling Take Down Club. In the middle of a very good story and completely lost my train of thought. I rolled through it with this is what happens with the age and they bought it. Then it came back. Had a world of fun doing it, but proves the point. I'm not the greatest.

This retirement is wearing me out. Tough working full time at funning. Actually fill in for whoever and there are quite a few whoevers. Just thinking about Clear Lake and got word from Al via the Newsletter that the lake is down 40". Curt's geese still have plenty of water, but Lady of the Lake Excursion Boat might have a little trouble floating. Plus the Bag O Burgers and Dog promo went good. Next month comes the bicycles (April).

Was reading a story about Babe Ruth who suffered from the humiliation of having the great Walter Johnson of the Washington Senators throw 3 straight fastballs past him. When he asked the umpire if he had seen any of the pitches, the ump said, "No." Ruth said, "Neither did I, but that last one sounded a little high to me."

Had a big storm last week. Started raining in the morning and then got cold and there was ice on everything. Lost the electricity and then a tree limb creamed the south end of our canopy. We finally closed about 8:00. Called Dick and he didn't lose the electricity, but most of the neighborhood did and he was really pumping it out. Where does he get that divine help and he isn't even Catlic.

Coach Timmerman is really a nice guy. He has 5 monikers—coach, professor, doctor, major and Lonnie. I have two—Gib and a dirty word.

Got to the Beverage Convention Monday night for the banquet. Missed Saturday and Sunday. Just as I came in here's Frank Clements with his protégé Connie. Frank has a bottle of beer in one hand, a pool cue in the other shooting pool. Only Frank could shoot pool with one hand. Everybody in the exhibit hall hollered at me. Good to see Ermal Loughry. Margaret asked Carol Winga to come up to my room and change for the banquet. Of course John had to come along. Old, old buddy John Hall and Teresa in attendance. Also had Monica Stence at our table. Inquired about her social life. Told me she was getting along fine and didn't need any help arranging dates. She left right after the dinner—I got lucky, Gib. With a twinkle in her eyes.

Dick Moore passed away first of March. Dick and Marge had the A & W since 1939 and retired in 1984. In the mid-seventies our two families had been on a cruise and the next week was the National Convention in Las Vegas. The wives were beat so Dick and I went together. We were at the M.G.M. and our gang was pretty much meeting at the Iowa Hospitality Suite. Dick was sitting with a group talking. I came in and whispered in his ear (actually nothing). Of course, everybody in the room thought we had something lined up.

It's 4/4 and snow is in the air. They cancelled the Little Cubs game. Good thing about snow this time of year the next day it is gone.

Was at Bussey one morning for breakfast before the NCAA final 4 started. They had a pick sheet that you picked the winners of every game down to the final. Would you believe I picked more winners than anybody else? I loaded the mini-van and pickup plus the grandkids and went to Bussey for breakfast and pick up the winnings. After feeding everybody that came in, house tips and taking care of the waitresses, won $156.00 and spent $176.00. Made a heckuva impression for $20.00!!!!!

Have a new love. The Little Flower bought a new mini-van from Lee Iacocca—Dodge Caravan. Of course, The Little Flower is my first love, then the '78 Merc then comes Mini. I couldn't throw off the old standby for this new pretty thing, but it is tempting. Have read both of Iacocca's books. Us journalists have to stick together.

Up comes Restaurant Day, our 8th annual Pork Cook Off. Netted about the same as last year, but gets more fun doing every time. Have a goodly number of other operators doing the pork thing and it is a help for our Special People.

I filled in for Larry at the Iowa Tourism Booth for Legislator's at the Fairgrounds. Of course I made the rounds and ended up with two bottles of beer, sausage, cake and candy and it was all during Lent. A pious little lady in the Centerville booth next to me said, "It isn't a sin if you really forgot." I can't be sure because I lie and cheat so much. Enjoy visiting with Father Greving, Head Honcho and Tourism Entrepreneur of the West Bend Grotto.

On to basketball. Our high schools boys won state consolation honors but more important the Sportsmanship Trophy. And on to the NCCA Final Four. Coach Jerry Tarkanian's wife Lois was busy working the rosary beads. The word is that she will rupture a rosary in three good games. While into Catlic, our new younger priest has a guitar Mass on Saturday evening. Kinda reminds you of the younger days at the Saturday night tavern. Harry DeCarlo and I have a lot in common. We both went in to the service at the same time and both got out February 1946. Both got into the restaurant right away and still in. Harry is an Italian and married a somebody. I'm a somebody and married an Italian.

Our economy has been down but maybe showing a little improvement and with the early rains it's a super year for mushrooms. A young lady brought in three bags in the course of a week and a half. She thought I didn't get out and would enjoy them. I told The Little Flower—Think she has a thing for me. She can take you home with her long as she brings in mushrooms. Some of you may remember Bobby Jones, A & W Rep (60's went to Whatta burger). He was a Texan that had never tasted our sponge mushrooms. Came by early one morning and set down to breakfast. We were having mushrooms. From then it was a ritual. Call at 6:00 in the morning—having mushrooms. I'll be there.

Now the Summer Social (IRA) is coming up at the Amanas. Golf outing at the new course. Was at a committee meeting with Carl Oehl. The course is beautiful but what do I know. Have thought about getting into golf but doubt if I ever make the grade. Delbert Stevens called to get his name in the pot. From Delbert—I play in the low 80's and if it's hotter than that I won't play. Yes and the beat goes on.

Can remember at this stage one of my favorite family members—Grandpa Doughman. A salty-type guy. I wouldn't trace back my ancestors. Might find a Republican. The McConnell side were scalpers and traders and you know what that would lead to.

#1 grandson Ross (8) is busy getting ready for Little League. I can see a star developing. Ross leans towards athletics and hopefully he will give us something to watch.

April 1$^{st}$—time for dandelion greens, bullheads and mushrooms. Our fisherman is #3. Tim is getting too busy with photography and he suggested I take up fishing. In the first place I'm not a water guy and in the second I can't sit still that long.

A young lady brought me in a bag of mushrooms. Said I probably didn't get a chance to hunt, so enjoy. Then she brought in a couple more bags. Told The Little Flower this lady must have a thing for me. She can take you home with her long as she keeps bringing in mushrooms.

For a few years I've been trying to line up #2 Larry with Monica Stence. (Jerry's Alibi, Elkader). It's all off. #2 Larry got engaged in April and they are working towards a wedding in October—November.

What a problem. Getting adjusted to the retirement. My basic schedule—20% work, 60% play and 20% just hang out. Was into a big dream the other night. Doing the Newsletter and one liners were popping out of my head faster than I could write them down then pop—woke up and couldn't remember a thing. Evidently, did entertain myself.

A buddy of mine came in the other night for dinner—a retired pharmacist from Knoxville. Had been to Atlantic for a golf outing. Got to keep active and you're even still working and know you have me beat and I'm 78. That took the fire out of my sails. I'm only 67 (but I'm on the go all the time and have been forever).

Dick and I had a great time at the National Restaurant Convention in Chicago. It took two full days to go through over 2,000 booths—outer drive McCormick Place. Vince Engl was working the Broaster Booth. That means there is still hope for us old guys. The "Doll" in Miller Beer commercials with the "Pool Shark" was working in the Miller Booth. She autographed her picture for grandson Ross (8). See you in 16 years. Ross wasn't too impressed. Thought the Cubs program was a lot neater. On Sunday night it was Chas and his entourage at the Big Hotel Ballroom. Dance, dance, dance. Monday night we went to Wrigley Field and watched Cincy beat the Cubs. Then rode the "L" down to Mike Ditkas joint for dinner. Full day and night. We headed for our home at Days Inn in a cab and here's John Winga walking up the street with a good looking girl. A little closer and it was Carol. Kappy met two ladies at the N.R.A. party on Saturday night from Heidelberg and Mannheim. He had bombed both of those cities in the war (WW II that is). Kap's name became "Boom-Boom." Dinah Shore was the head entertainment at the party Saturday night. The dad of Fred Sampson (friend of mine—Executive of New York State) was a singing waiter along with Jimmy Durante and Eddie Cantor in New York City and helped Dinah get her first job. That must make me something.

Our Summer Social July 8th at the Amanas. We were all set for a big softball game, but the Little League had the diamonds all corralled. The food was super as it always is at Amana. Prime rib, brats and sauerkraut. Typical Amana menu and then finishing off with a prize winning dessert from the Ox Yoke Inn.

The Little Flower and I got in with George and Daisy Sefrit in their van and we gave them an Amana tour. They had never been to the Amanas before. We actually won the softball game by default. Our team manager was Dick and Les couldn't fill a team plus they were all afraid of my pitching. The golf outing went over pretty good. Del Stevens was heard saying—Give me golf clubs, fresh air and a beautiful partner and you can keep the golf clubs and fresh air. The Little Flower and I don't golf, but we enjoyed the Amana hospitality with beer, wine and good food plus good music—German Oompah.

Our Metro Opera finished its run July 15th. The Little Flower and I make our appearance, but it doesn't match a Cubs game. Rocky came down with his sister Annie for a performance as an 82nd birthday present. We, along with Rocky and Annie, did the gourmet dinner at Michael's tent along side the opera building. Had a super good time and I suggested we sing "Happy Birthday" to Annie and Rocky said, "No, Gib. No!"

The Little Flower and I did a reunion at St. Benedict near Algona. It was Annie's niece and her gang. Great food, roast pig with all the trimmings with apple pie and ice cream (homemade and good). Finished off with a hay ride pulled by a steam engine. That was an all time first.

At this point it looks like a Chicago World Series. The Cubs are about ready to make the run. I'll order a block of tickets. Was proud of #3's wife Shelli. She spent a work week in Chicago (works as Food Editor for Better Homes & Gardens). Visited Ed Devaney one night and thought it was real fun. Ate at Harry Carey's restaurant another night and thought the food was super good. What Shelli observed and was Dick and I agreed is getting hang loose and out going. When I lived there in the mid 50's the people were frigid. Give Chicago a B+.

Had an Iowa Association outing with Les in the Southwest. Stopped for a beer with George and Daisy Sefrit in New Market and dinner plus conversation with Bob Berning in Creston.

Did the Cedar Rapids Beverage Association Golf Outing in Central City. Always a good time with those fun people plus the steaks are good.

Enjoyed the Leischenring's 50$^{th}$ anniversary party. Four couples of us went in Les's van. Just a plus for being on the Appetizer staff.

Went to Waukon to put away one of my best buddies Monday, July 31$^{st}$—Keith "Irish" Kelly. Keith and LaVerne had the A & W in Waukon from the early 60's and sold in 1976. He was a charter member of the Association in '66 and served many years on the Board. He had a small stroke prior to selling. Kelly was an all around everything in his area.

Finished up a very successful National Balloon Classic. Crowds were good. The weather was a little problem. Might have to call Father Burns back into service to straighten up the weather. Had word from Del Stevens. He is dropping golf and taking up bowling. Delbert says in bowling they send the ball back to you and seldom lose one.

Yes, I bad mouth the Wal-Mart store. They opened here in August and are bringing more traffic and everyone seems to be getting a little extra traffic and so far all are up.

During our very successful National Balloon Classic, a couple of nun friends (Sister sisters) came to see us from Nebraska and South Dakota. We gave them a ride in our hot air balloon. I got a very official looking card in the mail. "Angels Anonymous humbly immortalizes Gib McConnell a Saint for being totally divine and splendidly human. The glow of your halo is exceeded only by the size of your heart." Everybody I showed it to gives me the horse laugh. To me it's gospel.

Again I cried when the State Fair wrapped up. The new Tourism Building was, and is, a winner. Our good friend Joyce Ruth, Lighthouse Marina in Whiting, was doing a booth for the Bed & Breakfast Association. Good friends were manning the Ski Iowa Association—Valley Ski in Montezuma. Betty Stevens was making the pitch for Big Mo River Gambling and her a card carrying Methodist. Our good buddy Father Greving was holding down West Bend Grotto booth. Another fair plus, the Toby Tent Show was back. Toby Tolliver still has the white shoes like mine. Carl Oehl was doing an indoctrination for the new crew at the Amana stand. Father Greving had stopped by to say hello to his old buddy Carl Oehl. Carl acted like he didn't see Father. From Carl—About this time a Catholic priest will stop by and bless this whole operation. Father Greving jumped right in. Maybe this is the secret to the Amana success? I'm sure they will never make another two like Carl and Father Greving.

Now comes the I.R.B.A. Convention October 28$^{th}$ and 29$^{th}$. Our host hotel is the new Embassy Suites and our dinner will be the night of the 29$^{th}$. Surely our people from the north can't get lost. Of course they are not use to the Big City. Already heard from Betty. Keokuk is on the Big Miss not the Big Mo. My Iowa history book map was probably wrong, but also found out you can't get there from here.

Right now we are losing a lot of our operations. Haven't come up with all the reasons. John Jones, Osceola, decided he could do better off the interstate as an independent. He found out right away it didn't work. For highway business you definitely need a national name. John has sold what he had left for a convenience store. Dad, Scrappy Jones, was a charter member of the I.R.A. and had a restaurant up town before deciding to come out on the highway by the interstate. Think the A & W goes back to about 1960.

Now it's time to register for the National Convention in Chicago before November 1$^{st}$ and get the discount rate. I was late last year. Dorene got a new hip and the trip was iffy.

Had the most rewarding trip ever last month. Did the National Restaurant Association sponsored public affairs conference with the Iowa group in Washington D.C. There were 7 of us from Iowa with 42 states represented and 450 total restaurant operators. Got to meet with all our Legislators and explained our problems and wants. Expect good things from their next session.

Got to the Starlite Express at the Civic Center in September. Actually the bank bought my ticket as a reward for Bank Board and I popped for my girlfriend, The Little Flower. Dropped her off at the door and parked the car. Came in through the revolving door and caught sight of The Little Flower in the crowded lobby and I walked into the plate glass door. After 40 years, there is still that attraction. The lenses popped out of my glasses, frames fell to the floor and the batteries fell out of my hearing aid. Here is this Little Old Guy crawling around the lobby floor trying to find my belongings. That had to be a better show than the Starlite Express. Dorene on her cane led me to my seat. The whole thing had to be a big laugher. Eyes and ears are gone, but it is loud enough plus the characters were easy to see. A good story to tell the grandkids.

Back to the Public Affairs Conference in D.C. We actually rubbed noses with some of the Biggies in the Business. One of the members was introduced as one of the most successful bar operators in the world. Have you ever heard of Tom Kerchoff and Cheers in Boston? Fred Sampson was there with his gang. At least two of the Brennans (New Orleans) were there. Our good buddy Glen Gulsvig (McGarvey Coffee) was hanging out with a Minnesota entourage. The Wisconsin Executive had a fun group. I can talk to him eye to eye. He's an inch shorter than I am. (Yes, I like little people.) John Winga and Les seemed to know everybody. Asked Ron Godwin (Cedar Rapids' finest) if he would like to take a walk. I don't even walk up to my second story apartment when the elevator isn't working.

Now it is November and a hard month to crack for business. We could work a dozen promotions, but why give the farm away. Our business is decent so let it go at that.

Had a letter from Al Formanek. Al and Barb have Britt. Barb is a good looking filly and grew up with three sisters. We had only one daughter and kept me busy running guys off. Bet that road in front of Barb's house was bumper to bumper.

The 58th Iowa Restaurant Convention is now history. A really great show. Started with Howard Helmer (great entertainer) with Egg Council. Even I can make an omelet with his instructions. Herman Cain, President of the National Restaurant Association and heads up Godfather's Pizza, talked about business today. If he didn't get you motivated might as well call Digger O'Dell. The Little Flower and I even stayed overnight Sunday. Only 4 inches from home and we usually drive it.

Went on the road with Les to Bill Allen's grand opening of Chicken Store at Waverly. A cute young lady grabbed me for a Big Hug. One of my former banking buddies who had transferred out and now has a big position in Bob Schlutz's Waterloo bank. You can't imagine what a squeeze from a young lady does to an old guy.

It's coming up Christmas and a little house cleaning is in order. When I do the vacuuming you can hear things go up the tube. With the dusting there is a definite path where I have been. In fact, dusted the T.V. this week and then the T.V. wouldn't work. Getting ready to put the dust back on when #3 Tim came in and fixed it with 35 cent cable connector I had broken. How about a seminar for homemakers at the National Convention? I could head that up. On the other hand, I'm not too big on the diaper business.

It's Ho, Ho, Ho time. Still do the Santa Claus. I'm not the best and would make a better elf, but nobody has more fun doing it.

I took early retirement the first of January 1990—was 68. #1 Pat and #2 Larry took over and I'm around to fill in for whomever and this day and age there are quite a few whomevers. Said to #1 Pat the other day—You're kinda hard to work for. You taught me, Dad! The first word you get from the retired guy—Busier than when I was working. It's partly true. Takes me twice as long to accomplish half as much. Non-working about 20% and playing 90%.

My work with the Appetizer is very rewarding. Had an interview with Connie Zuber of the Amanas and widow of Bill Zuber who pitched in the Big Leagues. The memorabilia was well worth the time. Bill was a pitcher with a long arm and a ton of character stories about him.

This is the year the Cubs will go all the way. '91 will be a good year and kinda think the #'s will think I'm having too much fun and put me back to work.

# 35

## *1991*

The big family wedding, January 12th (#2 Larry) went off without a hitch. For our rehearsal dinner we hired a bus to take us from the church practice to Christopher's and back. The Geudicessi gang in Beaverdale did a super job. We loaded on the bus and #3 Tim passed out song sheets—Dad broke his glasses and hearing aid. Can't see or hear but his mouth still works good. So he'll lead the singing. After an introduction like that how could I refuse? Had a little trouble seeing the words, but knew the first two lines of most to get them started. Also did the bus aisle shuffle for added entertainment. Tim and Larry's buddies gave a slide presentation with a rhyming roast that brought down the house.

The wedding was big and beautiful with the normal amount of tears. The reception was what I was waiting for. I was at the food line and #3 Tim found me. Dad, what are you doing? I'm mostly eating the food and drinking the beer that Orrie is paying for. What am I supposed to be doing? You're suppose to be dancing. Wow, we had a good time. With my dancing abilities have trouble when I ask for a second dance, but with the big crowd never got around to a second.

The day after the wedding The Little Flower and #1 Sandy are booked to Europe. I am staying home by myself and will probably get in trouble (in fact, figuring on it). Was telling some little older ladies I gave Dorene a Europe trip for Christmas. Oh my, isn't that nice!!

A couple news items—Lynne Wilderman's Dad passed away in early January. Ray Doonkeen, Oklahoma City, won the car given away at the San Diego Convention.

The San Diego Convention was great. Laredo, Mexico is right next to San Diego and the big thing is don't drink the water and watch what you eat. Les had come with us and stayed a couple days to check out our Convention before he went to the N.R.A. meeting in Orlando. Les and I ate and drank everything we saw on the streets of Laredo. Plus we negotiated some good deals on jewelry and vanilla. We also met and talked with George Michel, our new A & W President. We sincerely hope he can turn this thing around. Joe Theisman gave a motivational speech opening the Convention. Ross got to sit by Joe and, of course, got his autograph. Doesn't get any bigger than that. I will say that will be a big topic at recess.

Got new stronger glasses and a redone hearing aid plus a big tube of Brylcream. I'm all set for the year plus it's coming up time to give your Valentine a big smooch.

The Little Flower and Sandy got home from Europe right on time and had a great one. Dorene hasn't stopped talking about her experiences. I've been a little close mouthed about my endeavors while they were gone. The Little Flower brought me a bunch of Italian chocolate bars. They do a good job with chocolate. The Barons of old used to every morning count their gold pieces. I fondle my chocolate.

Our good friend and buddy Betty Ahrens, Secretary of I.R.A., lost husband Ed last month.

There were over 400 attending the National Convention at San Diego and a good time was had by all. I asked Dick and Lynne to the Saturday evening Mass at the Cathedral in downtown San Diego. Dick was too busy, but Lynne went along. We both prayed for Dick, but that won't be enough. Maybe Lynne can talk her church to put in a confessional with a $20.00 window.

Business has come back in the Midwest and hopefully the East and West coasts will turn around by spring. We have a pretty good promotion put together. $100. in $5.00 gift certificates with all the participating operators names on the back.

Got an alert from the War Department. If there are air raids in Sioux City, might be called up. They remember the good job I did in WW II.

Our Summer Social is set up for the gambling boat in Davenport. Sounds good, but I'm not a gambler and I'm definitely in the minority.

Had a letter from Dick. He has started the Senior Citizens discount program. It should work with a plastic gold card. I hate the Senior Citizens, but they are a big part of our business. Pella has remodeled and took out the inside phones and went back to waitresses.

Got The Little Flower out last week for a two over nighter in Cedar Rapids. I took in the Cedar Rapids Beverage Convention and Dorene stayed with #1 Sandy. My mission was to help Sylvia in the Restaurant Coffee Day booth. Sylvia was able to get in over $800.00, so it was worthwhile. Restaurant Day is set for June 7$^{th}$.

Got a call from Dick and he's sending all his gift certificates down to me. That's okay. I'm sending all my Senior Citizens up to him.

It was great President's Ball at the Savery in February. Our first lady Linda never looked better. Hard for Dave to get past the ordinary. Our 6th Annual Legislative Dinner was also well attended. Seems to get better every year. I joined a new association. National Association of Short Adults. In fact, I am head of the Iowa Division.

Babe, the great one, Bisignano came down to visit me the other day. Paid me the supreme compliment—Next to me you're the Biggest B.S.er in Iowa. Babe has the Iowa Boy, Chuck Offenburger, writing about his life. That should be a simple job but hard to stop at any stage.

An old Satchel Paige Quote—"Age is a question of mind over matter. If you don't mind, it doesn't matter."

The Little Flower and I parked on Dick's lot and ordered the two chicken dinners. I ate the free one and The Little Flower paid. Thinking of hiring a bus to run my Senior Citizens up to Dick's on a daily basis. If he will continue that 'buy one, get one free', think I can fill up the bus. Told Dick we are putting the emphasis on the kids. Those S.C.'s are soon going to hit the great beyond trail. I'm an authority on that business.

Our Restaurant Day Honorary Chairman this year is Tom Davis, Basketball Coach at Iowa. In the latter part of March The Little Flower sets the table with dandelion greens, frozen buttered peas and pork chops. How could you ever be mad at a partner like that? Besides, she still controls the money.

Went with Les to the UPS Restaurant Show in Minnesota. Mike Hurst, the N.R.A. President, was their opening motivational speaker. Mike kept the audience's attention for a full hour. If you wasn't motivated by that, might as well call the Digger.

Took in the Kansas Restaurant Association Convention in Topeka the last of February. George Puckett, the Executive and his staff, plus the faithful cohorts from the restaurant industry tried and succeeded in treating us like V.I.P.'s. Pat Butter is a super little lady and long time (24 years) assistant and could very well be a clone of Betty Ahrens. The second assistant, Diana Jones, said, "You write in the Appetizer and I enjoy reading your stuff." Right away I like this lady and she's going to be on my Favorite People List. Besides, I came home with a sunflower pin in my lapel. Of course, it cost me 3 balloon pins.

You know things are a little shaky with you at the A & W when the gang comes out in new uniforms and you're still in that 80's garb. Really think they are sending me out with Les to get me out of their hair. Now The Little Flower has delegated some yard work to me. I'll tell you right now if this keeps up I'll either cement the yard or buy a condominium.

The Summer Social will be at Jumers in Davenport and then the riverboat about 1:30 and get off the boat at 10:30. More later.

Now it's the National Convention in Chicago. Great show—the biggest and best in the world. We stayed at the Days Inn on the outer drive just above the Chicago River. There were about 150 from Iowa at the show. Dick and I ran into many people we knew. Four people from Corporate plus Jeanne Harvey. Frank Sonoc and his son were in attendance. Frank invited us to stop on the way home and he'll buy dinner. We stopped last year (Sterling). Frank wasn't there and we tried to charge our dinner and the help threatened to call the police. We visited the "Doll" at the Miller booth. She said to Dick—Wasn't you here last year and not a word to me. Went to the big dance Sunday night. Great crowd, good show and band. Told Dick to ask his partner—If your mother is with you, can my partner dance with her? Did finally get a couple of grandmas.

Michael Morasco died of Alzheimer's in April. One of the premier restauranteurs in Des Moines from 1951 to 1979. He was named "Retailer of the Year" in 1972 by the I.R.B.A.

April 1$^{st}$ opened up riverboat gambling on the Mississippi. Our Babe was an honored guest on one of the boats. His words—Back in WW II I was running a few punch boards and doing a little bootlegging and now it is all legal. Babe, at the time, was doing a service entertaining the W.A.C.'s and soldiers on leave. I would say nobody in the world bought more drinks for servicemen and women.

I started in the restaurant business after the war in 1946. Ran punch boards until they pulled them in 1950. It was like a full ride scholarship. Gave me ready money during my business internship.

Visited Cedar Rapids (#1 Sandy) and we went to the Vernon Inn. Basil Hadjis is a real Greek and Dorene enjoys their gyros. Basil has been in business 15 years plus he's hardly dry behind the ears.

Yo Yo's are coming back. Dick and I can show these kids a few tricks. It really doesn't take them long to outmatch us. Are kids smarter today?

So President Bush throws out the first ball (a real southpaw) for the Texas Rangers, his former team plus one of my favorites. Hall of Famer Joe Morgan is helping announce the game.

K.F.C. is kinda new in town. For years we had the town chicken business with broasted chicken. Last week we got Gerald Knoll's bill and he got ours. Ours—1 case and his—12. Is there any justice?

Had perfect weather for Restaurant Day and it was down a fraction and the economy is supposed to be on the rebound. How do you figure?

My old buddy and sometimes called "stepson" turned 50 this year. I may have to be his crutch. We go to the National Restaurant Show in Chicago together and Lynne thinks I'm taking care of Dick and Dorene thinks Dick is taking care of me. A pessimist sees the difficulty in every opportunity. The optimist the opportunity in every difficulty!!

Back to Chicago. Wells Blue Bunny is good as Haagen Dazs. Miller is my favorite beer with Bud second, but Bud doesn't have the "Doll." With Dick at 50 not a big thing but actually the beginning of the end. No more up-up-up. No more ready smiles from the young lady on the dance floor. More like—I'll give the old guy a break and dance with him. You are no longer the helper, rather the helpee. Conversation is about three decibels higher and usually right in your ear. Then the eyes start to go and beginning of arthritis, but after 65 everything is beautiful.

It was amazing the people Dick and I ran into at the National in Chicago. There was probably about 120 at our hotel. The Fredericks, Happy Chef, had a contingent of people. Earl Utesch, McCormack Distributors, retired, was working the Taylor Freezer booth and I visited him while Dick was raiding the ice cream booths. He came back with two bowls but none for me. Glen Gulsvig, McGarvey Coffee, and then a picture with the "Doll." She said to Dick, "I remember you from last year." She said nothing to me. I'm better looking. Better in every category, just a little older.

Remember the M.A.S.H. episode with Chicago's Adam Ribs? We ate there Sunday night and they were good. Monday night was at Miller's Pub, landmark sports bar across from the Palmer House since 1935. Harry Carey used to hang out there before he opened his own restaurant.

Had a note from Knopps, Russell, Kansas—Looking forward to seeing you at the National. She related about me leading the song everybody would know. We're from Iowa. Once in awhile I hit a laugher. Besides, I got a dance with Lucy and have her on my card for this year. Beats those moms and grandmoms Dick pushes off to me.

Our Summer Social at Davenport was a real winner. I won $62.00 and not telling what I lost. Dick's smile wasn't too big and that tells me his story. Barb Knowles was working a red hot 25 cent slot. Gib, you pull the handle while I put the money in. My arm is getting tired. To be real truthful, did lose $124.00.

Now our opera is winding down. Went one night by myself. The Little Flower was doing a party and couldn't get away. Had the gourmet dinner at

Michael Lavalle's under the tent. The Executive Director and husband asked me to join them. I'm in tight with that opera crowd or what?

Hey, the middle of the year. Going super fast. A & W had a good year so far. The guys are doing a super job. Who says I couldn't be replaced?

We had the best first weekend of Balloons in our 21 years (that doesn't seem possible). The 3$^{rd}$ Annual National Balloon Classic. Remember way back when a trip to the bank was a load? Happy to say, with a smile, the past week the trips to the bank were delightfully heavy.

Our little County Fair fronts Balloons and then comes the State Fair. A busy three weeks for us. In fact, the best of the year. Dick and I save up so we can eat every item at the Fair.

Just got word Delbert Stevens passed away last night, August 15$^{th}$. Don't have any particulars, but will get them. Give me a call.

Last Saturday night was our bi-annual Bussey High School reunion. In the past have always brought the food and done the M.C. With the Fair and Balloons, wasn't able to do the food. I did a lousy M.C. job, but still get the plaudits. Maybe it's because I have so much fun doing it.

George Sefrit is selling George's Place and Daisy is retiring from the post office. He had been in the beverage food business since 1965 and Daisy already retired from the post office June 28$^{th}$. They rated right along with Alburnett on the dance floor.

Gen McNeil had stopped to say hello. She and Jack had run the Valhalla Supper Club for many years. Jack passed away about 3 years ago. Gen sold and moved to Missouri. A news item—Jan and Pete Norak make the best pickles in the world. They run the Prairie Moon Ballroom at Prairieburg and my next visit it will be a pickle sandwich.

In my interview with Pat Schade of the Best Western Regency in Marshalltown, she stressed good product, good quality, good attitude all of which she very obediently practices. She has a very outstanding personality characteristic of our industry people. Ever go to the Bankers Convention? About the same as a funeral.

About age—Our whole staff on the Appetizer are Senior Citizens. Les, Betty, Kap, Frank, me and Dick who just turned 50. From Dick—On their honeymoon in Chicago, went to a Cubs game then a Billy Graham Crusade. Didn't realize the Cubs were that bad an influence. At 50, it is the beginning of the end. No more smiles from the young lady on the dance floor. More like—I'll give the old guy a break and dance with him. You're no longer the helper rather the helpee.

I celebrated another birthday last week. The year before turned the big 7–0. Went to Lincoln, Nebraska State Fair and had prime rib with my carney buddies. Took in the Toby Tent Show. Things must be looking up for Toby (Jimmy Davis). He has new white shoes. I'm still wearing my old ones. Tried to trade in on new ones but my shoe guy wouldn't go for it.

Got down to Delbert Steven's funeral along with six other A & W's. Delbert was one of the best friends anybody could have. I will say the best storyteller, but they did get a little long sometimes. Betty hardly ever missed a meeting and from Keokuk every place was hard to get to.

The "Babe's" institution in the heart of Des Moines and a landmark restaurant on 6$^{th}$ Avenue closed August 24$^{th}$. Babe Bisignano at 78 and 52 years in the business threw in the towel. Think I've said it before, there's not many people that have been through Des Moines doesn't have a Babe story. He grew up on the near south side in the depression years shining shoes and hawking newspapers downtown. He got into boxing and attained the honor of Light Heavyweight Champion. Then he turned to Professional Wrestling under the name of Babe Carnera. We had a Professional Wrestler from California doing our advertising, also a movie actor. He was our advertising for a year. One day he asked me where I was from. How's my old buddy Babe Carnera? Good to know he is doing good. Great guy and give him my hello.

Ivan Gibson passed away August 18$^{th}$. Ivan and Maxine were long time operators from DeSoto, Missouri. The two, to my knowledge, never missed a convention. Ivan was also an auctioneer, among other things, and can remember late parties where a few big things changed hands with his chant.

From a magazine—When you are in business for yourself you have flexible hours. Just pick any 12 in a day you want to work.

A couple of weeks ago was an Honorary Pallbearer for an old buddy, 93. In fact, I was the only one. The last of his buddies were already gone. We were having lunch at the church after and a little older lady came in—Are you Father Ryan's brother? I may be getting too churchy.

Was at a meeting in Des Moines and sat beside a fellow (young) from Waukon. Irish Kelly always had ice cream for us. Had an overnighter at Okoboji. The Little Flower has a time share on the west side of the Big Lake. We didn't bother the water, but had some nice visits with operator buddies.

A buddy of mine is heading up Renew at church and asked me to be a Group Leader. I've always been kind of a Sunday Catlic and not get too involved, but John Roach and I were the two supervisors for the church from day one. Anyway, I did the Renew and we all enjoyed.

It's November '91. The business isn't too great, but we didn't get the ice and heavy snow that the north did of course. Besides, we can start thinking about the National Convention at Disney World. There will be 13 in our gang plus some foster kids. We had the whole gang in '72 and really had a great time. Plus we are getting smaller in numbers all the time. We had Father Burns along and we sat up a Saturday night Mass. Father couldn't make it this time. I'm getting churchy, but believe Saturday evening Mass is not in my scope.

Just got word that John Kosnovick is in the hospital with a brain tumor. John and Nancy were former Algona. Think John invented the word "Party" and one of the greatest. We sure wish him the best.

It's November and with Thanksgiving coming up we're waiting for an invitation from our great hunter Curtis Jante for the goose dinner. Okay, Thanksgiving passed and missed again.

Just talked to Dick and he was happy about losing 4 pounds with TOPs. Have known Dick about 20 years and he has always been on a diet. He has lost 400 pounds in that time, but the problem—he has gained 410.

Read an article about Lou Holtz. He was coaching at Arkansas. He has a slow quarterback. When he runs the ball we use quite a bit more film. As Dick reports, the business last of November could have been hard on the film. Also from Dick—Bob Loughman called and informed he was on two diets. He wasn't getting enuff to eat on one.

Now it's Santa Claus time and I decided to hang up the suit. It wasn't because some people thought the Jolly Guy should be bigger than an elf. On the same note, had a letter from Harry Ayres. Would sign on as foster kids if we would take him and Jean with us to the Convention. Would be happy to, Harry, but The Little Flower cut off the money. Spent too much at Christmas. Having to work a little extra this week business is so good. Now, that's a blessing.

It was a real happy for me to visit Larry on the fair circuit. He was in Ok City and I flew down to ride home with him. It was cold, especially working in a stick stand. I put on boxer shorts, long underwear and pants. Would you believe I put my shorts on backwards. Yes, it created a problem.

# 36

## *1992*

Hey, it's '92 and a great new year. Time for the annual inventory. The Little Flower brought home a large Brylcream and a new jar of Vicks. That means she is on the favorable side and will pick up the option. Will try to get her on a long timer. I'm 100%, but she has a few problems and gets around just fair on a cane. She works every day and I hardly ever work. Only one New Year's Resolution: Try to stay out of trouble and try to remember where I am going and where I put it.

Had a flyer from Taylor's Maid-Rite in Marshalltown. They are shipping frozen Maid-Rites anywhere in the U.S.A., second day air by U.P.S. Cliff and Emma Taylor started the Maid-Rite in 1928. Don Taylor Short is now the Manager—grandson and 4$^{th}$ generation of Polly Taylor. Wingas of Washington started in 1928. Now in 2$^{nd}$ generation.

Got the call from the C of C. Could I please fill one Santa day? Made with a lot of busy excuses, but took the job excited like a kid.

Did a weekend with Larry at the OK State Fair. A couple of good looking young girls came up to me. Remember us? We were at your place late on Labor Day night. I never forget a cute girl, even if I have to lie about it.

We had a super good time in Florida. The whole family, there were 11 of us, and the whole gang at Disney 4 days. The Little Flower doesn't get around too good so we checked out a wheel chair at the hotel. Everywhere is wheel chair accessible so we got along pretty good. I took out Wheelchair Collision Insurance so no worry. I was pushing up an incline and you would see this older couple feeling sorry for this little old dried-up type guy pushing the chair. I said, "Hey, there is nothing wrong with us. I push a while and she rides. Then she pushes and I ride."

Had a nice note from Marilyn Schlutz on her Christmas card. Gib, can't believe you've given up the expression "Little Flower." At this stage there is a little forgetting, Marilyn. It is still the "Little Flower" and she gets sweeter every day.

At home her moniker is "Sugar." In fact, woke up Christmas morn and there was an angel in bed with me. Then she got up and got my breakfast and February is coming up—Sweetheart month.

The local paper has been doing a full spread every week of a long time business with a story and picture. #2 Larry called and said—Dad, you do the interview. You can tell lies better than we can. I took that as a compliment. Also got a message from Santa Claus that Bo (their dog) is getting a brother or sister from the stork. That's our newlyweds #2 Larry and Jill. Our (not the greatest in my estimation) Priest Father Bruck had midnight Mass at 10:00. I call that sacrilegious. Since I am getting churchy, could very well hear your confession. Absolution might be on shaky ground. Then the New Year's Bowl percentage. Not good. But two of my #1 idols won—Joe Paterno and Lou Holtz.

I'm telling #1 Sandy all year we are going on RAGBRAI. She came home this summer. Dad, a group at work are going on RAGBRAI and I signed us up. I am in big trouble.

Closed in January and reopened February 5$^{th}$ and business bounced right back. We did put a new carpet down and refinished the woodwork. Plus work in the kitchen and a new ordering system.

Had a great time at the Convention in Disney World. We managed to get the gang in every night by 2:30 after we closed Treasure Island. Our party Friday night at M.G.M. was much fun. They put together skits from T.V. filling in with audience (A & W) talent. Iowa was presented by #2 Larry and Dick.

We were in line for dinner behind Chas & Lorraine Vegneri. Chas is second generation owner of Birchwood Meats, our hamburger supplier out of Kenosha. Dad Vegneri started the Kenosha Beef business 1936. Chas is very Italian. He and Dorene hit it off pretty well. One night we finished up at Venturer's Club t Pleasure Island. A scanty clad young lady was doing a good job of entertaining. Had #3 on the stage singing. Of course, all 11 of our gang was on the front row. She came down and rubbed the bald spot on my head and the left hearing aid popped out of my ear. She said—Gib McConnell, put the hearing aid back in. I want to sing to you!!

Went with Dick down to St. Louis for their Missouri State Meeting. Dick and I didn't get to St. Louis until about 9:00 in the evening and by the time we finished dinner it was fairly late. Dick said he would go out and run and I said good idea, I'll run too. Dick changed to his running clothes. Actually had a whole suitcase full of jogging clothes. I made it to the street and decided that was far enough. That really means that every working part of my body is showing a little wear, but my mouth still works 100%.

The University Park Holiday Inn did a great job hosting our Presidential Winter Outing and the Legislative Appreciation Dinner. Fun time (isn't that what life is all about?). At the Directors Meeting on Monday, accepted Restaurant Chairman for '92. (Kinda in my sleep.) One thing for sure, I will try to get more of the Beverage people involved. If you can keep them focused they do a great job. Have a lot of things going plus "Put your Mug on the Wall." The cut out mugs are $1.00 and taped onto the wall, door, etc.

Wes Skaden (President of Iowa Association) said Gib is like a Pit Bull with his Newsletter and the Restaurant Day. Pit Bull is pulchritudinous compared to the name Dorene has for me. (Where did I get that big word and what does it mean?)

Yes, there is still a recession. That's when the tough get tougher. We all have to work harder and better. All of our expenses are up and the net is harder to come by.

The Renew group began last week. I was into the opening prayer and got a call from Dick. Had to cut him off. That prayer is serious business.

Our girls basketball team are opening at State and and the boys, hopefully, will make it. Simpson is headed to the N.C.A.A. Division III tournament and if the Big Guy has a little extra time, my Cubs could use help. Not sure Father Bruck will agree with that philosophy.

It's time again for Coffee Days/Pork Patty Cook Off. Seems like yesterday we finished up on that. We have quite a few operators going with the Pork Patty thing and we hope to have 100 with the Mug on the Wall. This is developing money and helping the cause that coffee only didn't really develop enough to fool with, especially us fast fooders—A & W, etc.

Got The Little Flower out for a nice outing. Stopped at Ashton (diagonal road between Sioux City and Okoboji). Wanted to do a story for Cedar Cabin Lounge and Steak House—Al & Betty Mataloni. They will have my vote for "All American Nice." Then we stopped in Hartley and had dinner with Kenny and Sheryl Peterson of Pete's Steak House. They are youngish-type couple and also belong to the Pork Producers and Pete helps at the Pork Stand at the State Fair. At Pete's, happened to sit next to an old buddy from Bussey, Pete Spaur. Pete finished up in Spencer working for Stub Johnson. I imagine they made quite a pair. Pete was just a little on the windy side. Pete was telling them about me being the star on high school basketball team. I didn't correct him, but the only reason I made the squad was because they only had 9 guys. Did make the baseball team. Was so short they couldn't pitch to me. Coach would tell me—Act like you're going to hit it a mile. Don't you dare swing. Now desperately trying to get in shape for RAGBRAI. Might need divine help and Tom Harkin might be too busy.

The A & W meeting in Des Moines March 6th was a winner. Decided to give each Association Member a case of plastic promotion cups. It's good if we are all doing the same thing. The Association also purchased a new Bear Suit. Seven of us ended up at Christopher's for dinner. It is Dorene and I's favorite place in Des Moines. I actually carried them out to the restaurant in the Merc. Lynda got in. Is this your car? Never saw a car this big. Do you drive this? Lynda, this is a '78 Mercury and the love of my life after The Little Flower.

I'm getting heavy into the Renew Group. Our second meeting was hosted by an Irish WW II bride from Ireland. It happened to be on St. Patrick's Day and I was dressed as a leprechaun. Of course, Father Bruck came by and didn't really know the significance of St. Pat's Day. What does a German priest know about anything? Debbie represented Emmetsburg at the meeting. Second only to our Melrose for St. Pat's Day.

Spent most of two weeks at Vet's boys and girls basketball tournaments. The young people are great plus popcorn, Polish and sauerkraut. Don't get any better than that. Also got to Creston before for the substate. Stopped at the Windrow Restaurant then went across the street to the A & W to talk with Janet. Her husband Bill runs the Windrow. Janet informed me—Next time eat with me and then go across the street and say hi to Bill.

Father Bruck caught me, mark "Sainthood" off my probable list. What does he know?

Chuck Bisignano, (Babe's brother and a little guy) longtime successful and colorful restaurant operator in Des Moines, passed away last of March. He was at 6th and Euclid. Anita Mancuso, wife of Nick, passed away last of March. He was and is 2nd generation operator of Iowa-Des Moines Supply. I met Nick as a good friend of Father Burns.

Moved Restaurant Day to June 12th. It was going head to head with the National Pork BBQ at the State Fair Grounds. They draw a lot of people and take our farmer grillers from Pork Patty Cook Offs. It will give us another week to coerce more counties into our Pork Patty for Restaurant Day.

Our wanna be President, H. Ross Perot, and I have a lot in common. We're both funny looking little older guys and cut our hair the same way. On the debit side, he's big in the head and I'm big in the mouth. He is a billionaire and I have a '78 Merc!!

This year was the birth of the 20 oz mug. It moves every other up a size the age of super size. We bad mouth McDonald's, but they do put a lot of good ideas out and make them work. The old saying, if you can't beat 'em, join 'em.

Summer Social at Dubuque. Fun city. The next big thing on our agenda is Coffee Day and me as Chairman. Hopefully we can do better. In between we have our first Purchasing Task Force Meeting. Wisconsin has already started and there have been some big savings. The main reason we are franchises—the name and multiple buying power.

Dick is into antiques. Aren't all the younger generation? They don't appeal to me, maybe because I am an antique. Dick has a book on the value of different glasses. It's amazing to me. The Bear Pitcher and glasses worth between $10. and $20. each. The baby mug with the etched letter $20. No doubt the kids are on the right track and I am wrong. I've been wrong before!!

Last week Les asked me to ride along to the Colorado Restaurant Show at Denver. Good time, good show. Les got some ideas about their show and I had a good time with the operators and purveyors. I was a little loggy—probably the thin air. At the show they were pitching cell phones. I called Tom Cooney's daughter that lives in a suburb. This high tech world. Tom served on the first N.A.C. Board with me. He lives in Pueblo and has an A & W/K.F.C.

Slipped into a presentation from Jim Sullivan. Some of our people get to the place if it ain't broke—break it! Their party Sunday night had a country western rock and roll band. Kinda fit cause they are in cowboy country.

#1 daughter Sandy sent me a clipping from the C.R. Gazette. This young couple married on leap year day, February 29$^{th}$. Had their first formal date on June 2, 1991. Went to an A & W and then the movie. That would be Doug's on Ellis Boulevard. Have a lot of good stories from operators of long ago. I'm wearing one of those orange striped shirts. Any chance the Corporation could or would update me?

Have some new board members for the I.R.B.A.—Brian Godwin, Ron's brother of the Cedar Rapids Godwins. Brian is managing Winifreds. Clay Willie, Manager of the very successful Union 76 Restaurant in Altoona. Mike Jensen, Leona McGurk's son-in-law and Manager of the Highlander Inn & Supper Club. Paula Pieffer of the upscale Gallery Restaurant in downtown Cedar Rapids. Steve Henning of Swedes in Decorah. Young and successful. Last but not least, Al Mataloni of the Cedar Cabin in Ashton. Al is actually a re-run. He was on the Board in the 70's and now in semi-retirement.

I thank Jan Novak for the Prairie Moon Balloon Lighter. Don't smoke, but can light the candles at our prayer meetings.

Restaurant Day was a success in our county. Madison and Lucas were down about a 1/3. Hard to get the people motivated. Our 8th annual in Indianola. Did 500 sandwiches in 3 hours. Pre-sold and delivered a thousand. We moved to the Wal-Mart lot. Our take of $1,744.26 was doubled by Wal-Mart. Those people aren't all bad. Our jar collection were also up 1/3.

Our President Wes has suggested I do a prayer for rain. I will try, but not sure my connection is that good. The whole state is short on rain. I'll even do a rain dance. Do that about good as a prayer. Am I getting churchy or what? Besides, it's a funner to see the little older ladies get the float promotion and try to lift that 20 oz mug. Plus the Pricing Seminar is showing results.

Dick and I really have a good time at the National Restaurant Convention in Chicago. Norman Swartzkopf was the lead off speaker. Really did a good job. Sunday night was the big party and banquet at the Hyatt Regency with entertainment by Shirley McClain and Shelly West. Really a big crowd. A little older lady offered us a spot at her table (she had to be 85) right next to the band and dance floor. At one point said to the lady (thought I at least owed her a dance)—Would your husband care if you danced with me? He's just my boyfriend and he don't care.

Plus we got to see a ball game at new Cominskey Park. It was ½ price night and we got seats on the third base line, 3 rows back at $7.50 a piece. First we had popcorn, then nachos and finished with Polish and sauerkraut. Dick and I, of course, were entertaining everybody around us. Looked up and they had us on the centerfield big screen.

After the game we headed for Harry Carey's Restaurant, but had told the gang we would make the big dance at the Marriott. Would you believe that same older lady had good seats for us? The Shirelles were the entertainment and calling 3 people up on stage and, of course, they called me up and yes, I did my thing plus got a big smacker from the lead singer. John Winga caught me coming off the stage—You was the best. Made the show!!

May 1992: Had a great Restaurant Coffee Day as Chairman. I picked up all my markers. This Pork Patty thing picks up a little steam every year.

We've been losing a few of our distinguished operators. On May 30th we added a sweet young operator to our midst. Les's son Terry got married. It was an event worthy of wearing my Rolex watch. Wouldn't say all the dignitaries of the world were there. Dick and I plus I picked up #1 daughter Sandy. The Little Flower couldn't make it. It was at Cosgrove just east of Coralville. Certainly can't get there from here. A little community built around a nice Catholic Church. The priest was a black man from South Africa, Father Okuma, and the parishioners just love him. He had a lively homily, but I couldn't understand a word. Broken English plus one hear plug was on the bogus. Les had Dick Wosepka running a video of the proceedings and the communion route went that way. Les, like a Chinese juggler, was trying to keep the video in the clear.

On the way to the church, Les asked me to give the Invocation at dinner. I immediately wrote down a page and a half that ended up as two sentences. Stouffer's did a nice job with the food and Nasir did himself proud on the food and decorations. John Winga had a couple chairs for Sandy and I next to the dance floor. Ermal & Margaret Loughry (Ermal is confined to an electric chair) were there and Sandy and I gave Ermal one chair and we hooked up with Cosgrove people. We had a good time talking to them. They were pig farmers, etc., but the main topic was Kinnick Stadium and season football tickets. Anyway, Sandy and I were made honorary citizens of Cosgrove and were to be Marshal & Marshalette of the next grand parade. Plus we wish Terry & Brenda the very best. Next month will take up less important things.

This week we (A & W) are sponsoring an area Little League Tournament. All the drinks served at the complex ($1.00) will be served in that baseball cup (that didn't go very good in the promotion). Plus each team participant got a coupon for a hamburger, fry and root beer to be redeemed at the A & W. The promotion seemed to up things a little.

Neoma says we are close to 100% on Association dues. The Newsletter, I'm proud to say, has been a great asset for our Iowa operators. Had a letter from a Nebraska operator. An article in their paper related to a fellow from Nebraska that had stopped in an Iowa A & W and failed to get a smile. Think the biggest thing for our people—major business asset—"A Smile." We'll try to work on that.

Was working the Grand Prix last week (Des Moines). The Balloons had a promotion booth. Beth said, "Hi." It was Dick Christensen's manager at Ames a few years ago and she is now working for John Ruan.

Thanks to John and Jennie Jones, former A & W, Osceola, for letting #1 Sandy in for a hot shower when she goes through on RAGBRAI. Plus #1 grandson Ross was Honorary Bat Boy for the little Cubs at Sec Taylor. Can't get any better than that for a 10 year old. In the same light, The Little Flower's niece stopped by last week. Husband John is a promotion man for Sioux Bee Honey and covers 6 states. Gave them our last two tickets to the opera. They were tickled for the opportunity and I was tickled I didn't have the opportunity.

Set a goal of $50,000. for Restaurant Day, but possibly will reach $43,000. Got down because of the low figure, but compared to $5,000. to $10,000., that's not bad. Our Pork Patty Cook Off did 1,500 pork sandwiches and a total of $1,744.26 was turned into Wal-Mart and that would be matched and presented to Winifred Law. Yes, I'm liking Wal-Mart better every day.

The bright light of the year for Dick and I is and has been the May National Restaurant Association Show in Chicago. The good ole Merc delivered Dick and I there and back in good shape. Dick complaining about a muffler, seat adjuster and air conditioning. He has to realize us olders have a few parts wearing out.

It is a real challenge eating and drinking our way thru 1800 booths at McCormick Place. It takes Dick and I all of two days. Dick was disappointed the "Doll" didn't make it this year and Dick also failed to find Haagen Dazs. Norman Swartzkopf was just as entertaining as a civilian in person. We made the Big Dance at the Hyatt Regency. The entertainment was headed up by Shirley McLain and Shelly West.

Monday after our day at McCormick Place, we headed for Cominskey Park, new and beautiful. We got box seats back of Sox dug out for $7.50 a piece. Popcorn, nachos and Polish with kraut and even had good exposure on the centerfield big screen T.V. Don't know whether they thought we were the "Odd Couple" or a couple dummies having too much fun.

After the game we were headed to Harry Carey's Restaurant, but had promised the gang we would be at the Marriott for Rock—n—Roll night starring the Shirelles so we stopped off. Would you believe in this big crowded ballroom this same little older lady caught us at the door and made us the same offer? Carol Woklebon was at the next table with most of her 50 students from Kirkwood College brought for the Culinary Arts Contest. They were a really well behaved gang of young people.

We were dancing next to the stage watching the Shirelles perform. They needed 3 people on stage to help with the entertainment and, of course, grabbed me. I had on an Indianola sweatshirt and a White Sox cap from a cool night at Cominskey. It was the highlight of the trip and got a big smacker from Doris Jackson. John Winga was at the stage singing his praise for a fine job.

#1 Sandy went all week on RAGBRAI. Every year say I'm going all the way, but ... Was going to take Ross to meet Sandy and the 3 of us could ride together one day. We were loading into the van and started pouring down rain and we cancelled out. Ross hooked up later with his grandpa and did 30 miles. Maybe next year will go all the way. Got the helmet and gloves—$48.95. Don't let that out or I'm in big trouble.

Good meeting in Dubuque. Fun place and hard to sandwich a meeting in between. Plus I did a couple Appetizer interviews. Milepost Truck Stop in Clear

Lake and Dubuque Casino Belle. I enjoy doing the interviews and writing the stories almost much as playing Santa Claus. Jerry Krause (Milepost) was a history teacher in high school and was first alternate to go in Spaceship Challenger that blew up as it blasted off.

The 3$^{rd}$ generation is coming on with Pat & Lynn's kids, Megan and Ross, 12 & 10 with uniforms and working short hours. Now we have the 60$^{th}$ annual I.R.B.A. Convention in October along with A & W meeting plus National Convention in Las Vegas, the Mirage, January '93.

The Summer Social was a winter in Dubuque. The Casino Belle was a real treat plus the prime rib dinner was super plus the slots were hot, at least that's what we heard. You never hear from the losers, only the winners. I figured my winnings at about $170.00. Last year I lost $180.00 and only lost $12.00 this year. Dick and I got there and back in the Merc. Dick is still complaining about the air conditioning plus we didn't get into any trouble.

Just finished another Balloon event. #3 Tim was heading up the parade committee and asked me to be a judge. Went to the designated place and I was the only one there. So I did the judging plus entertaining everybody around. Tim caught up with me later. They had changed the judging point and forgot to tell me. It didn't bother me, but the people around me might be a little confused with the different winners announced.

Had a knock on the door Sunday morning before we opened. A little middle aged lady in shorts and barefoot, lived in Kansas City. Had been to the Amanas and asked to meet a Native Amanian. They pointed her to George Schuster (can't get any more Amanian than George). They fell in love with Amana and came back this year with an Amanas overnight and a dinner at Carl Oehl's. Then to Indianola for the early morning balloon flight. She saw Tim and the A & W balloon. She left happy with balloon pins, etc. Carl set this up. Anyway, they went back to Kansas City happy. This is what our business is all about.

Just got the call. New grandma and grandpa to Anna Marie. Larry and Jill are doing okay, but grandma and grandpa are a little shaky. I actually don't handle those things too well.

Our I.R.B.A. Convention is at the Convention Center and host hotel is the Savery. I'll suggest we have our meeting and join I.R.B.A. for the banquet at the hotel. Guido does a super job. Susan Clarke will be here with a new presentation on Sunday. If she doesn't motivate you, better call the undertaker. In between, this is my 20$^{th}$ year writing in the Appetizer. It is truly a labor of love.

Some of our industry's (Iowa) V.I.P.'s—Bill Leischenring, President of I.R.B.A. and serving on Board of N.R.A. Bob Schlutz, past President and finishing his first year as member of Iowa State Fair Board. Dave Heaton, past President and is in the Iowa Senate from his district. Our former U.S. President Dutch Regan with Iowa connections after ceremonies at Hoover Library Museum stopped at our buddy's Hamburg Inn II, Iowa City.

Got to judge at the State Fair with Les and Dick. Anything made with Spam. Des Moines Mayor's wife remarked—The big guy was real serious and you two seemed to be having fun. He had to be serious. Only one that really knew what was going on.

Dorene and I did get to Ray & Jan's grand opening September 21$^{st}$. I had listed Jan as "Judy" in the Appetizer and got that corrected. Ray and Jan had been in Oklahoma and Ray's "Oakie" will now be "Laplander." Curt and Florence were also down and about all we really did was entertain the customers.

Hard to believe but our A & W property tax is now $7,800. a year. Is that Kosher? More reason to get into the Pricing Task Force. Right now we're fighting that Drive Thru thing. I try to convince our customers we have 25 drive thrus with our speakers. So far it is a tough job.

Did get to the Public Affairs Conference in D.C. this year. Met with our Legislators. There were over 300 from 50 states and think it was well worth our time. You hear a lot of stories about D.C. and my main concern—might be accosted by a woman of the world. Sunday at Mass pulled a handkerchief out of the suit worn in D.C. It was covered with lipstick. In the first place, what was it doing on the handkerchief and second, that's the wrong place to discover it. Beside, John Winga was taking care of me.

1992: Seem to be having more "Now, Dad" meetings called by #'s (sons). Father Burns caught me and said no more fivesey, tensey in the confessional from now on it will be a $20. a visit. May go back to work full time to stay out of trouble.

Hosted Bill Clinton and Tom Harkin on September 27$^{th}$ at the Balloon Field. Three side hills sloping down to the stage a natural for an event of this kind. It was Harkin's fund raiser BBQ. Bobby Crouse furnished the dinner and we kicked in the coleslaw. Entertained 6,000 plus a lot of exposure. Brought Lynn and Megan along with my Host Badge. A pre-meet at the Tuttle House was $500.00 and I didn't go for that. #3 Tim took the pictures and gave us the story. I'm not voting for the guy anyway. He's trying to give away the farm. The Tuttles raised 12 children. Clinton opened with—If it's a close race and Tuttles vote for me, it's a shoo in. Harkin's opener—In Washington when I say "Barrow & Gilt" those people think I'm talking about a law firm on Pennsylvania Avenue.

A good meeting at the Iowa Hospitality Show. Les lent us the I.R.B.A. hospitality suite for our meeting—16 members. Numbers are down and I hope this turns around. We're now making plans for Las Vegas at the Mirage.

#2 Larry caught me on Friday night before the World Series which starts on Saturday at Atlanta. Dad, I have two tickets for Sunday night at Atlanta. You and I are going. No argument with that. We drove to Chicago Saturday afternoon and flew out of Midway Sunday morning at 6:30. Stayed in Holiday Inn, Oak Lawn. Got up at 4:30 and rode to the airport in the hotel van with the flight crew. At least you know you're on the right track. At Atlanta picked up the rental car and drove to Larry's buddies, our home away from home. Larry and I went to the stadium a couple hours early and did the whole thing. Walked all around the outside, inside and did the hot dog, beer, coke, popcorn, nachos, and salted in the shell peanuts. We watched both teams batting, fielding practice and grooms keeper groom the infield. Our seats were behind Ted & Jane, actually 14 rows up on the second tier. We stood at attention while our Marine Color Guard presented the Colors (Maple Leaf Flag upside down—Toronto) and we looked like pros doing the chop and chant.

Monday we ate at the Varsity Drive-In, billed as the World's Largest Drive-In and I believe it really is something. They still call on cars and hang the trays on the windows. About 30 stalls for this. Park 600 cars on a double lot. Inside have order stations where you give your order and pick it up. At 1:30 in the afternoon there were at least six people in line at each station and our friend-guide says it is always that busy. There are 6 different rooms to sit down and eat, larger than our dining rooms, with different T.V. programs in each one. The menu is limited. They specialize in homemade onion rings and also do their own potatoes (French fries) and coleslaw. Coney dogs are also a big item with hamburgers, about 5 soft drinks, shakes and fried pies.

You all know Atlanta is the birth place of Coca Cola. We spent half a day at the Coke museum. Of course at the ball park it was all Coke. I really didn't see any Pepsi the three days we were in Atlanta. They are really loyal. I imagine Coke is a big part of Atlanta's being.

Got the new Bear and established the rules for renting and keeping up. A charge of $30.00 for each operator using and that will be used for cleaning. Each operator is also supposed to pay for any needed repair.

Now Christmas is coming up. Especially happy with our new granddaughter Anna. So I'll have to get the Santa suit dusted off. That is probably most fun of any job I undertook and, of course, some of the kids are bigger than Santa.

The 60th annual Hospitality Show was a real winner. Guido did a great job with the food which he is noted for. Dorene and I even overnighted at the Savery. We had a fun table with our gang with new baby Anna and two couples that bought Rapids Wholesale (a restaurant supply house) in Cedar Rapids. Ted & Janice Dorwald have the Del Mar Drive-In at Fairbank. Janice is the operator and Ted is the fixer. Ted's real job is the maintenance man for the City of Fairbank.

A week later Dorene and I took a trip to Northeast for the turning of the leaves. We stopped and had lunch with Janet and had a good conversation with the natives. Had breakfast next morning at a café in Lansing. The owner wasn't in so I left my card. The card happened to be of Al Matalone. Al, if you get a call from Lansing, you know the reason.

#3 Tim had me as a program for Rotary. He evidently couldn't get anybody else and called me at the last minute. I enjoy doing it and whatever. Can't remember what the program was about, but did it.

Got a job modeling in January at Las Vegas. Why would they call me, but I sure wouldn't turn it down. Hope it's with the dancing girls. I don't look to good in those skimpy uniforms.

Dick is telling this story—Gib walked into a bar and asked the bartender if he could bring his cocker spaniel inside to watch the baseball game since it loved to watch the Cubs play. Business was slow and the bartender liked animals so he agreed to let the dog sit on the bar near the T.V. In the 5th the Cubs scored a run on a double and long single. The dog jumped around in circles and barked excitedly. In the eight they scored another run after two walks and a bloop single. Once again the dog went wild. "Gib, he really gets excited", the bartender said after the Cubs blew the game 3 to 2. What in the world does he do when the Cubs win? "I don't know", Gib said, "I've only had him 2 years."

We decided to pool our money and let Curt Jante invest it for us in Las Vegas. Curt is our best man in the category.

On our Northeast trip to check out the leaves we stopped to see LaVerne Kelly. Irish has been gone a couple years and don't think she will ever get over it. Irish was one of my best buddies and could write a book about our capers and we didn't get together that often.

Happy to report our gang is all fine. We have two new ones to celebrate Santa time with us this year. Our new beautiful little girl Anna and Sandy has an exchange student with her this year, Katja, and we're happy to have her.

Everybody in our area was shook with the death of Chris Street. He was everything you would like in a son and probably would have excelled in anything he undertook. He had those abilities and to the community he was just one of the family growing up.

A big social event of the year was the wedding of Dick's Melanie. Melanie is a real sweetheart and Dick pulled out all the stops. Les and our gang did the serving and the work. The weather was the very worst kind. We Catlics would call the Pope on a case like this. Guess the Protestants don't have an out.

A good convention in Las Vegas. Les, Dick and I shared a room, an experience in itself. Yes, Dick snores and he shakes the hotel. Even with my hard hearing it comes in loud and clear. It was really an upbeat crowd. More like the days of old. We got to see the Siegfried and Roy Show. Of course we were so far back another move and we would have been on the poker table.

The second night I slept in the bathtub. When we went to the show, I tried to make the crowd think I had made a score. Thursday night Larry, Ross and I went to the U.N.L.V.-Pacific game—great show.

At our Thanksgiving gathering the guys said we ought to have a party. Can't have any more wedding parties, ran out of kids. Decided to have a 5$^{th}$ anniversary party to Tim and Shelli. I popped for the band and they would take care of the rest. Turned out it was a retirement (surprise) party for me. I didn't catch on until the party was half over and then the tears started running down my cheeks half from laughing. The show with a video and slides plus a recitation lasted about an hour. They asked me to say a few words. For me like eating one peanut, but I refrained. Number one because they had been sitting long enuff, second because Dorene's embarrassed to tears and she deserved a break, and third was so choked up couldn't expound anyway. A good lady hug gets an old guy's motor running and Saturday night (Jan. 3) my motor never shut off.

Things are looking up for the little old guy. The #'s have agreed to get me a new uniform. Thinks it reflects the hit I made at the Convention style show. Ten years ago they decided it wouldn't be worthwhile to get me into new uniforms. Must've got a reprieve.

# 37

## *1993*

Have signed a contract to help Debbie Goeders when RAGBRAI overnights in Emmetsburg. Might even take Dick if Connie can spare him. Plus we have to start getting ready for St. Pat's Day, also a biggie in Emmetsburg.

Last year Linda made a call at the A & W on St. Pat's Day and I was a Leprechaun. This year she made the call on Tuesday before Ash Wednesday which is Paczki Day and for you Protestants that's the Polish celebration day fronting the start of Lent, similar to Mardi Gras in New Orleans.

Dick and I attended the Wisconsin A & W Convention and it was really a great show plus the operators went out of their way to make us welcome. It was held at the Dells and that has gotten to be quite a tourist attraction.

Was in charge of fun at the Clear Lake meeting. The crowd started out small due to the weather, but travelers giving up fighting the roads and tying up. They fittered into our party and helped our crowd plus the new people hadn't heard any of my stories. Took Dorene to the room about 10:30, but the party lasted until 2:00 when they turned out the lights. Danced with everybody at least once. Had one lady say—Gosh, you're a good dancer. I let it all hang out thinking of Lent coming up in a couple days and giving up everything on the good-bad list. Had one other lady say—Gosh, you're a good dancer (drinking, maybe?).

I really did pretty good on the Lenten season. Of course, I have a history of lying and cheating but my Renew Group is monitoring me, but it won't be easy.

We were closed again (3$^{rd}$ year) for Easter Sunday. It seems to be working. We're getting together for pricing from our wholesalers. Bread is the biggest item and next comes salad dressing. With the N.A.C., have negotiated a mile radius around our store. It was spot location before. George Michel helped our cause. He seems to be good for us.

Our Summer Social is set for Living History Farms. It's an important get together with all the front office planning to attend. There will be a nice program. Bring your concerns or problems to present to the A & W people. It will be an important meeting. Also our annual Association meeting that was wiped out by a snow storm.

We were expecting a new grand baby in August. On April 16$^{th}$ Shelli went into pre-labor and they battled all day and finally let nature take its course. At 10:30 pm the baby was born—took one gasp and expired. It was Gibson Thayer McConnell. It's always hard to lose these little guys. The little guy couldn't have had better parents, but it wasn't to be. You all are considered my extended family (A & W people) and it helps me to relate this.

Met Sandy in Washington D.C. the first week in April for 3 days of sight seeing. Sandy cautioned the first thing—Dad, I don't think you should talk to everybody on the street. This is a big city. That will never work for me. Sandy and I had a super good time. So many things to visit and the whole city is history. The Metro is clean, fast and safe. Really relatively easy and if I can figure out the Metro system, anybody can and it is also cheap. We got to see the Cherry Blossom Parade but the blossoms were about a week away. Sandy and I were visiting Arlington Cemetery and there were a few scattered magnolia trees with beautiful large blossoms. A couple of ladies behind us, one asked the other, "What are those blossoms?" "Must be cherry blossoms, that's what we're suppose to be seeing."

We thank Jim Nussle for the Gallery passes (U.S. House and Senate). Sandy was absolutely mortified when I jumped up and cheered as the senator from Minnesota announced on the floor that the University of Minnesota had beaten Georgetown in the N.I.T. The rule in the Gallery is—very quiet and I was warned very quickly from Security. We had a very nice guide at the Portrait Gallery. She was a native of the area and volunteered two days a week. She had the duty down pat, but was a little confused with Iowa-Ohio. She didn't realize Hoover was from Iowa and had never heard the Dutch Regan story. She couldn't imagine John L. Lewis growing up in our area. I was a little disappointed with that at the Air and Space Museum that they didn't have that B-17 I crewed on display. Could be that's on display at the Sioux City Air Base Museum.

Had the Little Flower out for an overnighter a couple weeks ago at the Village Inn, East Okoboji. Did some story interviews and made many stops. Our destination was the Spirit Lake Bakery Restaurant and The Inn. Had a nice visit with Deb Goeders in Emmetsburg, my old buddy from a RAGBRAI story. Stopped at Britt and visited Donna and swung by Belmond and caught former A & W Op's Don and Sherri. Happy to see us.

In another visit to the Northeast, got in a visit with Steve at Independence and caught the Bohemian, Doug, very busy in Cedar Rapids. They are called Czechs in Cedar Rapids, but Doug comes from Britt. Same, but different. "Houby" is the Czech word for morel mushrooms and the last two weeks have been Houby Days. Back home, The Little Flower and I had fresh crappies (#3 Tim), dandelion greens and mushrooms. It just doesn't get any better than that.

Temperature at 85 degrees and the sunshine overcome a lot of problems in the root beer business. The rain is still with us and that covers most of the state. In Indianola we're lucky enough to miss the big storms so far. Business is good so the gang is wearing the Big Smile.

Dick and I did the N.R.A. show last of May. Faithful Merc got us there in good shape. Over 1,800 booths to work which we did in 2 days. Former President George Bush was lead off speaker. Crux of his speech—Happy to be regular citizen and enjoying it. Dick and I hosted the I.R.B.A. Reception in our room. Great party, but they did make a mess. Dick and I flipped and I drew "Maid" for both nights. Did Dick cheat me on that flip? The Cubs and Sox were both out of town so we did the big N.R.A. parties at the Hilton and Marriott. Sunday night was country western and Monday night was 60's rock-n-roll. Happened to get a good dance partner from New Orleans. So one up on Dick and this will carry over to the A & W Convention in January.

Brother Jack had a bout with cancer in May so I spent quite a bit of time at Des Moines General. He's getting along fine—tough guy. One of his attendants was from Oelwein and her first job was car hop for Knute & Florence Sondrel. The big push at the N.R.A. Convention was expresso and cappuccino. They say it is hot in restaurants and bars in Chicago. Think Iowa is a ways from that. Dick spent a few days in the hospital to correct his snoring. It helped. Now it's similar to a brass band.

Had a great Summer Social at Living History Farms. We, of course, were in conjunction with the I.R.A. summer meeting and had a tour of the farms. We had a total of 25. The restaurant op's were amazed that Corporate President and Vice President would attend a social and picnic on Sunday night. We certainly thank George and Paul.

Now comes the floods of 1993. The Water Works (Des Moines) was under water and Des Moines is pretty well shut down. We have people coming in with jugs to fill and carry home for drinking water. We have a couple outside spigots and they are welcome to the water. The Des Moines Water Work says after the water goes down it will be another week to 10 days before they get the system cleaned and have pure water. Dick has been down a couple times to get a pick up loaded with pickle buckets full of water.

Dick asked me to go along to the Missouri meeting and I was happy to get in. He picked me up at 2:00 pm on the 29$^{th}$. He asked if the Cardinals were in town. I knew the answer—playing the #1 Phillies at 7:35. 400 miles from St. Louis and we were walking in the stadium at 8:00 pm. On the way into the ticket office we started talking to a couple. It so happened they had four tickets, third row from the field and would be happy to have us as their guests. Talk about Missouri hospitality!! I'll pop for the beer. No, we're going to a party after game and don't really need a head start.

It doesn't take a computer to figure out we made a fast trip to St. Louis. Of course, it's all down hill. Saw the Phils beat the Cards 13 to 10, with a total of 30 hits. Good game to watch and with those good seats. Always enjoy the people of Missouri.

Was talking to Juanita Popp from Cape Girardeau at the meeting next afternoon and asked what she thought of Rush Limbaugh, a native of the Cape. She told me Rusty and her son ran around together and Limbaugh ate many meals at her house. He was a bag of wind then just as he is now. Sort of got the idea Juanita and Richard may be Democrats.

Donna Hoop is working on the Iowa Scholarship. She has put a lot of work on this and thinks it is a great thing and will help all franchises.

We are selling a lot more Mozzaburgers now that they are on the menu. In June we sold 800 Mozzaburgers and the other hamburgers also showed an increase too. The 20 oz mug is another great addition. We used to sell the same amount of small as large. That's good for a real smile.

As usual, had a great Father's Day. The gang all had to bring me something and the card all related to the family head as a "Cool Guy"! In my book, that's a compliment. Plus our gang is probably the all time best.

President George was a good looking guy as a teenager in May/June Newsbearer. He's sure homely now and seems like Dick is going the same route. The Little Flower thinks I'm improving with age. Isn't life wonderful?

Balloons were a success again this year and A & W won the bathtub races. Our super little County Fair lucked out. A little muddy, but got all the events and ended in the black. Megan's first year in 4-H, 9 entries and 9 blue ribbons plus her apple pie will show at the State Fair and I'll be there with a sign "I'm Megan's grandpa." Plus I got the nicest award I've ever received. Was inducted into the 4-H Hall of Fame.

The summer is over and can't really say anything good about it and down economy will probably carry over into next year. Business was pretty good considering the floods and all. Had a great time at the Big Fair. Didn't get to judge the Spam contest. Les and Dick want to split the ante and consequently they didn't get any T.V. exposure.

Tom and Mary Cooney were in Des Moines during fair time and were having a family reunion. Got to see the whole immediate family at Tim's. There for a family portrait. Tom served with me on the first National A & W Board and operated Pueblo, Colorado.

Dick and I took an inventory and we ate at every concession stand at the Big Fair. The pitchman selling knives has caught my soft side for the last so many years and all my gang have knife sets. Got by the knife guy this year, but a petite little lady pitching chamois mops broadsided me. Bought a bunch. Might have to get a stand next year and sell mops.

Nebco is giving reduced bracket pricing to help the slow winter months and also the Buying Task Force hopes to hook up with Wisconsin. More operators = buying power. Also got the outline from Iowa A & W Scholarship. If everybody agrees and contributes $100., there will be $1,800. which could be 4—$450.00 scholarships. We'll see how that plays out.

Got word that Dick is bad mouthing the chamois mops. What does he know about mopping? Besides, that was a sweet girl selling them and I'm sure her pitch was gospel. Plus Dick's garbage pickup just went to $280.00 a month and he's thinking of buying a couple of goats.

We're praying for Lynne with her problems losing a lung. Has her name for a transplant and that usually takes a couple years. My Renew Group has a prayer for her at our group meetings.

Added the Hotel and Motel Association to the ranks for the I.R.A. Was a good move for all! Nice crowd for our Convention and the Marriott was great hosting. Dorene and I stayed at the mixer party Saturday night until the band quit. Got to dance with most all of the young ladies. Our guest speaker at the Convention Power Breakfast was Stephen Elmont, President of the National Restaurant Association. I had the pleasure of picking he and Linda up at the airport and later taking them to the Amanas, and also hobnobbing with the Biggies at Amana including George Forstner, granddaddy of Amana Refrigeration.

Seems like Dorene and I are funnin' too much. Attended the awards presentation at Pete's Supper Club in Hartley. Pete and Cheryl were awarded National Pork Restaurant of the Year. Next we did an interview at Palm's Supper Club in Fort Madison (opposite end of the state).

Now we're going into winter. Business changes 180 degrees. Coffee, soup and hot chocolate. The guys are also continuing the 99 cents bacon cheeseburger. Actually, most popular sandwich we have.

The National Convention coming up January 19–23 is at the French Quarter Marriott. Corporate is talking about conventions every other year due to expense. That puts more pressure on making this one.

Read an article why Don James, a Washington Football Coach, says he's grateful for "Playboy" magazine's annual "Pigskin Preview." It's the only time of the year my wife will let me buy the magazine, but she reminds me that "Playboy" is a lot like "National Geographic." Both have pictures of places I'm never going to visit.

An add on—Sold out on the chamois mops. Could sneak in a last minute order if you really need, but the price will have to go up due to demand.

We really do enjoy all the friends we've made over the years at Conventions and meetings. Our good friend from Sterling, Illinois, Frank Sonoc, has sold and moved with Kathleen and are living at Bonita Springs, Florida. It was Frank's lifelong ambition to retire in Florida. The Knopps from Russell, Kansas made the Convention with their three kids—8, 10, 12. I had it made up with the 3 kids that they would run up on the stage and sing the Iowa Corn Song. I got busy with family (we had 6 guests) and didn't get to pull it off. Sure it would have brought down the house.

And 1993 is coming to an end. The flood of '93 will live on forever, but there were a few blessings too. The kids put together a surprise birthday party for Curt Jante's 70$^{th}$ at Ronnie Newlins's Waterfront Restaurant. Over 200 people there and a ton of the old A & W gang. Al Dierks presented me with a bottle of A & W root beer and at that time, wasn't too much into root beer. The stories started stretching and was a party like the days of old and the next morning I remembered I am old. As we were leaving, the family invited us to breakfast—10:00 at the Holiday Lodge. Ray bet Linda $200.00 that I wouldn't make breakfast. The Little Flower and I made 8:30 Mass at St. Pat's plus a nice drive around the lake and walked into the lodge at 10:00. Linda hollered at Ray, "You owed me $200. bucks!" Had a super time. Curt and Florence with their family are the greatest.

Last month #3 Tim got an invitation to be the speaker at a father and son banquet at a country church (United Brethren) outside of Adel. He invited me to go along. I could visualize a passel of country ladies putting together an old fashioned dinner like the days of old. Not to be—Hy-Vee catering out of Perry. Tim said going up, "Dad, this is my program and you don't say anything." The Catlic boy did a great job, but doubt if he got any converts and I didn't say anything.

Busy time wrapping gifts for Christmas. Those chamois mops are really hard to wrap. Besides we're lucky to have all the grandkids within throwing distance. At Christmas we think of it.

# 38

## *1994*

Now we're into 1994 and New Year's Resolutions are in order or as us Catlics call it, "Yearly Confessions."

I resolve to: Do RAGBRAI with Sandy. To improve my Big Fair attendance. Missed 2 out of 11 last year; To be sweeter to The Little Flower. When I get in trouble, bring her a cookbook. She already has a ton; To quit bad mouthing Fathur Bruck. Maybe he can't help thinking he is the Pope; To refrain from bothering ladies at our dance functions. Referring mostly to the olders. Can't promise on the youngers; To not get my body pierced for rings, etc.; To write better for Betty's transcriptions in the Appetizer. This will be the toughest one.

The Little Flower goes along when I go out for interviews to write the Appetizer articles. She usually asks more questions than I. We did the interview last month for the Palms in Fort Madison. The head lady, Inez, with 3 children in their 20's and no grandchildren. We met a beautiful young lady that Niko is seeing. Maybe there is a chance yet, mom.

Remember two years ago at the Big Fair I was helping Les and Dick judge the Spam contest. In the November 8th issue of Forbes, sales for Spam was up 28%. Sure that was due to exposure at the Big Fair. I lost my job with Les and Dick and Spam sales have been down the last two years. Does that tell you something?

Doing the interview for Truck Havens. Was in Sergeant Bluffs next to the Sioux City Airport, site of my WW II battles. Brings back many memories. Still can tell those stories and they get a little better every time.

Passed my Homemaker Exam. Now "Hints to Heloise" is a must, right after Sports and Comics. Dorene and I, at this point, are getting along fine on our own.

Special news—The Little Flower and I have a new granddaughter as of 3:45 am, 1/27/94—Hattie Rae. A preemie at 7 months and at this point everything is fine. There will be a stay in the incubator etc. Appreciate all your prayers. Last one, last year, daughter-in-law Shelli was bedfast for 3 weeks. The big reason I was a little restrained at the Convention.

Hope everybody had a good Christmas. I get so many presents. Know I wasn't that good. Can you believe 5 different boxes of chocolates? The A & W is shaping up. We built in '75 and this winter did a complete remodel in the dining room. We had changed the dark paneling 10 years to light wallpaper and the plastic trim to natural finished oak. This year we changed the dark booths to light tables and brown seats. Changed the entries to light and also changed to oak plus new counters. Really looks like a new unit—lighter and brighter.

President Doug is missing and didn't get to the Convention. We will have our annual Association meeting with I.R.A. at the Highlander February 20–21. We'll get another look at the advertising and highlights of the Convention from Linda and N.A.C. report from Dick and then on to the fun. Bob and Leona McGurk are the very greatest and it's always good time at their house.

Really a super time at the New Orleans Convention. The correct pronunciation is all letters soft. "Norlean" unless you want to sound like damn Yankee. That's still one word in the South.

This is the 75$^{th}$ anniversary of the birth of our A & W company and it has been a great 75. Think the scholarship thing is going to work. There will be two $500.00 scholarships given, so everybody needs to get their entries in. Hopefully everybody will get a $100.00 check in. Need that to be eligible.

Another joke from Dick (where does he get this funny stuff?)—An archeologist was digging in the Negev Desert in Israel and came upon a casket containing a mummy. After examining it, he called the curator of a prestigious natural history museum. "I've just recovered a 3,000 year old mummy of a man who died of heart failure", the excited scientist exclaimed. "You can't know all of that from looking at him", the curator replied. "Bring him in and we'll see." A week later the amazed curator called the archeologist, "You were right about the mummy's age and cause of death. How in the world did you know?" "Easy, there was a piece of paper in his hand that said, '10,000 shekels on Goliath.'"

At one time we were considered one of the Biggies in the food industry. Hopefully we can get back to that status. In 1984 there were 666 A & W Restaurants with sales of 113.9 million. In 1994 there are 494 restaurants doing 187.1 million. We have a meeting coming up on Sunday, February 20$^{th}$. Maybe we can all get together and get on the road back.

We are already making plans for the Phoenix convention (1996). Contacted Harry Ayres for first dibs on his orange, grapefruit and lemon crops. The plans are for The Little Flower and I to rent a U-Haul and pull behind the Merc.

The New Orleans Convention continued—Slipped out the first chance I got to an oyster bar and had ½ dozen raw oysters on the ½ shell and a bottle of Jax Beer. Raw oysters aren't for everybody and tried Dick, but he backed up. One night slipped out for dinner of oysters, crayfish and bottle of Dixie Beer. Did the St. Charles Trolley and on Saturday afternoon Larry, Ross and I slipped out to the Super Dome to see North Carolina and LSU plus a good girls game. Just to be in the same area with those two coaches was worth the price of admission. Did Mass at the St. Louis Cathedral and tried to cover everybody with my prayers. My connection is a little shaky.

Just got word Terry McAllister from the Keokuk A & W, won a trip to Hollywood. Next trip down that way will get a celebrity interview.

News update: Hattie Rae now weighs 3 #, 15 oz as of 3/15/94. Weather is shaping up and business is starting to roll. Floods of '93 are and always will be on our minds, but now the floods are gone and the snow is mostly melted. Been in Des Moines the past couple of weeks to the girls and boys state basketball at the auditorium. Been there so much, am on a first name basis with the workers.

The Committee is working hard to get the Workmen's Compensation Insurance off the ground. One of our best Association benefits.

Inventory continued for the start of '94 with the White Glove Inspection of the Little Flower House. My homemaking duties aren't getting any better and I passed just barely. My spring house cleaning ended up overlapping my fall house cleaning. The Little Flower always had things ship shape, but I'm just barely. Anyway, at this writing all my parts and the Merc are showing a little wear, but still serviceable. Hope The Little Flower doesn't give up on us.

Every year it is and has been a ritual on New Year's Day to watch all the games and parades plus put the Newsletter together. My favorite color man is Joe Garagiola. Big Ten won 4 out of 7 bowls. I was pulling for Tom Osborne to win the National Title, but it wasn't to be.

Had a nice Christmas card from the chamois mop pitch lady. Ahead of Dick on that one. Have a new suit and Santa brought a shirt and tie. Start the dance music, it's going to be a good year.

The A & W Corporate is celebrating its 75$^{th}$ anniversary this year and will have signs up. Can see it now—the first customer: Nice, you're having a 75$^{th}$ birthday! Actually, not far off. Will be 72.

Back to the "Norlens" Convention. The crowds on Bourbon Street are still wall to wall, but the ages are 40 years younger than my WW II days. Jazz used to be 100% brass, but now 80% strings, but the loud is still the same. Had coffee at the original French Market Coffee Stand (Café Du Monde) plus beignets. The chicory takes a little time getting used to. In the 5 days, didn't hear the words "Damn Yankee." Had grits in the morning with my sausage and eggs. Got to do a Karaoke number and had 3 ladies lined up to dance with but they got away from me. We did a Mardi Gras parade in our hotel lobby and I got to be king following a "Norlens" jazz band (all brass). How many Mardi Gras parade kings do you know? We actually had 5 A & W's represented.

Back to business at hand. Yesterday went to the courthouse to renew the Merc license. It was a year in arrears. Wouldn't that have been funny if Dick and I had been picked up in Chicago at the N.R.A. show. It might have cramped our style. Not sure the Chicago jails allow big parties every night. The climax—calling Les to bail us out.

The President's Winter Outing at the Highlander—Hadn't been at the Highlander for a while, but it's still a class act all the way. The hor d'oeurves were super and dinner was a work of art. We think the McGurk family almost foundered us on the fun. Danced with all the ladies but two. Have them on the card for the next party. Think all should suffer through one dance with me.

Big News—Lippy Leo Durocher and Phil Rizzuto were elected to the Baseball Hall of Fame. Lippy played and managed 30–40–50's, mostly known for his saying, "Nice guys finish last." Phil was traded to the Cubs from the Yankees and Jack and I got to see him in the 1937 World Series in Chicago. Yes, this is the year for the Cubs.

I'm not a wrestling fan. Don't know much about it, but Indianola won the 3A Wrestling Title.

Hattie Rae update—The proud parents, not to mention proud grandparents, have Hattie Rae home as of March 28. Over 5# and doing fine.

#3 Tim and #2 Larry came to the house the other day. We're giving the '78 Merc to our buddy. That's a good car and I love that car. We know it's a good car, that's why we're giving it to the buddy and you have Mom and that's about all the loving you can handle, plus you can buy a new car. I'm not about to buy a new car, but got a real deal on an '89 Caddy with 18,000 miles owned by a little old lady that just drove it to church. Seemed like quite a few miles but maybe she went to church every day and a car salesman wouldn't story. Won't Dick be excited on our trip to Chicago Restaurant Show. Think he is still envious about the Chamois Mop Lady.

Can't get any bigger than the front page of the Newsbearer. My pardoner is D.r Thaicon from Bangkok, Thailand. He heads up a number of A & W units in the area and has been a buddy of quite a few years. He invited me to an international meeting they are having in Bangkok middle of November. It's a long shot and a lot of sweet talk to The Little Flower.

A fellow stopped in a couple days ago. We manufacture step ladders and you little people are our favorites. Everybody needs somebody.

Took The Little Flower out for a beautiful outing last of March. Stopped in Harlan—Kenny & Sue Kobold—Mickels. They do a heckuva job. Full house on a slower day. The 5 cars parked next to us were from 5 different neighboring counties. Kenny started no smoking in the restaurant last July 3$^{rd}$. It was a little slow at first, but when some competitors joined him it came back to normal and finished the year up 5%. Went on to Council Bluffs and the Blue Ox West for afternoon coffee. Bent Rasmussen, the perfect host, owner, operator and a good operator.

Stopped in Anita for dinner and a visit with Lee & JoAnn Poeppe, who have the Redwood Steak House. Lee remarked he had enjoyed reading since buying the Redwood in 1972. JoAnn also related quite a few of my past quotes plus she is Irish Catholic and I'm sure she's a good dancer which puts her on my most Favorite People List. What other qualifications could there possible be?

Plans are firming up for our Pork Patty Cook Off—Eighth Annual. This year's prices will be $1.50 each for ¼ pound BBQ (Cookie's) Pork Patty sandwich and a dozen for $15.00. We call for orders and deliver. This year we are shooting for $2,000. gross.

We grieve the death of Dinah Shore. She was the favorite singer—actress of many of us. Fred Sampson, Restaurant Executive Director of New York, helped her get started. Dinah migrated to New York City from the South looking for a job. Fred heard her sing and got her a job as a singing waitress at one of the bigger restaurants. A scout heard her and the rest is history. If that story isn't quite right, Fred will probably catch me at the National Restaurant Show in Chicago and straighten me out.

Checking on the smoke free restaurant. Zeno's Pizza in Marshalltown has been in business 40 years. Has been smoke free for a year. A few problems at first, but the year was up 5%. Happy with our move.

The past week Curt Jante was operated on for lung cancer and it was malignant. The operation went well and think they got it all. They gave Curt encouragement.

Along with A & W born in 1919, a couple of pretty big names with the same birth year—Earl May and Easter Seals. Nice to travel in good company.

Selling quite a few of the 75th Anniversary mugs and don't believe we're losing many. Maybe all the closets are full. Gallon sales are up 100%. Has to be from the neat labels.

Again it's time for the National Restaurant Show in Chicago. Greatest food show in the world. Colin Powell will be the lead off speaker with many seminars, new products, and equipment. It takes two days for Dick and I to visit the 2,000 booths. After 5 the fun starts—ballgame, dinner and then the Convention party and dance. Big name bands and entertainment. More fun than older guy should be allowed to have.

Larry and I were out for a ride in the new Caddy (I may fall in love again). Wasn't it nice of The Little Flower to let me have that car? Plus I had the house cleaning done by the 1st of May. Is that a record or what? Homemaker tip for the month—Hire the Homemaker Service to do the job and forget it.

The business seems to be going good. Report from President Doug at Carroll—RAGBRAI is again overnighting in Carroll. Doug is making plans. Last time through they set up next to a beer joint—beer floats. Not sure that would work. I've been around the RAGBRAI stops and from my experience these are the best people in the world. It is really like a week's vacation for the whole lot and they are enjoying. In my next life that ride will be first on the list.

The Regency Inn at Marshalltown was the host for our Summer Social for I.R.B.A. and A & W has a spot for our meeting. Sorry to say we only had 6 in attendance. Had a lot of Mesquaki stories. All big winners and no looser stories. The Little Flower and I were just back from a wedding in York, Nebraska. A couple nice kids that have been working for #2 Larry.

The Little Flower and I really had a couple of good weeks in Scandinavia. Trip was put together by our local bank—New Horizons Club. Senior Citizens 55 and over. You know how I hate old people. A total of 80 people on two buses and The Little Flower and I were second oldest couple. We landed in Copenhagen and bussed through Denmark, Norway and Sweden. The guide always makes it interesting and almost all the natives could understand English. He had some funny impressions. Breath of fresh air—Fresh Nose; Families switching partners—Switch Bitch; Long hour—Short Hour (haven't the foggiest). Crane is a bird of learning. Over here all they do is deliver babies. The guide gave us our first instructions—A toilet is a toilet, a wash room is a place to wash, and a rest room is a place to rest. The prices were high. Food was 2 to 3 times our prices. Gas was listed at the pump by the liter. $1.03 which figures over $4.00 a gallon.

Most of you have heard of Templeton Rye. For years I thought it was one word. In the days of prohibition the people in this German community made rye whiskey and had a steady pipeline to Al Capone in Chicago. A couple months ago, in my travels, had the pleasure of sampling Templeton Rye, probably 70 years old. Had to be the smoothest ever going down and then hit you like a Joe Louis right.

Aug. '94: As of July 18, the crops never looked better. The farmers may have to find something else to complain about. Farmers are super great, but there is always something not quite right.

In bragging about our successful Pork Patty Cook Off, forgot to mention had pre-sold for delivery 720 sandwiches. Larry was ramrodding and I was getting in the way. As he ran out of sandwiches, he discovered I had miscounted by 200. He needed 920 instead. From Larry—Dad, next year we will do this and you will be in Europe. My only answer—When I went to school they didn't teach big numbers.

Special News Release—James Lee 8 lbs. 9oz., 20 ¾", born 8/12/94. Larry and Jill are doing well. Grandpa, 5 foot moved up to 7 foot.

#1 Sandy did RAGBRAI XXII and had a great time. She had a good thing to say about all the stops and the great people. Put this down—figuring on joining Sandy for all of RAGBRAI XXIII next year.

Balloons are bigger and better every year. I retired undefeated from the Bathtub Races. My long suit was 3 horses to push me. There are a few things where age is cutting in and I hate to admit it.

The "Sherelles" were at the Big Fair this year at the Rock-N-Roll Reunion. I was on the stage with them at the National Restaurant Show in Chicago a couple years ago. Of course, Dick was at the Fair that night and filled me in. Did get with the Sherelles back stage after the show, but that's all I'm telling.

Larry has the Old Fashioned Soda Fountain in Pioneer Village. He let me be in front with the white shirt, bowtie, soda fountain cap to meet, greet, tell stories, sing, glad hand and in between clean a few tables plus do a little pitching, and I'm at the height of my glory.

Our new balloon "Root Beer Float" got in just 2 weeks before the Classic. Julie Craft had bought her Mother a balloon ride at one of Shelli's fundraisers. Mom and Dad, Julie's folks, had come down from Kinsley and they went up with Tim. It was my job to squire Julie around (a good looking News Reporter from Channel 5). Julie was doing the video of the inflation, take off, and then to the Chase Cars. Here comes a wire fence and I climb over. Julie had on a tight mini skirt (actually on her way to work). Gib, turn your head I'm climbing over this fence. Don't tell, but I did peek—just a little peek.

A line from Dick—I know a cemetery whose custom it is to bury lawyers 12 feet deep, because deep down they are good people.

Did perfect attendance at the Big Fair. There was a prettiest leg contest and I was a little bit late. I was the 52$^{nd}$ alternate and wasn't called, but will always think I could have won hands down. Julie Craft was on hand as one of the three judges and had promised me her vote. I was sitting in the audience with a shady entourage from Indianola and, of course, we were entertaining half the audience. Morgan Halgren (another Indy) works for I.P.T.V. and doing nightly Fair highlights and gave me pretty good footage.

Our Wal-Mart manager, Dave Schmidt, caught me at Balloons. Dave had given us a spot in front of the store for our Pork Patty Cook Off. Every year I pick up a form (response sheet) from the checkout counter and write a thank you for their help. For an $1,800 check I'm going to kiss their whatever. Dave's supervisor had read my note in front of the Regional Managers meeting. I told them what a great job Dave was doing, community, etc. Have no idea what I put in that letter, but it has a #1 position in Dave's trophy case.

Turned the Bathtub Races driving position over to Ross and he carried on the winning tradition. Had to go to the 3$^{rd}$ generation. The second generation didn't measure up.

Back to our Scandinavian trip. World Acclaimed Swedish meat balls,—between you and me, The Little Flower's are better. Second largest exporter of petroleum in the world. Lamb is prominent food, second to fish. Golf used to be very exclusive and many courses are still being made. Think they sent the last windmill to Elk Horn. Now all they have are large blade generators. Leggo's originated in a small town in Denmark. Had lunch in Knute Rockne's hometown, Doss Nowen.

Had a fun summer and good County Fair. Got to judge the BBQ cookout. The fringe benefit is tasting and eating. Also, was herdsman judge for the sheep barns. About all I picked up from that was sheep do in my rib-soled shoes.

In between Balloon events, got to Catherine Winga's 90$^{th}$ birthday reception. The Wingas, now in 2$^{nd}$ generation, are the very best and represent our industry very well. Marilyn Schlutz was in the line as I was leaving and asked if I flew in the Balloon event. No, just furnish part of the hot air.

It is Oct. '94 and the weather has been super which keeps the cash registers humming. There is just so much business available so we have to hone our skills to get more than our share. The operator that is content with what he is getting is ready to be put out to pasture.

Our Iowa Restaurant Association Convention is on and I was disappointed no dance on Sunday night. Had my dance card already filled with young good looking ladies. The Marriott Hotel did a super job as host. I'm probably a little partial because Willard Marriott's first year in the business world was with an A & W franchise in Washington D.C. Had an older fellow stop in this week from Council Bluffs. He was 17 in 1929 and at that time Willard Marriott had 3 A & W root beer stands in Council Bluffs. They only sold A & W root beer and had girls hanging trays on windows. Later on Willard wanted to move back East and sold the units to his manager and the old fellow went to work for him. That was probably when Willard obtained the D.C. franchise. Then when the cold weather arrived the Hot Shoppes developed.

In September an old WW II buddy stopped by. Hadn't seen him since 1944, 50 years ago. His name is Blackie Rivera from Rahway, New Jersey. We served together on the Flight Line at Sioux City Air Base. You remember there were no air raids over Sioux City. Blackie's wife, Joan, and I have a lot in common. She's Irish and married an Italian, me the same. Joan said—Blackie has been talking about you for 50 years. Funniest guy he was ever around. There were about 4 or 5 of us running around together. Four of us were in for anything and Blackie was our stabilizer. Always figured Blackie would make something of himself and I would be a total loss.

Finishing up 1994 and things are looking up. Had a good outing with Les. Stopped at Pine's Steak House in Atlantic owned by A. J. Poeppe, brother of Lee who is a successful operator in Anita. A. J. put together a sandwich that is formed like a pig. Calls it "Oinkies" sandwich. He also developed an all purpose sauce. He was giving out samples and hopes to get it on the market. Will check later.

Now it's time for the Ho Ho Ho and the Santa suit. The kids of Les gave him a retired greyhound for Christmas. Figured with Les exercising the dog "Lady", good for Les, (slim down) and also help the dog. The dog looks good at this point, but it isn't doing much for Les. Then we get dog reports: Betty has Snoopy, Dick has a feisty little dog named Cupid that makes like it will take your leg off—has to be a small leg. Kappy and I don't have dogs. Kap said he could use one if she could carry a golf bag. The Little Flower said I could have a dog with a few restrictions. My only requirement is if she could dance.

For the Christmas trade we have the 57$^{th}$ anniversary mugs full of root beer barrels and they are going pretty good plus it makes it more Christmas like. We're thinking of an operator Christmas party. Sounds good if we can get it set up. Everybody is busy. Got a note from Association President Doug from Carroll. He has a new girlfriend and wants to show her off. Better hurry with the party. He doesn't get very good mileage with the girls. Reminds me of my running days.

One of my best friends, Father Burns, passed away November. 23$^{rd}$. He was also my spiritual strength and holder of my punched ticket. Father came to our Parish in 1966 and was involved in all 4 of our weddings. He was our balloon pilot from day one and remained so until he could no longer pass inspection. Same for the balloon so we had to hang them both up. Father went with us to the first Disney World Convention in '72 (Contemporary Hotel) and also Las Vegas then Dallas, always bringing the mass kit along. In Dallas we were about a block from the church so we could walk to church and he could have a busman's holiday. Of course, the mass time had changed from the hotel's listing and we were going to be late for our flight out. Father was going to the Dallas Cowboys game and fly home later. Somebody had given us a ticket to the game. He ran back to the hotel and got his mass kit and got permission to say mass. There were quite a few in the same boat as us. A couple of big oil men from Texas were waiting too. They were quite impressed that we carried along our own Priest.

Father Burns was ordained in '46, raised in Beaverdale, served many Parishes and we were proud he called Indianola home. He also came back here for his final funeral services. It was the greatest honor of my life to be an Honorary Pallbearer and #3 Tim as a Pallbearer.

We all had Dick's Lynne in our prayers as she received a lung transplant. So far, so good. Put her in your prayers. She possibly isn't yet out of the woods.

For a smile—After trying unsuccessfully to collect an overdue bill, the grocer sent an emotional letter to the deadbeat along with a picture of his young daughter. Underneath he had written, "Here's the reason we need the money." A week later the grocer received a photo of a voluptuous blonde wearing a string bikini. It was captioned: "Here's the reason I can't pay my bill"

The Catholic hierarchy of Iowa—Bishops, Monsignors, etc. have come out against gambling and it's right they should. In the days of old, "Where's the action?" at the Parish Hall on Friday night. This is hearsay, but the word is the first year of seminary was devoted to teaching bingo, craps and roulette. Now the State is trying to take it over. It wouldn't surprise me if the Methodist, Presbyterians and Baptists get in next.

Congrats are in order for Dave Heaton, Iris Restaurant in Mt. Pleasant. Dave will make a good Senator and isn't afraid to speak his piece loud or soft.

The next problem, as in every year, remembering to move up a year as in 1995. No New Years Resolutions. I will clean the house twice a month instead of one and try to cut off the bulge around my middle and that's tough with The Little Flower's great cooking.

I've been Chairman of the Finance Committee of Balloons since day one (somewhere around 1972). My biggest job is to put together a gimme letter sent to everybody in around Indianola. Our new helper this year, graduate of Simpson, redid my letter—couldn't buy my grammar. I have been sending out this letter since before he was born. The problem with you changing, they'll think it is a counterfeit. Yes, we got along.

Was out visiting around the state in October. Stopped in Red Oak at Greg Berning's Redwood Inn and Restaurant and he's doing a nice job. Greg is the son of Bob and Freida Berning, Landmark Restaurant & Inn of Creston. A couple of the greats in our industry.

An article in the Big Paper. Big people are 3 ½ times more suspect for arthritis than a smaller—140 and under. I've always wondered does a guy like Les have a bigger hurt than my size? Sounds good to me!

# 39

## 1995

Here we go again. Postage went up to 32 cents on January 1st. In A & W news, a new President is taking the place of George Michel plus the Company has sold to 3 investors from Miami area. Our new President is Sidney Feltenstein, also from the Miami area. Oh my goodness!! In his words, would like to see accelerated growth and double the size of A & W in 5 years. George Michel will be with us until March. Most of us considered George a good President and also a good friend. We wish him well. We did think George had things turning around and we'll hope Sidney can enlarge on this.

For a smile—With the Pope's new book coming out reigning as #1 in sales (how is he doing the Rosary on a C.D.?), things are looking up. The Bishops have decided with all this money coming in that instead of asking for money this year there will be a dividend check for each Parishioner. They also announced they are not taking any Methodist converts.

With Tom Osborne winning the Hall Championship on New Year's night, it made 1994 complete and 1995 off on the right foot. By the same token, we welcome the member of Sabre's joining with I.R.A. The I.R.A. has a new name—Iowa Hospitality Association. We will try to get a representative from the former Sabre to contribute in the Appetizer. I've been writing in the Appetizer for over 25 years, have no schooled talents, have developed a little following and thoroughly enjoy doing it. The secret is that people enjoy and relate more to people they know and can have a hands-on relationship with.

I did it again. #3 Tim was standing beside me at Mass, into a song. Dad, you're on the wrong song!—and I sing pretty loud.

The guys did it again—a second retirement party. This time they just invited the fun people. They didn't come to me for money. Conned their mother out of it. She's a pushover for those guys. I have to sweet talk her for 3 days to get my allowance, but the answer would have to be—I married well.

It's February and we're opening the 7th. Closed the day before Christmas and then had a little fire. Cleaned up again and ready to go. Just got word, Frank's dream was to retire in Florida. He operated Sterling, Illinois and sold out 2 years ago. Frank and Kathleen had 3 daughters about the age of our gang. Frank got only 2 years in Florida. Our prayers are with the family. Also got word that Carl Johnson had a stroke last year, but is getting along. Carl served on the first N.A.C Board with me. They were longtime operators at Alexandria. Him and wife, Agnes, came up with the line—Yes, I'm a little larger but Minneapolis Tent and Awning takes care of my clothing needs.

Had a great time at the Regional Meeting in La Crosse. Good attendance and great hospitality. Those Wisconsin people have always been good at that. I won the contest for Best German Costume. Can't figure that. Throw back Irish but I accepted the award. Had a great fund raiser auction. Larry ran the A & W President up to $1,200 for an item and then dumped it on him. The Little Flower did think $6.00 was a little high for a roll of the toilet paper. Larry, Dick and I made the meeting and did enjoy.

The Little Flower got a new knee in January and so far is getting along fine. She's looking forward to getting back on the dance floor and she's the best. Norm Ruffridge got two knees about the same time and last report he was doing good.

Time for the yearly inventory. Hair—not much, Hearing—not much, Mouth—too much, Remember—not much. Everything else seems to be working okay. Bought The Little Flower a nice box of chocolates. This has been going on some time. She eats one chocolate and then I get the rest. This time she hid them and she is a good hider. Next year she'll get a homemade card.

President Sid seems to be moving right ahead. Has 4 areas he would like to build on: 1) Improved operations; 2) Accelerated development; 3) Enhanced image; 4) Become more aggressive marketers. With me, it's starting spring house cleaning. You've seen the housekeepers that clean and dust every day. At our house, nothing is cleaned before its time. Next it's helping Les at Variety Club. A shift with Les is 24 hours, the length of the telethon. Not sure I can still do 24 hours, but will give it a shot.

Came back from the Restaurant Convention with the real old time flu. Kicked the flu then sprained a big toe. Sounds silly but I couldn't walk for a day and couldn't get the shoe on for 4 days. Okay now and back on the bicycle.

Headline in the Big Paper—"Too Tall." People are getting too tall. They use up more resources, cause more pollution, more up keep and maintenance, plus they take up more room on the dance floor. Another win for us little guys.

Yes, in the 1950's had the candy, tobacco jobbing business. Got real mad at R.J. Reynolds for not putting me on direct. I fixed them and quit smoking (was averaging a pack a month). In the jobbing business was going head to head with Chariton Wholesale (Hy-Vee's Parent). It seems like Hy-Vee and cans are still around. Where am I? At least I married well. Spring house cleaning is here again. A homemaker's work is never done.

In Indianola we did the 10$^{th}$ annual Pork Patty Cook Off (May 5$^{th}$). Called and pre-sold 1,350 Pork burgers, $2205.07 plus $2,000 matching funds from Wal-Mart. Not a bad 3 hours work.

A report from the Variety Club Telethon. I did 22 hours of the 24 hour shift, but the deodorant went all the way. They raised a ton of money.

May of '95 and I did an interview at the Maid-Rite in Newton. Newton was the second Hamburger Shop opened by Fred Angel in 1930. The Angel family was the originators of Maid-Rite in Muscatine in 1926. He sold Newton in about 6 months. Marshalltown was also started about the same time by the Angel family and the rest is history.

Sue and the boys put together a surprise birthday party for Les. First time I ever saw him surprised and speechless. Also did 22 hours on the grill at the Variety Club Telethon. Les took one look at me and sent me home.

Now I'm mad at the Major Leagues and will give up baseball all together because of the players strike. Have a lot of baseball related clothes. Might have to do a garage sale. Was working lunch the other day at A & W and was doing my usual banter with the customers and whatever. A couple of young ladies were having lunch and threw me a smile from time to time which I threw back. Finishing, they came to the counter—What could I do for you? They threw down a $5 bill and said—This is for you. You made our day. Don't know whether they felt sorry for a little old guy working too hard or were really entertained.

Just back from the Ireland trip. First lost the carry-on bag at the airport with the passports, plane tickets, money, camera etc. The Little Flower about went into orbit and I was concerned. Two hours later and had the whole airport turned upside down. I had set it down in the hall and somebody had turned it in to the shop. Kissed the good lady twice and we were on our way. The Little Flower put the valuables in her purse and I never saw them again.

Lot to say about the trip to Ireland. Did go to the Wall Research Center for the family name history. McConnell is Irish originating in Ireland and there is Royalty in the history. No more of that Shanty Irish—treat me with respect. In Ireland I figured on kissing some sweet Irish girls. The only girl I got to kiss was the little Italian girl I was sharing a room with. Did get The Little Flower converted. She is now Irish.

Dick and I rolled into Chicago for the National Restaurant Convention. The Caddy took us there in style. The keynote speaker was Barbara Bush and she was great. Saw a lot of people we knew plus the dance was the best. Cindy (Nicker's Grill in Cedar Falls) grabbed us at the door and had a place for us at their table. Didn't miss a dance. Had 5 ladies at the table plus Cindy and the ladies from Michigan got in for a few dances. Never in my life did I have so much fun. Also got to a landmark BBQ on Sunday night and Monday night went to China Town. Hottest item at the show was Cappuccino.

Our Summer Social was a winner at the Ox Yoke Inn. Bill always does a great job. Dick came in without a room so he bunked in with us. It was great, but Dick and The Little Flower both snore. One would stop and the other would start. Like a battle of the bands, one snoring louder than the other. I couldn't go to sleep for laughing.

Back to the Ireland trip. Had a good gang to travel with. There were 48 on our bus and we hooked up with a couple from Red Oak. The lady had a foot giving her trouble. Her and Dorene made a good pair. He was a smaller guy like me and we went full speed. She was as fast with good one liners I ever saw. I was never nervous on the stage, but sitting in the audience always bothered me. She said—I'm the same, why don't we drop the other half and run away together. I can't do that, Dorene controls all the money. She said—With me it's the same. Guess we'll end up just as friends.

Now into this retirement thing. Being a spectator and a flunkie, odd jobs and fill in. Let's say it's all the same but different.

Had a letter from Donna Hoop. Their Hobo Days are a big thing in Britt and about the same time as our Balloon Days, then they have a Draft Horse Show. It's amazing that there are so many draft horses still around. There is Politics and there is politics. We like and respect Donna for what she is and honestly telling it like she feels it. Communication is the biggest thing in our world today.

The A & W Company is working on a new pre-mix root beer system that can be installed by Coke. The system we have used for years is the best and puts out the best product but in today's world it is a little behind. Too much work and too much room for error.

Had a letter from Paul McClellan with stamps for the Newsletter. They have Metro Fun Foods in Fremont, California. He was our Bear at Balloons for a number of years when he was in Des Moines. He related the Irish Heritage. With him it's easy with the map of Ireland on his face. On me, my face could say anything and mostly everything but Irish. I've been called a part of every nationality and that was some of the nicer things.

We ended with season tickets to the opera. To make it worse, we used every one. My favorite part is still intermission. The Chamber of Commerce was having an Indianola night and every member got a ticket. Told Dorene I was going early and they were having a reception for Sweeney Todd. Of course Dorene was ahead of me. There is no Sweeney Todd, that's the name of the opera. Oh, my, and still haven't figured out when to clap and say bravo. A cute little girl about 6 from our Parish was an extra in one of the Operas. The family with 3 children is heavy into sports. The little girl was confused when they played the National Anthem and didn't finish with "Play Ball."

Quiz of the day—My Grandmother started walking 5 miles a day when she was 60. She's 95 now and we don't know where she is. It's a good idea to obey all the rules when you're young so you'll have the strength to break them when you're old.

We went to Italy in '85 and hooked up with Dorene's relatives in Northern Italy. The one family had a pork wean-to-finish operation. I wrote an article for the Iowa Pork Producer and thought I should include it in this mass of words.

Italian Pork Facility: The hog farm is a wean-to-finish operation and handles 6,000 pigs at a time. The pigs are bought when weaned at about 20 days and weigh 20 to 30 pounds. They are confined in the pens from the start and are finished at about 300 pounds in about 5 months. The main feed is in the form of wet feed running automatically from the mix room thru 4" pipes. The feed for the mix tank is bran hay, which looks like alfalfa, and a big pile of bread sticks from the bakeries. All of this is chopped up and fed through the 4" pipes into individual pens. The Prunellis mentioned buying a lot of feed from Purina and had been invited to visit the Purina plant in St. Louis.

The manure is carried away as liquid into two large 20' by 40' holding vats. This in turn is pumped into honey wagons and spread on the fields. At the time of our visit, the hogs were at 200 to 210 pounds and would be ready to go in about a month. They were slim and trim and looked the picture of health. I also asked about sickness and that doesn't seem to be a problem. There is a law that the sow/pig operations are separated from the finish farms.

I asked about marketing. The local locker plant comes to the farm, buys the hogs and hauls them away. Evidently a ready market. Of course we were on the edge of Torino with 1.5 million people. They don't seem to market fresh pork to the degree Iowa does. The housewives still shop fresh every day and they aren't into refrigerators and freezers.

Last, but not least, the pig stuff smells the same as in Iowa. In Iowa the farmers all have caps and jackets with some company name. None of that in Italy. That market is wide open.

Back to October of '95. The political thing is the big splash. A ton of people running for President and to me there is not a really good choice. The Democrats want to give away the farm and the Republicans aren't much better. Senator Dole is still my choice, but he is a little old. Will check with Knopp's A & W in Russell, Kansas, the hometown of both Dole and Specter. The Knopps may give us some answers.

In jest—The new Minister's car broke down just after the morning service. On Monday he drove into the repair shop for repairs. "I hope you'll go a little easy on the price", he told the mechanic, "after all, I'm just a poor Preacher." "I know it," came the answer, "I heard your sermon last Sunday."

Wally Luedtke passed away at 69 this month (November '95). He was one of our premier operators when we opened in '56. He operated in Cedar Rapids and was an entrepreneur before Webster invented the word. He showed us how to make our first tenderloin. That was a big item with him and has been a real biggie with us.

The question came up at one of our meetings on what to put on the reader board or the road sign. So we will have the operators send in their favorites and it could help all of us. Samples: "Your wife called—bring home A & W"; "Shake it up, Baby." They should be funny and also relate.

For fun—Husband to male friend, "My wife talks to herself." "So does mine, but she doesn't realize it. She thinks I'm listening."

I've known Dick since '72 and he's always on a diet and usually a different one. Is it Kosher for a food operator to be on a diet? My line has always been we believe in 4 squares a day.

Sid Feltenstein has a lot of new ideas—some good and some not. He wants to bring in all beef hot dog (with that name he naturally would). We use an all-meat which is beef and pork which I like and we do sell a ton of them on Coney Day which promotes the rest of the week. The year is coming to an end. Homemaking is in order. Things are shaping up. Having happy thoughts about it all.

Now we have a new year and I have to get used to writing 1996. My prediction, it'll be a boomer. The whole family got together (13th) Saturday night to celebrate our 45$^{th}$. The accolades seemed to be all for The little Flower. Guess she deserves it living all these years with me. I got a bunch of clothes for Christmas. Keep this in mind—sure there will be a big garage sale the week after my demise.

Sure there will be a lot of new and slightly worn stuff. In case you didn't know, I'm average size—fit most.

Nice thing about being retired, subsistence checks every month from the kids. Next time around I'm figuring more kids. Will speak to The Little Flower about that. Now we're heading to Las Vegas, Caesars Palace, for the National A & W Convention. I have a secret I'll share with you. You've noticed I get more than my share of hugs from ladies of all ages usually finishing up with—you're so cute! We all know there's nothing cute about me and nothing necessarily good. The secret is, at our last convention at the Mirage I slipped over to Caesars and bought this cologne and after shave set. That's the come on. If you want to turn your life around get this set.

# 40

## *1996–1998*

Now it's '96 and the weather is old fashioned winter, couple of blizzards, extreme cold, etc. Chris Raab called the last of December and asked if could I come to Detroit first week in January to be in the commercials (A & W). After bouncing off the ceiling a couple times and verifying the caller I would, I started packing my underwear. I've had some biggies in my life, but this has to be a topper.

A & W showed their new insurance program and looks good. Dick, in comparison, can save $100. Haven't got ours yet, but competition is always good. Gets everybody on the ball.

We have a lot of new names as operators and hopefully that's good. Caesars Palace did us a good convention. We had 8 units in attendance at the convention and Indianola had 4 bodies. Next is our A & W Association meeting in Des Moines. The commercial is a big positive. Will even let you touch my Academy Award trophy presented to me at the awards banquet for "Best Actor."

In jest—"How can I help you?" the psychiatrist asked. "It's her," the man said nodding toward his wife, "for the last 6 months she has thought she was a lawn mower." "This is very serious," the shrink advised. "Why didn't you bring her in sooner?" "The neighbor just returned her."

Yes, a star is born or just uncovering an old one. Got into Detroit on a Tuesday morning. Livonia is a suburb of Detroit. My home was the Marriott across the street from the A & W office. In the city, real close usually means a couple miles but this really was close. I did the office, shook hands with the guys and hugged the ladies. Want you to know they have some good huggers. Jim picked me up and hauled me to the shoot. He was my babysitter. The shoot was all set up. Two actors from Detroit—Auntie and Uncle. Auntie asked—You're from Iowa? Yes. Where did you audition and read for the part? Weeeell. The first shoot the head cameraman says—Was concerned when they said a little old A & W guy would be Grandpa. You're not a rookie, you're a professional. Auntie said—Don't move to Detroit or we'll be out of a job. They might have been pulling my leg but I took it as 100% gospel.

Thursday was a wedding shoot and I wasn't in it. Jim took me down town to the International Auto Show and then dropped me off at the Henry Ford Museum. Told him I could find my way home. There was a cab sitting in front when I came out. I got in and heard that Livonia is a pretty big fare. It's either cab or walk and too old to walk. The cabbie might have been a couple bricks short of a load. He's asking me directions and my wagon isn't too full. We were kind of lost and I asked how far to Plymouth—just a mile. Drop me off at Plymouth square and I'll get home from there. The International Ice Carving show was on. Great show and got a ride from there home.

Friday was the Bowling Alley shoot. Jim and I walked into the bowling alley—You're the guy from Iowa. We heard about you. Evidently made an impression. I'm not selling the farm or trading in The Little Flower for a newer model, but it was one of my greater experiences.

Senator Dole, at this point, is coming along fine. Lucy appointed me as an assistant at L.A. and gave me plenty of buttons and bumper stickers. We were the only ones with Dole stickers. Been on that road before.

Into good weather sunshine and business is moving up a little and that's 100% better than down. I've been promoted to head of the Flunky Department. Is that good or bad? Donna has been working the scholarship thing. This year we will have four $250 scholarships rather than one at $1,000 Ray reports on "March Madness"—for them it is training the new help. Ray is 2$^{nd}$ generation A & W and the first of two Presidents—Father and Son. We'll all work together getting our members and formers at our meeting (turned out 13 of 16).

Yes, I still kiss the Academy Award trophy for the Best Actor every morning. Of course that's right after The Little Flower kiss.

Spring has sprung. The Little Flower brought in the dandelion greens and my lady buddy came in with a couple bags of mushrooms.

Do you get residual checks from the T.V. Commercials you starred in? Yes, I do, I get the check every month. In fact it comes the same day as the subsistence checks from the kids.

It's always with mixed emotions when we say goodbye to franchisees getting out of the business. We are losing 3 at this time.

Time marches on (May '95). Rain, cold and sunshine—farmers are in trouble. Our business is up a little and hopefully the farmers will pull out of it. We're putting together a Summer Social at Prairie Meadows. It will be our first time there. We put it in the contract with Prairie Meadows to loosen up the slots for a better pay out and we have somebody that talks directly to the horses so there is no way you can lose.

The weather was perfect and the Summer Social was super. Quite a few former operators joined us. The Little Flower and me first attended a convention in January '56 in Peoria and this reminded me of that. I didn't have time in between to play the slots, but sent money down with two or three operators. Still waiting for the return. Had a lot of horse tips and bet $2 on every race. One came in for me and got $2.80 back on the $2 bet.

Dick's count came up with over 50 present and former operators. Swapped stories and also had pictures from former shows, operators and conventions. A good time was had by all.

We lost Lynne Wilderman the 8$^{th}$ of August. A wonderful person and right in the prime of life. Her condition got to the point that it had to be.

Got to do every day at the Big Fair. Larry lets me stand in front of his Old Fashioned Soda Fountain in my fountain attire, a white shirt and black bow tie. Somebody asked Larry—Does your dad work for you? Work?!!?

I have friends all over the world and probably know more people than the average. Mostly it's a "Hello, how are you?" and not that many special friends. Dick and Lynne were very, very special. I go to a lot of funerals (I'm the designated funeral attendee for the family) and handle them pretty well, but Lynne's oldest son Mark's tribute to mom broke me down completely.

Our fellow operator, Curt Jante, passed away August 23, 1996. Really thought he was indestructible. Cancer did him in. Curt and Florence started Belmond (A & W) in 1958 and sold out in Forest City in '89. In the business 31 years and good progressive operators. First class all the way. From Florence—He was my best friend, buddy and husband. I was honored to be an Honorary Pall Bearer and Curt played to a full house on his last go around. We've lost two and hope that 3 in a row doesn't kick in.

Now it's back to business as usual. Really had a super time on the Alaska Cruise. The question—Did you see a lot of Polar Bears and icebergs? Actually was too busy entertaining the cruisers. There were 42 of us from Iowa, 1300 in all, and that's a bunch. Tough job, but we gave it our best shot entertaining. Did a solo at the Red Dog Saloon in Juneau. The gang designated me to lead "When Irish Eyes are Smiling" at the ship's piano bar. The leader thought I had a beautiful tenor voice. In 74 years I didn't know that and don't think The Little Flower did either.

The new insurance program is getting great kudos. Dick saved about one thousand dollars and we saved $868. Well worth the time checking it out.

The Little Flower and I did a Smokey Mountain bus tour last week. There were 40 on the bus—30 ladies and 7 men. Getting a taste of that—more widows than widowers. A lot of grits, gravy, sugar cured ham and Damn Yankees. We had a great time.

It's into November and business is a little slow. Believe we're basically holding our own. Usually picks up a little after Thanksgiving and runs decent into Christmas. Have a hunch I've slipped a little physically. My only concern is can I keep up with Dick next May on the dance floor in Chicago.

A golfer hit his ball into the rough where it landed on an ant hill. The golfer whaled away at the ball missing it each time but killing hundreds of ants with each stroke. Finally there were only 2 ants left. "If we're going to survive, we better get on the ball."

Vince Lombardi once said, "The price of success is hard work and determination. Whether we win or lose, we have applied the best of ourselves to the task at hand."

Had a note from a fellow I grew up with in Bussey. Both chasing girls and both ending up better in that category than we deserved. He ended up as a Preacher and me as a Pitchman at the State Fair. Funny thing—we both think we made the grade.

The A & W newsletter was started in 1967. It hasn't been work, but a labor of love. This year finishes up 50 years in the food business and loved every minute of it. A long time operator friend said the other day—After reading your stuff all these years I know more about your family than you do. Wrote in the Appetizer (Iowa Restaurant Association magazine) 25 years until I was fired last year. I really do miss it. Is that silly or what?

A lot of things happened this year—good and bad. Dick lost Lynne and Ray lost his dad Curt. For me it probably was my funnest year ever. For some the goal in life is to be President of the U.S. For me it was a standing ovation in front a large audience plus to be a Pitchman at the Iowa State Fair. I've had two standing ovations in front of over 200. This summer I was declared the greatest pitchman by the Big Paper at the State Fair. My life is complete.

Just did the Wisconsin Regional Convention January 19–21, 1997 at Lake Geneva. I know Webster copped the words "Fun" and "Hospitality" from the Wisconsin Convention Community. We had seven stores represented there from Iowa. In fact, over 100 stores in all represented. At the Convention Ray Jante was called up to accept a plaque in honor of his folks as franchisees for 50 years. It took awhile for Ray to regain his composure. Ray and his dad were pretty close. Paul Neirzwicki also acknowledged Lynne and Curt at the banquet.

Quote from Dick Vermeil—If you don't invest very much, then defeat doesn't hurt very much and winning is not very exciting.

At the Wisconsin Convention (Thanks to Larry and Dick for taking me along), Larry remarked, "Dad, you're not 18 anymore." I can live with 28. It is true I absolutely can't act my age. On Tuesday morning Dick remarked, "You look tired." Yeah, I chased bunnies up and down my hall all night. Remember the greased pig at the County Fair? Our hotel was the former home of the #1 Playboy Club. Got a lot of nice hugs and peaked out with Ray and Jan's little blonde sweetheart. Danced too much, but could you refuse Anna and Kari Johnson, daughters of Greg and Kristin Johnson, Austin. Gib, will you come dance with us?

Annie, mother-in-law of Verne Richardson (N.A.C)) Wisconsin passed away. She was 92. Two years ago she and I won best dressed Germans at their Wisconsin Octoberfest which was actually held in January. She was a good feeler.

Had a 46$^{th}$ Anniversary with the sweetest "Little Flower" in the world last week and she'll still be my valentine. Give that special one something extra. It will pay dividends.

The year seems to be starting out good. Know we're not breaking any records, but we've learned to live with a small up. Restaurant Association has the "Rise and Shine" to collect money for heat bills for the disadvantaged. Worked breakfast one morning at Hardees. Usually put together about $1,000. for the fund raiser. Saturday night is our biggest fund raiser for Balloons at the Embassy suites. Buy drinks and work the floor for the auction. Warren and I will help Les in the kitchen for the Variety Club Telethon. Great to help with the causes plus it's fun. For Christmas The Little Flower took the family (14) to Disney World the first week in January, Monday thru Saturday and stayed at the Contemporary. It was actually our delayed Christmas picture. Gram, Gramps and the kids had the most fun. Parents were busy trying to keep track of the kids.

We are coming closer to spring. Check the insurance, it should be time to renew. Then comes Valentine's Day and give the Love of your Life something special. This retirement is getting tougher every day. State Girls basketball is this week and next week is Boys and in between is St. Pat's Day which is an international fun day and the biggest day of my year. I try to work lunch then run to Vets for afternoon games. I go to Stella's Blue Sky Diner and then 2 evening games.

From Dick—We are getting some savings on paper goods. The group purchasing is paying off. Patty Halprin has worked for us a couple years as a County

Representative. She went to Barbados on vacation, fell in love and is getting married. It is the American way and we wish her well.

A church usher was escorting parishioners to their seats at funeral mass. When he came back to the entrance he found Les and Dick. Greeting them with a smile he asked where they would like to sit. Looking confused Les said, "Non-smoking please."

I'm getting a little closer to today's world. #1 Daughter Sandy got me a cell phone for Christmas. Dad, you have to carry it in the car when you go on trips. My first call—Called The Little Flower, but she didn't pick up the phone.

We have the Summer Social pinned down for Monday, July 21$^{s,t}$ at Prairie Meadows. Have a new area manager, Dave Martin, who is supposed to be at our Summer Social. He has had time in the food industry, which helps.

The Iowa Hospitality Show on April 6th is at Prairie Meadows and that gave us an excuse to go and also tie down our Summer Social. The P.A. was looking for Gib McConnell. A sweet young lady wanted me to cover her booth while she attended a seminar—Would I? It's an honor and a privilege plus it makes me feel important.

I don't work at the A & W that much. I just fill in but create such a commotion think they would rather do without. I'm 100% busy and among other things designated "Funeral Attendee." Last week attended a funeral, an Italian lady Dorene grew up with. There were 7 Priests and a funny looking Methodist Minister (his words) on the alter. The most Priests I had seen at a funeral was the 10 Priests at Bob McGurk's funeral and a "So Sorry" letter from the Bishop. I'm a pretty fair Catholic and probably will rate 1 ½ Priests. This lady was one of a kind. Called herself the "Little Old Wop." I found out 45 years ago—they can say "Wop", but a funny looking little Irishman better not.

The Little Flower went in Friday to get a ball replaced in her hip. She got a new hip 8 years ago. We're hoping for the best.

Good news about the hip ball. Replaced the plastic liner and rest was okay. Five days in the hospital and a month and a half getting back to normal. Everybody hollers about hospital food, but to me it's not that bad. Better than mine. Really don't want that to get out. I still have quite a few believers.

The Little Flower's hip popped out 10 days ago which means bad hurt and trip to the hospital. Yesterday, Tuesday, it came out again. Dorene has a high threshold for pain. I'd have been out of my mind. Dorene stayed overnight in the hospital and we brought her home this afternoon. They have a cast on the bottom of her leg and a brace for the upper, restricting the movement. Walks with a walker and can lie down. Sitting is little harder. Hopefully it won't go out again.

The Kids Meals are up 40% over last year and it has to be new items from Craig.

The N.R.A. convention in Chicago is coming up. Iffy with me because of Dorene's hip. She's insisting I go and I'm on the fence, but the mushrooms were really good!

Ray and Jan (Keokuk) are serving as President and 1st lady of the Association. Mom is getting along fine in Clear Lake.

We have Bob Loughman and Ray Jante for horse racing tips at the Summer Social. You're on your own with slots. We don't really have anybody that can talk to them. Already figured out Catholic prayers don't help.

The Crispy Chicken Sandwich seems to be the big deal this year and is going good. Dave Martin will be at our Summer Social.

Dick and I did go to the Restaurant Show in Chicago. We attended a seminar called "How to Work a Room." They paired me with a waitress from New York City. Our approach was far apart but ended up with good results from both.

A few definitions:
Dad: A male parent. From the Latin phrase Daddies Shin Plus Impactus, meaning "One who hits the roof."

Bum: See daughter's boyfriend.

Bathroom: A small room with a sink, and commode, available to dad approximately 5 minutes a week.

Grace: What dad yells out when mom asks if someone will say Grace.

Walk: What dad always did to school farther than anyone else, through deeper snow, up more hills, in flimsier shoes.

ZZZZZ: What dad says during any movie chosen by mom.

I brought Dorene home a cook book from the show in Chicago. Dorene has a passion for cook books and usually when I'm in trouble I bring one home and she has a bunch. Brought this book for you. Yes, it was great. The same book as last year.

On Monday night Dick and I got to Michael Jordan's restaurant for dinner. Across from us was a table for 6 and the young lady gave me the eye so I proceeded to go over and entertain them. It happened to be a group of restaurant consultants from Dallas with a booth at the show. Do you need any consulting? I certainly do. Could we do it on the dance floor?!?

The weather is decent and the crispy chicken sandwich is going good. The gross for May was up 9%. Up gets smiles—down gets tears and bad words. Along the same line, at the Pork/Coffee Day sold 2,150 sandwiches and netted $2,400.

Got to the Regional Meeting at Bettendorf and by all reports Dave Martin was received very well. The new insurance program is moving ahead with 146 participants at present. They are working on a diet A & W. It is already a pretty good product.

This week have been to the opera twice—just full of it. The Little Flower isn't able to get out yet so I gave her a run down of the happenings—mostly intermission. Next will be balloons and I'll be full of hot air. Then the County Fair followed by the Big One—State Fair. Goodness sakes, it's a busy time. In between we'll do the Summer Social at Prairie Meadows and we'll say—Good Luck to you.

Summer is winding down and time to repair, etc. A lady bashed in the side of our building last week. Thought her foot was hitting the brake and hit the foot feed. Took out the brick wall and hit the walk-in cooler freezer. It broke the seal on half the panels and at 25 years makes sense to replace it.

Had another birthday (every year it seems). Was enjoying the Little Cubs first playoff game with the gang at Sec Taylor in a skybox. In comes Les and Dick with a surprise birthday cake and ice cream. Can you top a birthday at Sec Taylor in a skybox? (Well, maybe Wrigley Field.) I'll put out some feelers with the proverbial sons.

The National Convention is coming up on February 15–19 at Orlando. Also a Regional Meeting on September 28th. Had a party at Dick's last week and played a game they called "Fantasy Football." It was kind of a gambling thing but it wasn't mafia related because there was no money up front.

This marks 30 years for the Newsletter. It is truly a labor of love. Hardest thing for me is to slow down and hate being a spectator. I want to be the entertainment. The Newsletter partly serves that purpose.

Had a good and extended summer, but this week is letting us know fall is here. We have to realize we get quite a bit of business off the highway from patrons going to Knoxville, dirt track capitol of the world.

After all the down, we are beginning to see a little growth. Most growth is with A & W restaurants that are connected to the end of a convenience store. Good reports from operators about Dave Martin. The Company has also been changing their Carousel Restaurants and Hot Dogs & More to become A & W units. The new crispy chicken has good reports plus the new chicken chunks. Chicken is a universal food plus also pigeons. Have traveled around the world and there was always pigeons. Kudos to Dave Martin and even Bob Loughman listens to him.

Dorene is still having trouble with a hip and is scheduled for a new hip on December 15th. The whole family did a week at Disney World and stayed at the Contemporary—a Christmas present from Dorene. This year I'll be alone at the Coronado in the Disney complex. Larry and his gang will also be there. Dorene hired Donna's Jared, 5'11", 279 lbs, to look after me. Sounds like a bodyguard to me.

Now comes December and Christmas. Have a few problems plus Dorene and a new hip. Laura had cancer, chemo and radiation. Myron is having bypass surgery the 15th. Harry Ayres' wife Jean had cancer of the pancreas and taking treatments. Betty Stevens is taking chemo. On the plus side we have the birth of septuplets in a neighboring village—Bobbi and Kenny McCaughey. I always had trouble with one at a time. Know I couldn't handle 6. Bobbi and Kenny were on the lot first night home. It was an honor to have them and we didn't bother them. We served Governor Brandstad a number of times, served root beer to President Lyndon Johnson, did breakfast for President Carter, but serving the septuplets is right up there.

What do you call a blonde with half a brain? "Gifted." People seldom improve when they have no other model to copy after but themselves. I know a cemetery whose custom is to bury lawyers 12 feet under because deep down they are good people. Plus The Little Flower and I are supposed to get a new grandchild about Christmas from Larry and Jill.

Indianola now has a full fledged winery. It's actually a little former coal mining community just north of Indianola called Summerset Winery. It's a younger couple (to me everybody is younger) and they also have a nice Bed & Breakfast. Can you believe 17 acres of grapes, plus the wine is good.

Did you know the Irish Santa Claus uses Leprechauns instead of elves? Next is fun in the sun at Disney World. We're putting together a night at Treasure Island while there for the Iowa people.

Our neighbor lady passed away and I was going to the wake at the funeral home. Went around the corner at the funeral home, hit some ice and went kerplop. The undertaker came around the corner—Gib, are you hurt? No, I'm okay. Wasn't about to let that undertaker get hold of me. Broke a small bone in my wrist, but it hurt big. Dr. put in a splint—bothered my speech and writing. Can't really talk without both hands free—absolutely can't tell a story. The Little Flower has decided not to try the trip so I'll be on my own. Have promised her I'll be good, but will need a lot of help to keep the promise.

Note from Dick—He is now typing with his computer. If he can do it, why not me? Did the Santa Claus at the Christmas party (A & W). Had the suit, hair, eyebrows and really thought I did a yeoman job, but didn't fool the grandkids for a minute—ages 5, 4, and 7, all knew Papa Gib.

Looking forward to Disney World. Both arms are now working.

New baby from Jill and Larry—Mary Grace at 7lbs 15 oz on December 22.

Did we have fun at the convention. Don't have enough adjectives to explain it. Broke all fun records. Iowa was represented with 2 tables at the banquet. In the old days, all were happy and outgoing and questions were constructive. Believe we are back. The mood was excited and positive. Seminars were good and well attended. Blondie and Dagwood will be our advertising theme and I'm excited about that.

Thanks to Donna Hoop's son, Jared, who bunked in with me and helped keep me out of trouble. The poor guy sunburned his back on Thursday and great pain for the plane ride home.

Roy Firestone was the meeting M.C. One of my favorite people with his whole speech related to athletics. Plus the biggest thing in the world happened to me Monday eve. The Iowa gang was meeting in the lobby to bus for dinner at the Rain Forest. I was early and slipped into the lounge for a glass of beer. This young fellow was sitting at the bar with a Miller Lite and looked down in the dumps. I'll cheer him up. Sat down and struck up a conversation and we were both laughing right away. I looked up into his face—"Did anyone ever tell you that you look like Greg Maddux?" "Yes." "Are you Greg Maddux?" "Yes." "Would you give me your autograph for my grandson?" "Sure." Told Jared on Tuesday morning I was so excited last night didn't sleep a wink. Jared said, "If my dad had sat down next to Greg Maddux he would have wet himself."

Yes, still have the splint on. Can wave it okay so didn't bother the storytelling or dancing. The first day I nicked myself shaving and AB spurted out. I did get a lot of hugs and sympathy. Had a lady tell me at breakfast one morning—Gib, you are an inspiration to all of us. Probably the oldest one here and more pep than any of us. Have to go fast. Time is running out on me.

Fourteen inches of snow on Monday, March 8th, plus high winds then cold. A rain fronted and we ended up with 6" snow and ice underneath—wouldn't move. Took us older guys back to the snow of 1936. Missed the first day of Girls State Tournament at the Barn. #2 Larry hid the keys to my car. Got to the tournament on Thursday. On the way home the car went dead on a hill and coasted onto an off ramp with bumper to bumper traffic. A nice young lady stopped and fixed me up—called a wrecker and the patrol. The patrol stayed with me till the wrecker carried me home. It was kind of a fun experience until I got the bill for a Cadillac alternator.

Yes, it was the big snow of 1998. The grandkids can tell their grandkids about this. The A & W was closed 3 days and school was closed for 2 (March 10).

Our meeting in Davenport was great and well attended. Dave Martin and Dave Miller put together a good and informative program on suggestive selling and employee rotation. Those are two of the biggest things we need to work on. Good meeting and the operators were very receptive.

Back to Disney—Donna Hoop's husband, Al, said of the Greg Maddux meeting—You gotta be the luckiest guy in the world. True, and I married well. I was introducing myself to this real neat lady. I know you. The Newsletter goes across my desk every month. She was President Sid's Executive Secretary Syndi Pease. The Little Flower was real pleased when I came home with money. Most everything was paid for and I did pick up my share of the extras.

From the Disney Convention—One of the few times I didn't lose my notes and now the big thing is trying to read them plus remembering why.

Played quarter slots for an hour on five bucks so figure I won. Plus A & W took us out to eat. At the convention with Dick, Donna and Larry, the talk turned to antiques. Gib, do you collect antiques? I am an antique. Was thinking of nostalgia last weekend and bought a can of Spam. Spam didn't get to my outpost at the Sioux City Air Base in the Big War.

Got the April issue of Delta Airlines "Sky" magazine. They had a 3 page story about last years RAGBRAI. It came through the hometown of Bussey. I worked the town as greeter under the arc of balloons. From the "Sky" quote: "I see people, I see money," chirps Gib McConnell, a sprightly senior citizen. I hate that Senior Citizen comment, but anything for a little publicity.

Wow, wow and this looks like the Cubs year. I will order a block of tickets for the World Series. As of April 6, six straight wins.

So I forgot Mother's Day and had to catch Dorene and celebrate later. The poor lady has had 47 years good or bad. By the same token, we're happy for Dick. Dick and Judy were married and both families we're enjoying. My highlight, Lynne's mother was there. She is in a care facility in Fort Dodge. Doesn't get around too good and could barely see. Gib, can't see you but picked up your voice right away. I'm so happy for Dick and he introduced me at the wedding as his mother-in-law. Wasn't that nice?

Weather is good, business is moving along and finished last of the mushrooms this morning. Did a couple of stories for the Restaurant magazine last week. The Winga family is having the 70$^{th}$ birthday of Winga's this year. Paul and Helen Abelson, Billy Boy Drive-Thru, are celebrating 50 years of marriage. Was doing an interview for the magazine and Paul and Helen gave me the grand Sioux City tour. On the tour we ran into Beanie Cooper. He was the great basketball coach at Sioux City Heelan and a character in his own right. Beanie was our banquet program at convention 25 years ago and he looks great. We both said we remembered and I think we were both lying.

Had a bout with colon cancer last week. Don't really do sick too well. In my 75 years haven't dealt with too much of it. As of now, all reports are good. Will keep you informed.

As per usual, Dick and I had a good time at the N.R.A. show. Dick was thinking about the new bride he left at home and I was thinking about my stomach. It's really a busy two days. Check out 2,000 booths at McCormick Place and catch a baseball game, this year the White Sox. Two dance shows and a Nike Town party (that was super). This year for our Restaurant of Distinction, we ate at Ed Debevic's—meatloaf, mashed potatoes and gravy, etc. We also visited Dennis Rodman's drinker with food and it was quite nice.

Yes, I did the colon cancer thing. They cut out about 6 inches of cancer and it was malignant. Did the 6 months chemo and so far so good. I did have fun entertaining the patients on the 5$^{th}$ floor after I was able to get out of bed. You all know I would rather be the entertainer than the entertainee. Putting together 8 pages of the operation highlights—holler if interested. Tomorrow I'm entertaining the Ladies Aid.

I'm back to about 100%—normally run 110%. In the hospital June 1$^{st}$ and out June 11$^{th}$. Started a mild chemo Monday. My thing is, "Hello, how are you?" Tim suggested maybe "Hi" would do it. Might get too much conversation with the question. Had a nice card from Harry—Jean is coping right now. Harry hung up his tools June 30$^{th}$.

At balloons sat next to a fellow from Freeport. He reports Curt Peterson is fine but getting fat with the retirement. Curt served with me on the first N.R.A.

Ray Jante, along with Jan, is serving as our Iowa Association President and doing a super job. They never miss a meeting and from Keokuk—you can't get there from here.

Had a call from Dick—Weather is bad, business is down, employees are tough and tougher. Really think he is envious of me and in the retirement mode.

The Dagwood sandwich isn't going that great, but the guys are having fun with it—Dagwood and the funny looking Little Old Guy.

July 7, the Opera office called. The lead lady had a bad throat and opera had to be cancelled. The Little Flower said—What will I do? You'll watch the All Star Game. It's what you wanted to be doing anyway. How lucky can you possibly get?

Just got a call—LaVerne Kelly passed away, Friday, July 17. Irish left us about 4 years ago. Irish and LaVerne were our two best buddies. No children, but a ton of friends.

Our busiest week of the year is Balloons. It was super this year with the near perfect weather. Plus our County Fair was the best ever which also relates to the weather.

Nice letter from Harry and Jean is continuing to improve. Paul Huber passed away. Paul was with A & W about 30 years in many positions. Was 83 when he left. Harry also mentioned the monsoon weather with the 45% humidity. If Iowa is that low, we consider it none. At this day 80 degrees with 70% humidity and near perfect.

Three nuns were assigned to paint a room in the church. It was a really hot day and the nuns were getting really hot in those black clothes they wear. They took off all their clothes and went on painting naked. Later they heard a knock at the door. "Who is it?" one nun asked. The man replied, "I'm the blind man." The nuns decided to let him in since he would not be able to see them. The man looked around the room, then looked at the nuns and said. "Nice bodies, sisters, where do you want the blinds?"

Sister Dawn is Dorene's niece and a nun for over 40 years. We had invited Dorene's side in for Balloons and most of the other cousins were Mormons. They had ideas of what a nun was supposed to be. Sister Dawn was crewing Tim's balloon and drinking beer with the crew. Don't think they ever got that straightened out. We had the whole gang all the 10 days. We made Winterset in between with the Bridges, Francesca's house and John Wayne's birthplace. The niece from California was sitting in the living room Thursday night. We've never had this much fun before!

Really doing pretty good from the cancer operation and starting the second month of chemo. The only effect so far is diarrhea which is not too bad plus a shut off valve that isn't working, just barely. No big accidents so far. Was going for a new suit last week and the guys caught me. Dad, I believe the clothes you have will run you in.

Me and the Bride are helping with lunch at the A & W. Dorene is working and I'm telling stories. Summer is almost over and it's time to get the soup kettle on. Dave is doing a super job and he will go down as one of the best. Two years is about the max length of time for our area men. We've had a little growth and this is 100% better than down. I'm in to my 4$^{th}$ month of chemo and getting along good. Stomach giving me a little trouble, but no big accident so far. Can you believe a guy with no job and nothing on the itinerary and still can't get caught up. The attendance wasn't the greatest at our meeting. We did have a quorum for the election of officers. Larry McConnell, President; Scott Dierks, V.P.; Donna Hoop, Treasurer. Our biggest problem is still hiring and keeping help and it seems to be universal.

Have had some nice letters from operators. Marcus and Karin Meyerotto, St. Charles, MO, just moved into their new house and would appreciate help with the payments. Letter and stamps from Al and Lois Dierks, former Forest City. Also a letter from Gene Benolken. They have settled in Tyler, Texas and sent a newspaper article that A & W is building a free stander. That's encouraging at the least.

#2 Larry is our new Association President and it is true that he was so much like me growing up I knew what he was going to say before he said it. Thank goodness he inherited his mother's smarts. It's Larry, Dick and I for the Newsletter. Not sure that's good or bad.

Next month is the last for chemo and so far so good. That last and double dose of chemo laid me out. Recovering gradually and Christmas cards and letters are waiting. On the positive side—the Hawks beat Kansas.

Happy to say President Larry included me in the reservations for the Regional Convention at Wisconsin Dells, Rain Tree Resort.

Larry reports up 15% for '98. He has given the A & W a new and young look plus doing a good job. He has a special sheet on each table with the daily specials for a whole month and thinks it's working good. He also got the new neon sign up—"All American Food." With the cleaning, painting and new sign, it looks like an all new 50's joint.

I bought a case of McCaughey's books "Seven from Heaven." Our A & W gets a mention and that's bound to go around the World. Yes, Warren County is the home of the McCaughey's and also the home of Summerset Winery, new this year. I bought a case of wine to give for Christmas presents. It is wine from their best year.

# 41

## *1999–2002*

It's January 1999 and I'm running at 100%. Usually do 120%, but improving. Down about one half of '98 with cancer and let's put that behind us. Right now we're babysitting Larry's dog. At least that gets me outside a couple times a day. At this time it helps to think about summer. Where did this come from? It's so hot I saw 2 trees fighting over a dog.

It's February and broken all the New Year's resolutions but one—spend more time on the Newsletter. I do enjoy writing that. Valentine's day coming up. Used to give The Little Flower a nice heart shaped box of chocolates. She didn't eat the chocolates so I got to eat them. The Little Flower got to eating chocolates so I don't buy them anymore.

Yes, the Wisconsin Convention was a real funner. The roads were clean and dry coming in (usually snow). Got up the first morning to 4" of clean snow. As hosts, the Wisconsin people are next to us as the very best. Thanks to A & W President Sid for purchasing the highest priced item at the auction. All the neighboring states were represented and 15 from Iowa. Plus Dave handed out a laminated check list and new handbook. Our N.A.C. President, Tom Thompson from Dubuque, is a computer head and we'll hope he can help us with the problems were bound to have. A & W also has about 50 stores taste-testing hamburgers and should help us get the best.

Yes, our Association is taking off from a state of limbo. At Dave's meeting February 23, we had 15 franchisees represented with 35 bodies. If it gets too aggressive, might have to replace "The Old Editor." St. Pat's is right around the corner for all of us Irish and wannabees which includes almost everybody in the World on the 17$^{th}$.

From Larry—This was Dad's original idea—as you know Dad was a waiter at the Last Supper, so it has worked well for years.

Was looking for the March Newsletter. #2 Larry came in—Dad, you evidently labeled the March letter "April." Larry, do you think there is any hope for me? Dad, you haven't changed that much. We're putting together the Summer Social and it will be August 3 in Indianola. The Balloons will be in full swing. Dinner will be by the A & W in the Hospitality Tent, meeting at the Apple Tree Inn and then we will tour the Balloon Museum and then to the Balloon Field. Weather permitting you will see the A & W Balloon called the "Root Beer Float" piloted by #3 Captain Tim.

We have received word that A & W has signed a purchase agreement to buy Long John Silver's. This is a company with 1,350 stores and does 55% of the away from home fish business. Company store average is $680,000 with 23% of their sales in chicken.

News—Harry and Jean both had major operations. Harry relates they are getting along now, but are both couch potatoes. Had a letter and check from Bernie Grady. He had 3 by-pass surgery and getting along fine and hopes to see us at the N.R.A. show. A note from Harold Bischman—lost his wife and remarried to his growing up sweetheart. The Clinton A & W had dropped the A & W sign in the 80's and ran as Dave's Root Beer Stand and is now being taken out by a highway change.

As we mentioned, Bernie Grady has been a super guy and friend. He called and sold us our first two broasters in 1958. He stayed all afternoon and then dinner and it was getting late—You have to stay all night. We had the big old house with 3 kids and a lady staying with us. Larry was about 2 and Bernie slept with him. See Bernie for the rest of the story.

A couple of quotes from Dick—Every job is a self-portrait of the person who did it. Autograph your work with excellence. Many of life's failures are men who did not realize how close they were to success when they gave up.

Life is good. Last Saturday had mushrooms for breakfast and grandson Ross hit a home run in the afternoon. Doesn't get any better than that.

My health is back and getting into things I'm not supposed to get into. The guys—Now, Dad! Now, Dad! Now I'm in trouble again. From Larry—Dad, the new lights under the overhang are neon—not fluorescent. Yes, the modern age is tough—neon, neon, neon.

The Summer Social is coming up. The Iowa A & Ws will be Special Guests at the balloon field. Plus we just finished our Warren County Coffee Day for the Retarded. The I.R.A. has dropped it, but we still carry it on and it is for a good cause and they do need the money. It's the annual BBQ Pork Sandwich Day. I call and pre-sell sandwiches for delivery orders and #2 Larry has to make it work. From Larry—Dad, we'll do this together. You stand in the corner and don't move. About 3 hours and it's over. More than 2,000 sandwiches and we netted over $3,000 for W.L.O.C. plus we all had fun.

A big change—our distributor has changed from Ameriserve to Reinhart. We were all a little maybe, but it seems to be working out great. Old people don't do changes too well. I did the Legion Parade on Memorial Day—8 blocks carrying the rifle. Didn't realize the rifle weighed 50#s. It was at least that heavy toward the parade end. Neon-neon-neon—that #2 Larry.

The Little Flower took me to the opera. Must've done something bad to deserve that—can't imagine how I was that bad.

There will be a new 2000 millennium mug available by Thanksgiving and also a small 9" bear. It will be nice for the Christmas season.

Yes, this retirement business is getting to me. You've heard the line—Much busier than when I worked. Half their time is spent trying to get the child proof lid off the pill bottles.

Peter and Marilyn Luetkenhaus stopped by on the way home from the Black Hills. They had the A & W at Wentzville, Missouri and dropped the franchise about 3 years ago and we are sorry. Good people and good operators.

It was our pleasure to host the Summer Social. We were guests at the V.I.P. tent at the balloon field for food and drink. #3 Captain Tim got the "Root Beer Float" up and was hauling a guy from Britt and a good looking girl from Des Moines (we had drawn names to get a couple winners). Dick was a little nervous. After sundown we had Nite Glow. It was Indianola's 30$^{th}$ year hosting Hot Air Balloons and would say, best ever. When our town hosted the "Nationals" it was sort of a "Dog eat dog" event and little too serious. Now it's more of a laid back fun event.

Here's the scoop—Monday August 16$^{th}$ is Gib's Big Day at the Iowa State Fair. I was chosen "Iowan of the Day." The Little Flower and I overnighted at the Marriott on Sunday and had a nice dinner. The whole staff treated us like royalty. Of course The Little Flower is royalty, but with me it's a stretch. Out to the fair for breakfast at the Cattle Barn (for atmosphere). Picked up the golf cart and $200, plus a whole bag of goodies. A sweet young lady, intern from Iowa State, was handling the details. Is there any restrictions on the cart? The Fair Board asks you not to drive on the sidewalk and try not to hit anybody. I didn't and didn't, but gave the cart a workout. Was around to the west of the Grandstand and a fellow hailed me—Would you take me to the Administration Building? Yes, sir. Why is "Iowan of the Day" on this cart? I happened to be the "Iowan of the Day." Oh my goodness! Was by the Agriculture Building and a Black man hailed me down. Could you take the family (4) up to the Pioneer Hall? You bet, climb in. On arrival—What do I owe you? Not a thing—It's a service of the fair and have a good time.

At 2:00 was the award ceremony. Cookie's BBQ Sauce was the sponsor. Speed Herrig, my buddy of 25 years, was the presenter. Then 4 tickets to a Reba McIntyre show at the Grandstand and we brought along Jack & LaDonna. The show finished off the day and I and The Little Flower were home at 12:00. Plus #2 Larry closed the A & W for the day and all came to the fair. No, I didn't have any accidents with the cart.

On the first day of the fair, Larry entertained Tom & Mary Cooney. Tom and Mary were longtime operators at Pueblo, Colorado. Kevin Cooney is Tom's nephew. Tom served on the first N.A.C. Board with me—great people. We were always pretty close. Just figured this out—they had 3 daughters and we had 3 sons.

Life is good and business has been steady to up a little. After being diagnosed with cancer, one doctor said—See you in 2 years That was nice to hear after one doctor wrote me off. Jim Duncan passed away first part of September. We buddied together when Dorene and I first got in the A & W business. He had the Ottumwa A & W at the time. We started the Iowa A & W Association together in 1967. He started as President and I as Secretary-Treasurer and would write a Newsletter. He served one year as President and I'm still doing the Newsletter. Right now I'm back to buying green bananas and making up lies to get out of work.

Looking forward to the meeting at Dick's next week (November). We'll have people from Corporate doing the new menus. Remember to make plans for the National Convention at Caesars Palace, January 24, 2000. From Larry—Dad booked a suite, but I got that cancelled. For his size a broom closet is all he needs. Don't tell Larry but I snuck a little extra money from his mother, The Little Flower. If I can sweet talk her out of more money, the party will be in my room.

Time really flies when you're having fun. The year has just started and it's over. Shopping is all done and Christmas letter ready to mail. Had a great Thanksgiving and looking forward to a super Christmas with the grandkids, then the Las Vegas Convention. Dorene is getting along pretty good on a walker after the new knee. She can now do about everything on her own. I did the cooking for 4 days and I got the pink slip, but wasn't completely fired. Still get to be helper and dishwasher.

The Las Vegas Convention should be great. A sock hop is planned for one night. That wasn't in my time, but I'll improvise. I've been designated as the "Party Guy" and I can handle that.

Outstanding Convention with good attendance at over 600. At the past Las Vegas Convention (about 6 years ago), would lose 2/3rds of the people after the first day. These people were more interested in learning than funning, or it could be they were playing all night.

From #2 Larry—Had to shorten Dad's dance list this year. Sorry if I missed any of you. So many girls, so little Gib. I'm certainly not the best dancer in the world, but nobody has more fun working at it. Last count at 420 hugs. Larry came in with—There wasn't that many ladies. Got into seconds and thirds.

A farmer named Muldoon lived alone in the Irish countryside with a pet dog he doted on. The dog finally died and Muldoon went to the Parish Priest and asked, "Father, my beloved dog is dead. Could you be saying a Mass for the poor creature?" Father Patrick replied, "No, we cannot have service for an animal in the church, but there is a new denomination around the road, no telling what they believe. Maybe they'll do something for your dog." Muldoon said, "I'll go right away. Do you think $50,000 is enough to donate for the service?" Father replied, "Why didn't you tell me the dog was Catholic?"

Went to Rochester to buy a little more time. Got a good report—back to buying green bananas. Hope you all remembered your sweetheart on Valentine's Day. The Little Flower gets sweeter every day.

Larry put in the new menu this week and also new phones. He figures 25 years was long enough. The outfit out of Oklahoma City that installed the original phones came in to install the new ones. The same gang of workers that installed the phones 25 years ago did the new installation. The kids don't have any trouble spending money, but for me it is getting harder. Honestly and truly any remodeling and updating always paid off.

Spring is sprung. Business is good. Weather is good. The Little Flower and I had the dandelion greens and next comes the mushrooms. Bullheads are next, but #3 Tim is our fisherman and is getting so busy he might miss the bullheads, so we'll figure on next year.

I really am semi-retired now. Still do a few things for the A & W plus help at lunch while the kids are in school. This is the first time in 77 years have worked in the garden. Today I put out 10 tomato plants.

A woman walks into the doctor's office and says, "Doctor, I hurt every place on my body." The doctor says, "That's impossible." She explains, "When I touch my arm it hurts. When I touch my leg it hurts. When I touch my chin it hurts. When I touch my head it hurts." The doctor shakes his head and asks, "You're a natural blonde aren't you?" The woman smiles and says, "Why, yes I am. How did you know?" The doctor replies, "Because your finger is broken."

At the past N.R.A. shows, Lynne wasn't able to do the walking with the lung problems. Dorene has had problems with the legs, so Dick and I have been on our own. This year Dick's Judy is going. This will be her final indoctrination into the family. She doesn't know what she is getting into. Keeping one in line, maybe, but both?

Tom Thompson's dad and mom are having their 50$^{th}$ anniversary this week. Can't believe Jack is that old. Haven't met Winnie, but she is an equal part of a great family and special like Jack. Anyway, congrats are in order.

Amused by the Sunday Register article about Templeton Rye. The Little Flower and I had a shot of the original from a good buddy. Not saying who, why, where, or when. It compares to a $50 Cuban cigar.

Now taking orders for tomatoes. Delivery in July—no delivery charge. Really think I missed my calling as a master gardener.

Very productive Regional Meeting on May 15$^{th}$. Good attendance and a lot accomplished. Ran out of time for the Association meeting and election. #2 Larry is getting nervous with the President's job. Didn't know it was for life.

May was good for us—up about 7%. The menu created no problems other than we throw away a lot of onions people have scraped off their sandwiches. Labor is still tough (help), which is a universal thing.

Belated Father's Day to you all. Mine couldn't have been better. Had all the kids and grandkids in. Plus I got to be the wrap-up man for Father Kenkel's 40$^{th}$ Anniversary Roast. Don't usually say it, but I held my own with the Big Heads and did myself proud. I have slipped a little, but don't believe it showed. Had a lot of—I don't know you, but you did a heckuva job on that roast.

The big thing today is the new menu. It's not a small deal and takes 5 to 7 weeks to implement. It was reported in March that reports from 79 stores with the new menu were up 6 ½ %, whereas 387 stores without the new burgers were down 8%.

I've known Dick since about 1972 and he has been on a diet from that date. Cabbage soup comes up quite often. Can't say I would like a steady diet of that. Think Dick sneaks a little from time to time. I have the same philosophy about diet and exercise as Dave Martin. It is well documented that for every mile you jog adds one minute to your life, which at 85 enables you to spend an additional 5 months in a nursing home at $5,000 a month.

We did have a great time at the Chicago Restaurant Show. Judy passed the test and kept us corralled on the exhibit floor and finished up jitterbugging Monday night to a Chicago big band. Judy resolved next year she'd bring two leashes and steel-toed shoes.

Tom is sending the e-mail and his IBM Microsoft is not compatible with my Apple computer. If you happen to see Tom's e-mail in outer space, send it on down.

Time is moving along and fast! Semi-retirement is highlighted with important events. Just finished the three operas, the highlight of the summer. I just conned Megan into taking Grandma to the last opera and I got to take in Ross' doubleheader baseball games. Next will step on a busload of Webster City people and give them a tour of our city. Then comes Balloon Days and the Fair starts. Most everybody I see asks—Will you be working at the State Fair? Yes and Yes! Isn't life fun?

The word I get from the guys—Now, Dad. Now, Dad! The Little Flower has her faults, but she did a good job raising the kids.

Right now A & W is moving from Michigan to Kentucky. Don't know what that entails, but I do know it's never fun to move. Plus, a lot of the staff decided to stay in the Detroit area.

Bus tour was fun with 47 people and had them laughing from the time I stepped on the bus. The Hot Air Balloon fest was good as I've ever seen. First Saturday was the largest people count of all time and that relates to money.

From Larry—We finished up July down about 10%. Not bad considering we had a first class Burger King open up and Taco Johns opened last week. We are getting about ten of the State Coupons a day. Dad is supposed to be working at the State Fair. All I get is stories about milking goats and pictures with the State Fair Queen. We may have to put a leash on the little guy.

Really did have so much fun at the State Fair it had to be sinful. The intern that babysat The Little Flower and I last year when I was "Iowan of the Day", caught me at the Corn Dog Kickoff fund raiser. Gib, we made the "Our State Fair" book. Picture of she and I with the "Iowan of the Day" golf cart—real biggie. Worked every day at the State Fair—anyway made roll call. Was in the Celebrity Goat Milking Contest on the last Friday. I kissed the goat, petted her and talked to her and even warmed my hands and still couldn't get those faucets turned on. Ended up 4$^{th}$ out of 7 and was happy with that. Did beat the State Fair Queen. Saturday morning the Queen came up to the Soda Fountain and wanted a picture of the cutest guy at the Fair and you are it. Oh my, if it could have been 70 years ago. Fringe benefit of old—old—old—after 70 everything is beautiful.

So most of the kids are back in school and elders get the work call. At least they have a couple bodies. The Little Flower and I are basically good—most parts showing a little wear. The mouth works too good at times.

Did have a good week in Okoboji. Stopped in Emmetsburg on the way up and visited with James & Janet Biever, relatively new in the business and doing well. Kissed the Blarney Stone and said hi to Doug Frank at Sibley. Had a nice visit at Sheldon with Jeff Freeman—great volume store. Even did a visit to West Bend and the Grotto—Dick's hometown. Got a lot of stories about Dick—a few of them even good.

A married couple were asleep when the phone rang at 2:00 in the morning. The wife picked up the phone, listened a moment, and said, "How should I know, that's 200 miles from here," and hung up. Her husband said, "Who was that?" The wife said, "I don't know, some woman wanting to know if the coast was clear."

News in the state—last month Florence Jante passed away. She and Curt were charter members and the very finest. Also Red Hauser passed away.

From Larry—We think the coupon was successful. The first day we got 49 back and then dropped to 10 a day. In all we redeemed 357 total.

Spent a couple days with Larry at one of his fairs and got to punch root beer across the counter—in the height of my glory. Thinking of running for the Legislature. My first task—mandatory 3 Iowa State Fairs each year.

Happy Thanksgiving to you all. Sorry to miss the Des Moines meeting on October 23 and sorry the attendance isn't too great. Dave does a real fine job and puts together a cool meeting. My excuse was legitimate. Stepped on a bus and gave an Indianola tour to 28 nice ladies from Keokuk and Betty Stevens was along. We had a nice visit. I really enjoy the bus tours and had them laughing from the start until they left town. At one point—I'm happily married but if you're available and worth over a million dollars, fill in this form and we'll talk about it.

The Stoners, Frank and Virginia, were killed in a car accident in New Mexico. They were on their way south for the winter. Sent the son a letter and he wrote back—One of Mom and Dad's passions was that they loved the A & W people. Had a letter from Harry Ayres. Jean passed away August 24—cancer got her. You remember the A & W jacket we got Harry at his going away party in 1982. He sent the jacket back and will put it in the A & W museum.

Poor little Donny wanted a toy of his own so he wrote a letter to God begging for $20 to buy one. After he mailed it, a kind-hearted mail clerk forwarded it to city hall where it came to the attention of the mayor. He wrote Donny a nice note, enclosed a $5 bill with it and mailed it to him. When the envelope arrived, Donny was furious. He grabbed a pencil, "Dear God," he wrote. "Thanks for the

$20, only why did you have to send it through city hall? Those politicians kept 75% for taxes."

Now it's time for the International Convention in Reno (International A & W that is). Lou Holtz will be the lead off speaker on Wednesday. Lou Holtz is the very greatest, probably the best motivator in the nation. Back from the Reno Convention that was on Saturday, February 2, 2002. One of the best run conventions in my 45 years attending. Do you really suppose we're having too much fun?

Just heard Pam Burr had passed away. She was a do everything gal for Allan and she will be missed. Allan has been President of N.A.W.F.A. since day one.

From Larry—Got the new menu housings—great. Plus a crew putting new shingles on the roof and canopies (orange, of course) and finished up new carpet in the dining room and cleaned every inch plus a new pop machine. Goodness, these kids spend a lot of money.

Dorene is really pretty good on a walker and we still are living on our own. She sits on a stool in the kitchen and tells me how to fix dinner—usually end up in a brouhaha. She said the other day—You'd never make a cook. If I had found that out 50 years ago might have gotten into a real profession and made something of myself.

Just got word from Tom and there is no snow on the ground in Dubuque. We'll be glad to ship him up a load. Our business is up so the snow isn't all bad. I actually don't have a job and don't do anything and still don't get caught up. We have the opera—black tie. In between the Reno Convention and after the fund raiser for Balloons, Puttin on the Ritz—another black tie.

Had a big time this Christmas. Over the years I've done it all from Santa Claus on down. This year I was an elf at the Lady Golfers Stag at the Country Club. Our high school art teacher was Santa Claus, #3 Tim was a Hershey Kiss. We gave them at least 30 minutes of entertainment in ten minutes. The next day at a buddy's funeral was coming into the church and the funeral director's wife was in the entrance and broke out laughing—at a funeral yet. Last night you was the funniest act I've ever seen. Oh my!

Back track—just run onto my older notes. It's February 2001—a real tough winter like the stories we told the grandkids and the same stories grandpa told me. The Little Flower and I celebrated our $50^{th}$ wedding anniversary on Sunday, January 28, 2001. It has been a smooth ride for me, but for The Little Flower there were a few bumps. Want you all to know the first 50 is the hardest—all downhill after that.

Larry couldn't make the Green Bay Regional Convention so he sent me with Dick & Judy to get notes on the meetings. Larry's words—Dad got the measurements of Lambeau Field and heard Vince Lombardi hollering on the sidelines. He had the names of all his dance partners, sang with the band and brought home a 45 year pin, but what knowledge did he get from the Convention?

We had a great time. In my mind, Green Bay was always two miles this side of the North Pole. I took long johns, extra sweaters and boots. For two days the temperature was exact same as Des Moines. Wisconsin people are second only to Des Moines for fun and frivolity plus they have some great units and always have been high in root beer sales.

Our Reno convention was great and in my 45+ years was one of the best ever. The hotel was super, accommodations excellent, the staff must have wrote the book about service plus a 5 star convention. The company has a new service manual for everybody and one item is training personnel. It was said—What if I train them and they leave? What if you don't train them and they stay? I went to have fun and accomplished that feat. Was riding down the road one day with Larry—I've probably had more fun than the average 6 guys. Would you believe 60? Says Larry—Well!!

The Little Flower and I celebrated 51 years of wedded bliss on January 28. Of course I forgot the occasion. Got a call in the evening from Larry & Virginia Whaley of Oklahoma City. They sang happy anniversary and woke me up.

Dick's A & W that was bought by the A & W Corporation is supposed to open the 25th. They put up a whole new unit with the A & W company brand and with a Long John Silver's connected to it.

My overall goal this year is to become computer literate. Was checking into email for the Newsletter. Got a few email replies, but general consensus is to stay with the snail mail Newsletter. So it will probably stay till the end of time—my time.

From Larry—Just had a letter from Sid telling us our family just grew by several thousand restaurants. Glad to hear everyone is staying on board. The future is so bright you have to wear shades.

#3 Tim just gave The Little Flower and I our first computer class. I failed big and The Little Flower didn't do much better. I'm sure Dorene will pick it up, but might take me a little longer. Dorene is making a little progress physically and my homemaker duties are simpler. She gave up trying to teach me cooking. She has now taken it over and I'm the assistant like getting the pans, ingredients, and moving the finished product. Will say we are eating better.

A & W Corporate has bought Long John Silver's. We have to thank Sid for the things he has accomplished and bringing us back from No Man's Land.

So, I don't have any problems. Have been up at the auditorium the last 2 weeks watching the Girls and Boys State Basketball Tournaments. Katy Grady was a forward on the Le Mars team. You all remember Bernie Grady. Katy is Bernie's niece. They lost on the first round.

The new Corporate A & W—Long John Silver's opened in east Des Moines on February 25 and so far the reports are real good. We certainly wish them well.

When Sidney Feltenstein appeared we thought this was the total end. He has certainly had everything against him, but things are beginning to look better.

Time really flies when you are having fun. Now it's time for the dandelion greens, next will come fresh bullheads out of the pond, and then the mushrooms will pop up. Tom, in his letter, is telling about the juicy Velveeta burger and the thicker ½ pound burger. They are really going pretty good for us. Larry is getting a new sign with an electronic reader board (Oh my goodness the younger generation spends money). Maybe it pays off. He reports up about 8% last month, March '92.

The mushroom season is past and actually it was one of the very best. Almost 2 weeks of mushrooms for breakfast. Had to pass on the bullheads and settle for catfish out of the meat case at the market. Ross went to the pond a couple times with Tim but they didn't score.

From Larry—Our new sign is up and have the "A & W—The All American Food" lit up plus electronic reader board. The great Root Bear and our World War II veteran and hero (Gib) were in the Memorial Day Parade representing the A & W. Dad threw out 30 pounds of Barrel Candy and he only threw it to people he knew. Isn't Larry just the greatest?!

The new Health Inspector was in. Makes you a little nervous at the best. She did a thorough inspection and asked the help a lot of questions. Her final report stated we had exceptional housekeeping and food handling skills and the restaurant was very clean. How come that kid is doing a better job than I ever did? Must be his mother's influence. Did get the kids a good mother.

A note from Jeff (Sheldon)—things are great. Weather in the North Half is especially good. All the operators Jeff has talked to are up. Maybe everything is looking up.

Success is the maximum utilization of the ability that you have—Zig Zigler.

Dick, Judy and I took the annual trek to the National Restaurant Show. On Sunday afternoon we caught a White Sox game at Cominskey Park. The Restaurant Association cancelled the night parties which were to be at a big hotel in the loop in a banquet room with a big band and program plus dance. We were disappointed. That was really the fun part of the whole show.

June 2002 and time has brought in colored pictures for the Newsletter. Really makes the Newsletter look classy. Now I'm trying to get the operators to send in pictures. Really don't want to look at me every month. A franchise owner in Western Iowa caught me at the Reno Convention. Just wanted to put a face on the Newsletter Editor. Think he was disappointed—funny looking little older guy.

It used to be work, work, work, work and now its play, play, play. I still work hard and play hard but accomplish half as much. In my 56th year in the food business and enjoyed every minute. A report from Larry—The "Thickster" hamburger is going better than we thought and the reader board sign seems to get everybody's attention and does create business. A girl that worked for me 30 years ago said—Gib, know you didn't have anything to do with buying that sign. You're too tight to spend that much money.

The Little Flower and I will finish up the opera this week, then Balloons, then County and State Fair—fun, fun, fun. Rocky Lavalle was down this week for an opera. He is the former Pizza King of Iowa Falls and currently Mayor. Rock's son, Michael, does the food tent for the opera so we all did dinner under the canvas.

Had 3 weeks of super fun—County Fair, Hot Air Balloons, Iowa State Fair. Worked all 3 full time. A person asked Larry—Does your dad work for you?—Work?!? Oh, well. From Larry—Dad finished his summer job at the Big One (Iowa State Fair). Now he's looking for work. Short day, high pay and no lifting—any takers?

The Fair duty was tough and it will take awhile to recuperate. On the other hand, nobody has more fun than I do and the hugs—goodness, gracious!!! From Jeff—We are faced with a series of great opportunities brilliantly disguised as unsolvable problems.

The Fair numbers (people) were not any higher, but the people were spending more money—that's the ultimate. It seems everybody is up—good news.

Corporate A & W belongs to I.F.A.—International Franchise Association. Some good meetings which relate to franchisees. Tom has attended a couple of their meetings. One at Hamburger U.—McDonalds Lodge in Oak Brook, Illinois and another at Washington, D.C.

Happy to say Dorene (The Little Flower) and I are getting dang good on our own at home. Cooking has been a big part of her life and there wasn't anybody better. At this point she's trying to get me to handle it with her instructions. It hasn't worked yet mostly because I don't have any talent. She gets pretty excited when I flub it. Try to keep the ball bat out of reach.

Most of the Big Events are over. Our little County Fair is very special. Larry and I are both on the Fair Board. He works and I watch. The Balloons were the best ever. Weather was good which also related to a good State Fair. I put the Big Fair down as my fun event of the year. I'm in mourning now!

Hey another Birthday came up—great party. Had to bring all the grandkids in to the blow out 80 candles. It was a backyard picnic at Shelli's. Had a lot of funny cards. Sandy left a $25 gift certificate at the Corner Sundry and I'm having fun spending that.

From Jeff—Our new owner, Yum Brands, is doing well with the transition. We are now playing with the Big Boys, but they do have a lot of good things to offer.

The Little Flower and I went on a bus tour sponsored by our bank to Manning, Elkhart, and Walnut. A nice group and real fun. Our Chamber of Commerce sends out invitations all over the state for a day's tour of Indianola. I step on the bus when they hit town and give them a day's tour. (A little stretch, but I make it work). That's one of my favorite jobs. In my next life think I will do that full time.

Just found out the real given name of Speed Herrig is "Duane." I always thought it was "Speed." Speed came to the Iowa Restaurant Association Convention when he first started Cookies and we have been buddies ever since.

Sharon Luedtke and Norm Ruffridge passed away during the last couple months. Cancer got Sharon and I think it was the heart that got Norm. They both were Charter Members of our Iowa A & W Association.

Larry reports business up about 11% for the year. (September '02). The new sign has helped a lot plus no new competition in the last 12 months. Dad turned 80, 5th of September. Larry came into the A & W the other day with a serious look on his face. I said, "What's up!" "Dad, do you know anything about Viagra?" I said, "No, not really. Why?" "Well, I think I'm going to the doctor. All I need is some half doses. I just want enough so I don't dribble on my shoes." Oh, my goodness—these young guys.

Enjoy working the Fairs with Larry. This year Dick and I flew down to Oklahoma City and worked a couple days, plus we stayed with Larry and Virginia Whaley—super people. Dick drove a van back on Sunday and I rode back with Larry on Monday.

Got the letter from Tom Thompson. Dubuque has a new hotel going up with a water park and a giant 500' water slide. He invited me up for a slide with the great Root Beer. My last ride on a Giant Slide was with the Iowa State Fair Queen. I don't think the Bear would measure up.

From Jeff—Make the mistakes of yesterday your lesson for today. When you're out of quality, you're out of business.

Was working the counter at the Oklahoma State Fair. A lady laid down the money for her purchase. Turned around to give her a dollar back and she was heading up the way. I hollered at her—You gave me an extra dollar! She thanked me and I heard her tell the person with her as she walked away—I can't believe that Carney gave me the dollar back.

It's time for Thanksgiving at Bussey. The first and second generation is laying back and the third are coming on and haven't had a bad cook yet.

In a letter from Jeff of Sheldon—All I want for Christmas is more business. The economy isn't booming but seems to be turning around.

We just passed Veterans Day. A few years ago the Legion asked me to do the program. Every year they have a little something that relates to the Service, War or like in general. I was relating some of my escapades in WW II. Wherever I went I was organizing something and having a good time. Pretty much had the whole crowd laughing in the aisles. After it was over, a lady came up to me—My husband was in the Service and I followed him around, but we never had any fun.

From Larry—The rookie cop was asked what he would do if he were to arrest his mother? "The first thing I would do is call for back up!"

I bad mouth Wal-Mart every day, but every week finds me there getting something I can't find any place else. They do give me money every year for my Retarded fund raiser. I was standing in the entrance the other day talking to the greeter. A sweet little older lady came in—Are you working here now, Gib? Oh, well.

Busy time—Christmas, New Year's celebrations. That New Year's celebration is mostly in my head, but still can talk a good party.

From Larry—It's been said that Adam and Eve had an ideal marriage. He didn't have to hear about all the men she could have married and she didn't have to hear about the way his mother cooked.

If there's a better way to do it—find it. Thanks, Edison.

# 42

## *2003 to 2005*

January '03: Here we go into '03. I didn't make the Lexington Convention. The Little Flower went into a stroke Wednesday and in the Hospital for three days. Back home on Saturday. There is no added problems with her manipulating—shuffles along a walker. Her head is intact and still gives me the orders with gusto

Larry got to the Convention. Tom Thompson, Dubuque, received our Chairman Sid's Mania Award. It compares to an Oscar or an Emmy. From Larry—At the auction in Dad's absence. Bob & Karen Cary bought a really cool cup (A & W) for a mere $1,100 plus Sid and Kevin Bazner opened up their pocket books. Customer Mania is the new word from the Convention. Larry came by and gave us an hour and a half about the Convention. It seems everything is positive and most all were up in '02. Maybe we really are on the way back and positive thinking is the best sign.

Got a lot of letters to The Little Flower and me about missing the Convention. I live and breathe A & W everyday, 24/7. I believe if this isn't your bag, follow another name down the street. A & W ranks #2 in my life, a close second to the family.

I don't believe the computer and I are going to hit it off. The Little Flower did make the remark—Must be getting a little better. At least you don't swear at it as much. Also the homemaking is better. The Little Flower's biggest problem is depression. She can't do the cooking thing like she used to and she was the best in the world. I've been in the food business 55 years and can cook just barely. I can get her on the chair in the kitchen giving me instructions. That doesn't work either. I can't even get that right.

Hey, we're on the downhill towards spring and everything is looking great. At least it snows everyday which keeps a clean look. Larry reports—The seafood catch is going good. Coach Bill came in and helped put together marketing for the year. He will get into Sweets and Treats this spring. The future is so bright we hafta wear shades.

Larry's business is good and seems like everything in general is good. Yum Brands and the merger with the Big Guys has to be good for us and were not the Little Guys, but part of. Was pulling The Little Flower up off the couch last week and pulled a muscle in my back. Was flat for 3 days but gradually get better. Can move my head a little this morning. Living with Advil. Never took a pill before. Plus the Conference calls from Larry, Jeff and Tom are great.

From Tom—I overheard a couple of guys talking while they were eating some great A & W food. One guy said, "My wife's cooking is so bad the flies in the neighborhood chipped in to repair our screen door."

A letter from Jeff, Sheldon, (March)—5" inches of snow and 14 below this morning. That's the big reason I live in the south—southern Iowa that is. We had 8 inches of snow but the temperature was like 3 above.

Think it was March 15th when we moved into The Village. Clean up your act, it could be your next stop. It's basically a Retirement Community and we live in a one bedroom apartment. There are about 180 inmates and it goes from living on your own to complete nursing care when you get to that stage. No, it's not what we want, but part of life. I think all the time but really can't figure out anything bad about the place. We still do our own breakfast and do noon at the dining area (food is very good for this type of facility). So far we are happy.

Larry just reported up 14% over last March. A nice day came up and Larry power washed the brick building and all the parking lot. That guy continues to do a better job than I ever did and that makes me feel good. I did get the kids a good mother.

I always view problems as opportunities in work clothes—Henry Kaiser.

Jackie Duncan passed away in April 2003. Jim had passed away a few years ago. Jim and Jackie were our first A & W buddies a few years ago. I helped them open Iowa City. Went to a few National Conventions together which makes for a few stories.

From Jeff—Gib, what is this "Village Place?" They mow your yard and cook your meals. Do they have an extra room? Jeff runs a good, solid operation. In my so many years have seen a lot of people come and go. Just recently—Kevin Bazner was one of the better ones and Sid Feltenstein brought us back from near obscurity and put up on solid footing.

Act as though it were impossible to fail

A new item on the menu is cheese curds. Dorene really likes them. Not too good in my book, but they are selling better than fair. It looks like a keeper.

Yes, Jeff, this retirement Village is out of this world at this stage of life, but don't sell your house until you have to. Plus a lot of new people to meet. A fellow just knocked on the door with a nice bag of morels cleaned and ready to go. Just don't get any better than this.

The weather is super terrific. My thing has always been—Hate old people and Methodists aren't too high on my list. We are with both here at The Village. The old people are getting better every day and my best buddy is a retired Methodist Minister.

From Larry—The chicken promotion is doing well and I think it has brought awareness to the fact we have good chicken products.

A Sunday School teacher asked the children just before she dismissed them to go to Church, "Why is it necessary to be quiet in Church?" Annie replied, "Because people are sleeping."

Next week I get to do another Bus Tour. There will be 40 or 50 from Manchester. Don't have many jobs left. This and the State Fair are two of the very best.

The Little Flower and I are getting used to these Methodists here at The Village. It is really ironic the 180 residents are made up of retired Ministers and workers within a school system. There are also a couple farmers. The Little Flower and I don't fit at all. It's amazing that we kind of like it. The Little Flower warns me everyday about stretching the truth on my story. I say—whatever it takes.

These people here (not all Methodist—my buddy across the hall is a Quaker) are accepting us and I've dropped all politics and religion, and getting along super.

The report from Larry—June was bad, bad. The Cruisin' Combos are going good and he also started the Sweet Treats. A & W is sponsoring with the Community State Bank dinner for 1,000 for 4-H and F.F.A. kids and families to kick off our County Fair. Dad is 80 and my kids are Mary—5, James—8, Anna—10. Do you think I need a babysitter for 3 kids and an Old Timer?

Hey, it's time to get ready for Fair, Balloons and the Big Fair—fun, fun, fun.

Now, I'm in mourning. The Fair, Balloons and the Big Fair are all over and now it's the kids with sad faces back to school. We have a lady across the hall that takes Dorene to lunch and kinda looks after her when I'm not around. Dorene usually does the Big Fair one day. Larry takes her around in a cart. We did make Balloons every night and all 3 operas. We do the wheelchair.

The Big Fair is one of my favorite things. I don't do much work but I'm the pitchman for Larry's units. When I was growing up and going to the Fair, rather than going to the fair midway I would follow the pitchman around. A few years ago as I was getting ready for the State Fair and Dorene said, "If you bring home another set of knives, there won't be a home."

In summation, summer is over, the Big Fair was strong, a lot of people there and they were spending money. We were set to break attendance records until the extreme heat set in. On the first Fair day was talking to a lady from Connecticut. She had always heard that Iowa had the best fair so they planned their vacation around it. People from Omaha said—We have a nice State Fair in Lincoln, but it's a County Fair compared to this.

Things are a little slow for me right now. Our local fairs are all in wraps until next year. I check on the A & W a couple times a day and mostly they run me off. Had a Tour Bus coming the 13$^{th}$ but they canceled because not enough people signed up. Next to the State Fair, that's my favorite thing. We had two buses this summer.

From Larry—Yes, we were up over 10% for August. Fantastic Balloon event (weather was good) and the Awesome Burger did pretty well. The Bike Give Away created a little traffic and was probably worth while. (Larry is making a mailing list from the sign up names and that makes sense.) Dick mentioned he would work part time somewhere. Remember if he calls, he was trained by Dad. Very messy, hard to get him started after he shows up late and rather expensive.

One fast story from Dick (he comes into see us about once a month)—A man walking a California Beach was in deep prayer. All of a sudden he said out loud, "Lord, grant me one wish." Suddenly the sky clouded above his head and in a booming voice the Lord said, "Because you have tried to be faithful to me in all ways, I will grant you one wish." The man said, "Build a bridge to Hawaii so I can drive over anytime I want." The Lord said, "Your request is very materialistic. Think of the enormous challenges for that kind of an undertaking. The supports required to reach the bottom of the Pacific. The concrete and steel it would take. I can do it, but it's hard for me to justify your desire for a worldly thing. Take a little more time and think of another wish that would honor and glorify me." The man thought about it for a long time and finally he said, "Lord, I wish I could understand women. I want to know how they feel inside, what they are thinking when they give me the silent treatment, why they cry, what they mean when they say "Nothing" and how can I make a woman truly happy." The Lord replied, "You want two lanes or four on that bridge?"

Health update—I'm getting along super. Dorene has stabilized after two strokes. She gets around slow on a walker. I do most of the housework—just barely. She does the cooking with me as a helper with quite a few arguments. Sometimes a real brouhaha.

Social event of the season (anyway for the McConnell family): #1 son Pat's daughter, Megan, married on a farm south of Cedar Rapids on September 20, 2003. The Friday night pre-wedding dinner was in the Hughes' big yard with our catering buddies, the Godwins, serving dinner behind the house overlooking a beautiful lake with lit torches all around. The Hughes family has 5 farms and grows trees to be replanted. As grandparents, we want the best for our grandkids. I think Megan got a couple levels above the best.

A fellow told me one day, a long time A & W operator,—I know more about your family than you do (from the newsletter since 1967). Yes, my veins run about 2/3rds. root beer. "A & W" isn't tattooed on my chest, but a lot of people think it is. My thoughts right now are to get ready for the Convention in San Diego. Right now it is October 5th and my Cubs are in the playoffs. I've been a Cub fan since 1938 and had about 3 winning seasons. Was in the War in 1945, but otherwise have been siding with them. Next year is now!

A Sunday school teacher asked her class why Joseph and Mary took Jesus with them to Jerusalem. A small child replied, "They couldn't get a baby sitter."

Yes, it's our 85th Anniversary birthday of A & W. Hopefully I'll get to San Diego for the Convention. Dorene won't be able to go and I'm not leaving her alone.

It's time again for Thanksgiving at Bussey. It's a good event and have been going for 50 years and the next generation just gets better. Of course everybody knows Bussey is the capitol of Marion County.

We have been fighting little Millers in the apartment! Instead of me gaining ground, they are multiplying and getting ahead of me. Finally I had to bring the bug guy in. Grain Millers house and multiply in open cereal boxes of which we had 10. Now we have no cereal and the guy put out something and sprayed. In about 2 weeks the little Millers were gone.

By most reports business is going along pretty good. With 6 people you can get many stories. I'm an "Up" guy and it's "Up" until proven otherwise. My Cubs lost again. Maybe next year. My next years are kinda running out.

Now to get ready for the San Diego Convention. First ever convention managed by the N.A.W.F.A. Larry and Anita are taking me along. I've always thought San Diego was the gem of California. Anita Vercellino searched all over the country and picked that for retirement.

From Jeff—Gib, there is no old age. There is, as there always was, just you. Passion is the log that keeps the fire of purpose blazing. Your work now is to find that fire and rekindle it and then let it burn.

I think back to the Convention at Disney World in 1972 and believe it was the best ever. It seems time the N.A.C. was running the Convention. We had Larry and Tim along and they had a super time. I've been with A & W since 1956 and it has been a great life. Had a dream the other night. I wasn't sure I wanted to come back for a second life. It couldn't possibly be as good as this one.

My converting these 180 Methodists here at The Village is going pretty slow. Might have to hire help like the time I told Larry he might have to hire somebody to keep me on the straight and narrow. Dad, it would take two!

From Larry—We're planning on San Diego in January. Dad, myself and Anita. Dad asked me for $80.00 for tanning. I think for 5' 1 ½" tall and 81 years old, that's a little vain. Besides, his shorts got to just above the knees and his socks just below so I think we could just paint his knee caps tan and get along fine.

Time again to wish everybody Merry Christmas. This is the third day of December and our first measure of snow. We got rain, ice and then 2" of snow. Dorene is still thinking about the house she left. My problem is I don't like old people and don't like them more every day. Religion doesn't kick in much. More and more of these inmates are "younger" old people.

Right now we're thinking Yum has to be a good thing for Corporate. I'm a positive thinker. When the positive runs out, I'll be going over another hill.

How about President Bush going to Iraq for Thanksgiving? Like him or not, that was an awesome move.

Yes, we'll hold court in San Diego. Might not have time for the meetings with so many stories of the past to tell. Bob Loughman said about an advertising meeting—hardly any new and re-working of the old ads. I've been writing in the Newsletter since 1967. Done it all and now rework the old stuff.

Larry didn't get to make the Convention last week and he's still pouting. Then comes the question—What did you learn and bring back? We talked to the animals at the zoo. Found an ape that looked just like Dick. We also found the #1 fish house.

We're a little confused with Yum, our partner. First International Convention was totally done and paid for by A & W. President Dale Mulder headed up the meeting and did a super job. Craig and Polly were also there with a ton of new and exciting products for the year.

"The Green Bay Packers never lost a football game, they just ran out of time."—Vince Lombardi.

The auditorium and convention center in San Diego was a block from our show. They were having a boat show and Dick slipped over to take it in. He came back with—Did you ever see a $3,000,000 boat? That might be classified as a ship. If Dick gets it we'll have our convention in it next year. How would it go in the Des Moines River?

January '04: A&W if back. The Convention was like the days of old. The final measure—the big banquet room was full for our final on Friday night. Dick and I were in charge of the fun and we handled it very well. Anita was in charge of riding herd on Dick and I and she had the toughest job. Thought there would be a lot of new faces, but mostly the gang of old. The people in general were happy, but a little confused with Yum and where we were heading. The setting was perfect. I consider San Diego the cream of California.

Report from The Village, our home to the end: My goodness, there are a lot of old people here. February 9, 2004—sunshine and 34 degrees. This is Iowa and everything can happen (weather) within an hour. Our apartment has three double windows looking out the south side and at this viewpoint the snow is beautiful. #1 Pat does snow and he's having a hey day (money).

Larry couldn't go to the Convention. Jill's mother was having a major operation (it was successful). Larry sent Dick along to be my buddy. Convention started with a film showing franchisees answering questions concerning co-branding and other related matters.

Dick's words—Gib was a definite hit, so I spent the rest of the Convention with a celebrity. Got lost in the zoo and asked a couple if they saw a lady and a short guy. You mean Gib? Also had to provide a pen so he could sign a can of coney sauce for someone.

Talking to one of my old priest buddies. A retired priests' home is called "Home of Unwed Fathers".

Yes, everything is positive. Weather is beautiful and business is great plus the high school basketball tournaments are on. One of my favorite times of the year and ranks close to the State Fair.

A couple drove down a country road not saying a word. An earlier discussion had led to an argument and neither of them wanted to concede their position. As they passed a barnyard full of mules, jackasses and pigs, the husband asked sarcastically, "Relatives of yours?" "Yes," the wife replied. "In-laws."

This is April Fools Day. That is fitting because there are a lot of fools here at the Methodist Retirement Community. Then The Little Flower comes in—Why are you writing the Newsletter? There's nothing in it. I thought it was full of good stuff and why am I laughing?

Dick and I were looking at a picture. The contrast: He with a Methodist face and me a Catholic face. Where am I going with this?!?

Paul Nierzwicki is gone from Corporate, the last of the old guard. He was honest, sincere and always ready to help.

Larry had the Great Root Bear on the square to help the Easter Bunny give candy to the kids for two hours. Yeah, that Bear is good for many things.

In this retirement community of over 180 inmates (is that the right word for Methodists?), they all know I'm from the A & W and they also tell me when they stop by to spend a little money. They are pretty active and ¾ of them are mobile.

Larry reports business is up 20% in April and the new item is cheese curds. Dorene really likes them, but not to my liking.

My schedule is: Take a run to the A & W at 7:00 and turn on everything. #1 Pat comes by and fixes breakfast. Take care of Dorene's needs and then to the bank for Larry at 9:30.

The Little Flower had the strokes about two years ago, but we get along good on our own. She's on a walker and gets around slow. There is always something going on, all the games the old people play. The Newsletter is a few jokes and not much meat. It keeps me occupied a couple days a month. My philosophy—A laugh is the start of something better. The food is real good here, but about every two weeks we bring in dinner from the A & W. How can you beat the broasted chicken, coleslaw or a Coney dog and root beer?

Larry is doing a good job with cheese curds plus broasted chicken is still the best chicken on the market and you have to eat Coney dogs on Tuesday.

"Hard work spotlights the character of people: Some turn up their sleeves, some turn up their noses and some don't turn up at all."—Sam Ewing.

Right now most of my talents are working towards nominating our high school art teacher for "Iowan of the Day" at the Iowa State Fair. I was awarded that in 1994 and it is quite an honor.

"Where does the time go?"—favorite line of The Village inmates. This week working the County Fair. I'm sure we have one of the best county fairs in the nation and it has always been in the black. A lot of the county fairs are in trouble financially. Our farmers are very proud showing their stock, etc. A & W has a good spot on concession row with the Lion's Club manning the counter serving root beer and floats.

Larry's report—Up about 7.7% in June. He gave me a new title: Head of the Flunky Department. Still get to the A & W a couple times a day and manage to work the tables once a week. Really don't talk the young people's language, but I'm trying to change.

Now our social calendar is in full bloom. Every morning have breakfast at the County Fair and every night at the Balloon Field. Then comes the State Fair. Balloons officially started about 1970 with Father Burns as our pilot. Can you top that? The good Father up in the sky working for us. #3 Tim is now our family balloon pilot and this year is sporting a brand new balloon. We used to run out of hot air and leased from Des Moines. Since The Village opened in 1990, we have ample hot air. The Village is for the most part retired preachers. They are professional propulsilators of hot air. Sometimes it's hard to tell who is converting who here at The Village.

The word today is busy. Not work busy, play busy. Everything is super good. The weather is better than normal which means the balloons fly and everyone is happy. Last year we only missed one flight in 9 days. Larry let me help with the dinner for the 4-H and FFA kids and their folks pre-fair. The A & W does this along with Community State Bank and it's a tradition for at least 20 years. Jeff (Sheldon) is supposed to be coming down for our fair on the 19th. You may get a report in the Big Paper. In any event, you will get a full report via the next Newsletter.

At our Balloon Hospitality Building located at the Balloon Field, our guys had a painter do a full size me on one wall. It is actually a better likeness than the real thing. The guys never fail to amaze me.

I'm in mourning. The County Fair, Balloons and State Fair are over and back to badgering these Methodists and whatever at The Village. The State Fair was the best ever from the first day thru the last. The total attendance had to be a winner. I had more fun than anybody doing my thing at one of Larry's stands. White shirt and black bowtie doing a little pitching. Have people come by and say—Just came by to see if you made it this year. It was my life's ambition to be a pitchman at the State Fair and at 75 I made it.

The biggest thing about running a business is a happy, cordial "Hello" and "Thanks, come back!" You need to really recognize the customer. The next big thing is a clean, well kept joint and, of course, quality and price enters in along with good service. I've been in the food business since 1946. I had no problem making money, but had trouble taking care of it. The Little Flower took care of that problem. If I were to start over again tomorrow (restaurant), a counter man in a joint would be my choice.

Had a visit from Dick last week and he left a joke—A husband and wife are getting ready for bed. The wife is standing in front of a full length mirror taking a hard look at herself. "You know, dear," she says, "I look in the mirror and see an old woman. My face is all wrinkled, my boobs are barely above my waist and my butt is hanging out a mile. I've got fat legs and my arms are all flabby." She turns to her husband and says, "Tell me something positive to make me feel better about myself." He studies hard for a moment and then says in a soft, thoughtful voice, "Well, there's nothing wrong with your eyesight." Services for the husband will be held Saturday morning, 10:30 at St. Joseph's Memorial Chapel.

News from The Village—Still a lot of old people here. That's a hard hump to correct. Could say I was King in the Horseshoe Pitching Tournament, but maybe at this stage I should clean up my act and not story as much. Teachers and preachers make up the greater percentage here. In my day, all I really knew how to do was make money and did that pretty good. Of course, I married well. My life's ambition was to be a pitchman at the Iowa State Fair and have done that for about 8 years. Larry turns me loose.

Retired three years ago, but still feel some root beer running through my veins. Dick and I did the state tour—900 miles and 14 different A & W's. It's a different world today from when I started with A & W in '56. More competition, higher expenses and the Company has changed the way business is done.

Great birthday with Sandy and an exchange student from Venezuela at Sec Taylor and the Little Cubs, plus we won.

Weather is good, crops are super. If the farmers make it, we make it. Into October and went to the Friday night high school football game in shirt sleeves. Don't remember that ever happening before.

The Big Election is over. I'm a known Catholic Irish Democrat and have voted for young Bush and also Dad. Of course, the people here at The Village think I voted for Kerry and can't convince them otherwise. Baseball is all wrapped up. I'm a National League fan and was in the Card's corner and Boston wins it in four.

News from The Village—I'm adapting pretty well after a year and a half. The Little Flower would still rather be home. It is Methodist sponsored, but a little bit of everything here. The couple across the hall are Quakers. There is one other Catholic family here. There are 5 retirement communities in the Wesley family and Indianola is known to be the most active and has the most fun. I make my share of noise and have more than my share of fun.

Carry over political joke—John Kerry was going to visit the Catholic National Cathedral outside of Washington as part of his campaign. Kerry's Campaign Manager made a visit to the Cardinal and said to him, "We've been getting a lot of bad publicity among Catholics because of Kerry's position on abortion, etc. We'd gladly make a contribution to the church of $100,000. if during the sermon you'd say John Kerry is a saint." The Cardinal thinks it over for a moment and agrees to do it. Kerry shows up and as the Mass progresses the Cardinal begins the homily. "John Kerry is a self absorbed hypocrite and a nitwit. He is a liar, cheat and thief. He is the worst example of a Catholic I have ever personally known. But compared to Ted Kennedy, John Kerry is a saint."

Last week I told Larry that December would be the end of the Newsletter. He said, "Dad, when we put you away, the Newsletter goes with you. Until then, you write the Newsletter." So, I got my orders. Guess it's better than no job at all. If anybody wants off the mailing list, just send me a card. Been sending the letter since 1967 and it's part of my routine. A true labor of love. Also we have to keep the N.A.C. working for us. As Corporate gets larger and stronger, the N.A.C. gets more important to us.

Yes, the Christmas season is on us. Our gang gets together as a family. As we move forward, there are a few things I can't do but still able to tell the story.

The Three Bears had been having some trouble recently and had ended up in Family Court. Mama and Papa Bear were splitting up and Baby Bear had to decide who he was going to live with, so the Judge wanted to talk with Baby Bear to see what he thought about living with his parents. How about living with your father? No, he beats me terrible. Okay, then you can live with your mother. No way, she beats me worse than Papa Bear does. The Judge was confused by this and didn't know what to do. Well, you have to live with someone, so is there any relatives you would like to live with? My Aunt Bertha who lives in Chicago. You're sure she'll treat you well and won't beat you? The Chicago Bears don't beat anybody.

Here we are, January '05, an already they cancelled the Convention and I had Larry talked into taking me. Looking out the window it is a sheet of ice. School was cancelled on the 3$^{rd}$ and 4$^{th}$ and the kids are super happy. Larry brought the kids out to lunch one day.

News—Paul Nierzwicki now has 5 Long John Silver's and three with A & W's. Bill Kelk passed away Thanksgiving Day—one of the better Corporate people. Bob and Jean Barnhill gave up their home in Florida and moved back to Oskaloosa. Bob has slipped quite a bit. Plus Larry has new competition—a new restaurant plus Arby's and still was up for the year '04.

Have talked about quitting the Newsletter. Back in '67 we were at a meeting. Jim Duncan (Ottumwa) and I got our heads together. We formed the Iowa A & W's Operators Association. He would be the first President and I would be Secretary-Treasurer and send out a Newsletter. Jim is now selling root beer in the beyond and I'm still doing the Newsletter.

An Irishman, Englishman and Scot go into a pub and each order a pint of Guinness. Just as the bartender hands them over, three flies fly over and one lands in each pint. The Englishman looks disgusted, pushes his pint away and demands another pint. The Scot picks out the fly, shrugs and takes a long swallow. The Irishman reaches into the glass, pinches the fly between his fingers and shakes him while yelling, "Spit it out, you bastard! Spit it out!"

Now Valentine's Day is coming up. Use to get my Valentine a nice box of chocolates. She didn't eat them, so I had most. She started eating the chocolates and I haven't given a box since. I catch her and plant a big smacker then give her another and she backhands me.

We just learned that RAGBRAI will cross Northern Iowa this year and overnight in Sheldon. Jeff is putting out pleas for help on that day. Yes, I think I'm free that day. They've never gone thru Indianola, but was down to Bussey when they went thru a couple times. It's nothing but good. Mostly an upper echelon crowd and they do spend money. Hardly a rider that didn't have a smile and greeting, and most stopped for a minute. The word has always been Iowa is the friendliest state in the nation. We are going to keep it that way.

Sandy and I did get to Sebring, Florida for a surprise 75$^{th}$ birthday for Jim Casey in January 2005. The party was at a hotel by a race track. Jim was truly surprised when he came in with Teresa and all these people were waiting for him and a good time was had by all. I was supposed to do a little thing for Dorene's side of the family in front of 150 people. I was in black tie and really looked important. Into the program and the pants hit the floor. Pulled them up and started again and down they went. There were little guys sitting in the front row and I said to one of the little guys—Would you hold my pants up while I finish this speech?

Sandy and I stayed with Jim and Teresa a couple of days and had a super time. Sandy is a good guy-gal to travel with.

From the Old People at The Village: Don't pass up the older set. They are pretty active and do have money. Going out to eat is a big thing for most. Every day I have someone say—Was down to the A & W last night. My answer—Thought there was an extra buck in the till this morning.

Had a nice note from a new operator, Louise Torrey, in Riverside. Think they are also getting a casino. My mind is a little shaky, but think I visited with them in Vegas. She sent a joke—A man and wife were having an argument about who should make the coffee in the morning. The wife said, "You should do it because you get up first. Then we don't have to wait as long to get our coffee." The husband said, "You are in charge of cooking and you should do it because that is your job. I can just wait for my coffee." The wife replies, "No, you should do it and besides it is in the Bible that the men do the coffee." The husband replies, "I can't believe that. Show me." So she fetched the Bible and opened the New Testament and showed him at the tope of several pages that indeed it says "Hebrews."

The weather is super terrific. The snowbirds have to be envious. Girls State Basketball is next week, March 7–12$^{th}$. Usually have a weather flare up by then.

Last Saturday was the American Cancer Society benefit. The top pie (auction), made and donated by Shelli, went for $275.00 and was bought by Larry with my card and I got the big write up in the paper. I did buy the first pie for $100.00 and, of course, Dorene jumped me for spending so much money. It's just money.

Basketball is winding down and now comes baseball. Girls and Boys Tournaments were great. I made it to a couple games of each. Now to follow the N.C.A.A. and also our three state schools were picked.

The N.A.W.F.A. Board (take from our original N.A.C.) is still going strong and at this time more important than ever with Yum Brands trying to squeeze.

#2 Larry still says, "Now, Dad. Now, Dad." Goes back to telling Larry he would have to hire somebody to keep track of me. "Dad, it would take two." Had Larry talked into taking me to Kentucky and now I'll have to get back into the sweet talk for the Las Vegas 2006 Convention on January 10–13$^{th}$ at Rio Suites. Right now The Little Flower and I are getting along pretty good in this den of iniquity (Retired Methodist Preachers). I was corrected. "Preacher" is next to street slang. The correct word today is "Pastor". Yes, I'm sure you needed that information.

Another joke from Dick—Into the Belfast Pub comes Paddy Murphy looking like he had just been run over by a train. His arm in a sling, his nose broken, his face cut and bruised, and he's walking with a limp. "What happened to you?" asks Sean the Bartender. "Jamie O'Conner and me had a fight," says Paddy. The bartender said, "He couldn't do that to you. He must've had something in his hand." "That he did, said Paddy, "A shovel is what he had and a terrible licking he gave me with it." "Well," says Sean, "you should have defended yourself. Didn't you have something in your hand?" "That I did," said Paddy. "Mrs. O'Conner's breast and a thing of beauty it was, but useless in a fight."

I'm in mourning again. The mushroom season is over. It was the second best crop in my time. Had mushrooms for breakfast ten days in a row. Back in '34 the economy was in the tank and the mushrooms were popping up everywhere. You couldn't miss.

Dorene's niece, the Nun, came to visit last week and told these Methodists whatever. I will have Sister give you a Blessing. Might be the closest you will get to the Promised Land. Sister Dawn went to the Nunnery at 14 and now in her 70's, and couldn't be happier. I'll take my chances with Father Burns for the Promised Land.

Dick was down for breakfast last week. He and I are a little short of work and we'll be happy for anything you can give us. I'll have to get 11 days off for the Big Fair. That's my most favorite thing, eating everything they have to offer plus lemonade shake ups.

Is this Heaven? No, it's Indianola at it's very peak. Finished up our County Fair on August 1$^{st}$ and the best ever. Balloons started July 29$^{th}$ and overlapped the Fair, but it seemed to work. The Balloons were super and ended on Saturday, August 6$^{th}$ and then a few rest days for the Iowa State Fair running August 11$^{th}$ thru 21$^{st}$. The weather has been perfect so far. Somebody must be talking to the Big Guy upstairs. My connection isn't that good.

Yes, the new line: "World Famous A & W Root Beer." I'll buy that.

It really is a different world. In my day, if we had money maybe we spent it. Today, they spend it and then try to figure out where it is coming from.

Sign at a restaurant front counter (not A & W): Effective immediately Helen Waite will be in charge of your rush or emergency orders. So in the future, go to Helen Waite.

At this stage there are a few things I can't do, but the mouth still works good and have many thoughts running out of my head. Not too much meat, but a world of frivolity.

From Will Rogers: Even if you're on the right track, you'll get run over if you just sit there.

Yes, the weather (October and November) was super terrific. Larry has the soup kettle on. The Soup of the Day was chili. Plus The Village has added Soup of the Day. So far real good. We are lucky here at The Village. Our lady in charge of Food Service is a real professional. Her husband is also a food purveyor and a good guy. How could we have it so good?

In my young days, opera and ballet were two things I'd never be guilty of participating in. Now in both up to my neck and a confession—they are both getting better all the time. The grandkids can do no wrong.

Thanksgiving at Bussey (only Dorene's is better), then Christmas with family and New Year's Eve at The Village. The Village had a New Year's Eve party from 8:00 to 10:30. That's the same as Father Spaghetti's Midnight Mass at 10:00.

It was a standard joke with Father Burns—Ten calls asking the time for Midnight Mass. Remember when we took Father with us to the National Convention. The banquet was on Saturday night and then catch the plane home on Sunday. He would get that Mass in some way and always have a full house.

Stopped in the grocery store this morning. I always put extra things in the cart that I'm not supposed to get. Think that's a guy thing. Anyway, I came up about $5.00 short at the check out. A young fellow next to me threw down a $5.00 bill. I said, "No, no, no." He would have none of it and, of course, he was a big guy. The world is full of great people and especially in Iowa. I always embarrass Dorene when I don't have any money and it happens quite often.

Our President (Larry) is on a sabbatical—likely pushing snow. Went out this morning and it was 4 below and by noon it was up to 1 below. The snowbirds are gloating.

The olders of you remember Prohibition. We call it the "Bootleg Days." I was thinking of Templeton Rye. Back in the Bootleg Days that was a hot commodity. I worked in the Chicago Loop back in the winter of '57 and got all the Al Capone stories. At our 5$^{th}$ Grade Basketball Tournament in Ankeny, a friend of Larry's (one of his boys' mothers) had a friend who had a sister living in Templeton (it might take a couple minutes to sort that out). Anyway, for Christmas I got ½ gallon jug of Templeton Rye. I know it was authentic because it's in a Captain Morgan jug with a cap sealed with blue plumber's tape. So, you're welcome to come in and get a story plus a snifter of the real thing.

From Larry—Making plans for the Convention in Las Vegas. Taking Dad along and would appreciate help babysitting him. If you can take a couple hours, let me know. Hope he gets a good looking young lady.

Neoma called. J.C. Glover was killed in a motorcycle accident. J.C. was one of the great ones in our era. He ran Electro Hop out of Des Moines and moved the company to Texas. He was always ready and able to help us with any problems we might have. At that time, Coors wasn't available in Iowa. He would stop in Colorado on the way up from Texas and bring in Coors for our Conventions. His bathtub was full of ice, water and Coors. Of course his room would be the hub of the show. Plus J.C. was a great guy.

The Newsletter fronting the Las Vegas Convention: If you can't make the Convention, send money and I'll invest it for you. Happy, happy, happy. Now back to the jug. It might last forever—my ever.

Life is good at The Village, but there are a lot of old people here. Can't seem to get that corrected. At this stage there are things I can't do, but the mouth still works good and have thoughts in abundance running out of my head. Not too much meat, but a lot of frivolity.

Busy never quits. Have a full plate plus soccer and football with the grandkids. James is in the 5<sup>th</sup> grade in tackle football. Wears a full uniform and even travels out of town. Our tax money at work.

The A & W is running better than ever. Let's blame that on Larry's Dad's teaching. Of course, did get the kids a good mother.

A lot of new ideas coming out of Corporate. That's the main reason for joining a franchise—everybody working together. Been working for us over 50 years.

The Newsletter of January was out early to beat the stamp raise to 39 cents. My first name isn't Scrooge. That's my middle name.

Was all set to retire from the Newsletter. Got so much static from the people at the Convention. Larry's comment, "Dad, when we lower you into the hole, the Newsletter goes with you." Plus at the cocktail party on the first night of the Convention must have had 50 hugs (Hello, how are you?) from ladies. We had a good representation from Iowa—Spencer, Riverside, Dubuque, Emmetsburg, Sheldon and Indianola. Thought there was 8, but only came up with 6. At our first night's party (drinker with hors d'oeuvres) had four ladies playing violins from 6 to 9. A little different, but it was good. Breakfast and lunch was served every day to try and keep the crowd together. Larry made the remark that it was the best set up and run Convention he has ever attended.

For a smile: The elder Priest speaking to the younger Priest said, "I know you were reaching out to the young people when you had bucket seats put in to replace the first four pews. It worked! We got the front of the church filled first." The young Priest nodded and the old one continued, "You told me a little more beat to the music so I responded to you and brought in that Rock 'n Roll Gospel Choir that packed us to the balcony." "So," asked the young Priest, "What's the problem?" "Well," said the older Priest, "my confessions have nearly doubled since I began all this, but the flashing neon sign that says, 'Toot and Tell or go to Hell' has to go."

At the Convention also was awarded a pin with 5 diamonds and a nice A & W watch for 50 years as an A & W operator.

# 43

## *50 Years with A & W*

By my calculations, on January 28, 2006 we celebrated 55 years of wedded bliss. From a general store, The Little Flower, to a restaurant sundry store for me. We finally ran out of toothbrushes and went to the grocery. "Joe, where do I find the 10 cent toothbrushes?" "That's in the next aisle right beside the 5 cent root beer."

Was talking to one of the inmates here at The Village. He had a story: There was an ecumenical meeting to get all the religions on the same page. They could make new rules. Catholics could eat meat on Friday. The Jewish could eat pork and the Methodists could drink in front of each other.

From Larry: The Convention was good. We are busy getting ready for our 50$^{th}$ season in the A & W Root Beer business. Dad wants every event to include dancing girls. I don't think Mom will allow that to be in the budget.

Larry hires me to come in and entertain and work the tables or is it me paying him to let me do it? Anyway, it tends to keep me out of trouble.

One of the inmate's daughters lives in Hawaii. They had a big storm with wind and rain. Their cottage isn't too substantial and one of the walls came crashing in. It was the dining room and the wall where she kept all her glasses and dishes. Broke every glass and dish she had except an A & W mug. She called Mom and told her to tell Gib.

Got to Girls State Basketball one day for four games in the new Wells Fargo Arena—great facility. Our boys won the sub-state so they'll be there next week. Have my bid in to ride up with Larry.

June 25, 2006: My biggest problem is repeating myself and I don't think that will get better. New stories, at this stage, are harder to come by. Goes back to Father Albers with instructions for our wedding in 1951. I was getting along just barely and Father Albers said one night, "Gib, what do you think the most of—God or the almighty dollar? Don't you answer that!" Father Albers was a real Priest. Think he passed away a couple years ago.

Really had a great time at the Las Vegas Convention on January 6th. The watch I got is still running. Really a nice watch. Larry has his eyes on it. "Dad, put my name on it in the Will." Las Vegas is the ultimate for a Convention. Everything around you says party, show, food and they relieve you of your money real easy. We didn't have a dance scheduled, but had the dance card filled just in case. Las Vegas is expanding at least one big hotel every year. They will eventually fill the desert.

Basketball is wrapped up and now were into baseball. Did you know at Spring Training the first week is spent teaching them to spit and they do it pretty well.

Mentioned last month that Dolph Pulliam was our Rotary program on a Friday. Big as a mountain, all black and gentle as a kitten. A question after the program to Dolph who is from New York City, "Why would you stay in Iowa?" Dolph said, "I'll try to answer that. The first fall I was at Drake and it was Iowa's hot, humid weather. One of my buddies had a motorcycle (a little ancient). I asked him if I could take it for a spin. So here I am out on a country road, barefoot and just shorts on. The cycle conks out. There was a farmhouse up the road a piece so I walked up and knocked on the door. A nice, older lady opened the door. 'I'm out here on a broken down motorcycle and if you would call this number a friend will come and pick me up.' 'You come in and call the number yourself. While you're waiting, why don't you let me fix you something to eat.' I thought right then if this is a sample of the Iowa people and the honest hospitality, I'm never going to leave this state." Dolph is still with Drake in something like Promotion. A story like that makes us proud to be Iowans.

Now it is mushroom time and this is evidently a good year. This happens every 5 to 7 years. #1 Pat came in with a nice sack. #3 Tim brought a nice sack and another older buddy brought in a nice sack all cleaned and said he thought I might enjoy a mess of mushrooms. Next time I see him I'll kiss him. In my next life, will have six boys. Wow, a ton of mushrooms.

Larry ordered 500 solid gold pins (that's what he told me) for the 50th anniversary party. Supposed to be a special day, maybe in July.

I've always been a positive type guy. Smile—it doesn't cost any more and sometime makes you feel better. "Smiley" is one of my nicknames (one of the better ones).

#2 Larry put in nice new menus last week. Not sure what that means, but they look great. Has a remodeling job coming up this fall.

It's July '06 and the weather is like—wow! But, we need more rain. At this point the crops look good. It's about every year for Southern Iowa that it is too dry or too wet. Had a fun thing a couple weeks ago. One of my buddies, Bernita

Barnum, was having a 92$^{nd}$ birthday party and would like me to be her M.C. Never turned down a job in my life and that's one of my favorites. Got about 25 Villagers in the bus and headed for Lake Ahquabi with song sheets in hand. Have about a dozen of the old favorites run off and I pass them out. In between tell a few jokes. One of Bernita's protégés had treats. Nice concession trailer with funnel cakes and fried ice cream. Nice lady was working the trailer. "How long have you had the trailer?" "Just got it yesterday." And a good time was had by all.

My time has been taken up trying to finish the book (autobiography). Tim's girls are typing it up. The biggest, toughest job is trying to read my writing. Had a high school girl lined up for a summer job. She took one look at my writing and backed away. Now Tim's girls are working on it. Asked them how they were getting along. Spend most of the time laughing. Is that good or bad?

Yes, I'm ready for the State Fair. The next couple of weeks will be the three operas. It's still Dorene enjoying the opera and me enjoying the intermission. There is the 4$^{th}$ of July at Bussey. Still see some of the people I grew up with. Larry lets me work the tables at the A & W and still give them the regular stuff.

Work on the Templeton Rye from time to time and the stories get better. To get it now is the same as the old bootleg days—you have to know somebody that knows somebody that knows somebody that has a relative. The effect is still the same.

On July 17$^{th}$ we celebrated 50 years in the Indianola A & W business. Larry had two custom billboards, a full page ad in the paper including "Mug Amnesty" for those who wanted to redeem themselves. Larry had 50 cent hamburgers, 50 cent Coneys plus 5 cent root beer all day. He opened at 10:30 and had 60 people in the dining room at 10:15. Mom sat in her wheelchair at one door and I was at the other door hugging the ladies. Not sure what Dorene did for the men. From Larry: Dad hadn't hugged that many ladies since the Convention. On the best day of Balloons Larry normally does about 150 gallons of root beer. On this day by 10:30 pm, he had done 400 gallons of root beer, 2,520 hamburgers and 1,300 Coneys, and that's a celebration.

Status of The Village: At the monthly Village Association Meeting, our President let off with: "This Methodist sponsored facility has many different religions and church groups plus 6 retired Methodist Ministers and Gib McConnell." Don't really know what that meant, but will take the recognition.

At the County Fair Larry called me to come out at 6:00 for an award. It was really an award for him, but he wanted me to share in the glory. The award was called "Friends of the Fair."

Now time for the Big Fair. This morning it started out cloudy and overcast. Washed my glasses and cleared that up. The Big Fair is my favorite thing of the year. It is 10 days plus a get ready day. Larry's Old Fashioned Ice Cream Fountain is where I hang out. He was awarded "Queen's Choice Award" from the Queen and her entourage. Everyone was so nice plus it was a fun place and the ice cream was great.

We do have a lot of fun. In fact, Larry is thinking of charging me to be there because I have so much fun. Quite a nice honor for Larry. Economy must be pretty good. Have a line most of the time and they are spending money.

Dick came down for coffee the week after the Big Fair. He and Judy took the whole family (14) to the Fair one day. Dick is pretty well ruptured and we may have to take up a collection to get him back on his feet.

After the Big Fair seems like the year is over. Still talking about 50 years party. The Little Flower hugged the men and I kissed the ladies (said hugged before). In fact, some of them had to kiss twice. Just didn't get it right the first time.

Dorene and I did make every night of Balloons. We hang out at the Sponsors Building. Dorene and I built the building so were still kind of considered the hosts and I work it to the fullest. Lunch, drink and doors open on all sides for good viewing.

Had a nice letter from Jack Thompson (Tom's dad from Dubuque) and he sent along: Ever wonder why sun lightens our hair but darkens our skin? Why women put on mascara with their mouth closed? Why don't you ever see Psychics win the lottery? Why is "abbreviated" such a long word? Why is it doctors call what they do "practice"? Why is lemon juice made with artificial flavor and dishwashing liquid made with real lemons? Why is the man who invests all your money a broker? Why is the time of day with the slowest moving traffic called the "rush hour"? Why isn't there mouse flavored cat food? Why didn't Noah swat those two mosquitoes? Why don't they make the whole plane out of that stuff they make the indestructible Black Box out of? Why don't sheep shrink when it rains? Why are they all called "apartments" when they are all stuck together? If "con" is the opposite of "pro", is "congress" the opposite of "progress"? Why do they call the airport "terminal". Oh, my. A smile is good for everybody.

Goes back to the conversation with The Little Flower about depression. "I've been with you for 50 years and never seen you depressed. You don't even know what the word means." "Dorene, that is the nicest thing you ever said to me."

Just finished up the ½ gallon of Templeton Rye. I'll have to get that refilled, but will have to figure out the know someone that knows someone that knows someone that has a cousin, etc.

Very special news. The Little Flower and I have our first great-granddaughter. Megan (granddaughter) Hughes and Tom on September 30$^{th}$ had Hannah Joy, dimensions of 8 pounds 2 oz and 21 inches long. The baby was 8 days old and Megan brought the baby to Indianola for show and tell. Megan put the baby in Dorene's arms and I know she thought it was 7$^{th}$ Heaven.

News from The Village: The old people are getting older and I'm still telling stories. The retired Methodist Ministers and teachers are all ears for my stories. Different from their regular line of conversation. The Little Flower and I are still accepted so we must be partly okay. They like to tell me about going to the A & W and I can't think of anything better.

Now the summer is gone and it's Halloween time. Anna, James and Mary plus their buddies visited Dorene and I in their best attire. The latest report from Hannah Joy. She is eating and sleeping. Guess that is good. Larry is into his remodeling of the A & W. So far is going great. Of the four kids, Larry is the most like me but he did get his smarts from Mom. I asked Larry what I could do to help. "Just stay out of the way, Dad. Stay out of the way." He has a 20' by 33' addition with full basement on the west side. From Larry: The basement is Dad's office and Hall of Fame.

I've already asked our newish, youngish Priest and he's agreed to do confessions wholesale.

By now it's Christmas and New Year's time. I retired from the Santa Claus gig. I was probably the lousiest Santa Claus plus the smallest but nobody enjoyed it more. What happened to the Santa Claus suit?

Larry asked a couple weeks ago if I would come in and work the noon hour. What do you want me to do? I'm short on help and you can keep them occupied until I can get them waited on. That I can do the best.

It's January 2007 and my one New Year's Resolutions is to beat somebody, anybody, in ping pong. It will be hard to beat a great '06. Things are looking good at the Old Folks Home. We had a Christmas party at noon. The inmates would treat all the workers to dinner and me, with a buddy, would be server entertainers. I got down on my knees to sing "I Love You Truly" for a lady worker and they had to help me up.

Our New Year's Eve party ran until 10:30. that is probably a record. The schedule is 12:00, but you are usually all alone by 9:00.

Did real good for Christmas. Got the normal things like a couple of shirts and probably enuff candy for 3 months. Also got a jug of Templeton Rye. Did I mention the shelf price is more than the bootleg price and not near as much fun. Went to Midnight Mass at the downtown Des Moines Cathedral at 4:00 and then to Shelli's for dinner. I ordered snow for the grandkids, but no snow. My connection up above isn't good and doubt if that gets better.

January '07—Enuff for now. Maybe more at a later date.

978-0-595-71608-1
0-595-71608-3

Printed in the United States
129852LV00004B/1/P